A

Century

Of

Secrets

By Teresa Syms

Disclaimer

A Century of Secrets is a book based on true life events and experiences.

The author has created dialogue in the beginning sections to add to the overall story, however, all events are true as told by family members throughout the generations.

The author has recreated events, locations, and conversations from her memories of them. In order to maintain their anonymity, the author has changed the names of individuals, dates and places. The author may also have changed some identifying characteristics and details such as physical properties, occupations, and places of residence.

The conversations in the book all came from the author's recollections, they are not written to represent word-for-word transcripts. Rather, the author has retold them in a way that evokes the feeling and meaning of what was said and in all instances, the essence of the dialogue is accurate. In writing about the personal lives of my characters, it was never my intent to discredit or create malice towards anyone. That was never the intent of this book.

The purpose of the book is to show the reader that they have the ability deep within themselves to overcome the obstacles in your life and past. Your background may be similar to the authors, or your experiences may be worse. However, the book is written to educate, motivate and inspire the readers.

Contents

Family Tree

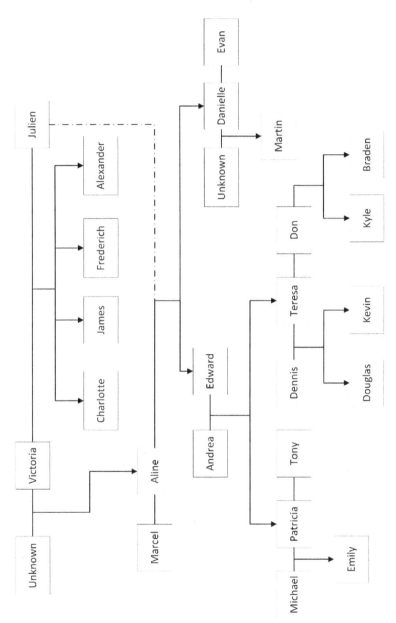

Introduction

A Century of Secrets is a multi-generational story of how one family's struggle with abuse, personal identity and deep-seated family secrets has caused suicide, alcoholism and lasting family scars.

This book is one woman's journey to uncover the lies, overcome adversity and finally set her soul free.

This story is based on the true life events and experiences of one woman, and the stories that were handed down to her over generations. The names have been changed in order to protect identities.

In life we have the choice to live to our highest potential or give away our power. In giving up our power we stop living a 'life' and we begin to just 'exist or survive.'

Each generation in this story, for different reasons, gave their power away and as a result spent the rest of their lives in their own personal hell.

Times and situations change, and for women, we have faced many challenges since this story began origin of 1911 Europe.

Trust me: It does not need to be this way! I now choose to be different.

"*You are now at a crossroads. This is your opportunity to make the most important decision you will ever make. Forget your past. Who are you now? Who have you decided you really are now? Don't think about who you have been. Who are you now? Who have you decided to become? Make this decision consciously. Make it carefully. Make it powerfully.*"

Anthony Robbins

The above words ring true for my life's journey. Now, at 56 years old, I have discovered and accepted my true self. Yes, I have suffered the torturous abuses from my family; overcome the disabilities I was born with; faced death head-on in a car accident; and live every day with chronic pain, and limited mobility; but I refuse to let these things define me.

Finally, my soul and heart have been revived. I am taking back the power I gave up so very long ago.

I am stepping into my true being as a person of sensitivity, integrity and great strength. No longer will I live in the shadows of others. I owe this to myself and future generations.

I **AM** living proof that with courage, determination and strong belief, you can gift yourself a brilliant future.

I owe this book to my grandmother, Maria, who taught me compassion. When I recognized the strength and courage she possessed, I was compelled to write the truth of the injustices she survived. I carry her strength, love and gentleness inside me and will miss her until the end of time.

My personal transformation has gone from victim, to a powerful being who is excited for my future.

My future is waiting...*I now stand and own it.*

CHAPTER ONE

Victoria's Story: A Victorian Era Saga of Servitude

A Century Past

To understand the dynamics of this story, allow me to share a brief background.

On February 2, 1891, a beautiful young girl was born in Koolscamp, Belgium. Victoria was a small girl, delicate in frame, but strong of will. The Victorian Era was a time when the distinction between the classes were evident. During this time, most families were large and patriarchal. They encouraged hard work and respectability of one's superiors.

Victoria was not born into wealth, but born to a lower-class family, who worked hard and demanded nothing less of their children. Not born to a life of privilege, money, and opportunity meant you were born into a life of struggle, hardship, and living for the servitude of others.

When a family felt their daughter was old enough to earn her keep, they would acquire the appropriate work situation for her. A good situation meant the girl would be sent to work in the home of the wealthy. The young girls, leaving their families behind, sometimes at a very young age, became a part of the "serving family" in the grand houses of Europe. Their futures would become embroiled within the "those behind the stairs are not seen" parts of the aristocracy.

The duties of the children would be to cook, clean, serve, or scrub their fingers to the bone, all for a few pennies. Such was the setting for a young girl born to the working-class. Victoria was born to such a life. She was that girl.

In Service of the Wealthy

The night before Victoria left her family home to enter her life of service, she listened to her mother's invaluable advice. "Do a good job for the master and his family. Remember always to do what you are told and do not question anything," her mother said.

"Yes, Mama," she replied.

Broken hearted at the thought of leaving her parents, Victoria cried herself to sleep that night. She was about to embark on a journey that terrified her. She knew her family was depending on her, but to do what? "What am I supposed to do when I get there?" she thought to herself.

Early the next morning, Victoria left her parents' home and began a life of service.

She was wonderstruck and terrified as she stood on the walkway outside of the grand home. This was to be her future!

Once she entered the home, she was given her uniform and a small room in the attic, where she would sleep. This small space she shared with another young girl.

Her duties included dusting, setting the fires, and assisting the kitchen staff when necessary.

"Do your job well and obey your orders," the main housekeeper told her, "and make certain you stay out of the way of the family."

"Yes, Ma'am," she replied quietly.

Victoria was set to work immediately. As she cautiously approached everything in the home, she found she was in awe of the beautiful furniture and treasures that surrounded her. Never before had she seen such large and beautiful paintings. Often, she would catch herself staring at some of the beautiful works of art or the statues.

After a few months, Victoria became accustomed to her daily duties and began to relax, ever so slightly. The master of the home had taken notice of her. The young girl did her best to avoid him and his advances, until finally, one day he caught her alone.

"Come here," he ordered her.

Timidly and with fear mounting, she went to him. She remembered the warning that was given. Not wanting to be disagreeable or disappoint her master, she obeyed.

Unsure of what she was doing, or if she was doing anything wrong, Victoria submitted herself to her master's whims. Like so many other young girls of this time, she soon discovered her future had been destroyed. She was pregnant. Once the pregnancy became known, she was immediately dismissed from her position.

Devastated, humiliated, and pregnant, Victoria returned home to her parents. She and her family did their best to hide the pregnancy and their shame. However, Victoria met and fell in love with a young Belgian man, named Julien. He was a tall strapping young man, who stood 6'2" in height. His piercing blue eyes and blond hair made him irresistible. The attraction was mutual, and despite her misgivings, they began their relationship. Victoria had held no hopes for the future.

But Julien would not give up on her, and their relationship blossomed into a serious romance. They loved each other.

"I must tell Julien the truth," she said to her mother one evening.

"Yes. Tell him the truth. However, be prepared, as most men will not accept someone like you," her mother told her.

The next evening, Victoria sat beside him on a park bench and said, "Julien, I'm not certain our relationship can go any further. I have something I must tell you."

With tears streaming down her face and her body shaking with sobs, she told Julien the truth.

Surprised at what he had just heard, he asked, "What do you want, Victoria?"

"I want a life and family with the man I love," she said.

"Julien, please forgive me for not telling you sooner," she begged. "I'm very sorry." She hung her head in shame.

She could not believe what happened next. Julien took her hand in his, while his other hand held her chin up to look him in the eyes and said, "It doesn't matter! Together, we will think of something." He knew the situation she was in was not her fault. It was a common occurrence these days. The girls could not say no when the master of the house decided he wanted to use them. After all, they were his property. Many girls found themselves homeless and destitute and were forced to resort to a life of prostitution to survive, and many didn't.

"I love you, Victoria!" Julien said one day. "I want to marry you and build a life with you, no matter what the cost. I don't care what gets in our way."

Her heart leaped with joy and love. "What about the baby?" she asked.

Julien wanted to marry Victoria, but it was evident that neither of them wanted to keep the baby she was carrying. Abortion was absolutely out of the question because of their Catholic faith.

Together, they would come up with a plan.

Victoria soon found herself ostracized by her community. The circumstances surrounding her pregnancy didn't matter to them. What mattered was that she was pregnant; ultimately, she was to blame. Of course, no aristocrat would take the blame, let alone the responsibility for a servant girl's problem. It was her own fault!

Victoria and Julien made plans for their future, but the future did not include her baby.

"Let's go to the United States," he said to her. "We can make a good start there."

"But what about the baby?" she asked.

"It's going to be very difficult in the beginning. We won't be able to care for a baby. Leave it with your mother," he suggested.

She struggled with the idea for months, but eventually, she gave into Julien's idea of a new future. Shortly after the decision was made on March 25, 1912, Victoria gave birth to a baby girl. It wasn't a difficult birth. Victoria was a strong girl, and the baby was small. She named her daughter Aline Magdalina.

Within months of the birth, Victoria and Julien were married. It was a happy time for the young couple. Their plans to travel to the United States to begin a new life together were about to happen. No one there would know of her past. If they left the "problem" behind, no one in the new world would know about it, and their shame would not follow them. Soon, they would be free to begin with a clean slate.

With tears in her eyes and pain in her heart, she hugged her infant daughter one last time.

"Good bye, my little one," she said as she kissed Aline's cheek one final time.

"Am I making the right decision?" she asked herself. "I have to support my husband. But my baby!"

Her heart was torn in two as she waved goodbye to her mother and child. She could barely see her daughter through her tears.

"Will I ever see her again?" she wondered. Only God knew for certain.

Julien and Victoria soon embarked on their journey to a new life, a life without the child born to a poor working-class girl, a child sired by a man she didn't know.

The young couple was excited about their new adventure, but Victoria's arms and heart ached.

The newly-wed couple arrived in Detroit, Michigan in mid-1912. The voyage was long, but soon forgotten when they set their feet on the ground of their new life.

Now, after much adversity, life was kind to the couple as they made their way in a strange new country.

In 1915, Victoria gave birth to a second daughter. They named their first child together, Charlotte Aline. Victoria's heart still ached for her first daughter, but she knew it was impossible to be with her.

"By giving Charlotte the second name, Aline, I can keep my first baby girl always close."

The young couple seemed very happy in their new life as parents. Victoria thought Julien was satisfied with their situation, until one day, he came home and said, "I've just heard of an area in Southwestern Ontario, where people can earn a good living working the land."

His wandering spirit had once again become restless.

"I have already made the connection for us, and we are going to move next month," he said, shocking his wife.

"Why do we have to move? We've just gotten started here," she asked Julien.

"Because there is lots of money to be made in that area," he told her. "We've already come this far, Victoria, what can it hurt to try?"

Victoria was worried, as Charlotte was a frail and sickly child. At first, she didn't appear to be a thriving baby, so the young mother spent all of her time caring for the girl. She did not know this would set the stage for the very spoiled and self-centered woman Charlotte would grow into.

Julien and Victoria decided to make the move to Canada and to delve in life of farming. They packed up their meager belongings and moved to Ontario.

What awaited them was very disheartening. Jobs were very difficult, if not impossible to come by and times were tough. These were the early days of the Great Depression, the time of poverty, starvation, and thousands of people abandoning their homes and wandering the countryside in search of jobs, food, and a place to sleep.

Victoria was beginning to question why they came to this country. Julien had told her this was a plentiful land, but from what she observed, life here was just as difficult as it was in war-torn Belgium.

"Was this a mistake?" she asked herself in fear. "What does the future hold for us?"

The Death of a Child

Julien's next move was to the Aylmer area in Southwestern Ontario. He heard great things of the farming in this area. Tobacco was one of the main crops between the Chatham and Delhi corridor at that time. Many other crops, such as corn, grains, and sugar beets were grown with great success.

They worked hard to make a good living for themselves, and they began to prosper. However, soon Victoria was pregnant again. She found it difficult to work in the fields and the strain of the pregnancy forced her to stop working. Julien was in a predicament. Charlotte was too young and frail to help, and his wife was unable. For the first time since leaving Europe, Julien was unsure of their future. "I must have help working the farm," he said to his wife. "But who?"

He was unable to afford to pay a hired man, even though many people were wandering the countryside, desperate for work. Times were hard and jobs were few. People were begging for work, but Julien was unable to afford this luxury.

Within a few months, there was a happy moment for the young family.

"You have a son," she told her husband proudly.

"Thank you," Julien replied with a tear in his eye.

They named their little boy James. Julien was relieved and happy to know he had a son, who in time could help him with the work and eventually take over for him.

Victoria was thrilled that after two daughters, she finally had a boy. She had fulfilled a wife's duty to her husband. Life was good for the first time in a very long time.

Their happiness was short-lived. Two years after his birth, James died suddenly. With the death of her little boy, Victoria became distant from her husband, while Julien grew more and more despondent.

"I've failed you as a wife," Victoria said to Julien as tears rolled down her cheeks.

"We will try again soon," he replied.

Victoria did her best to cope with the loss of her baby. Heartbroken, she felt the loss of two children, her little girl she had to leave behind in Belgium and her little boy, who succumbed to sickness, as many children did at this time. She was inconsolable.

Life became a struggle. In time, however, Victoria found she was pregnant once again. Things were starting to turn a corner for the couple. Fearful of losing another child, Victoria kept her distance from her husband. Having her soul ripped apart from the death of her baby was not an experience she wished to have again.

In October of 1923, Victoria gave birth, once again, this time, to a set of twin boys. The babies were small, and the survival rate was not very promising. She prayed to God daily for her children's health. The young mother was determined that her twins would survive.

"The babies need a warm environment," the doctor told her. "Warm your oven ever so slightly and leave the door open. Place the babies inside. This will help keep them warm when you can't physically hold them," the doctor said. "This will act as an incubator."

This homemade incubator was their only chance for survival. She was desperate and did what the doctor told her.

The couple was happy with the addition to their family. They named the boys Frederich and Alexander, after two of Julien's brothers in Belgium. One would assume this would be a joyous time for the family, but Julien's fears and apprehensions were growing daily. He desperately needed help on the farm to support his young, growing family. As the twins began to flourish, Julien became more and more desperate.

"What can I do? ***I need help***!" he yelled as he shook his fists to the heavens. He received no answer.

Several years passed, and Victoria found her time consumed by her daily chores of cooking, cleaning, and feeding her family, but her heart longed for her dead baby.

"Will the pain every stop?" she asked God.

She was having a very difficult time recovering from the death of James. Julien was becoming distant and withdrawn. He was working all day and long into the nights. He, in his own way, was trying to cope with the death of his first son. Julien was staggering from exhaustion, as he tried to keep food on the table for his young family. This was a hard life, a life that consumed every hour of every day. This was the life he chose for them.

"Did I make a mistake?" he asked himself. "I didn't think it was going to be this difficult."

The crops they were growing were very weather dependent. Not enough rain caused serious issues for the farmers, as did too much rain. But, what the tobacco farmers feared the most was hail and frost. Either one could completely destroy their year's work and, sometimes, their life's work. Many farmers found themselves bankrupt after a hail or frost. They just didn't have the money to survive until the next year.

In the 1920's, the farm families had the extra chores of caring for the many animals that helped them in the fields. Horses and oxen were used to pull ploughs, wagons, and tobacco boats. These animals had to be well-cared for. Their livelihood depended on them. Usually, the older children and the wife cared for the animals, but in Julien's case, Charlotte was terrified of the beasts, and Victoria had enough to do with the home and children. Since James' death, Victoria had become withdrawn from Julien. They were losing touch with each other, because neither knew how to cope with the death they had just experienced.

Soon, admitting defeat, Julien found he could no longer keep the farm going without help. He needed help if they were going to survive. The luxury of being able to afford a hired man just wasn't there. Where would they move next if this tobacco farm failed? What alternatives did they have in this new country that was riddled with poverty, on one hand, and wealth, on another? A successful tobacco farm could bring them the wealth and life beyond their wildest hopes and dreams.

"But how?" Victoria asked him one night.

Suddenly, he remembered the daughter they abandoned in Belgium. Aline would be over 10 years old now and able to do a full day's work. He could teach her everything that needed to be done.

"We bring Aline to Canada," he said to his wife. "She must be old enough by now to be able to work." "She can be the hired help we can't afford, right now."

So the plan was set in motion. Aline would come to Canada to be the "hired man" on the farm. It was back-breaking work, filled with long, hot days of dirt and sweat, but if Julien had help, he believed they could make a success of the farm.

One month later, Victoria left her children in the care of a friend and prepared for the voyage home.

"I'm going to fetch my daughter," she told her friend, almost busting with excitement.

She prepared to board the ship for the long journey to Belgium. Victoria was happy to be travelling back to her home country. Happy with the idea of seeing her mother again, she was also afraid of meeting her daughter. This would be her first time back to her home country, since leaving her daughter and mother.

"Will she even know who I am?" she wondered. "I haven't seen her since she was an infant. She probably won't remember me."

Trying to remain positive for the future, Victoria boarded the ship to Belgium. She was going back to the daughter she abandoned so many years ago. She was about to come face to face with the shame of her past and the life she left for her husband.

CHAPTER TWO

Aline's Story: A Life of Slavery, Sexual Abuse and Misery

A Little Girl in Belgium

Aline's childhood in Belgium was a happy one, but also one of many struggles. She lived with her Grandmother Emily (Victoria's mother) and her young cousins in a small house in Coolscamp. The children helped their grandmother and learned at her knee. Emily taught her granddaughter how to cook and sew, but her main specialty was making bread. The small house would be filled with the lovely aroma on bread days. The children's mouths would water in anticipation of that first slice being cut and the soft texture of the bread as they took their first bite. The heel of the bread was always the sought-after piece.

As a young child, Aline's life was one of poverty. The First World War was raging throughout Europe. Many children found themselves orphaned and desperate for food and shelter.

Emily's home was overtaken and occupied by German soldiers. She and the children lived under the constant threats from the soldiers, but Emily was determined to protect her grandchildren at any cost.

Their daily struggles for food were compounded by the soldiers, who demanded to be fed first.

"Madam, **you will** cook for my soldiers and do the washing of their clothes," the commanding officer ordered Emily. "My soldiers will sleep in this house.

You and these children will sleep in one bedroom." The small family was forced to live in an occupied hell. Their lives were no longer their own. Each day, they lived in fear, at the whim of the soldiers. You never knew what the soldiers were capable of. What little food was left after they served the men, Emily would use to feed the children.

Even though every day was a challenge for Aline and her grandmother, they were happy that they were together. The old woman loved and cared for her granddaughter. Aline grew up not knowing her real mother, but it didn't matter to her. She had someone here in this life, who cared for her, and to a young girl, that was all that mattered.

The simple life Aline shared with her grandmother was about to be destroyed. Emily knew this day might come, but she had grown so fond of her granddaughter, she hoped it never would.

Emily received a letter from her daughter, Victoria in Canada. The letter stated that Victoria would be returning to Belgium to "fetch her daughter." In her letter she told her mother of her expanded family and the work on a tobacco farm. They needed help! "They want free labour," Emily thought to herself. "Poor Aline. What in God's name will happen to her when she gets to Canada?"

Aline would soon be taken away from her Grandmother, a woman who loved her, taught her, and cared for her as if she was her own daughter. She had been the only mother figure Aline had ever known.

On the day Victoria arrived, the children were at school. She walked into her mother's house, and in an instant, all the shame she had endured here many years before returned in one second. She caught her breath in her chest and almost turned to leave, but she was here for a reason. Soon she could leave and never return.

"Hello Mama," she said to her mother as she kissed her mother on the cheek.

"Victoria, my daughter, you look well," Emily said to her.

As the women chatted over coffee, Victoria explained everything she had learned about tobacco farming to her mother. They talked about the future of living in Canada and how Aline would have a good life there.

"She does not want to go, Victoria," Emily said.

"She has to go, Mother!" Victoria snapped back. "She has no say in the matter. We need her help on the farm."

Suddenly, the door opened and Aline walked inside. She stopped immediately, frozen in terror upon seeing Victoria. The girl said nothing.

"Hello, daughter," Victoria said.

With tears in her eyes, Aline looked to her grandmother, who nodded to her.

"Go to her, Aline," Emily said to the girl.

Slowly and cautiously, Aline approached Victoria.

"Hello," she said to the woman. She stood at least two feet away from her mother. She didn't like the feeling in her stomach when she looked in this woman's eyes. She was frightened.

"Turn around and let me look at you," her mother said.

Obediently, Aline turned slowly, allowing her mother to examine her.

"She looks fine," Victoria commented.

Aline's heart was breaking. She looked to her grandmother for comfort. "It will be alright, my little one," her grandmother said to her, holding her hand. "You will be alright."

Aline's love for her Grandmother was unconditional, and the poor girl was horribly heart-broken. She didn't want to leave; she didn't want to go to Canada to live with people she didn't know.

"Who is this woman!" she screamed inside her head. *"She isn't my mother! She can't be!"*

Aline was desperate to stay in Belgium with her grandmother, but Victoria was her mother, and she had to be respectful. She didn't want to go to this Canada place. She wanted to stay here! In Belgium!

The young girl had no idea what the future would hold for her. How can she live there, when she doesn't know anyone or even know the language? Trying to keep control over her emotions, she looked at Victoria and felt hate for the woman. She was being ripped away from the only person she ever loved and the only family she had ever known, all for the sake of *"this woman and her family."*

The day Aline hugged her grandmother for the last time in her life was a day she would never forget. Victoria and Aline were strangers to each other. Victoria had left behind a baby, and standing before her now was a young girl, just beginning to bloom into young womanhood.

With one last hug for her grandmother, she began to cry. Tears poured down the young girl's face as she felt her mother pulling on her arm.

"I don't want to leave you, Mama," she said to her grandmother through her sobs.

"You **must** go now, little one. You're real Mama needs you," her grandmother replied back.

Victoria's tugging pulled them apart.

Deep in her heart, Aline knew she would never see this woman again. Her soul was destroyed that day, and she would never forgive her mother for causing this.

The voyage to Canada was long, and the seas were rough. Aline was sea-sick for many days. Never before had she felt anything like this, and she had never felt so alone. What would the future hold for her when she arrived to this new life? Would she be able to cope with the work? Would her family accept her? Only time would tell, and that was something Aline had a great deal of time.

The terrible pain of being separated from her grandmother never left her. She missed the woman so much. Every night, when she went to bed, she would cry herself to sleep, but even though sometimes crying is good for the soul, Aline felt lost, alone, and very afraid. She also began having nightmares that something terrible had happened to her grandmother. She would wake up in a terrible, cold sweat. Fear and agony was in her heart, but she didn't understand why.

A New Life with Strangers

When Aline arrived on the farm in Canada, she knew this was not going to be an easy life for her. Forced to live with strangers, who wanted nothing more from her than her ability to work, she felt more alone than ever.

She and Victoria walked into the house. Three children ran up and hugged their mother.

"Who is this?" Charlotte asked with a snarl.

"This is Aline, your sister. She has been living with your grandmother in Belgium. She has come to help us on the farm," Victoria told them.

The boys greeted Aline and quickly ran out to play. Charlotte, on the other hand, was shocked to discover she was not the eldest child. She knew better than to question her parents about such a delicate topic. "Take your sister to your room and show her where to put her things," Victoria told Charlotte.

Once in the room, Charlotte turned to Aline with an angry look on her face and said, "Why are you really here and who are you?"

"I am your sister, and I am here to work," Aline replied.

"Put your things over there," Charlotte snapped, and turning, she left the room.

Aline unpacked her trunk and neatly placed her clothing away.

The last item she removed from her trunk was a framed picture of her grandmother. Tears began running down her cheeks. "NO! I must not do that here," she scolded herself. "I have to be strong and do my best to get along with these people."

That night, just before dinner, Aline met Julien. He was a tall man, with piercing blue eyes and a large nose. He frightened her. "This is who I have to spend my days with," she thought. She knew it didn't matter how she felt; she was here for a reason. She must make the best of it.

Over the next few weeks, Aline found Julien was not an easy man to work for. He worked on the farm like a demon and only stopped for meals and sleeping, well after dark. Aline tried her best to please her stepfather. She worked as hard as humanly possible, but it seemed the work was never-ending. It was backbreaking work, but she never complained. If she did say anything to Julien or her mother, her complaints were usually met with a slap across the face, going without dinner, or extra chores. The work was hard, and Aline was hungry after being out in the fields. She found going without a meal was more than she could take, so she rarely complained about anything. She struggled every day to do her best, but it seemed her best was never quite good enough.

The relationship between mother and daughter was one of strain and tension. Victoria didn't enjoy being around her daughter. She was a constant reminder of her past life and the shame and humiliation she had left behind years before.

"This child ruined my life," Victoria thought many times as she looked at Aline. "Things could have been so different for me had I had not been raped by that man. Now this child is standing in front of me every day as a constant reminder of that shame," she thought. "I thought it would be alright, but I can't stand to look at her!"

Life in the house was not happy for Aline. Even though she was happy to find she had a sister and two brothers, her happiness was short lived. Aline's existence was kept a dark secret by Julien and Victoria. No one had ever spoken about her, who she really was and why she suddenly appeared in their lives, other than the girl was here to work. They knew Aline was their sister, but they treated her with disdain, and instead of making their new sister welcome, they treated her as an outsider, someone who was hired to help their father work the farm; she was just another labourer.

Charlotte's treatment of Aline was disgraceful. She was jealous and hated the fact that she had to share her parents with this 'new' girl. The boys didn't bother Charlotte. She was used to them, and they were boys.

Charlotte was a selfish girl, who demanded her parent's attention. She hated the fact that Aline was here. "I wish you had never come here!" she shouted at Aline, one day. The girls were in their bedroom, getting ready for church, when Charlotte decided Aline was taking up 'her' space. "Hurry up and get out of here," she snapped. "We were better before you came here," she said to Aline. The hate in her voice very evident.

The once happy home, according to Charlotte, was destroyed by this unknown girl. Confused and hurt by all the hate from her sister, Aline turned to prayer. Her grandmother taught her about faith in God, and this was her only comfort.

"Dear God," she prayed. "Give me the strength to endure this life and to be kind to these people." "Take care of Grandma. I miss her so." With those words, once again, the tears fell silently down Aline's pretty face.

After months of hard physical labour, Aline became quite strong. She was determined to make the best of her new situation. She accepted she must stay in Canada with probably no chance of returning to Belgium and the grandmother she loved so dearly.

One morning at breakfast, Victoria said to Julien, "I received a letter from Belgium, this morning."

"Oh?" He said rather disinterestedly.

"My mother died," she told him.

Hearing these words shocked Aline to the soul. She jumped out of her chair and ran out of the house. She ran blindly down the lane to the barn. Her eyes overflowed with tears and her heart was full of pain. Her mother/grandmother was gone! "How can that be?" she screamed. "She can't leave me here; she can't!"

Never before had she felt such loss. The only person she loved was gone. "Life doesn't matter to me anymore," she said. ***"Mama!"*** she cried out in the barn. No one heard her cries, and no one came to get her.

Hours later, exhausted and empty of tears, she went back to the house and went to her room. As she got ready for bed, and she said her prayers, as always, with one exception. Tonight, she prayed for the soul of her grandmother. There were no other prayers to be said.

No one returned to Belgium for the funeral; money just wasn't there for another sea voyage, and there was work to be done on the farm.

Victoria was living in her own personal hell and had little time to devote to anyone. The distance between Victoria and Aline grew larger. Aline was so heartbroken, she felt she would die. Her grandmother was the last binding-tie to a life she once had, a happy life, not this life of hatred, endless work, and no future. Aline desperately needed someone to hold her and comfort her. Her loneliness grew as the days passed. The other children did not share in the grief of their mother or sister. After all, they had never met the woman.

Victoria, in her grief, turned away from everyone. Julien was dispassionate, regarding the entire situation. It didn't matter to him. All he was concerned about was the crops and the endless hours of work that he had.

"Just keep working," he told Aline one afternoon. "In time, you won't feel anything."

Aline buried herself in the endless work. She was becoming a good help to Julien. The more she was capable of doing, the more he added to her burden.

As time went on, Aline was growing and developing into a beautiful young girl. She was physically strong, and her body was lean and muscular from all the heavy work she was doing. Everyone was beginning to notice her and her transformation.

Aline had not realized that her step-father was keeping a close eye on her. She was young and unaware of her beauty. After the loss of her grandmother, Aline buried herself in work and buried her feelings deep. She was numb. She felt nothing. Never again would she allow anyone to hurt her. She had endured too much pain and sorrow for someone so young. All she knew was that she was a pawn in this family, a tool to be used how 'they' saw fit.

Julien was tired of Victoria's distant nature. He was not the type of man to wait around for a woman. As a result, Julien spent more and more time with Aline out in the fields. Victoria had, however, taken notice of Julien's activities. She was becoming very concerned.

"We never see him," Charlotte said to Aline one day. "He only spends time with you! It's not fair...we are his children!"

The animosity was growing within the family, an animosity that would span generations.

You're Safe with Me: I'm Your Stepfather

Over time, Aline had developed a good working relationship with Julien. She had to spend hour after endless hour working side by side with him in the fields. As their relationship developed into a somewhat trusting relationship, Aline was beginning to let down her guard, slightly. He had provided her with the understanding and comfort she was so desperate for after the death of her beloved grandmother. Her trust of Julien was growing. For her, life inside the house was still one of indifference and struggle, but she found a bit of freedom outside, while working with her stepfather.

Aline was a young, naive girl when it came to men. She was given no guidance from her mother, and she felt approaching her mother with any questions would be inappropriate. Aline's knowledge of men was based solely on the German soldiers, who had occupied her Grandmothers' house in Belgium during the war. The soldiers were rough, angry, and very demanding. They ignored the children as long as they were quiet. Aline was not aware that her relationship with her stepfather was about to change.

Julien was a man, who was strong and handsome. He was very aware of the beautiful young woman. Since Aline had arrived to work the farm, Julien was distracted by the girl. Victoria rarely helped Julien with anything to do with farm work. She was busy with the house, children, and the daily struggles of farm life in the 1920's. Life kept her busy and exhausted, and she found she had very little time to devote to her husband, in any way. As a mother of four children, she had very little spare time.

"Keep away from me, Julien," she would snap at him. "We can't afford another mouth to feed."

Angry with the rejection of his wife, Julien turned and walked away from her. At times though, she was helpless to fend off her husband's advances. He did what he wanted, when he wanted. Women, at that time, had very few rights. It was dangerous to speak against your husband. Julien felt he had every right to use Victoria however he chose.

Victoria grew more and more distant from her husband. He was not the kind and loving man she had married. The struggles of farm life, the endless working, and hardships were driving them apart.

Julien began looking elsewhere to satisfy his urges. He found comfort and relief wherever he could. Things were so busy on the farm, there wasn't much of a chance to acquire female companionship, so he began turning his advances to the only other eligible female at his disposal, Aline.

Aline had no comprehension of what was happening. She had to spend her days with this man, and disagreeing with her stepfather would mean punishments. Going without food was one thing, but the beatings she would have to endure would make it impossible for her to do the work. She did what she was told.

With the summer heat streaming down on the barn, Aline walked in to get a bag of chicken feed. Julien was waiting there for her.

"I'm very upset today, Aline. Can you give me a hug?" he asked her.

Obediently, she walked to him. The way he placed his arms around her set off warning alarms in her head. She began to struggle.

"It's alright, girl. I'm not going to hurt you," he said soothingly as he stroked her hair.

"Everything is fine," he said. "Trust me."

She knew she could not disobey her step-father, so Aline allowed him to do what he wanted.

Not really knowing why this was wrong, Aline began to trust him. She was so starved for affection and attention from anyone, but Julien went too far.

She couldn't believe what was happening. This man was the only father-figure she had ever known. How could he be doing this to her? Before Aline had a full grasp of what was going on, Julien had already forced himself upon her. He knew this was wrong and very damaging, but it was too late. The deed had been done.

"I'm sorry," he said to her afterward as he held her. "This will be our little secret," he said. "No one must know. Promise me you won't tell anyone," as he looked her in the eyes. "No one!"

Hurt and completely confused about what had just occurred, Aline picked up the bag of chicken feed, then turned around and sat down on a bale of hay.

"What just happened?" she asked herself. "Why do I hurt?"

Julien had just walked out of the barn, as if nothing had happened. He left her sitting there, alone, with so many emotions welling up inside. She didn't understand any of this! She was only 14 years old, but she felt she had aged twenty years in ten minutes.

"I don't understand why I am here," she said out loud to the heavy, hot air in the barn.

An hour later, Aline emerged from the barn to continue her chores. She walked in a fog. One thing that was very clear to her, though, was her mother must never find out what just happened.

So alone, she desperately wished for someone to talk with. She was in pain, physically and emotionally. She had held her emotions in check for so long, but nothing like this had ever happened before. Aline thought that what she had done was wrong, but Julien had convinced her of the opposite. Since she trusted him (she really had no choice), "it must have been all right," she thought. But something deep inside her wouldn't let this incident lay quiet. "Is this what life holds for me?" she asked the heavens. "Am I supposed to live in this house full of a family who treats me as an outsider? Isn't my mother supposed to be happy I'm here and show me love? Am I supposed to endure my stepfather forcing himself on me whenever the mood strikes him? Please God, why am I here!" she yelled.

Aline ran back into the barn and curled up in a corner. Everything she had buried deep inside her heart came pouring out. The dam had burst, and she could no longer hold back the pain and tears. She sobbed so deeply her young body shook.

"You aren't finished here, Aline," she heard a voice say to her heart.

Not believing what she'd just heard, she looked around the barn. She could barely see from the tears that filled her eyes, but there was no one there.

It was then that she felt a pair of warm arms wrapping themselves around her shoulders. The warmth and comfort that she felt calmed her, and she felt safe.

"God, have you heard me?" she asked through her sobs.

Once again she heard the words, ***"You aren't finished here, Aline."***

Feeling safe and comforted, Aline fell asleep where she sat. Keeping watch over her was her Guardian Angel, ever present and ever protective of the young girl.

The Secret is Revealed

Recovering from the breakdown in the barn, Aline worked and cleaned endlessly. She kept busy, so she wouldn't have to stop and feel. She had grown used to Julien and the time he spent with her. Each time, before he walked away, he would always say, "This is our little secret." This had to be kept a secret. Aline was too embarrassed to tell anyone, and she was terrified someone would find out what was happening.

At night, she would cry into her pillow. Over and over again, she would ask, "Is there no one to help me?" Every night, she would ask the same question and received no answer.

Aline began feeling more tired than usual and felt ill. She thought she had been working too hard and not eating enough, but over time, she noticed her body was changing. Her breasts hurt and her clothes were getting tight. What was happening?

She found her mother staring at her one afternoon.

"When was the last time you had a cycle?" her mother asked.

"Three months ago," she replied timidly.

Victoria walked over to her daughter and slapped her hard across the face. "***Who have you been with?***" she demanded.

Crying out in pain Aline began to sob.

"You're pregnant!" her mother screamed. "**Who is the father**?"

"I don't know," Aline said through her tears.

"What have you done! You are a bad girl, and you have brought shame on this family!" her mother said to her.

"Mama!" Aline cried. But her mother would not listen to another word she said.

Victoria turned her back on her daughter and walked away.

"Mama!" Silence.

Julien was going to have to act fast. Aline was pregnant, and he had to come up with a solution. There was no way he could be named as the father. After all, everyone thought he was Aline's father. Julien was beside himself with panic. He would be ruined and would become an outcast, just like his wife had been fifteen years ago in Belgium. Everyone in the area believed Aline was their oldest daughter. They told the story of how they had to leave her behind to make a start in the new country. This was a lie, and Aline knew it. She had been forced to go along with the story.

"What am I supposed to do?" she asked herself. Being pregnant was the worst thing possible. "Will Julien help me?" she wondered. "Will anyone help me?"

Aline knew that girls, who got pregnant before they got married, would never be respected. The shame she was feeling was mounting. People would accuse her of being a girl of bad morals.

In the 1920's, it was a terrible scandal to be single and pregnant, but to be 14 years old and pregnant by your step-father, well, this would probably destroy the entire family. There was another scenario. This idea was even worse to consider. *Incest!* This could ruin the entire family for generations.

There was no one left in Belgium for Aline to go and live with. She was here in this country and would have to stay. "What's going to happen to me?" she wondered.

She soon learned.

"I'm the father," Julien told Victoria.

Victoria was furious. She hurled the bowl she was holding at Julien's head. "You horrible man!" she screamed at him. "How could you do such a thing?"

Julien ducked as the bowl went flying by his head. It hit the wall and smashed into thousands of tiny pieces.

"I'm going to help her," he told Victoria.

"Haven't you done enough?" she snapped back at him.

"I will find a solution to this," he said. "She won't tell anyone, and I'll make sure someone takes her off our hands."

"How?" she asked.

"I'll find someone to marry her right away," he said.

"Do it quickly," she said to him as she went upstairs to where her daughter sat.

Aline sat in her room, waiting for her mother. Suddenly, the door flew open and there stood Victoria. Aline was terrified. She knew her mother didn't like her much, but right now, she actually feared the woman. Nothing could prepare Aline for the onslaught of her mother. Victoria was enraged. She whipped her, verbally abused her, and locked Aline her in her room. She couldn't bear to look at the girl. Humiliated and shamed with the actions of her husband, Victoria vowed she would never forgive either of them.

Beaten and feeling like she wanted to die, Aline found solace in prayer. Every night, she prayed to Our Lady to remove her from this terrible life. She prayed for understanding and guidance. Was she mistaken with what she had heard in the barn that hot day?

"What's going to happen to me?" she wondered. Her life was in the hands of Julien and Victoria. The stress in the house was suffocating. No longer could the horror of the secret be kept hidden behind closed doors. The other children in the house were kept in the dark, but Charlotte knew something was not right, and she believed it had to do with Aline.

"This girl is upsetting my mother and father," she thought. Once again, she vowed to hate Aline. Charlotte continued to be relentless with her torment of her sister.

Luckily, by now, the farm was becoming profitable, and Julien had some extra money set aside. The solution to the embarrassment and problem of Aline was obvious. He had leverage. So, he decided he would marry off Aline to the first person he could find. The only problem with that was they knew most of the people in the area. What they needed was a stranger, someone no one in the area knew. They decided to bide their time, what precious little time they had, and find a suitable candidate and pay him to marry Aline and take the child as his own.

In the meantime, Aline was not allowed to leave the farm. She was not allowed to come in contact with anyone who visited the farm. They had to hide their shame at all cost, which was a challenge, most days, with The Great Depression ramping up. People wandered the countryside looking for food and shelter. 1927 was a very difficult time for many people. The jobless rate was high, and the homeless rate was even higher. Entire families were travelling around, from place to place, looking for work and begging for food.

The Great Depression was a time the world will never forget. Between 1929 and 1939, 30% of the labour force was out of work. One fifth of the population ended up on some form of government assistance, and in the

Canadian Prairies, two-thirds of the population were on relief. "We can't afford to plant our crops, and even if we could, we can't afford to hire workers to help bring in the crops," many farmers said. "We just can't do it."

The economy in Canada was shifting from primary industries, such as farming, fishing, and logging, to manufacturing. Wages fell drastically, which caused people to change their eating habits. Cheaper foods were used, and families made do with soups and beans and potatoes; foods that are more filling, can be used in a multitude of ways and made to last longer. Even the cheap cuts of meat were out of the financial reaches of many people. Families could not afford to eat beef, so they decided horse meat was cheaper.

People were struggling in so many ways. They couldn't afford to heat their homes or feed their families. Many people became sick, and many died.

Families were torn apart, as fathers would leave their homes in search of work. They would travel hours, days, and weeks to find work to feed their families.

Many women had a different approach to the situation. When their husbands left to find work, the women assumed an enormous burden. Some women took in boarders. They would cook and provide rooms for those who were travelling and could afford to pay.

Other women took in laundry and sewing to supplement income, or they went out to work long hours for those who could afford the luxury of help. It was such a horrible and difficult time for many women. The Catholic Church had always taken a stance against birth control, but it was the women who were left with the hungry mouths to feed. Pushed to the limits of what a woman can endure, many women began to defy the Catholic Church. They practiced whatever methods of birth control they could to prevent another baby and another mouth to feed.

The birth rate in Canada began to decline, despite Mackenzie King, the Prime Minister of Canada, telling everyone this crisis would pass. Because he felt this way, he refused to provide federal relief to his country.

To make matters worse for North America, in 1929, the crash of Wall Street happened. The Wall Street Crash threw the United States into turmoil. Many people lost their fortunes; people were committing suicide, and the future looked bleak for everyone.

Even though the situation was grim, many Europeans where still flocking to Canada with the hope of working the land and making a good living.

In 1926, two brothers, Marcel and Adolf, stepped foot on Canadian soil.

The Great Depression Travelers

In 1926, two brothers, Marcel and Adolf, hoping to change their futures and their luck, arrived in Canada from Belgium. Half-starved from the long journey, the brothers were here to seek their futures in the bountiful farming areas of Southwestern Ontario.

Once on Canadian soil, the men had their first of many disagreements with the authorities.

"Do you have a sponsor?" the authorities asked.

"No, we didn't know we had to have one," Marcel replied.

"You cannot stay in this area without a sponsor. You can go to Manitoba, Saskatchewan, or Alberta. You don't need a sponsor there," the officer said kindly to them.

A sponsor is a person, who would accept responsibility for the new arrivals and agree that they knew the two men in Belgium. They knew no one in this country.

"**You must leave Ontario now**," the officer stated. "I cannot give authorization for you to stay here. As I said, go west. **Leave Ontario now or there will be trouble for you**."

Marcel and Adolf thanked the man and turned to leave. Having just arrived from Europe, starving and poor, the brothers were two broken men.

"Now, what do we do, Marcel?" Adolf asked.

"We have no choice. We have to head west. Maybe things will be better for us out there," Marcel told his brother. He worried about Adolf. Adolf was the youngest of eight children. He had always been a sickly child. Marcel had always looked out for his younger brother, as he did now.

"We will find something, Adolf," Marcel said to him. "Right now, let's get started heading for the Manitoba border."

Adolf smiled at his brother. He trusted and loved this man.

"Somehow, I have to get us to the west," Marcel thought to himself. "First, I have to find Adolf some food and shelter for the night."

As Marcel watched over his brother as he slept, he vowed to their mother he would keep her son safe. To God, he promised the same and asked for protection.

On their journey, the two brothers walked for endless hours, begged for rides and food, and took odd jobs whenever they could. It was a horrible life, but it was better than what they left behind in Belgium. They slept on the sides of roads in the tall grass, in haystacks, and barns, provided they weren't found and chased off private property, usually with a shotgun leveled at them.

When the men were able, they would steal a ride on the rails. Each time, they ran the risk of being shot or beaten severely by the guards. Finally, exhausted and filthy, the men arrived in Winnipeg. What they saw made their hearts sink even deeper. They walked into a province of suffering and desperation. "Why did they send us here?" Marcel thought. "There is *nothing* here. The people are worse off than we are." This was the land of opportunity that they had heard so much about?!

The two brothers did their best to find work, taking on anything and everything. The word humiliation no longer existed in their vocabulary. Starving and exhausted, they traded work for food and a place to lay their heads at night. But Marcel's spirit could not be broken. He was determined to survive this brutal country. He was a strong willed man, equally strong in body, and it was this strength of character that drove him onward.

After a few weeks, the brothers were told by a government official to leave Manitoba. "There are no jobs here for you," the man said. "There are enough local people without work. We don't need immigrants coming in and adding to the burden of our province."

Confused, Marcel replied, "We were told to come here by the officials in Ontario."

"Then I suggest you go out east," the man offered. "You may find jobs out there in the fishing industry."

Marcel knew there was work in Ontario, hard work, but it was a place where a man could make something of himself. Marcel was a very headstrong man and decided they needed to go back to Ontario. Seeing this as their only solution, the brothers decided they would take the chance.

As they made their way back to Ontario Adolf was getting weaker. The men had been living on whatever they felt was edible. They ate grass, plants, garbage, and sometimes, stole from farm animals. Food was scarce. The younger brother was struggling with the hard physical labour and the lack of decent food. Adolf was a tiny man. He stood no higher than 5' 4". He was thin and fragile. Adolf's parents and their eight children had survived the harshness of a battered Europe during World War 1. Marcel wanted more from life and, with his brother, kissed their mother goodbye for the last time and left their home. Now, as Marcel lay beside his brother in the tall grass beside the rail bed, he remembered the tear in his mother's eyes as she wished them well and placed her rosary in his pocket, never knowing if she would see either of them alive again.

On their travels, they met a man who told them of a section in Ontario, where the farming land was very rich and fertile. Vegetables were plentiful, but the main crop grown was tobacco. The farmers were desperate to get their crops off the field and stored into the barns. In short, they needed labourers. Marcel and Adolf decided that was the place for them. Together, they headed for Ontario in hopes of being able to find work and a permanent life.

Suddenly, with a glimmer of hope for their future, and very tired of walking, they jumped a train.

In the years leading up to the Great Depression, if a "hobo" was found, they ran the risk of being shot on sight if they tried to run; beaten severely or jailed if caught. It was a crime to ride the rails, but the brothers were desperate. One night, they found shelter in an empty water tank car on a train heading east to Ontario. Being steam driven locomotives, if was necessary to make frequent stops to fill their water tanks.

Beaten by exhaustion, the two brother climbed inside the tanker car. The rocking and soothing sound of the train soon found the men fast asleep.

In a sudden panic, they both were awakened by freezing cold water pouring into the tanker. If they called out, they would be caught, beaten, and arrested. If they remained quiet, they would drown. With fear in his eyes, Adolf made his way to his brother. What was going to happen to them? Neither brother could swim. If they spoke up, they surely would be caught and arrested or shot. ***What were they to do?*** As the tanker filled up, terror began to take over. Drowning was evident now, but Marcel refused to accept this fate. His survival mode took hold of him. Nothing else mattered, but the fight for survival and protecting his brother. They took their chances and screamed for help. They kept screaming, and seconds before the freezing water covered their faces, two large arms grabbed them by the shirt and hauled them out.

"What the hell where you doing in there?" asked the train guard.

Unable to speak yet, Marcel and Adolf fell to the ground.

"I asked you a question," the guard snarled at Marcel as he kicked him in the ribs.

Doubling over in pain, Marcel managed to say, "we are trying to get to Ontario."

"There's nothing in Ontario for the likes of you two," the guard commented.

"Let's have some fun with these two boys," said the guard to his friends.

"Let's teach them a lesson," another guard replied.

For the next ten minutes, the guards kicked, punched and beat the brothers with their clubs. Once having satisfied their lust for power, the guards left the men beside the train tracks, bloodied and bruised.

Hours later, the two men managed to get to their feet and begin walking east. Suddenly, they heard shots being fired. Shot gun pellets flew past their heads and imbedded themselves into the wood of the trees.

"Run!" Marcel said to Adolf. ***"Run for your life!"***

Staggering and running for their lives, the men soon came to an old abandoned shed. Unable to continue, they opened the door and cautiously looked inside.

"It's empty," Marcel said. "We can stay here for the night. You find a place to lay down, and I'll see if I can find any food."

Marcel soon returned to his brother. "All I could find were some bugs, rotten apples, and grass," he told Adolf. "It will get us through until morning."

This looked like a feast to the starved men, and they heartily ate what their maker provided. For the moment, they were safe.

The next morning, the men had slightly recovered from their ordeal of the night before. They rose stiff and very sore, but knew they had to keep moving. The trains were not a safe place for them. So they walked. They walked for days, hoping they were heading in the right direction.

"God, help us!" Marcel prayed as they walked. "Protect us and keep us safe."

As their journey continued, they slept were they could, found work if available, and ate when possible. Taken to the brink of human suffering, the men resorted to stealing. **They had to eat!**

For weeks, they travelled, hoping and praying someone would help them. They saw starvation everywhere they looked. They knew what starvation looked and felt like.

Late one evening, Marcel turned to his brother. "We have to try the train again," he said.

"But it isn't safe," Adolf replied.

"We have to! We can't keep walking like this," Marcel said as he grabbed his brother's shoulder in comfort. "We have to try."

In the dark of the night, they were able to jump another train. They took shelter behind some barrels stacked in a corner of the cars, and soon, the rocking of the train lulled them into a deep sleep.

Half-starved, filthy, and exhausted beyond belief, the two men arrived in a little town. They had no idea where they were, but were hoping they had finally arrived in Southwestern Ontario. To their shock and horror, they discovered they had gone too far. There was no way for them to tell how far they had gone.

Stopping a fellow traveler, the brothers were stunned when they were told they had arrived in Quebec. They had completely missed Ontario. How could this have happened, and what were they to do now? Determined to find their dream and very concerned for the health of his brother, Marcel soon found he had no pride or dignity left. His brother's life was at stake!

"I must fix this!" he thought to himself. "But how? I promised mother no harm would come to us."

Gathering what little strength he had left, Marcel helped his brother to his feet.

"We must keep walking. I know God will protect us," he said.

Looking his younger brother in the eyes, he said, "just a little farther."

The two men wandered down a narrow road on the outskirts of a small town in Quebec. Rounding a corner, they saw a small farmhouse. With great caution, they approached the house and timidly knocked on the door. A kind older lady answered.

"What do you want?" she asked as she stared at the very thin and filthy men.

"My brother is hurt and ill. We need a place to sleep and a bit of food," he told the woman. "I will gladly do any work in exchange for food and shelter. Please help my brother," Marcel begged.

Noticing the tears welling up in Marcel's eyes, the old woman said, "Come in. Take your brother upstairs to the last room on the right. Get him undressed and into the bed. I will be up shortly to tend to his wounds."

"You are a gift from God," Marcel said to her as he helped his brother across the threshold.

Once Adolf was settled and resting comfortably in the bed, Marcel went back downstairs. The old lady had prepared a meal and was waiting in the kitchen for him.

"You can go in that room," she said pointing to a small room just off the kitchen. "Take off all your filthy clothes. I've laid out some of my husband's old things for you. Put them on and then come and eat." Marcel ate what he could that night. Never before had food tasted so wonderful to him. But he had gone without real food for so long, he found his stomach could not hold much.

When he had finished eating, the old woman said to him, "My name is Mme Moreau. You and your brother can spend a few days here. I will feed you, but you must do some work around the farm for me."

"I will do anything you ask," Marcel said to her. He was moved to tears by the kindness and giving of this gentle woman.

"There is a tub filled with hot water in the outer kitchen," she told him. "Go and wash yourself. You will find soap and a razor as well.

"Thank you for your kindness," was all Marcel was able to say to her.

The hot water soothed his sore and tired body. He soaked away the thousands of miles of dirt and grime that had stuck to his body.

Shaved and dressed in clean clothes, Marcel approached Mme Moreau. "How will I ever repay your kindness?" he asked her.

"Just do some chores for me. That will be enough," she said. "It's difficult for me, because I am alone, you see."

"I thank you, my dear woman," Marcel replied. "But I must repay you in some other way."

She would not hear of it. She told him to go back upstairs and visit with his brother.

"There is a second spare room beside the one your brother is in. There you can rest and sleep well," she told him as she lightly touched his arm.

"You are the answers to my prayers," he said to her before bidding her good night.

It had been a very long time since the men had been well-fed and clean. In a matter of minutes of lying down on the soft bed, Marcel fell into a deep and restful sleep. Tonight, there was no need for fear. "We are safe," he thought. Tonight there will be no fear of beatings, being chased, shot at, or exposure to the elements.

Marcel prayed with sincere thanks that night. He gave thanks for the woman, who reminded him so much of the mother he left behind in Belgium all those months ago.

The men stayed with Mme Moreau for four days. Adolf became stronger, and Marcel did everything the woman asked of him and more.

On the day they decided to take their leave of the lady, she had prepared a wonderful breakfast for them. "This is a feast," Adolf said to her. "Thank you." She asked them to sit at her table, once again, and to share one last meal with her. Together, they thanked God for everything they had.

The brothers felt the horrible sting of humiliation and shame. They could not repay the kindness of Mme Moreau. They had no money to give her in payment. Marcel offered her his last remaining possession. "Please take this rosary," he said to Mme Moreau as he stretched his hand out to her. "It belonged to our mother."

Seeing the pride and determination in Marcel's eyes, Mme Moreau knew she must accept the gift. "Thank you," she said to them both.

Marcel handed her the last remaining possession he had of his mother. It was a beautiful rosary from Lourdes. His mother had gone on pilgrimage many years before, and this rosary was her most treasured possession. Emily, their mother, gave Marcel the rosary and blessed both her sons before they left her. "Keep them safe, Blessed Mother," she prayed.

Marcel had carried this precious gift with him for the last several months.

Mme Moreau saw what this rosary meant to them, but to refuse the gift would hurt their pride.

"I will keep it safe, here with me," she said to them. "When you have made your way in this country, come back and visit me. I will give it back to you then." She kissed each man on the cheek and handed them each a little bundle of food to help them on their way. This simple act of kindness and giving was one that neither brother would forget for the rest of their lives. Truly there are God-sent people in this world.

The Future that Awaits

Two weeks later, Marcel and Adolf finally arrived in Southwestern Ontario. Once again, they were surprised at the prosperity of the area. The only hurdle they saw was that so many people had flooded to the area looking for work, the farmers had their choice of labourers. If the people had tobacco experience, they would be selected first. Marcel and Adolf had no experience with this crop, so they continued to travel, learning everything the could and continually begging for food.

One day, in mid-September, they came upon the farm that Julien and Victoria owned. Julien was looking for good, strong men to help finish the harvest and to work in the barn during stripping. He needed a replacement for his step-daughter, now visibly pregnant and unable to do hard labour.

Victoria and Julien gave them a place to sleep in the barn for the night. The brothers agreed to work for food and shelter. The type of work didn't matter to them. They were very thankful to Julien and his wife.

Julien, being the sort of man he was, recognized an opportunity when he saw one. Here were two young men, desperate for work and food. Once he heard their story, he knew they would do anything. Julien was also desperate. It was becoming more and more difficult to hide Aline and her pregnancy. He needed a father for her child, now! What he really needed, he decided, was the girl taken off his hands, with no reminders of his enormous mistake. He was running out of time; he must act soon.

"I have an idea," he said to Victoria one evening. "I will make an offer of $10,000 to the man who will marry Aline and give the baby his name."

"Julien!" Victoria screamed. "How can you do that?"

"We are out of time," he told her. "These are desperate men. They want money, and if one of them will marry her and claim the baby as his own, then no one will ever know of my shame."

"I don't like it, but we must do something. She is about one month away now," Victoria replied.

And so it was decided. The next day, Julien made the offer to the two brothers, hoping that one of them would accept. To sweeten the offer, Julien also offered to set the couple up on a farm of their own.

Quietly, he awaited their reply.

Both men were shocked and appalled by what Julien just offered them. They couldn't believe a man could be so desperate, as to sell his daughter.

Neither brother had ever seen $10,000 dollars; a King's ransom to be sure! Marcel thought about the idea. He was a single, 25-year-old man, who had nothing in this world. He and Adolf had left everything behind in Belgium to find a better life for themselves in Canada. Their mother would be devastated if she found out that both her sons had failed. So Marcel contemplated the offer.

"With that kind of money, I could take care of Adolf and send money home to Ma," he thought. "She's not an ugly girl, and she knows everything about farming. I could learn from her."

Adolf did not want a wife and family. Even the offer of money could not pull him in the right direction. He was a bachelor, and that was the way he was going to stay. They had made their decision. It was Marcel who would marry Aline and give the bastard child his last name.

"I will marry your daughter," he told Julien the next day.

"Good," Julien said to Marcel as the two men shook hands on the deal.

That night, Aline was called to the kitchen table. Frightened about the summons, the poor girl shook with fear.

"We have decided you will marry Marcel," she was told. "The two of you will be set up on a farm in Norfolk County, and he will give the child his name."

"What?" she asked.

"You heard me!" Julien shouted. "You will marry him, and he will give this bastard child a name. You have no say in the matter. Now go to your room!"

Aline's world came crashing down around her. She ran into her room and buried her head in the pillow.

"Why do they hate me so? I've done everything they have ever asked of me. I didn't want to come to this country in the first place, and now, they are selling me off because **he** used me!" she screamed into her pillow. Her head hurt and her eyes stung from tears, but she couldn't wash away the words her parents had just said to her.

"Dear God, how can you do this to me? Why?" she cried out.

As she fell into a fitful sleep, she once again heard the words, ***"You are not finished here."***

Marcel didn't particularly care for Aline when they met. He found her very quiet and removed. But that really didn't matter. He was going to be a wealthy man very soon. No longer would he suffer from starvation. His plans and reasons for coming to this country were finally, after so long, falling into place. To him, it didn't matter how it happened.

On October 11, 1927, in an official ceremony, Aline was sold to Marcel as his wife. She was so close to her time now and had felt the cramping of early contractions for days now.

It was a cold, wintery type of October day, more resembling a late November day. The sky was grey and overcast, and the clouds hung heavy in the sky with the threat of looming disaster.

Aline was forced to wear a large fur coat to hide her pregnancy from the Justice of the Peace. It was imperative the secret was kept as long as possible.

"We'll be free of this problem very soon," Julien said to his wife.

Pleased that the 'problem' was being taken care of, Victoria hated Julien for using her daughter in such a way. "I will never forgive you for this," she said to him.

Struggling to keep her sanity during the short service, Aline still could not believe what her parents had just done. "They sold me!" she thought. "What have they done to me?"

Still in a daze and struggling with her emotions, Aline felt a stabbing pain in her lower back. Not understanding what was happening, she kept quiet.

Julien believed he had made the deal of a lifetime. His embarrassment and shame would soon be gone. They had kept Aline hidden on the farm for many months now. Soon, they could tell friends and neighbours that Aline had been gone back to Belgium for a visit and returned with a husband and child. They were finally rid of her.

The newlywed couple travelled to the small town of Harrow, Ontario.

Aline, terrified beyond belief, was now at the mercy of this stranger. "Who was this man? He's ten years older than I am! What am I supposed to do?" she thought to herself. But she didn't have much time to think of the answers.

They arrived at a quaint little hotel, where Marcel thought they could have a good meal and possibly spend the night. Aline went into labour twenty minutes after arriving.

Marcel, not knowing what to do for his new wife, turned to the hotel owner. The owner's wife quickly took the girl upstairs and got her safely into a bed. It was fortunate that Aline was a strong, healthy, and young girl. Her body withstood the several hours of searing labour pain, until finally, exhausted and drenched in sweat, she gave birth to a healthy son.

"What will you name your baby," the woman asked her.

"Edward," replied the 15 year old new mother.

"You need to get some sleep now," the woman said. "I will take care of your baby for a while. You just rest."

"You have a healthy son," the woman told Marcel. "Your wife is doing very well."

"That's good," was his reply as he turned back to his beer. "Glad that is over with."

His lack of emotion was cause for concern.

Marcel was concerned with getting his money. He really didn't care about the kid. He was pleased Aline came through the labour well; after all, she was his ticket to $10,000.

Aline, completely exhausted after the birth, found her emotions running wild within herself. The feeling of the last few months of shame, embarrassment, and humiliation now came boiling to the surface. She was emotionally and physically drained. No longer able to contain the pain in her heart and soul, the young girl burst into tears. The old woman assumed it was a typical reaction to giving birth. She had no idea how much Aline had suffered. The older woman held the young girl while she sobbed her heart out. After ten minutes of crying, the older lady became concerned.

"My dear, are you alright?" she asked Aline.

Unable to answer, Aline just nodded her head.

"I'm here, my dear, you just go ahead and cry. Let it out," the woman whispered to the girl as she stroked her damp hair. "Shhh! Everything will be alright."

With this act of kindness, Aline was immediately taken back to the love and care she had received from her grandmother. She was taken back to a simpler time in life, before she was forced to come to this country. She hated it here, and now, she was tied to a man she didn't even know! "Will he be kind to me and my baby?" she prayed later that night.

"Oh dear God...help me!"

The Opportunity

A few weeks after the birth of Edward, Aline and Marcel travelled to the small town of Bothwell, Ontario. The owner of the hotel, where they stayed when the baby was born, told Marcel of a small hotel in Bothwell, owned by their friends, Odiel and Paula. Odiel had mentioned to his friend that he was looking for a couple to hire who could help them with the work.

Odiel and his wife were getting on in years and didn't have children of their own. They had no one to turn to for help.

A letter had been sent ahead, as a means of introduction for Marcel, but as he approached the hotel, he pulled from his breast pocket a second letter confirming the introduction.

The hotel was a very old building standing three stories tall. It stood majestically on one corner on the main intersection of town.

"This is a very nice place," Marcel commented to his wife.

"Yes, it is," she replied back.

As they walked through the main doors, Aline immediately fell in love with the place. The homey atmosphere and lovely décor made her feel very at home.

Marcel approached the older gentleman behind the bar.

"Hello sir," the man said in greeting.

"Hello. I am looking for Odiel. I am Marcel," he said.

The older man, with a smile on his face, turned to his wife and said, "they're here, Paula!"

A kindly lady turned around and looked at the young couple standing before her. Her eyes lit up with happiness.

"Oh my dears, I'm so glad you are here. Let me hold that baby!" she said as she took Edward out of Aline's arms. "He's adorable!"

"Thank you for your hospitality," Marcel said to Odiel, as the two men shook hands.

"You are welcome," he replied. "I hope you are eager to learn. The Mrs. and I are getting on in years, and we could really use the help of an eager young couple, such as you."

"I will learn whatever you wish to show me," Marcel replied back.

After a lovely dinner, Paula showed Aline where their room would be. "I have a cradle here for the baby," she said. "Lay him down, and I will show you where everything is."

"You are so very kind," Aline replied. As she followed the older woman down the hall towards the washroom, she felt her eyes sting with the beginning of tears. This time, they were tears of happiness. The next morning, after a good night's sleep, Marcel was put to work behind the bar. He interacted with customers and vendors. Odiel watched the young man as he talked easily with people. "This young man is rather impressive," he thought to himself. "I like this fellow."

Even though Marcel only had a grade five education, Odiel found the young man was very clever. Soon, Marcel was managing the bar and learning to do the accounts of the hotel. Marcel had a gift with numbers, and soon, he became indispensable to his new friend.

Aline was soon strong enough to begin working with Paula. She spent many hours with the kindly woman, learning everything she could about the care and operation of the hotel. When she was not caring for her baby, she was to do the cleaning and cooking. Odiel insisted on paying the young couple for their work and refused to take money in repayment for their room and food.

During the day, while Aline worked, Paula looked after Edward. She cared for the little one as if she was his grandmother. Each day, her feelings depended for Aline and her baby.

By January of 1928, life was beginning to settle for the two young people. Aline worked hard in the restaurant and hotel, cooking and scrubbing all day. She was proud of her work and tried her best not to disappoint Paula.

Marcel poured drinks, chatted about current events, and followed his mentor's lead. He was learning everything possible about running a profitable hotel. Odiel wanted to pass on his wisdom to the younger man, because he saw in him the desire to strive for something better from this life. Odiel seemed to understand the horrible hardships this man had survived, and his respect for Marcel grew. He saw a future for the young couple in this hotel.

Within two years of arriving, Marcel and Aline knew how to run a successful hotel. As the two couples had dinner one evening, Odiel set down his glass and said, "I want to sell you the hotel."

After catching his breath from choking on his beer, Marcel said, "You cannot be serious!"

"I am very serious," he replied. "We've been thinking about selling for several years now, but we want the hotel to go into the right hands."

"We cannot think of two people better suited to have as the new owners," Paula said to Aline, as she grabbed the young woman's hand.

Aline had grown to love the older lady. She was everything in a mother Aline had ever wanted.

"We accept," Marcel said as he stood from the table and shook the hand of his friend. He respected Odiel as a friend and businessman.

"Will you both stay on for a while after the sale," Marcel asked.

"Of course we will," Paula replied. "You are our family! We couldn't love you more if you were our real children. That is why we've made this decision to sell to you."

With a smile of contentment on her face, Paula turned to her husband and said, "We've made the right choice." Her husband nodded his head in agreement.

Odiel and Paula stayed on for a couple of years to help with some of the smaller jobs around the hotel. Paula had grown very attached to Edward. Her time spent with the baby was the best and most rewarding of her life. She enjoyed caring for her 'new' young family. Aline, on the other hand, found time slipping away from her. Morning turned into night and days turned into weeks. She was completely wrapped up in the hotel, she was losing track of time.

The young woman was exhausted by the end of the long days. At night, she would kiss her little boy on the forehead and then fall into bed, completely fatigued. She slept soundly until the next morning came, and she would rise and begin her day anew.

Time found a way to heal old wounds. Aline discovered she no longer feared her husband. She believed that he too had been a victim of Julien and Victoria.

Together, Aline and Marcel worked hard towards their future dreams. They developed a mutual respect and liking for each other. As a couple, they found their relationship was growing. Together, they would talk over the day's events and, in time, shared their ideas for the future.

In the meantime, the hotel was becoming prosperous. Marcel was a good businessman and knew the value of hard work of money. He was becoming a shrewd hotel owner, who was respected by his peers and friends.

Aline felt their lives were settling nicely, developing a sense of contentment for the first time. Marcel, on the other hand, was beginning to hear the call of his restless spirit. It was these feelings he kept hidden from his young wife. He knew she loved it here, but he was beginning to question, "Is this all there is?"

A Change is Needed

The wandering spirit in Marcel remained restless and ever present. He had learned from several farmers from Norfolk County that the tobacco industry was still thriving. Marcel wanted to cash in on the opportunity. From a friend, they had learned of a seventy-acre farm for sale just on the outside of Delhi, Ontario. The little town had gained in popularity for being one of the richest areas for tobacco in Southwestern Ontario.

"We're going to Delhi to look at buying a farm," he told Aline one afternoon. "You can leave the kid behind with Paula for the day."

"But Marcel, I thought we were going to stay here!" Aline exclaimed, shocked by what he had just told her. The last thing she wanted to do was go back to farming. She was happy here and had put all those terrible years on the farm behind her.

"Get ready to leave," he said and left the room.

She knew better than to challenge her husband on his decisions.

Upon arriving on the farm property, Aline found she could no longer remain silent.

"There are no buildings here!" she said to her husband.

"Adolf and I can build something quickly for us to live in. You can stay at the hotel until the building is ready.

Then you will come down and help us with the land," he replied to her.

The farm was in a good location. It was on the Coal Road, just outside town. In Marcel's eyes this farm represented a veritable gold mind. Aline, on the other hand, viewed the land as more back-breaking work that she prayed she would never have to do again.

Once the deal was signed, they returned to the hotel.

"Adolf and I will return tomorrow and start building," he said to Aline that night at dinner. "You stay here and manage things while I'm gone. Once the building is ready, I'll send for you."

Realizing she had no choice in the matter, she knew she had to do what her husband decided. "Yes, Marcel," she replied.

Later that evening, as Aline sat in a chair in her room, she stared out the window, recalling all of the wonderful memories she had made here.

"I don't want to leave this place or Paula," she whispered to the night air. Silently, tears began to roll down her cheeks. "I know I have to make the best of this, but I'm happy here!" She would always cherish the memories of this place and the people here, but her life was going in a different direction, once again. She must adapt.

After some consideration, the men decided it would be a good idea to build the garage first. They could live in the building, store their food and grains, and work on any machinery when necessary. The three people spent the first spring and summer erecting buildings and clearing the land. Marcel bought two horses, cows, a pig, and some chickens. He built a lean-to against the back of the building as shelter for the animals.

The back-breaking work of clearing the land for farming tobacco had begun. Stones where gleaned from the fields and used for fence rows or as foundations for buildings. Trees were cut down, and they enlisted the help of the horses to pull out the stumps.

The daily routine of work became a ritual. Fields were ploughed, animals were fed, and food was prepared. It was a very hard life. Aline had been used to this type of work, but Marcel had only worked for Julien briefly. He didn't have a full grasp of what 'farming' entailed. They worked like slaves. Hour after hour, day after day. They fell into their beds every night, exhausted beyond belief.

Everyone was doing their share. Even Edward was being put to good use on the farm. At his tender age, he was put to work helping to remove stones from the fields; he fed the chickens, collected eggs, and helped whenever help was needed. The young boy quickly learned there was no time for play. He soon settled down to the life of a farm child. It was not a very happy way for a child to grow up, but this was typical of the times and the life Marcel had chosen.

Fall came and the rye crop was in the ground, and the farm was bedded down for the winter.

"We're going back to the hotel for the winter," Marcel said to Aline.

"Really?" she asked excitedly. "Are we staying?"

"We will stay for the winter," he told her. "Adolf will stay on the farm and care for the animals in our absence. We will run the hotel during the winter. Come late February, we will go back."

Aline's heart sank. She was happy to be returning to the hotel, and that is where she wanted to stay. But she realized this wasn't possible.

During the winter, Marcel decided he was going to look for someone to run the hotel while they went back to farm. "We will keep the hotel and have someone run it for us," he told Aline. "Just like we did for Odiel and

Paula. That way, we'll have extra money coming in, and then if something goes wrong on the farm, we can always come back."

This made sense. "It's a good idea," Aline told him. However, she secretly hoped they could remain at the hotel.

"Dear God," she prayed every night. "Will my life ever settle down?"

A New Year, A New Beginning

Early the next year, Marcel, Aline, and Edward travelled back to their new home in Delhi. Marcel was ready for his future as a tobacco farmer. Aline had made her peace and resigned herself with her husband's dreams. With the tobacco seeds sown and sleeping soundly in their greenhouse beds, Marcel and Adolf began the construction of the family home. He had already decided not to return to the hotel in the fall, but had not made the announcement to his wife. He knew she would take the news very hard. That would be a conversation best saved for a later date.

While on one of his many trips into town, Marcel met and became fast friends with several prosperous farmers. One man, in particular, stood out to Marcel. He was successful, wealthy, and respected by other men. Marcel made a point of getting to know Mike. The two men spent many Saturday afternoons discussing farming and business over a glass of beer in the hotel Mike also owned. Marcel soon learned what a shrewd businessman his friend truly was, and he admired the man for his many accomplishments.

Mike had been a successful tobacco grower for many years. He and his wife had made enough money to expand their holdings. They now owned three farms and two hotels in town.

The common bonds between the two couples grew as time passed. There were many common bonds, especially their beloved home country of Belgium. The four friends spent much time reminiscing about their homes and families they had left behind.

Readying themselves for their very first crop of tobacco, Marcel said to Aline, "I'm going to bring Adolf here. He can work as a hired man."

"That's fine," she replied. She knew they needed help, and she had grown fond of her brother-in-law. "As long as he does his share."

"Never mind, Aline! Adolf does the best he can!" Marcel replied quite sharply.

The family began the long and arduous process of getting the farm ready for planting. They worked long, hard hours, and at the end of each day, they washed and scrubbed themselves clean. After a day out in the hot dry fields, sand was everywhere! It was in their eyes, ears, nose, and mouth. While outside on the back step, Aline would strip Edward down to the skin and shake out his clothes. Then the boy was told to scrub his head with his hands in an effort to remove more sand before washing. Once clean and scrubbed, he could have his well-earned dinner.

This was a time of hard work and pride for the family. Aline was teaching her son how to care for the horses and other animals. Edward developed a special bond with the horses. They were massive animals used for hard labour. At night, before Edward would brush down the horses, he would walk under them and scratch their stomachs. The horses loved all the special attention they received from the boy. Edward was learning how to milk the cows and kill chickens for dinner. The boy loved farm life, and he was proving to be very useful to Marcel. "He can almost do the work of a grown man," he told Aline one evening.

"He is very strong for his age," she replied.

"That's good," Marcel commented back. "Soon, he will have to help us with the bigger projects."

The construction of the barn had begun a few months earlier. Things were moving along quite well, and Aline soon felt a sense of comfort in the life they were making here. Being back on the farm wasn't as bad as she had anticipated.

"The plants will soon be ready for planting," Marcel said over the breakfast table. "Maybe three more days of hot sun. Edward and Adolf will do the planting. I've hired an extra woman to pull plants with you, Aline," he told her.

"That's fine Marcel. I like being in the warm greenhouse," Aline replied.

Life was going well for the family. Everything seemed to be going in the right direction for them. But the news they were about to receive blindsided them completely.

After a very long and hot, dry day out in the fields and greenhouse, the family sat around the dinner table talking. Aline had received a letter that afternoon, and as she opened it, everyone could tell it was bad news.

"Aline, what's wrong?" Marcel asked. "You're turning white as a sheet!"

Aline couldn't speak. She just stared at the paper in her hands.

"Aline!" Marcel shouted at her.

Shaken out of her trance, Aline looked up at her husband and said, "Ma and Pa have bought a farm five miles away from here."

"Godverdomme!" Marcel swore in Dutch, as he stood up and slammed his fist down onto the table. ***"I thought we were rid of them!"*** Suddenly fearing her husband, she cowered in her chair. She could see the dark and violent temper rising in him. She was afraid of what he might do. Aline didn't want her family here, either, and the shock of the news terrified her. All the horrible memories she had managed to bury came flooding back to the surface. But she would have to deal with this on her own. In his anger, Marcel stormed out of the house slamming the screen door behind him. ***"Godverdomme!"*** was all she heard him say.

Victoria and Julien had secretly purchased a farm outside Delhi the previous fall. Not thinking the time was right, they told no one. Victoria didn't want to be this close to her daughter. It had been Julien's idea to buy another farm. She was afraid of what her husband was going to do when he saw the girl again. She dreaded the first meeting of Julien and his bastard son. For all these years, they had managed to fool everyone into believing Marcel was Edward's father; he was, but not biologically.

"What's going to happen to us now?" Aline wondered as she stared out the window. "Why now?"

In the days that followed the news of the arrival, Marcel had grown quiet. However, after spending the afternoon in the hotel with Mike, he would come home and take his anger out on his family. It didn't matter who got in his way, when he was enraged. Both Aline and Edward suffered equally from his verbal and physical attacks.

Aline grew afraid of her husband. She did her best not to step out of line, but at times, it was impossible to avoid. On one particular occasion, she found the courage to challenge her husband. Marcel was in a foul mood, and Edward had made a mistake with the plants. Marcel removed his belt and began whipping the boy across the back with it.

"Marcel!" Aline screamed in horror. ***"Stop! He's just a boy!"*** In his anger, Marcel couldn't hear his wife's pleas. He just kept swinging. ***"Stop!"*** she screamed, as she tried to grab Marcel's arm to prevent him from striking the boy again. In his rage, he stopped hitting Edward, but turned his attention to his wife.

"This is all your fault," he sneered at her.

Crouching down in fear, Aline felt the first sting of the belt across her back. Screaming out in pain and falling to the ground, she began to cry.

"Marcel, please stop. Please!" Aline said as she sat down in the dirt.

Suddenly the beating stopped. With tears streaming down her dirty face, she looked up. Adolf stood beside his brother, holding the belt in one hand and his brother's arm in the other. In terror, Edward had run up to the house to get his uncle. He had to protect his mother somehow.

Calming down and catching his breath, Marcel realized what he had just done. He pulled his arm away from his brother and walked away, not saying one word. He looked like a man who had just lost everything.

Adolf and Edward helped Aline to her feet. "Oh Aline," Adolf said. "I'm very sorry."

Unable to speak, Aline gathered up her son, and together, they walked back up to the house.

The next day, the endless work began, once again. Everyone worked hard to get the crop in.

The relationship between Marcel and Aline had turned to one of mistrust and misery. The several years they had spent together developing a family bond had been shattered in an instant. She now feared him and did her best to not anger him.

Soon, Aline became isolated and very lonely. She missed the comfort she had found with her husband, but in his anger, he had turned his back on her. Once again, the walls of despair and depression began closing in around her.

"I have to keep going," she told herself over and over. "Things will get better in time." But in her heart, she knew things could only get worse. The time was coming when she would have to come face to face with her past. She couldn't avoid her parents for much longer.

The Past Revisited

Later that fall, when the crops were tucked away neatly in the barn, Marcel took Aline and Edward into town to have a meal with their friends, Mike and his wife Alyce. Aline and Alyce had become dear friends. They always had so much to talk about when they got together. The two couples would sit in the hotel and have a beer together and visit. It was good for Aline to get off the farm, once in a while. She needed the break from the constant drudgery of farm work and the daily tasks in the house. As the women talked about their interests, Marcel and Mike talked business. Marcel was a quick study, and he learned a great deal from his friend.

The next evening, Marcel said to his wife, "We're going to see them tomorrow."

"What?" she asked.

"You heard me! We are going to see your mother tomorrow," he replied. "We can't avoid this any longer."

Panic caught in Aline's throat, and the fear rose. She knew the day would come, but as she heard the words from her husband, a hand closed around her throat and began squeezing.

She had not seen or heard from her mother, since the day they sold her to Marcel several years earlier.

Suddenly, Aline grew afraid for her son. Edward believed Marcel to be his father. She feared Julien would do something to jeopardize the boy's relationship with his 'father.'

"Dear God," she prayed. "Give me the strength to face my demons," she begged before falling into a fitful sleep.

The following afternoon, chills ran down Aline's spine as they walked to the front door of her mother's house. They were welcomed into the home by Victoria, who gave her daughter a polite smile. There was no warm hug or gentle touch on the arm. Aline greeted her mother cautiously and stepped aside.

"Edward, this is your grandmother," she said to her son.

Victoria froze in her spot. Her eyes grew bigger as she stared at the boy. "Oh my God," she said. "He looks just like…" and then she caught herself. Immediately, she turned her back and walked into the living room. "They're here," she snapped at Julien.

Marcel, Aline, and Edward walked into the living room. There sat the man, who was the cause of their torment. Aline instantly felt like she wanted to turn and run screaming from the house. Marcel immediately raised his guard.

When the usual pleasantries had been satisfied, Charlotte, Alexander, and Frederich walked into the room. The boys greeted their sister kindly, but the loathing she saw in Charlotte's eyes spoke volumes. Charlotte didn't want her sister back. Her world was a better place without Aline.

"You look well," Victoria said to her daughter. "Is he treating you well?"

"I'm fine, Ma," Aline replied. "Everything was going well until you and Pa came back."

Upset by her daughter's words, Victoria walked away from her.

Aline returned to the living room to find Julien talking to her son. Fear of what he might say or do rose in her throat. "I have to get out of here," she thought.

"Edward, say your good-byes. It's time to go," Aline said to her son.

She had to get Edward away from Julien. She couldn't risk the truth coming out.

Marcel and Aline quickly said good-bye to the family and left.

Once outside, Aline realized that stress had taken over her body. She took a deep breath and let her shoulders return to their normal position. "I am very glad that is over," she said to her husband.

"The old man still won't give me the money," Marcel snapped back at her.

"I'm sorry Marcel, but I..." he didn't let her finished.

"We're going home. *Now!*" he commanded.

Obediently, she followed.

The fear in Aline was beginning to rise again. She knew Marcel wanted the $10,000 Julien promised him to marry her. It wasn't her fault Julien was cheating him. "Maybe if I talk to Julien, he will give Marcel the money," she thought.

The visit home had been difficult for the adults. Edward, on the other hand, had enjoyed himself. Frederich and Alexander were only seven years older than Edward, but age didn't matter. The older boys showed Edward around the farm. The boys enjoyed themselves. They talked about fishing, animals, and farm life. All three got along quite well. Edward was happy to spend time with the other boys. Friendships like this had been missing in his life, and "these two are cousins," he thought to himself.

During the next few months, the two families began to make peace with each other. The extremely hard feelings and awkwardness of the first visit had past. On many occasions, Aline spent time at the home of her mother in an effort to get to know the woman. Since his anger had subsided, Marcel allowed the visits to happen. However, he never completely trusted Julien.

During planting time, no one had time for visiting. Everyone was settling down to the routine of life on the farm.

Until one fateful afternoon.

Adolf had noticed Marcel was in a very angry mood again. He knew something was seriously wrong. But when he tried to approach his brother, Marcel took a step back from Adolf and said in a most threatening tone, "**Mind your own business. You will find out soon enough what that whore has done.**"

Left standing at the barn and wondering what on earth had happened, Adolf felt fear from his brother for the first time. Looking off into the fields, he saw Marcel approaching Aline. She was out with Edward, hoeing tobacco all day. It was a beautifully warm and sunny day, and mother and son enjoyed spending time together.

Seeing the way Marcel was approaching set Aline's guard on high alert. She has seen Marcel angry, but this time she was terrified. "Run off now, Edward," she told her son. "Pa is coming and looks angry. Go up to the barn and brush the horses," she instructed him.

Edward, afraid for his mother, but more terrified of his father, did what he was told. But he didn't go to the barn. He stayed nearby in case his mother needed help.

As Marcel approached, his hand came out and landed on the side of Aline's face. **"Godverdomme, woman,"** he screamed at her. **"What made you do it again?"** he asked. Not waiting for an answer, his hand came down on her again. Aline cried out in pain. "Marcel stop!" She cried. But he didn't hear her cries. He was enraged at what he had just discovered. ***"You whore!"*** he said to her. ***"How could you do this again!"***

Sitting off in the distance, too terrified to move, Edward witnessed his father beating his mother. Knowing he was too little to stop his father and fearing his own beating, Edward stayed put. When he saw Marcel rip the hoe from his mother's hands and beat her over the back with it, Edward knew he had to get help. Sobbing and blinded by tears, he found his Uncle Adolf at the barn. ***"Pa's beating Ma!"*** He screamed at his uncle. ***"Help her! Stop him! Please! He's going to kill her!"***

Adolf ran to the field. He had to stop Marcel from hurting his wife. Adolf saw Aline stand up and run down the row of tobacco. She was trying to get away from her husband. But Marcel caught her and continued the beating. **"Marcel! Stop!"** Adolf yelled to his brother.

Seeing the watering bucket close by, Adolf picked it up and threw the water on his brother. He hoped the shock of the water would stop the beating. Standing, soaked and breathing heavy from the physical activity, Marcel now looked at his brother. For the first time, he saw the shock and disgust in his brother's eyes. "Oh Marcel," Adolf said to him. "What have you done! **Look at her!** *LOOK what you've done!*" Adolf screamed at him.

Marcel turned and looked down. Lying on the ground, covered in dirt lay his wife. Lying there whimpering, her face streaked and muddied from crying, Aline was unable to move. Marcel stepped forward to help her stand, but in terror, she pulled away from him. "What in God's name have I done," Marcel said to the air. "Aline, I'm sorry."

Sobbing and unable to speak, Aline tried to stand. Adolf went to his sister-in-law and helped her. Together, they got her to her feet, and she staggered back to the house.

Now, completely disgusted and shamed by his brother's actions, Adolf turned to Marcel and said, "I'm leaving at the end of the week. I will not stay here and watch you kill her." Adolf turned his back on his brother and walked away. What Marcel had just done would cause a rift between the brothers that years could not fix.

As Aline approached the house, her son come running out of the barn towards her. The boy was crying and feared for his mother. He ran to her and threw his arms around her. Aline flinched, but didn't want to let her son see her pain. **"Oh, Ma I was so scared!"** Edward cried. She held the boy tightly as tears continued to roll down her face. She tried her best to sooth his pain and fear.

Twenty minutes later, the two walked into the house. "You go up to your room and lay down for a while," Aline told Edward. "I'm going to have a bath and wash the dirt off me before I start dinner.

Keep your door closed, Edward," she said. Still sniffling, Edward replied, "Yes, Ma."

Now stripped of her clothes, Aline could see the red welts and the beginning of several large and nasty bruises growing. "A hot bath will help," she thought. "Oh dear God, I hope everything is alright."

Stiffly, she stepped into the tub. The water felt good on her battered body. "I knew he would be angry, but I didn't expect this," she thought as she sunk deeper into the water.

An hour later, Aline emerged from the washroom. Gingerly, she walked down the steps towards the kitchen. She had to get dinner on the table.

"Edward, come down for dinner," Aline called up to her son. With extreme caution, the boy came into the room. He was afraid of his father and was terrified of being near him. Edward no longer felt safe at home.

As Edward sat down at the table, he noticed his father was still in a foul mood, but he spoke not one word. Adolf sat in silence next to the boy. Carefully looking around at each person to gauge the situation, Edward noticed how slowly his mother was moving. He noticed her difficulty in moving and bending, but not wanting to speak out, he remained silent and ate his meal. That night, the meal was eaten in silence. The tension in the room was explosive. Edward wondered when the bomb would go drop.

Aline remained quiet and withdrawn for the next few weeks. She barely spoke a word. Edward helped his mother as much as he could, but when his uncle left the farm for good, only saying "Good-bye," to the boy, more chores fell on the young boys' shoulders. Edward was afraid to leave his mother's side. He could see the fear in her eyes, but he knew he had to obey his father.

Weeks later, Marcel was still in a black mood. Edward could not understand what was happening, and no one was telling him anything. One thing that was becoming obvious were the bruises on Aline's arms and legs.

A few months after the beating, when Aline was putting Edward to bed, she sat down on the bed beside her son and said, "I'm going to have a baby." Edward was excited by the news, but he couldn't understand why his mother was so sad. "Why isn't she happy about the baby," he wondered.

That night, as he lay in bed, he thought of the new baby. During the night, Edward cried out in his sleep. In his dreams, he saw his father beating his mother again. Screaming in fear, he woke himself and his mother. She came rushing into his room to comfort him.

"Ma, I'm scared!" he cried out.

"Shhh, everything will be ok," she said as she held her son. She wrapped her arms around the boy and kissed his forehead.

"We will be fine."

Welcome the New Arrival

A few weeks after Aline told Edward she was pregnant, she went into labour. Marcel went to get the doctor for her.

Struggling through several very painful hours of labour, Aline gave birth to a daughter. Relieved the ordeal was over, she lay resting in bed. Her friend, Alyce, had arrived a couple hours earlier. She had been taking care of the house and Edward while Aline laboured. Alyce walked into her friend's room and sat beside her on the bed. "How are you Aline?" she asked.

"I am alright," Aline replied. "Can you help me change my nightgown, Alyce?" she asked her friend.

As Alyce lifted the sweat soaked nightgown from her friend's body, she saw the remnants of Marcel's abuse. There were several large bruises still showing on her back.

"Aline!" Alyce exclaimed in horror. "What on earth happened?"

Once Aline had finished explaining what had gone on that horrible day in the field, Alyce took hold of her friend and hugged her. "So the baby isn't his, is it?" she asked.

"No," Aline replied. With shame in her voice and on her face she said, "It's Julien's."

"YOUR FATHER!" Alyce yelled out with complete shock.

"NO!" Aline exclaimed. "He is not my father. He is my step-father. He showed me great kindness and comfort when I first was brought to this country, and when Marcel began beating me and Edward, I was afraid. I went to him for comfort only, but I made a mistake." Aline began to sob. Alyce held her friend and let her cry. She cried for a very long time. Alyce felt pity for the young girl. The sobs that came from the girl were an outpouring from her soul. Her soul was in pain and torment.

"There, there, Aline," Alyce said soothingly. "It will be fine."

Aline continued crying.

"What will you name your pretty little daughter?" Alyce enquired.

With her sobs subsiding, Aline looked up at her friend, her face swollen from the hours of labour and the crying. "I will name her Danielle," Aline said. "I've always been very fond of that name."

The following Sunday, Danielle was christened in the Catholic Church.

After the service, a few friends were invited back to the house for coffee and cake. It soon became evident to their guests that something was wrong in this house. People were noticing the indifference Marcel was showing towards his family. He barely spoke to his wife, he was short-tempered with Edward, and he ignored the new baby completely.

Marcel, stuck in his own world of anger, was oblivious to what others thought of him.

The only person Marcel spoke to that day was his brother. Adolf had come for the christening. He congratulated Aline on the baby, but to his brother, he asked, "Are you alright Marcel?"

"They've all lied to me!" Marcel said in a voice that caused his brother to take notice. "I don't have the $10,000 the old man promised me, and then she went and did it again! That kid isn't mine! She's a whore!" he exclaimed.

Adolf tried to calm his brother. "Let's go outside and have a glass of beer," he said. And with that, the two men walked out the back door and sat on the stone wall that surrounded the back of the house and had their beer.

"You must make peace with this somehow, Marcel," Adolf finally said to his brother.

"I know," he replied as he hung his head and stared into his beer. "She can't do it again."

Deep in thought and buried in his own torment, Marcel went quiet. He had to think. Somehow, he must come to terms with the betrayal of his wife.

As time passed, Marcel was indifferent towards the baby. The only thing that concerned him now was the extra mouth to feed.

Edward was very sensitive to the atmosphere in the house, and he knew something was wrong in his family. When he visited his friends, he could feel the difference. Their homes were happy, and even though it wasn't spoken, you could feel the love in the house.

Edward always felt comfortable and happy when he was with his friends. He could tell his friends were happy at home, and he wondered why he was so different. He wondered why his father was always so angry and unhappy. "Why doesn't my mother ever smile?" he asked himself. I see other mothers smiling. "I don't understand," he said to the horse he was brushing.

After a few years, Marcel decided to sell the farm they were on. He didn't want the constant reminders and bad memories. He wanted a clean break.

Marcel and Aline bought a farm on the other side of town. The couple made quite a nice profit from the sale. The farm they bought had more acreage than their first farm and had more buildings. On this farm, Marcel could bring in more animals. He wanted to get into cattle. His friend, Mike, had told him that cattle farming could make a nice profit. Marcel decided to invest in several dozen Herefords. Among his purchase were two prize winning bulls. One he named Royal Rupert, and the second was Prince Royal Rupert. Both were magnificent beasts, and they sired many offspring, which pleased Marcel.

Marcel developed a very successful cattle business. He carefully tracked the lineage of each and every animal born. It was important to keep very detailed documentation on each animal for veterinary records and ultimately the auction.

As Danielle grew, she developed a love for the animals on the farm. She particularly liked being around the cattle. Marcel had made his peace with the birth of the girl and decided he would raise her as his own. Since Danielle exhibited a great love of the cattle, Marcel decided to teach her. Together, they cared and protected the beasts.

As each calf was born, Danielle would name it. "I think I will call this little girl Miss Royal Princess," she said to her father. "She's pretty, Daddy."

"Yes, she is," Marcel replied. "Are you going to be able to name and keep track of each one?" he asked.

"Oh yes!" she exclaimed excitedly. "I know each one. They are my friends," she replied.

Danielle loved spending time in the barn. It was her favourite place.

When it was time to sell off some cattle, Danielle always went with her father to the Toronto Stock Yards. She enjoyed looking at the animals and found the process of the sale fascinating. The young girl was becoming very knowledgeable about Herefords.

His success in the industry and breeding had produced several championship bulls, whose lineage could be traced back several generations. Marcel planned a major cattle auction on his farm. Along with the bulls, they had listed ten championship females, who had been bred by Marcel and sired by his prize bulls.

The excitement was building for the sale. Danielle knew the sale was all part of the business, but she found she was going to miss her pets.

Since the sale was such a huge success, Marcel decided to buy Danielle her own calf. "Oh, thank you, Pa," she said as she hugged her father. "I'm going to name her Pearl."

"She is all yours. Make sure you care for her," Marcel warned her.

"I will," she replied.

Marcel and Aline watched the girl as she loved and cared for Pearl. After a couple of years, the calf had grown into a majestic beauty, just like her owner.

Danielle had grown into a beautiful young girl, who had sandy-blond hair and big, expressive brown eyes. She was a beauty. Unfortunately, she attracted the attention of many a man. At first, she found the attention unsettling. She soon understood what she could do with this attention.

"Danielle is turning into a flirt," Marcel snapped at Aline one evening. "She has to stop behaving like that! We don't want something happening to her!" he warned his wife.

The parents knew their daughter would walk in her sleep. The girl had no idea what she was doing. At first, her sleepwalking seemed harmless. Until late one night, Marcel heard a commotion coming from the bunk house, where the summer labourers lived while they worked on the farm. Danielle had walked into the bunk house and began yelling at the men to get up out of bed and get into the fields. "You're all lazy men!" she screamed at them. "Move it! We have to get the crop in!" she yelled. At first, the men thought her actions were funny. They soon realized there was something wrong with the girl.

One of the farm hands went running to the house to get Marcel and Aline. "We didn't touch her!" the man tried to reassure Marcel. "She just walked in and started yelling at us." All the workers were afraid of losing their jobs. Their lives depended on the money they received from Marcel. When her parents arrived at the bunk house, they found Danielle laying down on one of the beds, sound asleep. The shame they felt was written all over their faces. They collected their daughter, and as they left, Marcel said, "Go back to sleep. Forget what just happened."

"Yes sir," they all replied as they breathed a sigh of relief that the girl was gone.

Aline woke her daughter and guided the sleepy girl back to the house. Once she was safely back in her bed, Aline closed the bedroom door on her daughter and said a quick prayer.

Unaware of the previous night's events, Danielle went on as though nothing had happened. As she grew older, she proved to be a very difficult girl to control.

Two years later, Aline and Marcel took their daughter on a very different type of trip to Toronto. Danielle had no idea where they were taking her until they arrived at their destination.

"What are you doing!" she screamed out to her parents.

"Just get inside and don't cause a scene," Marcel threatened her. "You have caused us enough shame and embarrassment."

The young girl stepped out of the car and looked up at the building that awaited her. ***"Oh my God!"*** she thought as panic rose in her throat. ***"They've brought me to a convent!"***

Marcel had warned Aline repeatedly over the last several years to keep a closer eye on Danielle. Aline tried her best, but she found the girl rather uncontrollable and impossible to deal with.

Now four months pregnant, Danielle found herself at the mercy of Nuns. "You will stay here until after you have the baby," her mother told her. "Then you can come home."

"What about the baby?" she asked her parents as tears began to run down her face.

"I will not have another bastard child running around my home!" Marcel yelled out in frustration. ***"I've had enough! The child will be given up for adoption."***

"NO!" Danielle screamed. ***"No!"*** But her cries fell on deaf ears. Her parents had signed the necessary paperwork, and she was handed over.

"Bad girls must pay the price," the Mother Superior said to her.

Danielle had no idea just what that price would be. She thought it was just going to cost her the child, but there was more.

What she did not know was Marcel, in his anger, had made another arrangement. Yes, the child was to be immediately placed for adoption, but he also took measures to ensure Danielle would never have another child again.

When Marcel met with the doctor who delivered the babies at the convent, he told the doctor, **"Fix her! She better not have another kid!"**

The poor girl was unaware of the last part of the deal.

Just after Christmas, 1955, Danielle gave birth to a beautiful, healthy baby boy. Immediately after she gave birth, the Nuns removed the baby from the room. Under no circumstances was she allowed to see the child.

The girl cried and screamed for her baby. The Mother Superior approached her and said, "There, there my dear. It's always better this way. The baby will go to a good home. It will go to a married couple," she told the girl soothingly.

Danielle was sedated and then sent for surgery.

When she woke the next day, Mother Superior was sitting beside her bed, once again.

"What happened?" Danielle asked.

"You've had surgery," the older Nun replied.

"Why, what was wrong?" the girl questioned as she tried to sit up in bed. "Why does my stomach hurt so badly?" she asked.

"You've had surgery," the Nun repeated. "You will never have another child."

Danielle's eyes grew to three times their normal size. Shock, horror, and anger hit her all at the same time.

"Why?" she asked through her tears.

"Your father didn't want you to have any more children," she said in a kindly voice. "It is for the best."

Unable to utter another word, Danielle rolled over and turned her back to the Nun. As she began to cry, tears ran down her face onto the pillow. Her father had broken her completely. There was nothing left. Nothing except anger and hatred for the man. *"How could he do this to me?"* she screamed inside her own head. *"HOW?"*

CHAPTER THREE

The Unfulfilled Life of a Man

The Life of a Son

Edward had grown into a fine and handsome young man. His muscular body, along with his sandy-blond hair and alluring blue eyes, made him irresistible to most girls in the area. He was quite the catch until the girls went home and told their parents about him.

Somehow, the families of the area heard that Edward was a product of incest. Being shunned, as if he carried the plague, local parents discouraged their daughters from getting serious about him. Edward never understand why he was always rejected. "Everyone seems to like me, and people get along with me, but why do they seem afraid of me?" he wondered to himself many times. "Why won't people be honest with me?" he thought. He carried these thoughts with him everyday. They were part of him, just like his hair and eye colour. But he didn't understand.

Edward, with some friends on Saturday nights, would go to one or more of the local hotels and dance halls. They wanted to enjoy some beer and dancing.

The music in mid 1940's was a great part of the culture. The younger people would congregate to the local dance halls to socialize and dance for hours. They danced away the hours to Tommy Dorsey, Bing Crosby, Glen Miller, or Benny Goodman. The music was always great. The young people needed one night off before returning to the work that awaited them early the next morning.

It was on one of these occasions that Edward met a girl. This girl didn't seem to judge him like all the others. She was friendly, and they danced together and talked for most of the evening.

He soon discovered that Andrea was the eldest daughter of Belgian immigrants.

Andrea's father had emigrated from Belgium to St. Boniface, Manitoba just after World War I. Alphonse had such high hopes of a good life in Canada. What he found was a country of back-breaking, honest, and filthy work. Like so many before him, he discovered farming could give him a better life.

Because he had no one to sponsor his landing, Alphonse was sent out west. Soon, he learned there was nothing out there for him. Then he remembered the stories he heard stories about the Southwestern Ontario farming industry. "I have to go," he told a friend, one day.

When Alphonse first entered Ontario, he went to Leamington. He had been told about the vegetable crops Leamington was famous for. Not afraid of hard work, he soon acquired a position in the vegetable and sugar beet fields. Both are labour-intensive jobs, but it was good, honest work. He loved working the fields.

One day, while working in a field of peppers, Alphonse met a beautiful young girl, named Elvira. She was the eldest daughter of a Belgian immigrant who, as a widower, was trying to raise two children on his own in Detroit, Michigan, a challenge he found most difficult as did many widowers in the early 1900's. In his frustration with his children, Henrique hired a young woman, named Yolanda, to work as a domestic. Watching the girl, he soon discovered she would make a good mother to his children. Three months later, the two were married.

As it happened, Yolanda was not a good mother to his children. She wanted a family of her own, not someone else's. She began to manipulate her husband. She convinced him to send his Elvira and her brother Cyril to work in the vegetable fields in Leamington. "Out of sight, out of mind," she thought to herself as she smiled. "It worked!"

The two children worked in the vegetable fields by day and boarded on the farm of their employer by night. Their money was sent directly to their father. Neither child saw a nickel.

Henrique missed his children terribly. Yolanda had a cure for his loneliness. She soon gave birth to a son she named Andre. He was an adorable baby and became the apple of his mother's eye. She dedicated herself to him.

Elvira and Cyril soon found themselves as unwelcome visitors in their father's house. Unfortunately, Cyril had fallen ill and had to return home. Elvira, saddened and lonely for her brother, remained and continued to work.

In the vegetable fields of Leamington, Alphonse met Elvira. They talked while they worked, and a caring relationship developed.

At the end of the harvest, Alphonse returned to Michigan with Elvira to ask permission to marry her. Henrique was pleased with the strapping young man who stood before him. He gave his permission for the marriage immediately. Yolanda was very happy about the upcoming marriage. "That means the girl will be gone for good," she thought to herself. She smiled. Her plan was working perfectly.

The following April, Alphonse and Elvira were married. They were happy. Together, they made plans to move to the LaSalette area in Norfolk County. LaSalette was part of the heart of the tobacco belt. The land was fertile, and the couple knew they could make a good living.

They were fortunate to find work on the same farm. The farmer offered them a small home on the farm to rent. Alphonse and Elvira began their lives together in a small farm house. Happiness is what mattered to them, and happiness they had, for Elvira soon discovered she was pregnant.

"A baby!" Alphonse exclaimed. "Already!"

"Yes, Alphonse," she replied. "I'm sorry."

"No, no, don't be sorry," he said to her soothingly. "I think it's wonderful."

Elvira continued to work on the farm as long as she could. When she grew too heavy with the child, she worked in the house for the farmer's wife.

Alphonse proved to be a quick learner. He absorbed everything about starting the plants, readying the soil, planting, harvesting, and curing. The curing was the tricky part, but Alphonse soon mastered that aspect of the crop.

Later in Elvira's pregnancy, she found life was good to her. She was happy. Until one afternoon, she heard a loud explosion. It shook the house. She and the farmer's wife walked outside to find out what happened.

The farmer came running up to the house with a look of terror on his face. **"Call the doctor, now!"** he said to his wife.

"What's happened," she asked.

Elvira, with panic and fear rising in her throat, screamed out, ***"Alphonse!* Where is Alphonse?"*** she asked.

"He's been hurt," the farmer replied. "Over there by the greenhouse."

Not waiting to hear anything else, Elvira ran to her husband. At first, she couldn't see him from the tears in her eyes. Then, she saw a shape laying on the ground under a tree.

He lay in the shade of the tree unconscious. Debris was everywhere. "Alphonse! Alphonse!" she screamed. "Can you hear me?"

Slowly, he began to wake. "Elvira," he whispered.

Suddenly, there were other people around. The farmer and other farm hands had arrived. "Let me through," she heard someone say. "Let me through. I'm the doctor!"

Elvira saw a kindly old gentleman approach her husband. "Help him," she said as the tears began to overflow her eyes.

Once permission was given, the men carried Alphonse to the house and to bed. "He must remain calm," the doctor directed Elvira. "I will tend to his burns now and will return everyday to change the dressings."

Working quickly, but carefully, the doctor cut away Alphonse's clothes. The burns were bad. "He must lay on clean white sheets only," the doctor said to Elvira. "We must prevent infection."

Elvira, shaking with fear and anxiety over her injured husband, took to heart everything the doctor told her.

"We were starting up the steamer," the farmer was telling his wife. "I went off to get a wrench from the barn, and the next thing I heard was the explosion."

"Where was Alphonse at the time," she asked.

"He was working on the steamer," he replied with incredible sadness in his voice.

"The poor man!" she said.

Alphonse suffered burns down the right side of his body from his ear down to his knee. The pain was incredible. It felt as though his skin was being cut away from his body in very thin sheets, layer by layer. The doctor kept him sedated. "That will help him get over the worst of the pain," he told Elvira. "He is healing, but it will take time."

Suddenly, their lives changed. Now, very much pregnant, Elvira took up the reigns and went to work in the fields. She had to help her husband.

Alphonse lay in pain and agony for months. He was able to see his baby daughter when Elvira gave birth, but under no circumstances could he hold her. Heartbroken and trying to remain positive, Alphonse smiled at his wife. "She's a beauty," he said to her. "Thank you!"

Smiling, Elvira leaned down and kissed her husband on his cheek. "Anything for you, my dear," she whispered to him. "I've named her Andrea after your mother." A smile and a tear appeared on Alphonse's face, as he succumbed to sleep.

It took months before Alphonse's burns healed. Unable to farm again, he had to look for an alternative to make a living. He had a wife and a little baby girl to provide for.

Opportunity came knocking, one day. A friend, who was a fine carpenter, said to Alphonse one afternoon, "When you are better, I can use your help building homes."

"You will teach me?" Alphonse inquired.

"You are a good man Alphonse, and I believe you would make a great builder," the man replied. "Come work for me."

Alphonse's prayers had been answered. As he shook his friend's hand he replied, "I would be honoured. Thank you."

The carpenter soon discovered Alphonse had a very analytical mind. He had a gift with figures, and in the building trade, that would serve him well.

Alphonse absorbed himself in the carpentry business. He was learning everything possible about the many different types of wood, drawings for homes, barns, and other buildings. Alphonse was a gifted man with wood. Soon, he was discovering the finer arts of carpentry and began creating beautiful pieces of furniture and cabinetry. He knew, in time, he would be able to put the past trauma behind him. He was beginning a new life and a wonderful career.

And Baby Makes Four and Five

Ten months after giving birth to their first daughter, Elvira gave birth to a baby boy, Peter. Alphonse was thrilled beyond belief. "A son!" he said. "I have a son!" His dreams were coming true. One day, Alphonse wanted to own a carpentry business with his son, and Elvira made that possible.

It seemed as though the little family was complete. However, two years later, Elvira gave birth, once again. She had another daughter.

"I would like to call her Angela," Elvira said to her husband. Thinking this was a good name for the tiny little girl, Alphonse agreed.

Now, their family truly was complete. "We have enough," Elvira said to Alphonse.

"I agree," he replied.

Angela was a tiny baby. She wasn't a sickly baby, but her mother devoted endless hours to her. This didn't concern Peter. After all, he was a boy. Andrea, on the other hand, found the favouritism overwhelming. She became angry and resented her sister.

Elvira found her days filled with cooking, cleaning, washing, and caring for her children. She was unaware of the animosity growing between her daughters.

Within a few years, Alphonse was able to afford a small home in town. Now, his children could get to school easier, and Elvira found work in the local tobacco factory.

The family prospered. Alphonse became a great carpenter and builder and completed many successful building projects in the area. He was well-respected in the town as a man of quality. Elvira worked hard, holding the jobs of factory work and wife/motherhood.

Over the next few years, their children grew to young adults. Peter and Angela became very good students in school, as Peter excelled in math and Angela in business.

Andrea struggled in school. She didn't like school and couldn't do the work. She was held back for two years, in hopes that she would, eventually, learn the material. She did not and soon found herself sixteen years old in Grade 8.

Believing she had no talent for education, Andrea quit school. "I just can't do it," she said to her parents as she admitted defeat. "I can just go work in the factory with you, Ma," she said to her mother. Her mother was hoping for better for her daughter, but knew Andrea. "Fine," Elvira said. "I'll see about getting you in."

One week later, Andrea began her life of factory work. "It's better than school," she thought to herself. It was steady work, and the pay was reasonable, and in 1946 Delhi, tobacco was the main source of income.

Andrea was content working in the factory. She and some friends would go out dancing together, and on one particular Saturday, in 1949, she went to the dance hall for an evening of dancing and fun. She had the most wonderful time of her life.

"Mother, I met the most wonderful boy, tonight!" she told her mother excitedly.

Her mother looked at her with caution. "Who," she asked.

"His name is Edward. He's a farm boy and is so handsome and tall," she replied. "We had so much fun dancing together. I'm going to see him again next week," she said.

"Oh Ma, it was love at first sight!" she exclaimed.

Elvira was happy for her daughter. Andrea was getting older, and her prospects were few. This news gave her hope for her daughter's future.

Edward was happier than he had ever been. Andrea was his equal, and together, they talked about their pasts and looked forward to building a bright future together.

On one special occasion, Edward looked deep into Andrea's eyes.

"Will you marry me?" he asked.

"Oh Edward!" she screamed with excitement. She hugged him tightly and whispered in his ear, "Yes. Of course, I will marry you."

Andrea was beside herself. Her heart was filled with happiness and love.

Her happiness and joy would be short-lived.

When the young couple told their parents of their plans, they soon learned their happiness was not shared.

Alphonse and Elvira knew of dark clouds that loomed over Edward's life. A family with incest was not the ideal place for their daughter.

"We wanted better for you," Alphonse said to his daughter.

"But I love him," she cried. "I'm nineteen years old! You can't keep telling me what to do!" she screamed at him.

There were so many skeletons in the closet, and like any parents, they wanted more for their daughter.

Alphonse stood up and slammed his fist onto the dinner table. "***Godverdomme***," he said.

"You WILL listen to me!"

"Alphonse," Elvira said. "She is old enough. Its her decision."

Red in the face and still angry, Alphonse listened to his wife's reasoning.

"Alright," he said. Alphonse sat back down and understood that nothing he could say would change his daughter's mind. Defeated, he gave in.

"Alright," he repeated to Andrea. A feeling of dread loomed over his head like a black cloud.

"This is not right," he thought to himself. "Just not right!"

When Edward told his parents, they were stunned.

"You can't marry her!" Marcel shouted at his son. **"Everyone knows there is something wrong with her!"**

"Pa!" Edward challenged back. "I don't care what people think."

"Well, you should!" Marcel yelled. "You can do much better than that!"

Coming from very humble beginnings did not prevent the parents from wanting the best for their children.

Neither family felt this match was right.

"We will see," was all Marcel said to his son. He turned and walked away. As he walked into the living room, he called back over his shoulder, *"Aline! Get over here. NOW!"*

Edward left the house quickly. He knew what that tone of voice meant.

He came back to the house late that night after his parents were in bed. Edward knew it wasn't smart to upset his father like that. He hoped he was safe.

What faced him the next morning, rocked him to his core. He was about to discover exactly what his father meant by, *"We will see,"* the night before. Edward was about to be offered the deal of a lifetime. It was the biggest decision of his life, a decision that would change his life forever.

Edward's Decision

Determined that their son's relationship should come to an end, Marcel came up with what he thought was a devious plan.

"You have a choice," Marcel said. As he stared down at his son, he said, "We will give you an all-expense paid trip to Belgium for six weeks, or we will buy you a new car, and you can stay and work the farm. Those are your two choices, provided you don't marry Andrea."

Edward stared up at his father, but remained silent.

"If you marry her," Marcel continued, "you get nothing. You will stay on the farm and work and make due."

Shocked and repulsed by what he just heard, Edward replied, ***"You're trying to buy me!"***

Edward stood up from the table and walked out of the house.

Angered by Edward's reaction, Marcel turned to Aline. He raised his fist in her direction and said, ***"This is your fault! He's your bastard son! Do something with him!"***

"Marcel," she replied. "He's 21 years old. He's a man!"

"He gets nothing, but farm work," Marcel replied. "That's all he deserves."

His plan had backfired, and Marcel was furious. He walked out of the house, slamming the door behind him. Aline didn't see him for several hours.

They had tried, once before, to give Edward a different chance at life. As a teenager, Edward was sent to St. Jerome's College, a Catholic Boys' high school in Kitchener. St. Jerome's was a boarding school for students from all over Canada and the United States. They provided a unique atmosphere for the young men who attended. The facility, run by Catholic Priests, was very strong on sports. These were strong-willed men, teachers, and athletes, and they demanded respect. What some of the priests lacked was compassion. It was here Marcel sent Edward for an education. He wanted the boy to have a better, easier life than farming.

Edward wasn't impressed with life away from home, but he was a good student. He excelled in physical education. It was here he learned how to box. Edward found boxing a good release for his anger and aggression. His other favourite sport was football. He was a strong, agile young man, who was quick on his feet and great at ball handling. He played quarterback for the school team. During one particularly rough game, Edward was removed from the field with a broken nose. Blood poured from his nose covering his jersey and pants.

Life at St. Jerome's wasn't all bad. Even though Edward missed his best friends, who stayed behind in Delhi, he soldiered on with his classes.

Edward found the priests to be hard men who were very firm on discipline. If you stepped out of line, you were punished, sometimes severely. Edward, being a stubborn young man, suffered many such punishments. One priest, in particular, an amateur boxer, used the boxing ring as a form of physical exercise and punishment. Forced to step into the ring with this terrifying priest, each boy soon learned his place. It was during one of these "discipline" sessions where Edward suffered his second broken nose. Believing his parents would come to his aid and reprimand the priest, he was devastated by their silence.

Marcel refused to interfere. He was pleased Edward was gone.

"They're beating him," Aline said quietly to Marcel one evening. A tear rolled down her cheek.

"It will make him a man," was all Marcel would say back. He rolled over and went to sleep, having no pity for the boy.

The Catholic Church was the ruler of most homes. The priests were revered and their word was law. Few parents ever challenged their authority.

Beaten, bruised, and emotionally destroyed, Edward grew despondent, and his school work began to suffer. The dreams he had of becoming an accountant, with his gift in math, soon became a nightmare at the hands of his tormentors.

After one particularly harsh discipline session in the ring, Edward decided he had had enough. Turning his back on his education, he packed his trunk, boarded a bus, and headed for home.

Stunned at seeing their son standing on the doorstep, Marcel said, ***"Wat doe je hier in Godsnaam?"***

"I left school," Edward replied. "I can't take the beatings any more, Pa!" he said as a tear escaped his eye.

In his anger, Marcel raised his fist and backhanded his son across the face.

"Marcel!" Aline cried out. ***"Enough!"***

Edward, knocked down to his knees from the blow, did not say another word. He stood up and faced his father. ***"I WILL NOT* go back,"** he said.

Standing before them as a grown man, Edward had made the decision of his life. "I'm going to marry Andrea and stay on the farm," he said to his mother. "That is ***My*** decision."

The choice had been made, and Marcel soon realized he had lost this battle. Aline was proud of her son, but was still disappointed with his choice of bride.

"My life is all set," Edward thought to himself. "I made the right decision."

But had he? Only time could answer that question.

The Wedding

On October 12th, 1949, Edward not only celebrated his 22nd birthday, but he also celebrated his marriage to Andrea. He awoke that morning with a new lease on life. He was happy.

Their day began early, with a 10 am marriage service, followed by a typical wedding breakfast. After breakfast, the wedding party went to pose for their official portraits. Andrea looked beautiful in her ivory satin wedding gown. Elvira was very busy that morning, doing up twenty pearl buttons on each sleeve and seventy pearl buttons up the back of the dress. Her daughter never looked lovelier.

The photographer's wife, an exceptional artist, hand painted the photographs to add colour to the usual black and white pictures of the day. She captured Edward's blue eye colour exactly. The bridesmaid's dresses were a beautiful rainbow of colours. Danielle's dress was an apple green, while Angela wore a soft pastel pink. Andrea carried two dozen blood red roses in a stunning trailing bouquet. It was a gorgeous contrast to her ivory gown. As the wedding party posed for the pictures, they all found the heady fragrance of Andrea's bouquet intoxicating.

Edward and his ushers looked extremely handsome, standing regal in their identical pitch-black suits. The ivory handkerchiefs and ties brilliantly matched Andrea's dress.

Even though Alphonse and Elvira had reservations about the marriage, they couldn't help but breathe a sigh of relief that their daughter was finally married. They had been concerned for her and her future. Their concerns were put to rest as they enjoyed the wedding day celebrations.

Andrea and Edward celebrated their day in style. They enjoyed the meals, dancing, family, and friendships. What they were not aware of was the constant tension between the two families.

Marcel still refused to accept Edward's decision, but for the day, kept his opinion quiet.

The entire day was a beautiful celebration of young love.

"How naïve these children are," thought Aline to herself. "They really have no idea what they are in for."

Alphonse found he was able to set his opinions of his new son-in-law aside for the day. "At least, he makes her happy," he whispered to his wife.

"Yes, for now," she replied. Elvira found it difficult to ignore the stories of incest that surrounded Edward's family, but for her daughter's sake, she buried her fear deep.

Neither family wanted to spoil the day for Edward and Andrea.

The rest of the wedding day went smoothly.

Later that evening, they both kissed their mothers and waved goodbye to family and friends, as they departed for a short honeymoon. The time away together would be exactly what they both needed. It would be a time for the two of them to bond as a couple and to build the strength they needed for the very difficult future that awaited them.

The Bad Beginnings of a Marriage

Right from the beginning, they discovered life was going to challenge them.

Andrea went to work every day in the factory, while Edward struggled on the farm to please his parents. He found it very difficult to satisfy his father. What he found most troubling was the erratic behaviour of his wife. He was beginning to see his wife had some emotional issues.

In all the time he had known Andrea, he had never noticed her odd behaviour. "I guess you never really know someone until you live with them," he thought to himself. "It will pass in time."

However her behaviour did change, but not for the better.

At first, it was little things, but then, his friends would make off-hand comments, which Edward chose to ignore.

With increasing pressure from his parents, the long hours of work and the demands of his wife, Edward found himself looking for an escape. His method of escape was a destructive one. He drank more than usual in an effort to numb his feelings. As Andrea became more aware of his excessive drinking, Edward felt she was becoming the proverbial 'nag'. She hounded him the minute he stepped foot into the house.

"Why do you have to drink so much every night?" she said to him.

"Be quiet," he shouted back at her.

"Stop it!" she yelled.

"Shut up and leave me be!" Edward would yell out in frustration at her. "Shut up!"

Each night, he would drown his feelings in beer and hard liquor, but he was unable to escape the demons that followed him.

Noticing the declining personality in their son, Marcel and Aline made Edward another offer.

"We have an extra house on the farm," they said to him over coffee one afternoon. "Come and live here. That way, both of you can work on the farm."

"Why do they want us out there with them?" Andrea asked. She was not thrilled at the idea of living so close to her in-laws.

"They are my parents, and they want to help," he answered her.

"They just want to spy on us," she replied, raising her voice in anger.

"You don't know what you're talking about," he said. With his anger rising, he said to his wife, "We are going, and you had better just deal with it!"

In February of 1950, they moved on the farm. Edward could take a more active role in the crop, allowing Marcel and Aline more spare time. They prayed this arrangement would work, for it was time for them to consider retiring.

Andrea quit her factory job and began her new career as a farm wife. She still dreaded this plan, but for her husband's sake, she would try.

Busying himself with the daily routines, Edward began to feel better and emotionally stronger. He found time to spend with the horses, one task he had always enjoyed immensely.

He steamed the greenhouses in preparation for sowing the beds with seeds, worked with his father preparing the machinery, and planned out the crop.

Keeping house kept Andrea fairly content. "Maybe this was a good idea after all," she thought. Until the day came when she was called to the big house to begin helping her mother-in-law with washing, ironing, and preparing the bunk house for the farm labourers. She hated working with Aline.

"I don't want to work with her!" she shouted at her husband.

"Andrea," he said, "we have to make this work. Do what is necessary to help!" he shouted at her. Then he turned around and went for a beer.

Heartbroken and disappointed with her husband, Andrea went to bed and cried into her pillow. "How will I tell him?" she asked the empty room. There was only silence.

Two weeks later, Andrea cautiously said to her husband at dinner, "We're going to have a baby."

Completely taken by surprise, Edward jumped up and hugged his wife. "That's wonderful news!"

"I thought you would be angry," she replied.

"Never," he said to her soothingly. It was a beautiful moment that shone only briefly.

Much to their dismay, his parents arrived. Sitting at the table having coffee, Edward told them of the happy news. ***"How could you be so stupid!"*** Marcel yelled at his son. "We don't have time for this, now!" he said. Bursting into tears, Andrea ran to the bedroom and slammed the door. She was devastated. Her anger for her in-laws was growing like a festering boil.

"Pa!" Edward screamed. "How could you! I think you better leave now," he said.

"Let's go, Marcel," Aline said as she grabbed her husband by the arm. "Now!"

Not able to face his hysterical wife, Edward reached for a beer...then another...and another. Later that night, he staggered to bed too drunk to deal with Andrea.

"How could you!" she said to him the next day through clenched teeth. Then she walked up to him and slapped him across the face.

As anger built within him, he said to her, "You still have to work on the farm. Just because you are pregnant changes nothing!" Edward turned and left the house, with his wife standing there.

When planting season arrived, Aline and Andrea went into the greenhouse to pull plants. Familiar with this job, Andrea settled in. She sat her behind on the board that lay across the width of the bed of plants. In front of her was a thin bar about two and one half feet away. Here, she rested her feet as she leaned over between her legs to pull plants. Only the tallest plants in the bed where pulled or, at times, if a spot was sewn too thickly, she had to thin out the area. Andrea didn't mind the job, but she didn't want to spend that much time with Aline.

Aline loved pulling plants. She enjoyed pulling all day, even on the hottest of afternoons.

Most people pulled until noon and then, after lunch, went out planting. Sometimes, they would have people pull all day to be ready for the next day.

Mostly, women pulled plants, probably, because they are more flexible than men, but this job was also seen as women's work.

The greenhouse had a narrow walkway down the centre, running the full length of the building. On either side of the walkway were the plant beds. It was here the farmer sewed his crop of tobacco. He would water, fertilize, and care for the plants, just like they were his own children. After all, this crop represented their livelihood. If the crop was a failure, at this point, you faced the possibility of ruin. When the plants grew to the appropriate size, it was time to "pull plants."

While pulling plants, because her bottom rode only inches above the plants, Andrea sometimes ended up with very wet pants. In the morning, the plants were tall and strong, but as the heat of the day wore on, the plants became saggy and spindly.

To pull plants, you would gently grab the top leaves of the plant and pull slightly. The plant should lift right out of the soil. Andrea would place the plants in a nice bunch beside her, and when the pile was too large, the farmer would gather the plants and put them in boxes. The boxes would then be taken out to the field for planting.

Typically, if you pulled plants in the morning, you went to the fields and planted in the afternoon. Andrea was fed up with being around her mother-in-law all the time. "I want on the planter," she demanded of her husband. "Make it happen!"

"I'll ask," he said to her.

"ASK!" she screamed. "You are supposed to be the boss around here. Make it happen!" she demanded.

The next day, Andrea was out on the planter. She'd won! That was all that mattered to her. Aline was put in her place.

Planting wasn't a difficult job. A person just had to have some timing and coordination skills. You laid the tender plant down, root end toward your body, while a pair of grippers came over and grabbed the plant taking it down to the ground. Water and fertilized were dropped in the trench at the same time. Then a shoe came along behind and closed the trench around the plant. Plant after plant, acre after acre went into the ground. "The good part of this job is I'm not in the greenhouse with her anymore," Andrea thought to herself. She smiled to herself thinking she was victorious. Time would tell.

"Told you it would be better," she said to her husband that night.

"You better be quiet, Andrea," he warned. "Ma and Pa are angry with you."

"I don't care," she said, "They don't own me!" she snapped at him.

Edward left her standing and went outside. He refused to fight with her.

Andrea continued to plant tobacco every day. She had to ensure she dressed appropriately for the changeable weather. With no covering over them, they were constantly exposed to the elements. The hot sun would beat down on their heads or on rainy days, they were pelted by cold rain and wind. Sometimes, the weather could be so bad, there would be no way for anyone to keep warm. But they had no choice; planting had to be done.

Each day brought new challenges at the greenhouse, in the field, and at home for Edward.

The ride of the planter was beginning to cause major discomfort for Andrea. She suffered from sitting on a freezing cold metal seat all afternoon, while the bumps and jostling from the tractor going over the uneven ground made her afternoons a living hell. She had no choice, she told a friend, "It's expected of me."

Mother Nature could be a cruel mistress to farmers. There were years when the farmers would have their entire acreage of tobacco planted and hoed and cultivated only to have a killing frost hit and have the entire crop wiped out in a single night. If there were no extra plants available to replant, they had to look around to buy plants and quickly replant their crop. If no extra plants were available, they either tried to find an alternative crop or work off the farm for the year. This crop represented their income for the year.

The fact that they lost their crop to frost was one thing, but all the money invested for that year was instantly gone, as well. More money was not always available. The banks usually felt second loans were a bad risk. They wouldn't consider helping after a lost cause. Sometimes, other more profitable farmers would consider loaning money to help other farmers in need, but the interest rates would be high.

Mother Nature could also be a kind and compassionate mother, as well. Luckily, this year went well for Edward's first crop. Within a couple of weeks, his 30 acres of tobacco was planted, and Marcel and Aline breathed a sign of relief. "The crop is in," he said to her.

"Yes," she replied. Her son was successful...so far.

The two women spent the next couple of weeks walking the fields hoeing. It was their responsibility to hoe out any grass or weeds. They had to protect the tobacco plants at all cost. Row by row, hour after hour, they walked and hoed. Sometimes, they could spend up to half an hour or more in one spot if the grass and weeds were bad. So the women hoed, bent down, pulled out weeds, and walked. That was their day.

Andrea was having a good pregnancy, so far, and as she grew stronger, so did her baby. Spending her days with her mother-in-law was not a treat for her. The two women didn't like each other, but managed to be civil. The hours walking the fields passed slowly. Aline didn't mind the silence in the fields. She liked it. She was taught that there was a time and place for talking. Working and talking didn't mix.

Andrea was left to her own thoughts to help pass the time. She thought of her baby. "Will it be a boy or a girl," she wondered. "I want to give Edward a son." She personally didn't care either way. Andrea just wanted a baby.

Life in the house for the young couple was changing. Edward spent a great deal of time working on the farm and not with his wife. "He's never here," she told her mother one afternoon.

"Andrea," her mother replied. "He has a farm to run and crops to grow. He can't spend his time in the house with you."

She understood what her mother was saying, but she didn't like it.

Andrea felt that, instead of Aline and Marcel interfering, they should help her husband more. She didn't know that Marcel wanted Edward to have the full experience of growing a complete crop from start to finish on his own.

Farming meant long, hard hours. You can't just turn it off and on. Marcel wanted Edward to be successful and resourceful. He pushed his son to stand up and be a great farmer. All his life, Edward wanted to be on the farm. This was his choice, and this was his chance.

"His parents are trying to help him," Elvira said to her daughter.

"You just don't understand, Ma," she replied. Andrea thought of Edward's treatment from his father after he left school. "This must be how he is punishing Edward," she thought. The more she thought about the situation, the more her resentment of her in-laws grew.

Towards the end of June, the tobacco plants were growing strong and tall. It was time to cultivate. The cultivator is a piece of equipment that is pulled behind either the tractor or horse.

While Edward drove the tractor, Andrea and Aline sat on the cultivator, ready for a long day out in the field.

The cultivator is similar to a pair of scissor blades that slip under the soil. Aline and Andrea used the handles to operate the scissors below ground to cut weeds down. "You must have impeccable timing," Aline said as she looked at her daughter-in-law. "We can't afford to lose any plants."

Angry at her mother-in-law, Andrea just glared down at the blades and remained silent.

The ride was rough, and Andrea found she was very uncomfortable with her pregnancy. She did her best to not let her discomfort show. At night, she would tell Edward how much pain she was in. "I can't afford to hire anyone else," he said to her. "You **must** finish the crop for me, Andrea."

Over the next few days, Andrea's discomfort grew until she could no longer bare it.

Noticing the girl's discomfort, but not wanting to acknowledge it, Aline remained silent. "There is still a lot of work to do," she thought to herself. "We have to help Edward get this crop in! Just deal with it!"

The Tragic Loss

One day, when the women were out on the cultivator, Andrea was suddenly gripped by a severe pain in the abdomen. She doubled over from the stabbing pain in her stomach. Unfortunately, at the same time she fell forward, she cut down a few tobacco plants. Angered by the costly mistake, Aline turned toward Andrea to reprimand her. What she saw instantly changed her mind. **"Edward!"** she screamed. **"Stop!"** Looking down at Andrea, they both saw the pain in the young woman's eyes. As Edward stepped down from the tractor, he glanced at the row behind his wife. What he saw shocked him to the core. A long trail of blood laid behind his wife. Tearing his eyes away from the bloody trail, he turned to his young wife. Her face was white as snow. Sweat stood out on her forehead, and tears poured from her eyes.

In panic, Andrea tried to stand from the cultivator. She fell in the dirt. Edward picked her up and held her. A silent tear slipped from his eye. He knew what had just happened. He had seen this before from the animals in the barn. "Dear God!" he thought. "She's lost it."

With sadness and an understanding of what had just happened, Aline quietly got up off the cultivator and walked back to the house. Andrea, in her torment, thought her mother-in-law to be cold-hearted. "How can she just walk away from me!" she screamed to her husband. "Why?" she asked as she sobbed onto his chest.

Aline walked to the house to get the truck. She and Marcel drove back to the field. They found Andrea still sitting in a pool of blood, crying, while their son held her and tried to be brave.

Marcel and Edward gathered up the poor girl and put her in the truck.

To Andrea's horror, her husband didn't get in the truck with her. Aline got in the driver's side and drove away, leaving the two men standing in the field.

"What are you doing?" Andrea screamed as panic began to rise up in her throat. *"Edward! Why aren't you coming with me?"*

"He has to look after the plants and equipment," Aline told her. "He will see you later," she said.

"This is his responsibility," Andrea ranted. *"Not yours!"*

"Calm down," Aline said soothingly. "You aren't helping yourself."

Finally, at the doctor's office, Andrea's greatest fears were realized. She had miscarried their baby. Her next journey was to the hospital for a D & C.

"A D&C, or dilatation and curettage, is a procedure where the cervix is opened (dilated) and the lining of the uterus and its contents are removed by scraping and scooping," her doctor told her. "It's just routine after this type of event."

After the procedure was complete, Andrea woke with a terrible sadness and emptiness. She had been well into her second trimester, and there had really been no problems.

"I'm sorry, Andrea," the doctor said to her. "It was a boy."

Her heart was immediately ripped from her chest. The pain of the loss was magnified. "He wanted a son," she whispered. "And now, I've lost it." In her torment, she turned away from the doctor and sobbed. Her entire body shook. She was inconsolable.

Two days later, Aline went to collect her daughter-in-law from the hospital. "Don't you do any work for at least two weeks," the doctor warned her. Marcel had lost his compassion, and he was furious. "Now we are one person short," he bellowed at his wife. Frustrated with the entire situation, he left the house.

Aline tried her best to look after Andrea. During the day, she would stay in the big house with Aline and do simple tasks, like cutting vegetables for the meals or folding towels. Edward worked hard on the farm during the day. After dinner, he and Andrea would return to their smaller house on the farm.

Edward buried his pain deep inside. There was no one he could talk to, so he bottled the pain and soldiered on. Andrea saw that her husband was in pain, but found herself incapable of helping. She no longer had the energy to deny him one or two extra beers per night.

In time, Andrea recovered physically, but she did not recover emotionally. She even tried to talk to Aline about her loss, but the conversation was quickly shut down. Aline had gone through her own horrors in her life; she couldn't deal with anyone else's. "I'm sorry girl," she thought to herself one day. "I truly am."

With her grief laying undealt with and her loneliness growing, Andrea's demeanor began to change. She grew short tempered, reactive, and more unreasonable. A very nasty combination.

Everyone walked on eggshells around her. No one knew when or what would cause her to explode.

The First of a Few Harvests

Harvest time was quickly approaching, and Edward had to take action. He hired five men to go out in the fields to prime, one man to hand tobacco sticks into the kilns, and two other women to hand and tie. In a few weeks, an older gentleman would arrive from South Carolina to cure the crop.

Out in the fields, the men walked bent over to prime the bottom three leaves off the plant and tuck them under their arm. Armed with a huge bundle of leaves, the primer would place his armful in a long structure, called a boat. The boats varied in size, but the majority of them were seven feet in length, approximately eighteen inches wide and three feet high. Usually, they were constructed of a steel frame, similar to that of a sled, with side angle pieces that curved up the structure for stability. In between these raised ribs, the farmer would place wooden boards to hold in the tobacco. The design of the tobacco boat was similar to that of a giant bathtub on a sled frame.

When filled to the brim and sometimes beyond, the horse or tractor would pull it up to the kiln-yard, where the women would be eager to get to work tying the tobacco leaves onto the stick. Once the stick was completed, it would then be handed up to the kiln-hanger for strategic placement into the kiln for drying.

It was an incredible process of timing and very hard work.

Andrea and Aline worked as a team at the kiln. Andrea handed, while Aline tied. "Make sure you only hand three at a time," she reminded Andrea abruptly. "We must be exact."

Aline, with three leaves in hand, quickly tied string around the leaves and turned them over one side of the stick. The next bundle would fall on the opposite side. They would alternate the leaves from side to side. Three leaves on the left side and three on the right. Back and forth they went until they had the proper amount of leaves. Hour after hour, day after day, the same procedure was followed.

The weeks began to drag on with the constant non-stop of work that was their lives.

Rarely did they have a day off.

For the farm wives, the work was even harder. They spent most of the day at the kilns tying, but also had to prepare meals for all the men who boarded on the farm. Three full and hearty meals a day were expected from the wife. The men lived in a small 'bunk-house' on the farm, while the cure-man had his own little house, because of the odd hours he kept. He was up all hours of the night keeping a watchful eye on the drying tobacco.

Everyone knew their job on the farm, and they were paid accordingly. The primers made, on average, $10 to $12 per day for priming a full kiln. The women who were tying could earn up to $8 per day for their skill. Most of the time, the women who handed leaves received slightly less than $8 per day, because the skill most valued was tying.

The men of the farms thought their work was hard, but for the farm wives, the work was endless.

Andrea and Aline spent many long days cooking, cleaning, doing laundry, and baking. The primers were usually out in the field by 6:30-7:00 a.m. "Hurry up, Andrea," Aline scolded her daughter-in-law. "The primers will be here for breakfast soon. You know the meal has to be on the table by 6:00 a.m.!"

"I'm hurrying," Andrea snapped back as she gathered up the butter and jam for the table.

There were no simple meals for the men. A typical breakfast consisted of oatmeal or some type of cereal, bacon, ham and eggs or sausage, fresh bread and butter, jam, and coffee. They needed fuel for their bodies.

Once breakfast was finished, a quick clean up began. Andrea cleared the table as Aline began washing dishes. "When you are finished clearing, get the stock started for lunch," Aline told Andrea. "We have to hurry and get out to the kiln. The first load should be there shortly." The women had to utilize their time wisely.

With their kitchen duties complete, the two women headed for the kiln yard and another day of handing and tying. These women were skilled at their craft and very important on the farm.

Andrea and Aline would stand in one spot for hours at a time handing and tying leaves. By the time harvest came to an end, the women were barely able to stand from exhaustion. Andrea, however, found herself beyond exhausted. She could barely move from being tired by the end. It was then she discovered she was pregnant again.

Another Try at a Family

Edward and Andrea were thrilled at the prospect of a baby. Edward was pleased they were given a second chance at a family. However, the timing was never good when you farmed. You could make a good living for your family farm if you were successful. If things didn't go your way, and at times this happened, you could develop huge debt or run the risk of bankruptcy.

All these things plagued Edward's mind. Marcel was around to help most days, but he was trying to give Edward enough space to learn the art of tobacco growing.

Aline, on the other hand, was always around on the farm. As far as she was concerned, there was always work to be done, and you worked until the work was done. She was totally indifferent to the news that Andrea was pregnant again. Aline never had the time to be the maternal type. Like many women, she just had them because it was expected of her.

Andrea felt Aline's presence at every turn. They worked together, cooked and bake together. She felt the ever-growing presence of her mother-in-law, even in the home she shared with Edward, for the house was was owned by his parents. If Marcel felt a discussion was needed, he walked into the house, sat down at the kitchen table, and talked with his son. Aline didn't 'visit' as often as Marcel, but the presence of her in-laws loomed over every aspect of their lives.

Once harvest had ended and kilns were emptied of their precious golden leaves, Andrea and Edward piled the tobacco neatly in the barn. Now, they could breathe a bit easier. The primers had returned home for the winter for a much deserved rest from the intense farm labour. The cure-man stayed on the farm until the last kiln of tobacco was packed away. He had to ensure the crop was perfect. His reputation depended on it. If you were a successful cure-man, your invitation to return the following year was ensured.

Marcel and Edward learned every possible detail they could from the cure-man. They wanted to be able to cure their own crops in the future.

As fall and winter quickly approached, life on the farm began to settle down. They began to look forward to the birth of their child.

"I hope and pray everything will be fine with the baby, this time," Andrea said to her husband. "I can't lose another child." Andrea prayed every day for the life of her unborn child.

Edward never told her, but his prayers matched hers. He was very concerned for his wife. After the miscarriage, he found his wife's behaviour had deteriorated. She was very moody, short-tempered, and at times, irrational.

Andrea kept herself busy. She and Aline busied themselves with putting away preserves for the winter. They made jams, jarred fresh pears, peaches, and plums. Some of Edward's favourites included apple sauce and pickles. These two women packed away as much food as possible for the long winter months.

Andrea enjoyed these domestic chores. "She seems better than she has in months," Aline told Marcel over dinner.

"Good," he replied gruffly. "She needs to pull her weight around here." He had very little compassion for the young woman. He just didn't like her.

Excitedly, Andrea approached her husband one Sunday afternoon. "I've passed the day," she said with a huge smile that completely lit up her face.

Confused, Edward asked her "What day?"

"I've passed the time when I lost the first one," she replied.

A huge smile appeared on Edward's face. He hugged his wife to him and said, "I'm so happy." As he hugged her, a single tear fell from his eye. He prayed this baby would help his wife recover.

Even though she was still working every day in the strip room grading tobacco, Andrea felt good. Now that the pressure was off, they only worked five days a week. Andrea enjoyed her Saturdays and Sundays off. They would go to town to buy groceries, see friends, and visit with other families. She could save the housework and laundry until the weekends, now. On Sundays, they attended church, and prayed to God for the safe delivery of their baby.

Andrea was beginning to settle down and relax. "Everything will work this time," she said, one day, as she stood in the baby's room.

Christmas of 1951 was a happy time. Edward and Andrea hosted her family for Christmas dinner. Everyone was having a good visit, until Marcel, Aline, and Danielle came walking in the door. Andrea tensed immediately. She was hoping to have this one day with her family and **not** with his.

A fourth person walked in the house. It was Edward's uncle Adolf. He hadn't seen the man for a few years. Edward was pleased with the surprise visit.

"Uncle," Edward said to Adolf, "come and share a beer with me." Soon, after several bottles of beer had been consumed, the men's conversations grew rather boisterous, and the women grew disgusted with them.

On the other side of the room, Elvira and Aline were sitting in the living room, surrounded by Andrea, Angela, and Danielle. Andrea was happy to see her sister. They hadn't had a chance to spend much time together the last few years. Danielle, being the youngest of the three younger ladies, talked about the boy she was interested in this week. Andrea was in her eighth month of pregnancy and felt more positive than she had in months. She was happy.

Elvira and Aline moved to another part of the living room, to have a quiet conversation over a cup of coffee. The two mothers, who didn't like each other, seemed like old friends today, sitting this Christmas day, chatting like old friends. They talked about their families, what the children were involved in, and even chatted about some mutual friends they had in town.

Christmas Day 1951 ended rather nicely for the two families. Everyone was cheerful and was full of happiness and blessings and looking for a great future for the beginning of 1952.

"It was a great day," Andrea said to her husband late that evening.

"It certainly was," he responded. "How great that everyone got along today."

The happiness of Christmas would soon be forgotten. Two weeks later, Andrea's stomach pain began.

"NO!" she cried out. ***"It's too soon! This can't happen again!"***

Why Did This Happen Again?

Still a few weeks away from her due date, the doctor remained positive. After he examined Andrea, he said to her, "Everything is fine. There is nothing to worry about. Go home and get some rest and stop working in the strip room."

"Will the pain stop?" Andrea asked him.

"Yes," he replied. "If you rest, it should stop in a few days."

Andrea was hopeful. She had been over tired the last few weeks, but just assumed it was from Christmas.

"I'll hire someone to take your place in the strip room," Edward told her. "Just take the time and look after the baby."

Andrea enjoyed the rest, but the chronic fatigue didn't go away.

Suddenly, one evening, Andrea went into labour. "Oh no!" she screamed. "I did what I was told! Why is this happening?"

Edward rushed his wife to the hospital in Simcoe.

"I'm not worried," the doctor told him. "She is close enough to the date, now. Everything should be fine."

In a very short time, the labour turned hard and heavy. Andrea was growing more and more exhausted. With sweat dripping off her body, she screamed at the doctor, ***"I can't do this much longer. The pain is horrible!"***

"Ok, Andrea," the doctor said soothingly to her. "We are going to take you in now. You will be put to sleep, and when you wake up, you will be holding your beautiful little baby."

She smiled at the doctor just before another massive contraction grabbed hold of her entire body. Andrea screamed out in agony.

"Relax," the doctor said, "everything is going to be fine..."

After a few minutes, the doctor had dispelled her fears. "Soon I'll be holding my baby," she thought.

"I'll see you soon," she said to Edward as he kissed her forehead outside the delivery room. She was unaware of the fear in his eyes.

"Dear God," he prayed. "Let them be alright."

Hours passed that seemed like an eternity for Edward.

Drowsy when she woke, and in a fog from the anesthesia, Andrea found herself alone in a room. Looking around, she noticed the absence of flowers, cards, and gifts. There was nothing 'baby' in the room. "Where is everyone?" she asked the empty room. "What's going on? Am I dreaming?"

Pushing the buzzer, she rang for the nurse.

To her surprise, the doctor walked in the room with Edward. She could tell by the haggard and drawn look on her husband's face that something was wrong. He looked horrible. His eyes were red and swollen, and the corners of his mouth were down-turned.

She tried to swallow the terror that was rising up from within.

"What's going on?" she demanded. "Edward! ***What's wrong?"*** Quickly, she began to lose control.

Suddenly, the doctor was beside her, sitting on the bed. Edward remained standing behind the doctor. He was unable to make eye contact with his wife.

"Doctor?" she said in a questioning tone that was filled with panic.

Grabbing Andrea's hand and patting the top, he began talking. ***"There's something wrong, isn't there?"*** she screamed, without even hearing his words. ***"Where's my baby?!"***

Even without hearing his words, she knew something was wrong. "Not again," she thought.

The doctor was still talking, but she looked up at her husband. He had tears silently rolling down his cheeks. "He never cries!" she thought.

Then, the doctor's words penetrated her hearing. "Your baby was stillborn," he said soothingly. "He was a beautiful boy, weighing 9 pounds, 2 ounces."

"I want to hold my baby," she screamed.

"Andrea..." the doctor tried to say.

Andrea sat up in her bed with a wild look on her face. ***"I want to hold my baby! NOW!"*** she shrieked.

"I think that's not a good idea, Andrea," the doctor said. "It will be harder if you bond with it."

"I WANT TO SEE MY BABY, RIGHT NOW!" she shouted in the doctor's face.

Edward didn't want her to hold the baby, either. He thought it would drive his wife over the deep end. She was moody and not quite herself after the first miscarriage; this could be the end.

"Why do you want to hold him?" Edward asked her.

"It's my baby!" she cried. "I have to see him." Her face, now drenched in tears, and her sobs rocked her entire body. She was able to say, "I need to see if I can make a baby." Her hands went to her face. She wept from a heart filled with great torment and pain.

"Calm yourself a bit," the doctor said to her. "You can see your baby."

Ten minutes later, after Andrea had calmed herself, a nurse came into the room carrying a large bundle in her arms.

Immediately, Andrea held out her arms. Edward sat down on the bed beside his wife. "I can do this," he thought to himself. "I must put my feelings aside for her."

The nurse carefully placed the bundle in Andrea's arms. Carefully, she grabbed each corner and pulled open the blue baby blanket.

Nestled inside the blanket was the most perfect, chubby baby. He had a head full of dark, curly hair. His head was beautifully shaped, and his tiny little ears framed his head perfectly.

Andrea looked down at her child and smiled. "Look," she said. "He's smiling. He's an angel. Oh Edward," she cried, "look at his chubby little toes. He's perfect!" she screamed.

Unable to control her emotions any longer, Andrea pulled the baby to her chest. Her breasts ached as the milk demanded to be expressed. "But to whom? I have no baby to feed," she thought.

As she held her baby tight to her chest, she began rocking back and forth. Her sobs became uncontrollable. Both the doctor and nurse wiped tears from their eyes.

"Oh dear GOD!" Andrea screamed. ***"How could you take another baby from me!"***

Edward tried to console his wife. He put his arms around her and his son. Quietly, he wept.

"WHY?" she screamed as her eyes looked to the heavens.

"Andrea," the doctor said, "we need to take the baby now."

Coming out of her torment, she looked down at her little boy. "Richard," she said and looked at her husband. "Yes," he replied.

Andrea's tears had washed her baby's face. Carefully, she took an edge of the blanket and wiped his little cheeks dry. "I love you," she whispered to him.

The nurse took the baby from his mother's arms. She left the room quickly as her own tears escaped, once again. "I'm sorry little one," she said as she carried the baby down to the morgue. "I'm so sorry."

"Andrea, Edward," the doctor said to them both. "I need to tell you what happened."

The young couple looked up at the doctor. He felt such pity for them. The doctor looked at their tear-stained faces and said, "The cord had been around the baby's neck," he began. "Every time there was a contraction, the cord tightened. He had been dead for awhile." Looking at them both with sorrow in his heart he said, "There was nothing anyone could have done."

The doctor left the room. "They need to heal this wound together," he thought to himself as he hung his head in sorrow, while walking down the hallway.

They held each other and cried. Nothing could ease the pain that was tearing their hearts apart.

Plans had to be made for the burial. Their little one would be laid to rest in a beautifully quiet place in Delhi. He would sleep for eternity, ever shaded by the beautiful and majestic trees that stood guard over him.

They wanted to have their baby baptized, so the next day, their parents and priest came to the hospital room. It was a beautiful service as the lifeless baby was blessed, anointed into the Catholic faith and given the names Richard Alphonse.

After the family left, Andrea's doctor came to talk with her.

"You lost a great deal of blood during the delivery," he told her. "You are weak, and I will not release you from the hospital for one week," he said in his official voice.

Shocked, as if he had slapped her across the face, she looked at him. With tears building in her eyes, she replied, "But I will miss the...the service."

"I am sorry, Andrea, but you are ill, and it's my job to look after you. I will let you see the baby once more, here, but you must stay in the hospital!"

Later that day, the doctor brought her baby to her. She wept as she held him to her chest. The pain in her heart was unbelievable. Andrea had wanted a baby more than anything. But once again, God had taken her child away.

Edward walked in the room. He immediately stopped and stared. He rushed over to his wife and son and held them both.

"It's time," the doctor said very gently to them. "Say your goodbyes."

Together, they leaned over and kissed their little boy on the forehead. "Until we meet again," Edward whispered. "I love you," Andrea breathed as Edward took Richard from her arms to hand back to the doctor. Turning, the doctor walked out of the room and went back to the morgue.

Their pain was so raw and so real. Andrea had not really recovered from the loss of her first child. This loss could send her over the edge.

"I'm a failure!" she told herself. "A failure as a wife and mother." After trying twice to give her husband a son, she had failed. Twice, she would return home empty-handed. She began to fall into a deep, dark depression.

Edward would be able to spend some time with her at home. Life on the farm was at a slow point, so he could afford some time with his wife. They both needed time to deal with their grief. "But how?" he wondered. "How can I help her?"

Andrea's grief was excruciating. It was ripping her apart, and she was inconsolable. Unfortunately, when she arrived home, everything for the baby was still in the room. She walked in the room and looked around.

She ran her hand along the nice solid crib that was just begging to have a baby curled up asleep on the mattress. There were a few dozen diapers, some hand-knitted and crocheted outfits stacked neatly in the dresser, powders and soaps, a brush and comb, and tiny little shoes sitting on the table all waiting patiently to be used on a newborn. Everything would remain unused.

Andrea sat on the floor in the middle of the room and cried. Edward left her for a while. "Maybe if she cries it out, she'll feel better," he thought. He truly didn't know what to do to help. Honestly, he couldn't figure out how to help himself. His own misery was taking hold.

As his wife cried, Edward turned and walked to the case of beer that sat on the back porch. He sat down on the bench and grabbed for a bottle and opener. He would attempt to drink away his pain. "If I drown it, I won't feel the pain," he thought.

With the fourth beer downed, he reached for another. Off in the distance, he heard his wife's cries.

A Period of Recovery

The first few months following the burial of their son were very difficult for Andrea. She suffered greatly from the black moods of depression that covered her like a shroud. Edward, however, was feeling much better as he went back to work in the fields. His heart and soul came to life in the open space of the farm. The soil was his life blood, and he intended to prove to his parents he was a great farmer.

The crop of tobacco he produced each year was of very good quality. The buyers paid just slightly higher than top dollar per pound, which satisfied his parents. Marcel and Aline were beginning to believe retirement was possible. Their son was proving his worth as a tobacco grower.

Like many retired farmers, they made their son another deal.

"We will set you up on the farm. You will have total control, and we will take quarter crop from the profits," they told their son over dinner one evening. "Andrea must do her share on the farm, Edward," Aline said. "You know how imperative it is to have a good wife to help."

"I know, Ma," he replied. "She's getting stronger every day."

"She had better get herself under control and get to work to help," Marcel said abruptly. "You can't afford to have a liability on your hands."

Edward glared at his father. Not wishing to cause an argument, he remained silent.

Retirement proved to be difficult for the older couple. Having worked extremely hard since their arrival in Canada, they found retirement a great challenge.

Marcel had always kept himself busy. He found tinkering with machinery enjoyable, and it occupied a great deal of his time.

"I have to do something!" he said to Aline one evening. "I can't just sit here!"

"Why don't you see if you can help with fixing the machinery on the farm for Edward," she replied. "That will keep you busy and help him at the same time."

Both found they could not break their connection to the land and the habits of a lifetime. Aline would be found walking out in the fields. She loved spending her time out looking at the crops and soaking in the sunshine.

Edward agreed to have his father work on the machinery. "It would be a great help, Pa," he told his father.

Marcel smiled and slapped his son on the back. "Thanks."

In time, Marcel soon forgot he was no longer growing the crops. He offered his opinion and comments at every turn. Edward found his father's constant comments and interference troubling.

"He doesn't trust me," he said to his mother one afternoon.

"It's just his strong will," she replied. But she knew about a very opinionated and strong-willed man. It was a challenge to get him to see reason or change his mind.

They needed to find a way to make this arrangement work. Edward was struggling with his father during work and his wife at home. He had no peace.

After the death of her second baby, Andrea became more disagreeable and moody and showed a definite lack of enthusiasm for being on the farm. To Edward, it seemed that Andrea blamed his parents and the farm for the loss of her children.

"I don't understand what your problem is!" he said to her one night. "You need to just get moving and keep busy," he said. "You will feel better."

"Get out!" she screamed at him.

He stood frozen in shock. "What is wrong with you?" he yelled. This all seemed so ridiculous to him.

"Just get out," she shrieked.

Rejected, once again, by his wife, Edward left and went to the barn. Earlier that week, he had hidden a case of beer in the tool shop. He walked in the barn and headed for the beer. "The only source of comfort I have," he thought to himself.

Andrea's actions became more erratic as time went on. She became more disagreeable, her anger issues were out of control and no one knew how to handle her.

If she quarrelled with someone, she would scream, throw things, and at times, run away. Everyone was beginning to worry. Edward was left standing, embarrassed at having to explain his wife's conduct.

Andrea's behaviour gave her parents serious cause for concern one afternoon while visiting. She disagreed with her mother at every turn. Elvira tried to talk with her daughter, but to no avail. **"I'm fine!"** she snapped at her mother.

Over the next few months, everyone kept a close eye on Andrea. Eventually, she was able to deal with her great loss, and her moods began to improve. Edward was relieved.

Even though she improved during the day, Andrea found the nights unbearable. She was having nightmares.

She had been seeing the family doctor regularly and, finally, decided to confide in him about the dreams.

"In one nightmare," she told the doctor, "I hear Richard crying in the other room. No matter which door in the house I open, I can't get to him. He just cries and cries," she said. "I hear the pain in his screams, but I can't help him."

"What about the second dream?" he asked her.

After some hesitation, she responded. "I find myself in the delivery room of the hospital. I'm happy and sitting up with Richard in my arms," she said. Tears began to roll down Andrea's face.

"Go ahead," the doctor said encouragingly.

"The room is filled with flowers, toys, and people," she began. "Everyone is happy. I'm holding Richard in my arms, but then I look down, and I see my baby is dead!" she screamed. "I see his face over and over again."

"Andrea," the doctor said sternly. "In time, these memories will become easier to deal with, and eventually, they will fade. Keep yourself busy on the farm. Go back to work. Get back to life!" he urged her rather strongly.

In the spring of 1955, Andrea gave Edward the news that she was pregnant again. She had held off telling him for a few months. She didn't want to get his hopes up again. Much to her surprise, Edward was very happy about the news.

"That's wonderful!" Edward yelled out as he picked up his wife and swirled her around the room.

"Oh, Edward," she said to him, "I'm so afraid."

"Don't think about it," he whispered back to her. "Everything will be alright."

Their happiness was short-lived. When they told his parents, Edward could see the disappointment in his father's eyes. The next day, in the barn, his father approached him. "Why did you do that again!" he demanded.

"Pa," Edward replied. "I want a family."

"You need help on the farm more," Marcel replied. "She can't do the work if she's pregnant all the time.

"Leave!" Edward bellowed at his father. ***"Now!"*** he said. "I don't want to see you for a while."

Marcel turned and stormed out of the barn. Edward had never spoken to his father in such a manner. He had no idea what the repercussions would be. Only time would tell.

By the time they told everyone of their good news, Andrea was almost 5 months pregnant. Edward didn't want her out in the fields, so she was put to work in the big house with Aline. She cooked and cleaned and did laundry, day in and day out. The two women were appreciative of each other's help, but Andrea did not relish spending so much time under the constant gaze of her mother-in-law. They were civil to each other and worked towards a common goal, but the tension was always there.

In time, Andrea found she learned a great deal about baking from the older woman. Aline was an expert at making pie crust and bread. Together, they made dozens of pies and 6-8 loaves of bread every day. They had a large, ravenous farm crew to feed three times per day.

Aline felt sympathy for her daughter-in-law. One afternoon, in particular, Andrea was looking very tired. The old woman came to her and said kindly, "You go and rest. I'll wash the dishes."

Shocked by the comments, but feeling very tired, Andrea said, "Thank you. I am rather tired today."

"Maybe she does care," Andrea thought to herself as she rested on the bed.

She found the afternoon of rest a blessing. She felt rejuvenated.

In the months that followed, tensions between father and son began to grow. Edward was overwhelmed with the work that needed to be done during harvest. Marcel, being bored with retirement, would find little projects to keep himself occupied. However, he ended up being in the way more than anything.

"Go into town and have a beer with Mike," Edward would suggest. "Go play darts, Pa," he would offer. Once in a while, Marcel would leave and go into town to the Belgian Hall. He enjoyed visiting with his friend, Mike, who had also retired from active farming.

Edward appreciated the time his father was away.

Harvest time had been very successful for Edward. The crop was harvested, cured, and stored in the barn, waiting for stripping to start.

Two weeks into the stripping season, Andrea began having severe pain. Terrified that something was wrong again, she remained silent. "If I rest, it will stop," she thought to herself. "Thank goodness it's Sunday." She went to her room and lay down on the bed to rest. Several hours later she screamed, "Edward! Help me!"

Her husband came running into the room. His wife lay on the bed in a pool of blood.

"Oh my God," he thought. ***"Not again! Dear God, not again!"***

"We have to get to the hospital," he said to her. "Hold on! Please!"

The Horror of it All

Andrea's pain continued hours after arriving at the hospital.

"Oh dear God, why is this happening again!" she screamed, as another agonizing spasm shook her body. As each new pain took hold of her, she sank deeper and deeper into despair. ***"Please, please!"*** she begged. ***"Don't take this child from me!"***

"I will give her something to calm down," the doctor told Edward. "We must let nature take its course."

Edward was beside himself with fear. ***"Why am I being denied a family? What have I done wrong?"*** he begged God. But his prayers remained unanswered.

"Will I be able to keep the baby?" Andrea asked her doctor.

"You are just over eight months now," he replied. "There is a good chance you will give birth to a beautiful baby."

Relief washed over her, and she began to relax.

"Rest," the nurse said to her as she gave Andrea an injection to help her sleep. "Your strength will help the baby."

Exhausted and feeling the immediate effects of the drug, Andrea closed her eyes and slept.

Her sleep was not peaceful. Repeatedly, she saw the face of her infant son Richard, who had died without ever knowing his mother's face.

The next morning, Andrea was subjected to a battery of blood work and examinations. She was still groggy as the doctor was keeping her sedated.

Meeting Edward in the hallway, the doctor pointed towards a quiet room and said, "Let's step in here so we can talk."

"What's going on doctor?" Edward asked.

"I'm very sorry, but your baby didn't survive, Edward," he told the young man. He placed his hand on the man's shoulder and said, "I thought you should know before I tell your wife."

Edward's anguish was evident on his face. With tears starting to roll down his cheeks, he asked the doctor, "What happened?"

"I thought the vital signs were a bit different last month when I examined Andrea," he uttered. "I assumed it was due to the stress she was under and the approaching time. Today, when I checked on her, there were no vital signs. I'm sorry, Edward."

Hanging his head, the young man began to weep. "We just want a family," he whispered to the doctor. "Will she be alright?"

"Your wife is strong and healthy," the doctor answered. "Physically, she will recover, but she will need your help to recover mentally."

"What happens now?" Edward asked the doctor.

"Her labour was brought on because the baby has been dead for a couple of weeks. It's nature way of cleansing her body," he replied. "We have taken steps to prep her for delivery."

"Have you told her?" Edward asked.

"No, I wanted to tell you first," he divulged. "I thought we could go in together and tell your wife."

"NOT AGAIN!" she screamed in agony. **"Why!?"** she wailed as her eyes overflowed with tears. The grief she expressed brought the nurses in the room to tears.

"Give her the shot, now," the doctor instructed. In two minutes, Andrea fell into a deep sleep. "Kiss your wife, Edward," the doctor told the young man. "We are going to take her in now. Why don't you go and call your family? I'll talk to you afterwards."

"I will," was all Edward was able to say. He left the room with hunched shoulders and tears streaming down his face.

He hated the two phone calls he had to make. Both his mother and his wife's mother were lost for words. They understood what he had just conveyed, but were unable to speak.

"I'm sorry," was all he was able to say to them. "I'm so sorry," he repeated. After he ended the calls, he leaned against the wall and wept uncontrollably. "How am I supposed to get through this?" he begged for an answer as he pounded his fist onto the wall. There was no answer.

Sometime later, the doctor approached Edward in the quiet room. "It's over now," he said.

"And?" Edward questioned.

"You had another son," the doctor replied.

With a look of utter despair on his face, Edward asked in a calm tone, "Tell me the rest."

"It's as I had suspected," he began, "the cord wrapped around the babies neck twice. He was a beautiful boy," the doctor told him. "Chubby with the face of a cherub."

Edward began to lose control of himself. "I'm sorry," he murmured to the doctor.

"Your wife will need you," the doctor said. "I have to register the birth, Edward. Have you decided on a name?"

"Yes, we did," he replied. "Edmond."

"Thank you," the doctor said. "You can see your wife shortly. Be gentle with her!" he warned.

Later that day, sitting with his wife in her room, Edward had the feeling of déjà vu. "How many more times do we have to go through this?" he thought. But his train of thought was broken as a nurse walked in the room, carrying their baby.

She handed the bundle to Andrea and stepped back to keep a close eye on the family.

Wrapped in a soft blue blanket lay the most beautiful baby boy. Andrea fought back her tears as she tenderly kissed the little forehead. "I'll never see him with his eyes open," she whispered. ***"Oh God, how can you be so cruel!"*** she screamed.

The nurse was ready for action. She knew, at any given second, she may have to remove the child and sedate the mother. "They need this time together," she thought to herself. "This is the part of my job I hate."

Edward, sitting beside his wife, gently touched his son's chest. He desperately wanted to feel a heartbeat. "Edmond," he uttered and kissed the baby on the cheek.

"Give him one more kiss," the nurse said to them. "It's time."

"NO!" Andrea screamed at the nurse. ***"YOU CAN'T TAKE HIM!"*** Just as she said this, the doctor came into the room and approached Andrea.

"Give the baby to the nurse, now," he urged her gently. As he spoke, he injected medication into her I.V. tube. "You're going to have a rest now, Andrea."

Andrea hugged her baby tightly to her chest. Slowly she released her grip, and the two parents planted loving kisses on his face, then handed Edmond to the nurse.

"Good bye my little one," Edward said as the nurse left the room with his son.

"Go home now, Edward, and get some rest," the doctor ordered him. "There is nothing more you can do."

Completely destroyed and feeling like dying, himself, Edward went home that night and drank himself into a stupor.

Five days after the delivery, Andrea and Edward stood in the Cemetery at the gravesite of yet another child.

Andrea looked to the sky and her heart asked, "Why God?" She looked back at the open grave, where her baby would lay, and felt the life completely drain out of her. She fell in the soft grass. The stress and strain of yet another stillbirth was too much for her. She had passed out.

Do We Dare Try Again

Afraid to tell her husband, Andrea decided to wait until Christmas to tell Edward her secret.

Christmas morning, she cautiously said to him, "Edward, I'm pregnant."

Happiness and fear showed on his face and in his eyes. "That's wonderful," he said to her as he hugged her. "When are you due?" he inquired.

"Sometime in the middle of May," she replied. "Are you happy?" she asked rather carefully.

He smiled at her and replied, "Yes, yes, I am. We have been given another chance," he said to her.

They spent a glorious Christmas morning together.

Later that afternoon, Marcel and Aline came over for coffee. They found spending time with their daughter-in-law a challenge. She had been extremely moody and irrational, but today, she was in an exceptional mood.

"Ma, Pa," Edward said to his parents. "We are going to have a baby!"

Neither parent spoke, at first. After all that had happened, they didn't know how to respond to the news. Suddenly, Aline knew she had better say something. She could feel the eyes of Andrea burning into her. "That's lovely news," Aline commented. "Congratulations."

Unhappy with the news from his son, Marcel just glared at him. "Edward, I would like a beer," he commanded.

"Pa," Edward replied. "Be happy for us."

"Why do you keep doing this?" Marcel demanded. "It's obvious she can't give you a child!"

"Marcel!" Aline shouted. "That's enough!"

Losing complete control of herself, Andrea stood up and screamed, "***Get out of my house! I don't care who you are! Get out!***"

Marcel slammed his fist on the table. He glared at Andrea, but said nothing to her. "Aline!" he yelled. "We are leaving."

Feeling ashamed of her husband's actions, but knowing not to say a word, Aline rose and walked towards the door.

"I hate him!" Andrea shouted after they had left.

Edward tried to calm her, but found it nearly impossible. Her mental stability had declined over the past several years. He assumed it was the trauma from the loss of their children. But now, as he spoke to her, he discovered she actually was not hearing him. "Maybe she is just too upset," he thought. "Maybe that is why she isn't hearing me."

But his wife didn't calm down. She actually picked up the glass Marcel had been drinking from and threw it against the wall. Shocked by her lack of control, Edward said, "Andrea, calm down!" Once again, she didn't hear. She just continued to rave.

Over the next few months, Edward noticed more episodes of his wife's lack of hearing. When he mentioned it to her, she would get very angry with him. "There's nothing wrong with me!" she would shout back at him. "It's all you and your family! That's what's wrong here!" she would yell.

Andrea was beginning to have difficulty with her hearing. She was just too terrified to face it.

When they would listen to the radio or watch television, Andrea began to realize she was missing certain pieces. Edward would laugh at jokes or funny stories, but she didn't always catch them. She assumed that maybe the equipment was faulty or someone turned down the volume.

Unfortunately, as time progressed, she admitted to herself she had a problem. "Do I really want to know the truth?" she asked herself, "or do I just keep going as I am?"

Shortly, she had to admit something else was going on. Her due date was coming closer.

"It's May!" she shouted excitedly to her husband. "I've never gotten this far before! It's a good sign, I just know it!" she screamed with excitement.

Two weeks into May, she went into labour.

Edward got her to the hospital immediately. "Is everything alright?" he asked her on the drive in.

"Yes," she replied calmly. "This time is different."

After the delivery, the doctor approach Edward in the waiting room. "I have good news, my boy!" he said as he clapped the young man on the back. "Your wife just gave you a baby girl!"

Thrilled, but cautious, Edward asked, "Is she alive? Is Andrea alright?"

"Yes," the old doctor replied. "They are both fine. You can go see them shortly."

"Thank you!" Edward replied as he shook the doctor's hand. "Thank you!"

The doctor smiled at him and returned to the delivery room, relieved.

One week later, they took their infant daughter home.

Both sets of parents put their differences aside and celebrated the very happy occasion. They had cake and coffee ready to greet their first grandchild.

Several weeks later, Andrea began to notice she was struggling with her hearing. She began to worry.

"Andrea," Edward would say to her. "The baby's crying." But Andrea had not heard her daughter cry.

"If I can't hear her cry, how will I be able to care for her?" she wondered. "Will I miss something?" Her fears were becoming real.

That evening, she worked up the courage to talk to Edward about her hearing. He was relieved when she finally admitted there may be a problem. Now the big question was, what where they going to do about it?

The next day, they went to see their family doctor for a regular check-up for the baby. The baby was in perfect health and growing rapidly. The doctor was very pleased. Edward and Andrea didn't want to take any chances with this baby.

While at the doctor's office, Andrea timidly raised the problem of her hearing. She mentioned to him that this had really been going on for about 5 years. They were afraid of what the future held. All sorts of ideas had been milling around in Andrea's mind. She believed the three infant deaths were some type of punishment for her. Now, she was beginning to believe her hearing loss was another form of punishment...but as for the reason, she drew a complete blank.

Their family doctor ran some tests, but felt it was imperative for Andrea to see a specialist in London. "These doctors specialize in hearing and deafness," he told the couple. "I strongly urge you to go and find out what is happening."

Before they could attend their appointment for Andrea's hearing tests, the families joined together to celebrate the Baptism of their first infant daughter. It was a beautiful, sunny day in mid-June in 1957. Together, they prayed and thanked God for the gift of their child.

It was a beautiful service. As Edward looked around the church, he admired the beauty of the stain-glass windows, the soft lighting from the candles, and the soothing sound of the music softly playing in the background. Another sound he thoroughly enjoyed was the tiny little whimpers coming from his first child as the holy water was poured over her forehead. Life was beautiful today. They christened their daughter, Patricia Maria.

The pride Edward felt was about to burst forth from his chest. He invited everyone back to the farm for a celebration.

As the celebration continued, the men grew louder. After three cases of beer had been drained of their contents, the men turned their attention to whiskey. The women grew disgusted by the spouses' behaviour. If it had been any other day of celebration, the women would have reprimanded their husbands, but today, they let everything go.

"Andrea," someone said to her from a few feet away. "Andrea!" the women repeated. Unaware she was being spoken to, Andrea continued slicing the cake. **"Andrea!"** the woman yelled.

Edward, seeing what was happening, went over to his wife and touched her arm. As he did, he whispered in her ear that she was being called.

When Andrea turned around to face her guests, she was shocked by the look their faces. All she saw was pity and confusion in their eyes.

"What's the matter?" Andrea asked. "I was busy," she said.

"Bertha, will you please serve the cake for me?" she asked her friend. "I will be right back."

She ran to her room and closed the door. Embarrassed and humiliated, she fell on her bed and began to cry.

Outside the room, someone was softly tapping on the door. Andrea heard nothing. The next thing she knew, her mother was sitting beside her, gently stroking her shoulder. As Andrea sat up, Elvira offered her a handkerchief. "Wipe your eyes," her mother told her. "What's going on, Andrea?"

Andrea wiped her eyes and blew her nose. Then she bared her soul to her mother.

The two women talked for about an hour. Andrea informed her mother that in two days she would see a doctor in London, someone who specializes in hearing impairments. Hugging her daughter tightly, Elvira said, "I'm glad you are getting help." She noticed her daughter's hearing difficulty for quite some time, but given her daughter's explosive behaviour, she was reluctant to mention it.

Andrea hugged her mother and began to cry. "What will happen to me?" she asked.

Stroking her daughter's hair, Elvira replied, "I don't know, my girl. I don't know."

The Specialist

The day for the hearing specialist had arrived. No longer able to hide the fear, Andrea ran around the house doing chores that had already been done. Her hands shook as she tried to put away drinking glasses in the cupboard. When she finally dropped one, she broke down. Sitting on the floor amongst the broken shards of glass, she lost her composure. Her sobs reached the ears of her husband. Edward ran into the kitchen to find his wife sitting in broken glass.

"What are you doing?" he asked her.

Her crying was the only response to his question.

"Come on," he said to her as he raised her to her feet. "We need to go."

After a few minutes, Andrea regained her self-control, and together, they left for London.

After the extensive examination, Edward and Andrea chatted with the specialist.

"It's nerve damage," the specialist told them. "You will eventually lose all your hearing," he said.

Terrified by the words she just heard, Andrea began to lose control. She brought her hands up to cover her eyes and began to cry. Edward gently rubbed her back, and the doctor remained quiet. He knew this was difficult news to hear.

His nurse brought coffee into the office for the couple. The doctor offered them each a cup. In time, Andrea regained her composure. The doctor continued to explain his findings.

"We are finding a direct link with this type of deafness and family history," he indicated. "There are probably other family members who have had or have the same type of problem. Do you know of anyone?" he asked.

"I know my maternal grandfather had hearing difficulties, but he's dead," she told the doctor. "My father lost some of his hearing from an explosion and burns," she mentioned. "My mother was pregnant with me when the explosion occurred," she said. "The doctor, at the time, wasn't sure how it would affect me."

"I would like to run more tests," the doctor said. "You can stay here overnight, Andrea, and we will do the tests tomorrow." He turned to Edward. "You can pick her up tomorrow after 6:00 p.m. I want to run a battery of tests to learn the direct cause of the hearing loss problem," the doctor said. They both agreed to the testing.

The next day, Andrea was subjected to a barrage of tests. They needed to determine how much hearing she had lost already, what the cause was, and how quickly it would progress.

After a very long day, Andrea was drained of all energy. Edward took her home. As she stood at the stove making his dinner, a horrible feeling of foreboding hung over her heart like a black raincloud.

Later the next week, they returned to the specialist's office for the results.

He offered them each a cup of coffee. Edward accepted, but Andrea declined the offer. She was sitting on pins and needles, waiting for the news. Secretly, she was hoping for good news.

"It's as I thought," the doctor began. "It is nerve damage."

Andrea's heart began to sink. "Is there more?" she asked.

"The nerves are quite damaged, and I found scarring on the ear drum," he said. "I believe this is a hereditary issue. You should look into both sides of your family, Andrea. Ask questions. Find out if anyone else has suffered hearing loss," he continued. "I would like to study the family cases."

"How soon will she lose all her hearing?" Edward asked the doctor.

"We will get her fit with a hearing aid, now," the doctor began, "that will help her hear better."

"And?" Edward asked.

"Within about ten years, she will have lost all her hearing," the doctor told them. "I'm sorry," he continued. "But other than the hearing aid, for now, there is nothing I can do."

Accepting the answers offered, Andrea was fitted for her first hearing aid. Immediately, she hated it. The unit was uncomfortable. The base unit was clipped to her bra, which showed on her clothing, and the cord running from the ear piece to the base unit was obvious. She discovered she was able to hear better, but as her hearing loss progressed, she realized she was straining to hear anything people said to her. Over time, she became more nervous and uptight. Everything in her life became a constant struggle. She wasn't able to use the telephone or hear the television. But above all else, the two things she wanted to hear the most were the sound of her husband's voice saying, "I love you," and the voice of her little girl calling her, "Mommy."

Over time, Andrea was not coping well with her life. She was angry and lashed out at everyone. Her moods declined, and she didn't want to leave the house. She was closing herself off from the world in fear of her deafness.

Edward was living in his own personal hell. He was unable to deal with his wife and her constant irrational behaviour. They began to grow apart.

Edward, once again, found solace in beer. The more unbalanced his wife became, they more he drank to ease his pain.

The only bright spot in their sorrowful lives was the little girl they had. She could occupy their minds and hearts for hours. They doted on her.

"She is the only child I will have," Andrea said to her mother. "That little girl is my only chance at happiness in this life."

Elvira worried for her daughter and her mental health.

1958 Harvest

The harvest of 1958 seemed busier than usual for Edward. He was everywhere on the farm. Edward ran himself ragged and had lost fifteen pounds since planting time. Even if he had downtime, he wasn't at home. He always seemed at odds with Andrea. Her moods declined at the same rate as her hearing. Home just was not a place for Edward.

Suspiciously, he always seemed to have errands to run in town. Andrea assumed he was just having a beer with his friends, bowling, or playing darts. Either way, she was content to spend her spare time with her daughter. Patricia was the apple of her eye. The girl could do no wrong.

Andrea took great pride in her daughter. She had her princess, and together, they played, read stories, and went for walks. Andrea was finally content with this part of her life.

Once again, friction was heating up between the families. Only Andrea's mother was allowed to babysit Patricia. Aline felt shunned, and the snub angered Marcel.

"Who does she think she is!" he yelled. "That's your granddaughter, too," he said to his wife.

Aline knew what he meant, and it saddened her that he still felt this wasn't his family. A tear approached the edge of her eye, but she wiped it away.

One afternoon, Andrea had to run to town because she ran out of eggs. Just before walking in the store, she spotted her husband walking into the hotel. Looking again, she saw he had a woman on his arm. She had heard rumours of his escapades, but would not believe them. Now she had proof.

Looking in the window, she saw her husband sitting at a table having a beer with the mystery woman. "I'll wait," she thought.

Twenty minutes later, Edward and the woman left the hotel and drove to a small house on William Street.

Andrea's anger was about to burst forth, but she knew she had to be smart about this. She knew life had been very difficult for her husband, but this was not the answer!

The couple walked up to the house. After unlocking the door, they walked in together and closed the door behind them.

"Wait!" she thought to herself. "I have to wait. Then I can catch him."

Half an hour went by, and slowly, Andrea crept up to the house. "He's cheating on me," she thought. "I'll kill him!"

Ever so carefully, Andrea crept to the living room window. Slowly, she lifted her head to the glass. Her life almost came to an end with what she saw. "Oh my God," she mumbled. The reality of the view was sinking in now. "How could he do this to me!"

There, on the sofa, was Edward, completed naked. Beside him, Andrea spotted the woman from the hotel. After blinking a couple of times to clear her sight, she looked again. Her heart was utterly destroyed in this moment. There was a second woman in the room. Both women were as naked as her husband.

Stunned, horrified, and unable to catch her breath, Andrea staggered away from the house. She tripped and fell over a short fence that edged the garden. Clawing her way back to her feet, she found her way to her car.

Unable to drive far, she went to her mother's and father's house.

When they saw their daughter, they knew something was wrong. But the girl was unable to speak. She sat and cried.

She wept for quite a while.

Her parents sat and waited for their daughter to collect herself.

When she finally did speak and had told them what she had witnessed, Alphonse stood up and slammed his hand onto the table. ***"Godverdomme,"*** he said. His voice boomed throughout the house with the curse he had just uttered. The very walls seemed to vibrate with the anger from his words.

Andrea shrank in fear. She knew her father and his temper.

Alphonse wanted to go after his son-in-law and give him the thrashing of his life, but Elvira managed to convince him not to. "Let it be, Alphonse," she said to him. "They have to work it out for themselves."

"Andrea," Alphonse said to his daughter in a very stern voice. "You better go home, now. You are upsetting your mother too much."

Shocked that her father would just toss her aside like this, she stood and headed for the door.

When she arrived back on the farm, she noticed her husband had not returned yet. Waiting for her, though, was Marcel and Aline.

"Where is he!" Marcel demanded.

"In town with his women," Andrea replied. She walked in the house and slammed the door on her in-laws.

Going through the motions, she made dinner for her daughter. Andrea had no appetite. Once the dishes were put away, she bathed her little girl and put her to bed.

"Sleep well, my little one," she whispered as she kissed Patricia's forehead.

After mid-night, Edward came staggering into the house. He was so drunk he could barely stand.

By this time, Andrea had worked herself into a frenzy. She was not thinking clearly or rationally.

"I saw where you were and what you were doing today!" she snapped at him.

"I don't care what you saw," he said with a very thick tongue.

She had never seen him this drunk before. She had never been this angered before. There was a demon inside her that wanted to escape and beat the life out of him.

The argument started and continued for a couple of hours. Back and forth, they threw insults, names, and threats. He was too drunk to stop, and she was too angry to let it go.

Suddenly, Edward had enough of this. "Shut up!" he yelled to his wife.

"No!" she screamed. She continued to badger and emotionally beat him down.

"Enough!" he hollered. He turned to her and swung his arm in her direction. His hand connected with the side of her body. She fell to the ground and screamed.

He leaned over and grabbed her by both arms. ***"Shut up, Andrea and listen."***

But she heard nothing. In her crazed state, she was beyond hearing.

He held her as she tried to lash out at him. He had never seen her so overwrought before.

"This is my fault," he thought. "What was I thinking? *Oh my God, what have I done!"*

In this moment, he realized how severe his loneliness and grief had been. He also recognized the turmoil his wife was living in.

"Andrea, listen to me," he said to he as he shook her. He was trying to snap her out of her wild mood.

"Andrea!" he screamed. **"We have to fix this!** *Do you hear me! WE HAVE TO FIX THIS!"*

Then the horrible realization hit him between the eyes.

"What have I done!" he whispered to himself.

Debt and Hatred

In the months that followed, Edward continued to drink heavily. He no longer had visits into town, but that didn't seem to appease his wife. Her anger towards him continued to grow. Neither person knew how to deal with their anger, and the situation escalated.

Unable to stop needling her husband, Andrea would constantly drag up Edward's sexual exploits and his drinking habits.

He was unable to control his anger towards her any more. Many times, when she verbally battered him, he would lash out in the only way he knew. Several times, he would push her away with such force that she would trip, or he would slap her across the mouth. But she just wouldn't be quiet.

Out of frustration with her and disgust with himself, Edward spent many nights sleeping in the barn. "Life with her is destroying me," he thought.

He managed to get the tobacco crop off and ready for stripping. The stress and strain Edward was suffering was visible to both families. Neither would interfere. It wasn't their place.

Edward was able to get his crop stripped, baled, and ready for sale.

In the afternoon, when the buyer arrived, Edward was in London with Andrea. She had another appointment with the hearing specialist. Aline and Marcel were going to sell the crop in his place. They still owned the farm, so it was their right to accept or decline the price offered.

This decision was the beginning of the end for Edward.

Aline felt the price offered was too low for the quality of tobacco. She rejected the bid. The buyer was shocked and rather put out by what he felt was a lack of respect for his position and offer.

Aline knew her tobacco and was very aware of current pricing.

"Will you accept the price," the buyer asked again.

"No," Aline said. "That isn't high enough."

The man turned to Marcel and said, "Then you will wait until the second round of buying." With a sneer on his lips he continued, **"I guarantee the price will be less."**

Angered by the arrogance of the man, Marcel gave him five minutes to get off his farm.

"You did what!" Edward asked, shocked by the behaviour of his parents. ***"We needed that price to break even!"***

Furious at his parents, Edward stormed out of the house. ***"How could they be so stupid?"*** he yelled to the sky as he looked to the heavens. **"I need that money!"**

Two weeks later, the buyer returned. After examining the quality of the crop, he looked at the two couples waiting for his price, and he said, "Most of the buying is completed now. I can't offer you top dollar."

After thinking for a few more moments, he gazed at Edward and named his final price.

"What!" Edward yelled.

"That is the best I can do," the buyer replied.

"Ma," Edward said, turning to his mother. "That's one third of what the crop was originally worth!"

"Take it or leave it," the buyer said.

Hanging his head in shame, Edward replied, "sold." He just lost his shirt on the deal. The majority of the money would go to his parents as the owners. He was left with very little money, and huge debt.

Because Edward's drinking got worse after this event, his parents no longer trusted him on the farm. They tried to blame him for the loss, claiming his womanizing and drinking were at fault.

He found himself unable to take any further abuse or punishment. In 1959, since he found himself $13,000 in debt to his parents, they demanded he leave the farm. So now he had nowhere to live, and his wife just informed him she was pregnant again.

He knew she was very angry about the pregnancy. She did not want more children. She had the one she wanted.

"I hate you for getting me pregnant again," she sneered at him one day.

Edward discovered the pregnancy was the only bright spot in his life.

"I don't want the baby," she screamed at him.

"I do!" he said. "But first, we have to find a place to live. We're leaving here!"

An Era Gone

With his hopes and dreams as a farmer shattered permanently, Edward and his small family moved off the farm forever. Secretly, Andrea smiled. Now, she would finally be free of his parents.

They moved into a rented town house owned by Andrea's father in March of 1960. It was small, but they would make do.

Now, with his future uncertain, Edward found himself a beaten man. With rent that had to be paid, and mouths to feed, he pulled up his courage and looked for work. After all, there was no personal respect if a man accepted something for free.

Driving transport truck for a local fertilizer factory was not his dream job, but one he gladly took to feed his family. It was steady, honest work for most of the year. At other times, he flew with a local crop-duster, mapping out hydro lines, and in the winter, he worked slugging bales of tobacco in the warehouse.

He worked hard and tried to make amends with his wife.

Nothing he did could appease his wife. After all, it was his fault she was pregnant again. She did not want another child.

Saddened by her son's departure from the farm, Aline did her best to cope. "It could have worked out differently," she thought, "if he had a better wife." She still found life around Andrea extremely challenging. "She is such an irrational person...almost crazy!"

On the other side, Elvira was glad her daughter was off the farm and away from, "**Those people**."

She, like most people, also found her daughter's behaviour very draining, but she relished the thought of spending time with her granddaughter.

After the family moved into their new home and life settled into a routine, Andrea began to prepare a room for the baby. The grandmothers-to-be sewed, knitted, and crocheted until, at last, everything was prepared. They gathered what friends Andrea had left for a baby shower to help celebrate the upcoming birth. But Andrea did not enjoy herself. "She actually appears angry," her mother thought to herself. Her guests left her home with the feeling of uncertainty.

By mid-June Andrea began to feel the tell-tale signs of early labour.

Edward made the necessary calls to the doctor's office and then to his mother-in-law. Now, with the appropriate calls taken care of, he took his wife to the hospital.

He was excited at the prospect of another child. Even though he could see his wife was extremely content having one child, he had wanted a larger family. His excitement for the new baby grew. "I can't let her see how excited I am," he thought.

During the labour, Andrea's outlook changed slightly. "Maybe this baby will help keep my husband at home where he belongs," she thought. "Maybe it will be another girl." This idea made her smile. She knew another girl would upset her father-in-law greatly. He preferred boys.

On the afternoon of June 16th at 2:00 in the afternoon, Andrea was taken into the delivery room. The time to get this over with had finally arrived.

"Push, Andrea!" the doctor urged her. "Push!"

Clenching her jaw and holding her breath, Andrea gave one final, massive push.

"Ok, Andrea, you can stop now," the doctor said.

Exhausted and drenched in sweat, Andrea lay back on the table.

"You have a girl," the doctor told her. "She is small, but..." The sudden wails of the newborn baby interrupted the doctor's words. "She has a strong set of lungs."

Tears began to flow down Andrea's face. She had barely heard her daughter cry. Her hearing was going to make this an enormous challenge.

In a flurry of movement, Andrea noticed her baby was being rushed out of the room.

"What's happened!" she screamed! "Where are you taking my baby?"

"Relax," said the nurse soothingly. "Your daughter is fine. We are just taking her for an examination."

Andrea began to relax slightly, but she had the feeling of dread deep in the pit of her stomach.

Three hours later, Andrea still hadn't seen her baby.

"What is going on?" she demanded of the doctor.

"We just needed to do a complete examination and run some tests," he told her. "I will be back shortly to speak with you and Edward."

"But, what's wrong?" she asked, as panic was beginning to grow within her.

"Calm down," he said. "I will be back soon." The doctor stood up and left her room.

Andrea's heart began to pound out of control. "What's going on here," she wondered. "Why won't they tell me anything!"

She quickly began to lose control of her emotions. Her body began to shake uncontrollably, and tears were streaming down her face.

Edward walked in her room, excited about the birth of his new daughter. The scene that met him destroyed his happiness immediately.

"What's wrong?" he asked his wife as he ran to her bed.

"They won't tell me!" she screamed. "Something is wrong, and they won't say!"

Andrea began to completely come apart.

Edward ran out and returned with a nurse.

"I'll give her something to settle her down," the nurse commented.

"Good," he said. "She's almost out of control, again."

Once Andrea began to feel the effects of the injection, she started to settle.

Her doctor walked into her room with a nurse beside him.

He sat down on her bed on the opposite side of Edward.

"Your daughter is beautiful and very healthy," he announced to them.

Relief washed over Edward.

"What's wrong?" Andrea asked impatiently.

"Your baby was born with a serious deformity," he told them.

Edward's heart dropped out of his chest. He had not been prepared for this news. "Oh my God," he thought to himself. He was unable to speak.

His wife did hear what the doctor said. Her eyes opened like a deer in headlights. Shock took hold. She began to cry. Her sobs were deep and shook her entire body.

The doctor turned and nodded his head towards the nurse. She approached and gave Andrea another injection.

"Sleep, for now," the doctor said to her as he patted the back of her hand. He met Edward's eyes. "I'm sorry," he said. "I've called in a specialist."

Edward broke eye contact and looked at his wife. He was unable to reply.

Looking back towards the couple, as he left the room, the doctor saw Edward break down. Unable to watch the young man lose control, he left.

As the doctor walked down the hall to where the specialist was examining the new baby, he looked heaven-ward and asked, "Why?"

CHAPTER FOUR

The Gift of a Child with an Unbreakable Will

The Birth of the Unwanted Child

June 16th, 1960 was a warm and sunny spring day. This was the birth date of Edward and Andrea's second daughter.

"She is small," the doctor said to them. "Even though she only weighs 5 lbs. 7 oz., she is strong and a fighter. I do have bad news, though." He dreaded this part of his job. "I am sorry to tell you that your daughter is crippled. She has what we call 'clubfeet'," the doctor continued. "I have called in an orthopedic specialist to examine her. You can meet with him shortly after his examination."

Edward was finding it difficult to hear what their doctor was saying. His wife's loud sobs created a storm of noise in the small room.

As their family doctor left the room, he thought to himself, "This family has already been through hell and back. Dear God! What do you have in store for this innocent child?"

The orthopedic specialist, Doctor Parker, lifted the pink blanket from the newborn. There's a little beauty," he said to her. Both of her legs were twisted around in an inward motion, right from the hip joint. Moving downward, he saw her left foot was turned completely inward, causing her toes to be facing behind her. Her right leg was twisted, which caused the foot to lay ever so gently over top of the left heel.

"Her feet look like someone clasping their hands one over the other," he said to the nurse. "You would almost think the right leg is laying over to protect the left from harm."

"I'm going to tickle your little feet now. Oops, it looks like she has good feeling in the right foot," he said to the nurse. Then he moved over to the left foot. He ran his car keys up her little foot from heel to toes. All he received in reaction to this was a little twitch. "Hmm, not so sensitive on this one, are you, sweetheart." As he continued to examine the baby, he talked to her and cuddled her to make her feel safe. He took his time inspecting the little legs. He checked her hips for mobility, bent her knees, and moved her ankles, all the while speaking softly to her. As he looked at her, he hoped she would overcome life's obstacles. He hoped she was going to be able to do some sports to help keep her legs and back strong, for this disability not only belonged to the legs and feet, it also can cause problems to the spine. Some babies are born with varying in degrees of spinal bifida. Others suffer from curvature of the spine.

"The legs are very pliable at this stage," he said to the nurse. "We can manipulate the legs into the corrected straight position and cast her. That will be a very good beginning."

Once Dr. Parker had completed his examination of the baby, he asked the nurse who was with him to clean her, wrap her up, and feed her if she is hungry.

"Yes, Doctor," the nurse replied.

He said to her, "Now I have to go and talk to the parents." He left the room with confidence, but his heart was hurting.

With Andrea still in tears, but beginning to settle, Edward stood as the two doctors entered the room.

As soon as Andrea saw the men, she screamed out, ***"Give me my baby! I want to hold her...now!"***

"Please Andrea, calm down and listen," Edward cautioned her.

Ashamed at her own outburst, Andrea quieted down.

"This is Dr. Parker," their family doctor said as he introduced the specialist to the young parents.

After the initial greetings were complete, Andrea, once again, demanded her baby.

"Please," Dr. Parker said to her. "You will see your daughter shortly. I need to explain to you, first."

He looked at them and began. "As far as we know, there isn't a true reason for a child being born with clubfoot. However, medical theories are that women who smoked during pregnancy have a higher risk of their child being born with clubfeet. The other theory believes that mothers with low amniotic fluid levels may deliver babies with clubfeet. But a third theory does exist," he stated. "It is possible Andrea contracted a virus when she was 8 weeks pregnant. This particular virus can cause the deformity, but I will need to do a bit more research on that aspect, though," he said.

"What does all this mean for our daughter?" Edward asked Doctor Parker.

Dr. Parker looked at the parents who sat in front of him and a great sadness rose up in his heart. He knew the couple had suffered greatly in trying to have a family, but he was confident he could help their daughter.

Doctor Parker took in a deep breath. He said with a smile, "Your little girl is beautiful. She has a full head of dark curly hair and a cute little smile, but she does have problems with her legs."

"Will she ever walk?" Edward asked him.

Dr. Parker looked the young man in the face and said, "As of right now, we cannot guarantee anything, but I will do my absolute best to help her to walk. Her legs and bones are soft and pliable now, so this is the best time to take action. I will gently straighten her legs from the hips and then place them in plaster casts with a steel rod between her feet, keeping the feet hip distance apart and perfectly straight. This is where we will start," he told them.

"What then?" asked Edward.

"Well, we have to take things slowly. She will be in the casts off and on for a year, at least, maybe two. After that, her ankles will be taped to hold the steel bar in place. The bar is vital to keep the legs exactly hip distance apart and to prevent them from twisting again," Dr. Parker continued.

"What does all this mean?" Edward asked.

"First," the doctor began, "your daughter needs to be your main focus." He stared at them in earnest, "She will need a great deal of care if she is ever going to walk."

Suddenly, Edward became angry. He stared at his wife, who was sitting with a blank look on her face. He stood up and pointed his finger in his wife's direction.

"She didn't want this baby at all. Is there anything she could have done to cause this?"

Andrea screamed out in horror. **"How could you say such a thing?"** she yelled.

"Edward," Dr. Parker said to the man. "Stop this, right now. No one is to blame! Your baby needs the love and care of both parents," he scolded.

Calming down, Edward asked about medical expenses. "We can't pay for any of her treatments."

"Edward," said Dr. Parker, "the majority of medical expenses and treatments for your daughter will be paid for by the Rotary Club in Simcoe. I also believe, when she is a bit older, your daughter would benefit from going to the Crippled Children's Hospital in Toronto." Then he looked at the mother and father and said sternly, "We all have our duty to ensure this little baby grows up happy and healthy, and I will do everything in my power to ensure she walks."

Unable to speak, Edward bowed his head in shame as tears began to flow from his eyes. He wondered why God was punishing him all the time.

"Thank you, Doctor Parker. When will you begin the treatments on her?"

Doctor Parker knew the pain this man must be feeling, so he softened his tone when he answered.

"With your permission, we will begin treatment today. We will start with massaging her legs, hips, and feet to give them the idea that they need to work and to prep them for straightening. At around 17 days old, we will put on her first set of casts. They will be from her toes to her hips. We need to cover the complete legs and feet to have them in the straightest form we can. Then a steel bar will be placed between her feet for the first year or so. As I mentioned before, she may be slower to walk than an average baby, but hopefully, she will walk."

Edward stood and shook hands with the doctor. "Thank you for everything," he said.

"You are very welcome," the doctor responded. "I know this is very difficult. Now, I think it's time you met your daughter," Dr. Parker said with a smile.

A nurse walked in the room carrying a tiny pink bundle. "Here she is," the nurse said as she handed the baby to Andrea.

Together, they looked down at their daughter. "She really is a cutie," Edward said.

Then, Andrea laid the baby on the bed and unwrapped the blanket.

She screamed! "Oh my God!" she said as tears rolled down her face. Truly horrified by what she saw, Andrea fainted.

Immediately, the doctor and nurse were at her side. Within a few minutes, she was back with them.

"Give her time," the doctor said to Edward. "It is overwhelming."

"She didn't want the child," Edward whispered. "Is this the punishment?"

In his heart, Edward knew his mother and mother-in-law would help with caring for their daughter. He could no longer resist. He gathered the tiny baby and held her close to his heart.

"Thank you, Dr. Parker," Edward said, and he looked into his little daughter's face. "Thank you for caring for her."

"You are very welcome," said Dr. Parker. "I have seen a few of these cases over the years, some not too bad and some very severe. Your daughter's case isn't the worst one I've seen."

He was not sure Edward heard a word he had said. He seemed mesmerized by his newborn daughter and her tiny little nose and dark eyes. Edward was happy, despite everything. Finally, as he hugged his baby again, he thanked God for her life. He knew in his heart this little one was going to be a fighter.

No one really knew of the true horrors this baby would face in her life. That was yet to come.

The Challenges of Home

Edward and Andrea asked their parents to suggest names for their baby. Aline was to be Godmother, so she had the privilege of the first name. "I want to name her Monica," she told her son. "But Ma," he replied. "There is already a Monica in our family. We can't call her that."

Aline rethought and suggested, "Teresa. It means diligent harvester. Please Edward?" Aline asked her son.

"Yes, Ma, Teresa is a good name," he replied.

On the day Edward and Andrea left the hospital with their new baby, life was a true unknown.

The ride home was a tense one. Neither person spoke much.

Even though Andrea was shown how to care for and bathe her daughter, she was very unsure about all of it.

She was not to immerse the baby in water as that would soften the casts. This meant nothing but sponge bathing. The other obstacles were chafing and keeping urine away from the casts.

They knew that, as the baby grew, she would have to be subjected to nerve and muscle tests. It was important these tests were done each time the casts were changed. The parents were in for a long ride.

Looking to his wife, Edward said, "It will be alright."

She glared at him and remarked, "We didn't need another child. I was perfectly happy with Patricia. This is your fault!" and with that burning comment, Andrea turned her head away from Edward, using her deafness as a means of purposely avoiding him.

Her comments stung as much as if she had slapped him across the face. Quickly, he wiped away the tears that rimmed his eyes.

As they drove into their driveway, he saw that his parents and in-laws were at the house. "More challenges for the day," he said to himself. Then, the front door burst open and Patricia came running out of the house to greet them.

She was elated to see her daddy. "Daddy, Daddy," she said. "I'm so happy you're back. Grandma and Papa have been playing out in the garden with me."

"That's great kiddo," he said to her as he hugged her. "Go in the house and tell your grandparents that we are here and have grandma put on some coffee."

"Yes, Daddy," Patricia said as she skipped off into the house.

Edward went around the car and opened the door for his wife. She handed him the baby. Gently, she got out of the car. Before he was able to close the car door, she looked up at him and said, **"No more children, do you hear me! No more. I've had enough,"** and with that, she walked into the house, leaving him standing there holding the baby.

When Edward walked into the house with his new daughter, Patricia was already sitting on Andrea's lap, cuddling. Both his parents and Andrea looked up and smiled. Both grandmothers had been desperate to hold their new granddaughter, but they were both a bit unsure.

Edward said, "Ma, why don't you sit, and I'll give you the baby."

Aline sat in the chair and looked up at her son. He smiled at her and said, "It will be alright. She won't break." In an effort to lighten the moment, Edward added, "You can't hurt her legs, Ma. She has casts on."

When Edward placed his little daughter into his mother's arms, tears escaped her eyes. She was happy, but her heart ached for the burden her son had to bear.

Aline whispered to her son, "Will she ever walk?" Edward saw the sadness in his mother's face. That was the first time he could ever remember seeing that look from her. The woman had been through her own personal hell, but had never shown any emotion, not until now.

"The doctor is very optimistic," he replied quietly. "Have faith. She'll be walking before you know it."

Things did not go so smoothly when Edward showed Patricia her baby sister. "I don't like her. Take her back," she screamed as she pushed the baby away from her and ran to her room.

All four grandparents looked at each other with that knowing look that older and wiser people have, but no one said a word. No one wanted to upset Andrea. She was too volatile.

Andrea's father welcomed Teresa into his strong arms. He cuddled her and spoke ever so softly to her. A huge smile exploded across his face as the baby smiled back. My little *Engel*, he said in Flemish, calling her his little Angel. The baby looked up at him and cooed. He looked into her eyes and he smiled. "You are going to be my favourite," he said, tears slid down the wrinkled old cheeks. A tremendous smile lit Alphonse's face, and he knew from that moment on, he would love this little *zoetje* (sweetheart) until the end of time.

A Year Later

Teresa was growing into a healthy and strong little girl. She was flourishing. When the baby woke from her naps, everyone in the house could tell. The noise that came from the bedroom was getting louder the older and stronger she got. When she woke up, Teresa would lift her legs straight up and drop them back down onto the mattress. To her, it was a game. Every time her legs hit the mattress, she would bounce. This was her wake up call to her parents.

One afternoon, Andrea sent Patricia to the bedroom to see what her sister was doing. "What do you want?" Patricia said to her sister sarcastically.

Teresa lifted her legs up and dropped them down again. Happy and content from her sleep, she wanted to play. "Put your legs down," Patricia snapped at her as she pushed Teresa's legs down hard onto the bed. "Stop that. You make too much noise. Mommy doesn't like you making all that noise." Patricia said. Teresa looked at her sister. She didn't understand.

Just as Patricia was pushing Teresa's legs back down again hard, Edward walked into the room. "You stop that, right now!" he yelled at her.

"But Daddy, she is making too much noise with those legs of hers, and mommy doesn't like that," Patricia told him.

"I don't care what your mother likes. Don't you dare let me catch you doing that to your sister again. Do you understand?"

Patricia started to cry. With tears running down her face, she ran past her father in search of her mother. She knew her mother would protect her.

Patricia found Andrea outside hanging up laundry. "Mommy, Mommy, Daddy yelled at me," she told her mother.

"What happened?" Andrea asked her.

"Teresa was making too much noise, and I went in and told her to stop, and then Daddy came in and got mad at me," she said to her mother, conveniently leaving out the important part.

Edward then bounded outside to find Andrea.

"What do you think you're doing to her?" demanded Andrea. "How dare you treat my daughter like that?"

Edward was stunned by the comments, but he knew what the tone in his wife's voice meant.

He tried to explain to his wife what Patricia was doing, but her deafness came into play, once again, and she refused to hear.

"Patricia did nothing wrong," she snapped at him. "Teresa is the difficult one. Patricia was trying to help. She makes so much noise, the entire neighbourhood knows when she's awake," Andrea complained.

"Listen Andrea," Edward said to her as he began to lose his patience, "I know you didn't want the baby, but we have her. **You should at least make an attempt to be a mother to her.**"

"What did you just say to me?" she screamed. *"You bastard!"* How dare to tell me how to act. I enjoyed being a mother. Then you wanted that one, and now you expect me to pretend nothing is wrong. You're crazy!"

Edward could see Andrea was beginning to lose her control again.

"I didn't want another child," she ranted at him.

"I don't care what you wanted," he hollered back at her. ***"We have her, now be a mother!"***

Anger boiled up inside him. He had to get away from her at all costs.

Seething with anger, he stormed off to the house and went down into the cellar for his beer.

After quickly downing two beers, he let off a huge belch that rumbled the walls. Still furious, he grabbed four more bottles from the case to take upstairs with him. **"No stupid bitch is going to talk to me like that,"** he said to himself. Never making it back upstairs, he downed those four beers in succession and belched once again. Removing two more from the case, he staggered his way upstairs.

By the time Andrea and Patricia were coming in, Edward had a good buzz going...until Andrea opened her mouth again.

"Here you go again, drinking yourself stupid," she snapped at him. "That's all you ever do. You don't do anything around here except drink beer," she said with venom in her eyes.

"What do you know, you stupid bitch," he threw back at her. His words slurring out through a beer thickened tongue. "You are so tied up in the poor me, I can't hear, that no one else matters."

Refusing to say another word to her, Edward stood up and headed for the cellar and the beer that awaited him.

Later that evening, Edward sat on the front step, enjoying the oblivion his beer provided until late at night. "Why should I go up to bed," he thought to himself. "There was no one to hold or cuddle." He knew his wife had completely turned away from him, and right now, he wasn't sure he even cared if she ever came back. Life with Andrea had been a huge disaster, and she was becoming more disagreeable and unreasonable as time went on.

Someone was going to have to confront her, but he knew she would blame everything on him and her loss of hearing. "Her hearing," he thought. "Her excuse for everything."

Deciding he wasn't up for the fight, Edward turned and grabbed the only comfort he could find...another beer. He sat in the cooler night air drowning in his own agony.

The First Steps of Freedom

At one year of age, Teresa had her last set of permanent casts removed. The freedom was incredible. She giggled as she felt the air tickle her legs. She kicked each leg up and down and laughed out loud from the freedom and happiness she felt.

"There you go, sweetie," Dr. Parker said to her as he rubbed her little legs. "You won't ever have to wear those nasty pieces of plaster again." Teresa looked up at him with love in her eyes. Another laugh burst from her. She was a strong little girl. Her core muscles had developed well, and Dr. Parker was pleased to see her progress.

"If her core is strong and stable, that will give her a very good chance for walking without worry," Dr. Parker told her parents.

"Now," he said to the little girl. "Let's stand you up and see what your strong legs can do."

He picked up Teresa and attempt to stand her on her feet. At first, she pulled her legs back up. What an odd sensation. She'd never done this before.

"Try again," he said to her.

His soothing tones touched the little girl, and she trusted him. Cautiously, she touched one foot down. Quickly, she pulled it up again and looked at the doctor. She smiled and laughed. Slowly, she set the foot down on the table. She liked the feel of standing. Teresa suddenly looked in the doctor's eyes.

"I'm not going to let you go," he told her.

Down went the second foot. With the doctor still supporting her, she began to bounce up and down.

"Wait a minute! Slow down," he said to her as he picked her up. "One thing at a time, little one."

He was very pleased with the results. He hoped and prayed that she could do the rest.

"Her legs are straight, now, with no signs of twisting," he said as he turned to Teresa's parents. "She is strong and very determined to walk. However," he continued, "she will need to wear the braces at night for at least six months. Her legs are straight now, but we need to ensure they stay that way. It is common practice to keep the legs at a good angle, while the child sleeps. This will help with the structure and calm the legs after the activity of the day. I'm sure she will be running circles around her sister in a very short time."

"Thank you, Dr. Parker," Edward said as he and the doctor shook hands.

"Make sure she wears good solid shoes and keeps them on while she is awake," he instructed. "At night, use the second pair of shoes with the steel bar between the feet to keep her legs apart. If she keeps going like this, she will be walking before you know it." Dr. Parker said. "Always be mindful of her ankles, though. Be extra careful that she doesn't step into holes. She may twist or sprain her ankles, and that could be a huge setback for her."

"I will see you in six months," he said as he leaned over and tickled Teresa on the stomach.

As they walked out of the office, Edward turned to Dr. Parker and said, "Thank you. Thank you for everything you have done for our daughter." Emotion caught in his throat. "We owe him so much," he thought.

The kindly doctor smiled back at the man and said, "The next time you visit, I want to see Teresa walk into my office. What do you think little one? Can you do that for me?" Dr. Parker asked Teresa as he pinched her cheek. Teresa giggled and smiled at him.

It wasn't long before Teresa was up and running, just like the doctor had said. With each step she took, her leg muscles strengthened.

Six months later, on her return visit to the doctor, she not only walked into his office, she ran to him as he held out his arms in greeting.

"She has done remarkably well," he said to Teresa's parents. "I'm very pleased with her progress. She has great movement in all the joints. Her flexibility is good, and there are no signs of nerve damage. The reflexes in her left foot are slightly slower than her right, but that should come in time." The only tell-tale sign was a tiny scar on the top of her ankle. It was a tiny burn from where the cast cutter had touched her delicate baby skin.

Pleased with the results after his examination, Dr. Parker turned to Edward and said, "She is doing exceptionally well." He smiled down at the little girl and said, "I think I will only need to see this feisty little darling once per year, now."

With that great news in his ears and happiness in his heart, Edward scheduled Teresa's next appointment. As Teresa waved good-bye to Dr. Parker, the old doctor smiled, laughed, and waved back. "Bye sweetie," he called after her.

At home, Edward bubbled over with joy. Excitedly, he relayed the facts of the appointment to his wife. She was pleased at her daughter's progress. Internally, she was thrilled that part of the huge burden this child represented had been taken off her shoulders.

Life with a crippled child was difficult, both emotionally and financially. Andrea found the constant care of her daughter very tiresome. Ensuring the casts were clean and odour free had been a nightmare. Now, she had to ensure the child didn't step wrong and hurt her feet and legs. The struggles continued. "How am I supposed to watch her every minute," she asked her husband. "I have other things and another child to care for," she shrieked at him.

"We will just have to watch her, that's all. Our parents will help," he suggested.

Andrea glared at him. "My parents will help!" she announced and turned her back to him.

They both found the next few months draining, as they tried to slow their daughter down. Once she had started walking, there was no slowing her down and the little girl had no fear.

Over the past year, a little green monster had been festering within Patricia. She hated Teresa for all the special attention she received. Everyone treated **her** special because of her feet. "She's nothing special," Patricia thought to herself.

Once the centre of attention as the only child and grandchild, Patricia had never been taught how to share. Too young to understand what was happening, she lashed out at the only person she could...her sister.

Angry and jealous, Patricia took every opportunity to demonstrate how much she hated her sibling. She pinched, hit, and kicked at her when no one was looking. Once in a while, she even bit the little girl.

But being the clever little girl she was, Patricia made sure no one ever witnessed her actions. With her parents ignorant of her behaviour, this set the stage for a lifetime of loneliness, jealousy, and hatred.

Five Years Too Late

Teresa's transition into her school life was not an easy one. As for many children, it can be a traumatic experience, and for most children, life at school usually sorts itself out after the first few days. Teresa enjoyed being with other children. They talked and played and learned together. She was thrilled not being with her sister so much. Everything about school was great, except for taking naps. She just wasn't tired and didn't see the purpose. Being forced to submit to the demands of the teacher, she still found sleep wouldn't come. Teresa would quietly whisper to the other students. Of course, she would always end up in trouble with the teacher.

"Teresa! ***Lie down and close your eyes! Stop disturbing the other students,*** " the teacher would say to her in her matronly manner.

"But I'm not tired," the girl would reply.

"I do not care if you are tired! You are to lie down with your eyes closed and do not speak until I say nap time is over. Do you understand!" the teacher would snap at her.

After a repeat offense, the teacher would gather the young girl by the ear and say, **"If you cannot lie quietly, you will go out in the hallway."**

"Yes ma'am," Teresa would whisper as she hung her head in shame. She noticed all her little classmates were staring at her. Some of them even giggled, which made Teresa feel even more ashamed.

One week was as long as Teresa could remain quiet. During the second week of school, the teacher was becoming frustrated with the little girl. Teresa constantly heard, "be quiet," "stop talking," "I will phone your parents tonight," or "go stand outside in the hallway." Teachers usually have their favourite children and those children they despise. The 'good' ones received praise and privilege, while the others received punishment and humiliation. Teresa was one of the latter.

When the school day was over, Teresa was told by her mother to meet Patricia at her classroom, and the two girls would walk home together. "But that means I have to walk into the 'big' side of the school," she told her mother. "It's scary with all the big kids."

"That doesn't matter," she replied. "Just get your sister! Don't you dare leave the school by yourself," her mother warned. "Do you hear?" her mother questioned her.

"Ok," the young girl replied.

Andrea insisted Patricia, as the older sister, would be responsible for the younger girl. She was to walk Teresa to and from school and babysit her until Andrea returned from work. This would be fairly normal, if the two girls got along.

Sometimes, Patricia's friends would walk part of the way home with them. Teresa was always forced to walk several paces behind. "These are **MY** friends," Patricia would snap at her. "You stay away." This time of the day was the beginnings of the Jekyll and Hyde times. Teresa would watch her sister transform from a happy girl at school to an evil tormented being that inflicted suffering on her little sister daily.

Once the friends left the two girls, the torment would begin. "So what did you get in trouble for at school, today," Patricia would ask as she pushed her sister off the sidewalk.

"Nothing," Teresa would respond.

"Liar! I know you were bad. One of my friends told me. I'm going to tell on you." These lines were her favourites.

"I didn't do anything," Teresa would scream at her sister, but it did not matter what the little girl said; she knew her parents would believe the older girl.

Once Edward and Andrea absorbed what Patricia had to say, the punishment was not far behind. Teresa was never given a voice to defend herself. Even while they exacted the punishments, her screams of innocence fell on deaf ears. She was always guilty, but never given the opportunity to prove herself innocent.

Secretly, laughing behind their back, Patricia enjoyed the events.

Edward and Andrea were fond of several favourite forms of punishment. The simplest one being starvation. This was their "go to" punishment. Teresa had to sit at the table during dinner and watch everyone else eat.

"Sit up straight with your hands in your lap," her mother would order.

Teresa found sitting completely still a challenge. "Sit on your hands," Andrea would scream at her.

In fear of her mother, she did as commanded.

Hungry and frustrated at the restrictions, tears began to well up in her eyes. The smell of the food made her little mouth water. She knew better than to ask her parents for something. They were stubborn people, and their word was law.

Close to the breaking point, Teresa would look up at her sister.

Sitting across the table from her, Patricia would be smiling. When certain her parents were oblivious to her actions, Patricia would make teasing faces at her sister. She wanted the girl to yell at her. Then the little 'angel' would pretend she was just eating her dinner.

"Stop it!" Teresa would yell at her sister, unable to take the torment any longer. "Stop it!"

Immediately, Edward would respond by telling her to "shut up at the table. You are not allowed to speak." Teresa would feel the tears welling up inside her from the pit of her empty little stomach. When her eyes would meet her sister's again over the table, Teresa saw the happy look of triumph on her face. The other horrible thing she saw in her sister's face was hate. Unable to understand, Teresa would begin to let the tears run down her cheeks; this was the cue her mother had been waiting for.

"Stop your damn crying this minute, or I'll give you something to cry about," Andrea would snarl at her.

"But she started it!" Teresa struggled to get out.

"Stop it! Stop it this minute!" Andrea's voice would hit a frenzied level, as she jumped up from the table. Grabbing Teresa by the arm, she dragged her off the chair, knocking the chair to the floor. *"I told you to stop crying,"* Andrea would scream at Teresa.

Holding her little girl by the arm, Andrea raised her hand in anger. Suddenly, the hand would fall, and Smack! Smack! The sharp sting of Andrea's hand left a perfect imprint on the girl's little face. Within seconds, red welts rose up on her face. Teresa would scream out in pain. "Mommy, Stop! Please! Mommy stop! Ouch!" she wailed. Conveniently, her screams fell on deaf ears.

Unable to stop her crying at her mother's command, the brutality continued.

Depending on his mood, and the state of his drunkenness, Edward would react. Andrea would finish with her part of the beating, then demand that Edward, ***"Do something with this kid of yours,"*** Andrea would scream at him. Teresa would scream out at the top of her little voice, ***"No Daddy, No! Don't hit me. I'm sorry. I'm sorry."***

If Edward felt sympathetic towards his daughter, he would simply turn her over his knee and hit her across her bottom only once or twice to ensure his wife's anger was satisfied. How hard he hit depended on how enraged he was or how drunk he was. When he beat her in one of his drunken rages, Teresa would scream in pain. Edward's anger would explode, and she would be severely beaten, leaving her unable to sit properly in her school desk for days.

Once their anger had been quenched, they would command Teresa to stand up. Her little bottom so sore from the beating, and her little heart torn to shreds, she would stand and face her abusers. Unable to cry from the beating she had just endured, she would stand straight and look down at their feet. The only evidence of her pain was the odd teardrop that left her eyes, rolled down her cheeks, and vanished into a damp spot on her shirt.

Inside, she screamed out for understanding. ***"What did I do wrong? Why are they beating me?"*** she thought to herself. ***"Why does Mommy and Daddy hate me?"*** Her immature five-year-old mind was unable to deliver an answer. "I have to be tough," she thought. "Maybe, if they don't see me cry, they won't hit me."

But when Teresa looked up at her sister's face, she saw pleasure, joy, and satisfaction. How is that possible? **"She is happy they are hitting me,"** she said in her mind. **"She likes this!"** Shocked and disgusted by her sister, Teresa thought to herself, **"One day, YOU are going to regret this!"**

The Big Move

In the summer of 1965, Edward and Andrea bought a house. It was the first real break they had financially, since losing the money over the crop sale. Edward felt a sense of pride in his new job, working at a garage. "This is my break," he thought.

They were thrilled at the thought of owning their first house. Still blaming Edward's parents for most of her problems, Andrea found the independence of the home would be exactly what she needed.

The established three-bedroom home they purchased was only one block away from the house they had been renting from Alphonse for the last 5 years.

A doctor had originally owned the property. He had his office in the basement, so the main rooms had been renovated. There was linoleum on the floors and paneling on the walls. He used a second room for his office and patient examinations. It was a nice house that would serve their family for years.

This was a new adventure for Teresa, and she was quite excited about the new prospects. She was happy, until she learned she was to have the smallest bedroom in the house, right beside her parent's bedroom. The only good part about the location was she was right beside the bathroom. "Very handy," she thought.

The children had not been allowed in the house until moving day. Teresa was delivered to the house in the first load, just like the furniture. Her mother grabbed her by the hand and walked her into the house. "Here, this is your room," Andrea said to her. Teresa was excited to have her own bedroom. Finally, she would have some privacy. She was tired of sharing the same room and bed with her sister. For the first time in a long time, Teresa was happy. She hated sharing a bed with her sister. Patricia was always pinching her or kicking her in the legs at night as she tried to sleep.

Like most children, when they are sent to bed, they were told to, "Be quiet! I don't want to hear a peep out of you, or I'll come in there and you **WILL** be sorry." This was a nightly warning the girls received from their parents. But Patricia took pleasure in causing her sister's troubles.

"Tonight, I won't get in trouble," Teresa thought to herself. "I can go to bed by myself!" She was filled with excitement at the prospect.

When she entered her room, she immediately felt uncomfortable. Yes, the room was small, but the paint colour looked funny to her. She had never seen a colour like that before. But after considering for a moment or two, she thought it might do.

Suddenly, Patricia came running into her room, laughing and teasing her. "I've got the bigger bedroom, ha ha ha, Brat!" she snapped at Teresa.

Patricia walked over to the closet door and opened it. "Oh yuck!" she yelled. "That's ugly, just like you!" she taunted Teresa.

When Teresa looked into the closet, she thought it was a dark and scary tunnel that only creatures of her nightmares could live in. The little girl immediately jumped back away from the closet in terror. Her sister thought it was funny. She was going to enjoy this.

Patricia grabbed Teresa by the arm, dragging her into the closet and threw her in and closed the door. Teresa screamed, "Let me out! Please, let me out." She hated being trapped in dark places. Only scary, evil things lived in dark places.

Teresa kicked, screamed, and beat on the inside of the door, as she heard her sister's psychotic laughter on the other side. The terror rose up inside her from deep down at her toes. It was so dark; she couldn't even see her hand in front of her face. The shock of being locked in was overwhelming for a five-year-old.

She let out a blood-curdling scream. Her terror of being trapped overwrote the fear of her parents and what they might do to her. After a second piercing scream was let go, Patricia opened the door and stood there, smiling at her sister. Bursting forth from the closet, Teresa ran into the kitchen for fresh air. It was then she heard her sister laughing at her. "You big baby! What a baby you are, such a cry baby!" she taunted. "Baby's so afraid of her closet. Poor baby."

Something snapped inside Teresa. She felt anger and hatred growing in her heart. Teresa had suffered so many abuses at the hands of her sister. One day, when she was sick with the flu, Teresa was taking a drink of ginger ale. Her grandma had told her it would settle her tummy. As she drank from the bottle, Patricia hit the end of the pop bottle with her hand, causing Teresa's top front teeth to chip. Later that evening, Teresa had told her mommy what her sister did. What she received was a spanking. "You know you are not supposed to drink out of the bottle," her mother said as she spanked her.

With each tormented session she remembered, her anger grew.

Now recovering her breath after being trapped in the closet, Teresa looked at her tormentor. ***"YOU MEAN***

BITCH!" she yelled out at her sister as she pushed her across the room. ***"I HATE YOU!"***

Patricia fell down in the middle of the kitchen floor. She began to whimper. Finally, standing back up, she whimpered, **"I'm telling, and you are going to get it."** She ran out of the room towards the front door. Trying desperately to calm herself, an enormous feeling of dread flowed over Teresa. She knew what was about to happen. Patricia would run to her parents and tell on her. Believing her lies, her parents would be so angry that Patricia had been hurt. Furious, they would blame Teresa...again.

Teresa waited. It was only a matter of time before they stormed into the new house. Then her punishment would begin.

"Welcome to our new house," she whispered to herself as the stress of her captivity left her little body. As she sat down on the floor, the first painful sobs escaped her lips. After a few minutes of gut-wrenching crying, she crawled her way back to her 'new' room. She sat against the wall, afraid and terrified of the doom that awaited her when her parents walked in. This room, with the disturbing closet that led to the underworld, was to be her new cage.

She knew her parents would send her back to this jail, once they were finished with her. Here, locked away in this room, she would struggle with many demons of this house, demons created by her sister and her parents. Dread and fear grabbed hold of the little girl, and she opened the closet door and stepped inside.

In one brief instant, she thought, "If they can't see me, they surely won't hurt me." Oh, how wrong she was.

The Punishment

Shaking with fear and dread as she waited for her parents to return with the moving trucks, Teresa stayed hidden and quiet in the horribly ugly closet.

She knew from past experience that her parents would believe what Patricia said. Teresa had never lashed out in anger towards her sister or anyone, and she knew, today, she gave her sister the evidence she had always wanted.

Inside her small and dark closet, she could only hear the odd little muffled noise. Terrified beyond belief, she was only barely able to breathe. Ice cold terror struck her heart the minute she heard her father scream her name. Suddenly, she knew her waiting was over, and her torture was about to begin.

"Teresa! Kom hier nu! (Come here now!) Edward yelled in Flemish as he stormed through the house. *"Where the hell are you?"*

Teresa curled herself into a small little ball; she wanted so desperately just to disappear. Her entire body shook with the beginnings of what felt like a seizure.

So hyper-aware of her surroundings, she could almost hear and feel the walls breathing. She was glad the walls were breathing, because she noticed she wasn't. So afraid of making any sound, Teresa had no idea how long she had been holding her breath. She just wanted to blend into the walls and go away, where they wouldn't find her.

Suddenly, the closet door flew open.

Absolute terror stuck in her throat as the blinding light hit her eyes. The cool air that greeted her felt nice.

It was refreshing, not stale closet air. As she inhaled a massive breath of cool air, she felt a man's hand reach into the darkness and grab her by the arm. She knew immediately it was her father pulling her to her fate. ***"What do you think you're doing in there?"*** he yelled at her as he dragged her from her hiding spot.

"Ouch, Daddy that hurts. Please, let go," she cried. Then she looked up and saw his face. The rage that was staring back at her was something Teresa had never seen before. "Daddy, my arm!" she cried again. He looked like he was going to kill her.

"More than your arm is going to hurt by time I'm finished with you," Edward growled at the little girl. **"Why did you push your sister? Why do you always have to be so stupid! Can't you do anything right! We don't need this extra shit from you, today."** As he finished speaking, Edward swung his arm around and dragged his little girl over his knee. As he held her arm, his large roughened farm-worked hand came crashing down on her little behind. Teresa screamed out in pain and terror. ***"Daddy! No! Stop! I'm sorry, I'm sorry. She started it,"*** Teresa tried over and over to get her father to understand, but her voice fell on silent ears and a brain that was dulled by drinking. Over and over, the hand came crashing down on her bottom. Soon, she went to a place where she no longer felt the blows. Teresa felt numb. As she emotionally went to a safe place, she stopped crying. If she cried, she knew the punishment would always be worse.

When the physical hitting had finally stopped, Edward let go of her arm. ***"Get up,"*** he growled at her. Teresa fell off her father's lap and onto her knees. The stinging in her buttocks was beginning to return. She struggled to move, but she refused to show him any signs of weakness. She stood up and faced her abuser.

Teresa wasn't sure she understood his next words. Angrily, he repeated them.

"Pull up your pant legs to above your knees," he commanded. **"And hurry up about it! I'm busy with the move, and I don't have time for the stupid games you are playing today."**

Teresa gingerly bent over and pulled up her pant legs. Her bottom hurt! When she finished pulling up her pants, she looked back at her father.

"I'm busy, so you are going to stay put for the rest of the day," he snarled at her. He pointed his strong dirty finger at the register grate that lay on the floor. **"You are going to kneel on that metal register grate right there, and you are not going to move for the rest of the day. *DO YOU HEAR ME!* You are not going to move; you are not going to slouch; you are not going to talk to anyone...you are just going to kneel there and shut up until I say you can move."**

Disbelief and horror filled the little girl. "Yes, Daddy," Teresa said in a low voice.

"Now move," Edward commanded.

Teresa carefully knelt down on the metal grate and straightened her back. When Teresa looked up, she noticed a full-length mirror that had been left behind, hanging directly in front of her. Glancing into the mirror, she saw a pathetic, beaten, and tortured little girl staring back at her. "I know you," she said to the reflection. As she looked at the reflection, she noticed the little girls' face was stained with tears, her arm showing signs of dark red finger marks from her father's tight grip. "I wonder if her bottom hurts as much as mine does," she thought.

After what felt like an eternity in this position, her back and knees were burning with pain. She made the attempt to slouch only once. When her bottom touched her heels she shrieked out in pain. Quickly, she covered her mouth with her hands.

Inside her heart, the tears flowed like a river. The pain she felt in her knees was nothing she had experienced before. If she cried out, they would hear, and Teresa knew she couldn't risk that. She had to remain silent.

She stared hard at the girl in the mirror. As she stared at the little girl's expression, she wondered, "Why is everyone so mean to you? Why does your sister hate you so much?" There was no answer. She desperately wanted to know why no one loved and hugged her.

With sympathy growing for the little girl in the reflection, Teresa could see the only thing the girl wanted was to be loved.

Not understanding any of this, Teresa did realize one thing..."**never** trust anyone, **never** let anyone get close to your heart, and **YOU ARE UNLOVEABLE**, because **YOU ARE BAD**."

After being on the torture grill, Teresa lost feeling in her knees and lower legs. Tears had stopped rolling down her cheeks. The sadness and anger she had been feeling was replaced with rage. She was developing a burning hatred towards her sister for causing this.

Forty minutes later, Teresa's mother walked into the house. *"Get up!"* was all she said as she walked into the kitchen. Teresa was not sure what to do. She wasn't sure she *could* move. It took a couple of attempts to stand. Suddenly, all the pain she had been ignoring since this ordeal began came flooding back, and she cried out.

Sharp stabbing pain in her knees caused her legs to buckle. Oh, how she wanted to cry out and say, "Mommy, I hurt; please help," but she knew better. Her lower back was stiff from kneeling that long. Teresa was not sure she would be able to stand up straight (and of course, standing up straight was important. If you did not stand up straight, you could expect a backhand from either of your parents). Andrea came storming into the hallway where Teresa stood. ***"Stop your damn crying, or I'll give you something to cry about,"*** she screamed.

Unable to answer for fear she may burst into tears, Teresa nodded to her mother.

Slowly, Teresa walked into the kitchen, where her mother was waiting for her. She noticed her sister sitting at the table. Teresa's heart sank with horror. Patricia's face said it all. She had the look of a satisfied serpent that had just swallowed a large rat. It was then, Teresa saw the hate in her sister's eyes, and in that instant, she knew this was not a true sister. This other girl would be the source of Teresa's torment for a very long time.

Lifes Goes on, and More Lessons Learned

After the 'move' and the horrible events of the day, everyone seemed to settle down to their own routine.

Alphonse and Elvira were regular visitors, much to the delight of Teresa. She had developed a very special bond with her 'Papa.' Teresa and her Papa were always together. During her regular visits to their home, she and her Papa had adventures in the garden and enjoyed stealing Elvira's tomatoes. While they ate, they chatted. Alphonse would talk to Teresa in Flemish, and she would answer him in English. It was their game. She loved being with this man, and she admired him more than anyone on this earth. Once finished with their snacks, they would explore other options from Grandma's garden. Some days, it was carrots, beans, cucumbers, or peppers; it didn't matter to Teresa. What truly mattered was the time she spent with this man, who showed her nothing but love and kindness. She loved and trusted this man a great deal.

When they returned to the house, Elvira was always suspicious that "Phonse," as she called him, was up to 'no good' and teaching his granddaughter to do the same. Of course, he always denied everything, with a wink to his wife.

The only place Teresa ever felt safe was with her grandparents. They protected her from her parents and sister. Many times, she would spend the entire day at their home and beg to spend the night. She learned how to sew from her grandmother, who was a great seamstress. Teresa was taken into the kitchen and shown how to cook and to do preserves. Her grandma had delicious recipes for peaches and chili sauce and headcheese. It was here, Teresa developed a love for cooking and baking. Elvira made wonderful cakes and the best strawberry-rhubarb pie ever, but it was her honey-cake recipe that was Teresa's absolute favourite.

Teresa flourished in this environment and was happy. Her Papa began teaching her wood burning. This was an art form the two shared and developed, together. Alphonse bought Teresa her own wood burning pen, and together, they spent hours in the basement, working side by side on their projects. If they weren't in the basement, they were in his extensive wood working shop. He taught her how to use the table saw, tools, and most important for a carpenter...the hammer. She soaked up everything they taught her.

Alphonse and Elvira lived three blocks away from the elementary school the girls attended. Teresa knew this was her safe house, but she could never bring herself to tell her Papa of the brutal beatings she received at home. She didn't feel safe telling anyone.

Early one very cold winter morning, in 1967, Teresa was rudely awakened by her sister.

Even at this young age, the girls were responsible for getting themselves up and to school. Their parents began work before 7:00 a.m.

Storming into Teresa's room, Patricia yelled, **"Get up, now!"** as she kicked the side of Teresa's bed with her foot.

"Ok, I'm coming," Teresa replied. She was tired from not sleeping well the night before. The young girl had been plagued by nightmares since moving into this house. She hid under the blankets for a few extra minutes.

Suddenly, a cold draught ran over her as the blankets were violently torn from her body. "I said get up, **NOW!**" Patricia screamed as she punched Teresa in the arm.

"Ouch," Teresa cried out in pain as she grabbed her arm.

"If you don't get up now, you are going to be in so much trouble. I'm going to tell on you." Patricia sneered.

"Ok," Teresa said as she got up. Then suddenly, another punch in the arm came, followed by a slap across her head. Dazed by the sudden blows, she screamed out. **"Stop it! What's wrong? Why are you hitting me?"**

"You have five minutes to get out of this house, or you are going to get it," Patricia threatened as she raised her fist to her sister's face.

In fear, Teresa threw on yesterdays' clothes, pulled on her boots and grabbed her favourite little red winter coat. Terrified, she ran from the house at 7:30 in the morning, wondering where on earth she would go? "It's too early for school, and I can't disturb Papa and Grandma," she thought.

Hungry, cold, and with no prospects of anything to eat for the day, Teresa found herself crying. Her tears froze on her chubby cheeks as she ran towards the school.

Now, another fear hit her. "I'm going to be in trouble, because I'm not supposed to walk to school by myself. For some reason, her parents thought it better to beat her at home, but not let her cross the highway by herself to get to school. "What am I supposed to do," she wondered.

Freezing, cold, and starving she had no idea where to go. If she went to her grandparents, they would tell her parents, and Patricia would find out, and the beatings would get worse.

"Where can I hide," she thought as she ran down Argyle Street. Teresa was beginning to panic. It was too early for a girl her age to be out walking around. Now running, she found herself standing in the parking lot between the Catholic School she attended and the Catholic Church she belonged to.

Catholic priests were dominant figureheads in the homes of their parishioners. If a family had a problem, they were supposed to approach the church for help. The priests were always ready to give advice. As most priests were the figureheads of the schools, the teachers, nuns, and principal would, ultimately, answer to the priests.

To a girl of seven years old, the priest was a man of great power, respect, and awe. Teresa was terrified of the man, but it was to the church that Teresa found herself being pulled.

Once inside the side door of the church, she stood deathly still, frozen to the spot, afraid to move for fear of being heard or found. If found, the priest would call her parents and demand to know what this child was doing. This would give credence to her parents' argument that Teresa was doing something bad, which would lead to another 'punishment.'

She spotted a little cupboard under the back stairs in the church. There was a little door covering the opening. "The perfect place to hide," she thought. Quietly, she crawled inside and sat down. Her little legs felt like thousands of tiny needles were being poked into them. They hurt badly. When she looked under her tights, the skin of her legs was bright red. Her body shook from the freezing cold she felt. Then her stomach started to growl. "Shut up," she said to it. It had been over 12 hours since she had eaten, and she knew it would be at least 6:00pm before she could have dinner if everything went well.

Hearing the church bell ring 9:00 a.m., she knew it was time to leave her shelter.

She had warmed up and felt a bit better, but her legs still hurt. As she heard the school bell ring, she quickly ran across the parking lot and walked into her entrance of the school as though nothing had happened.

Teresa found it easy to get through the day without food. It happened often, and she was an expert by the age of seven of not drawing the attention of the teacher. When it was time to eat lunch, she would go to the bathroom and spend several minutes there, doing nothing. She would return in time to go outside and play. No one ever knew she was starving, not even her best friend. Sometimes, hunger got the best of Teresa, and she would ask her best friend for a piece of her sandwich or a cookie. Occasionally, her friend would oblige and give her something, but not very often. Her mother would complain because it was her daughter's lunch, and Teresa had no right to ask for it. "You should bring your own lunch," she told Teresa one afternoon, while playing.

She was absolutely right. But Teresa didn't have a mother, who made her lunch. The girls were to get their own breakfast and make their own lunches before school. Usually, Patricia chased her out of the house, so she rarely had a chance to get any food.

Later that day, when school was finished, she went to the senior wing of the school to find her sister. They were supposed to walk home together. Teresa knew she was going to be in trouble for running out this morning and didn't want to add to it by not walking home with Patricia.

While walking home, Patricia started teasing Teresa. **"You are so fat! Look at you! You are fat and ugly! So Ugly."** These were the constant and common remarks from Patricia. Thinking she was immune to these words, Teresa didn't realize how deeply they cut her. They cut so deep that she began to believe she was 'ugly and fat.' Teresa was a chubby child and constantly described as "big-boned." She was beginning to believe what people were saying. It was this thought and the comments from her sister that initiated the eating disorder Teresa developed, but it also forced her to become physically active.

Once home, Teresa went to her room and closed the door. She wanted no more interaction with her sister that day. However, Patricia had other ideas. Patricia banged on the outside of Teresa's door and screamed, "You have to come out and do your chores, or you're going to get it. If you don't come out, I'm going to tell on you."

"Go away!" Teresa yelled back. Fear and guilt began to settle in. Teresa knew she had to go out and do what her parents expected, or there would be hell to pay. Quietly, she opened her door and stepped out. She tiptoed into the kitchen and began setting the table for dinner, while Patricia sat in the living room, watching Bewitched on television.

When Teresa had finished setting the table and peeling potatoes, she felt she was in the clear and away from her sister's wrath. She began to relax a little. Placing the pot of potatoes on the stove for cooking, she went back into her room and closed the door.

Dinner was rather uneventful that night. But within an hour, the mood of the house changed.

Edward got up from his chair and went downstairs for a beer. Everyone knew, when Edward went down for a beer right after dinner, they were in for a bad night.

His usual routine was to have one or two beers, while in the cellar, then bring up two with him. He always hid the bottle caps in his pocket, because Andrea had a nasty habit of keeping count. The more he power-drank, the faster he got drunk and drifted into oblivion for the night.

After giving instructions to her daughters to clean up the dinner dishes and kitchen completely, Andrea walked into the living room, sat in "her" chair, and began to crochet. While she crocheted, she watched television and keep a constant vigil on the outside world as she spied on her neighbours. With her mental illness taking control of her, she would create all sorts of exotic stories of what went on next door. She was becoming agoraphobic. Andrea used her deafness as a weapon and wielded it like a double-edge sword. Rarely speaking to anyone, because, "I can't hear what they are saying," she would fabricate stories of her own, living in a fantasy world of misery. In this world, she raised her children.

Life After Dinner and Kitchen Wars

While their mother went to crochet, Patricia and Teresa were left alone in the kitchen to clean up the dinner mess. Being the eldest, Patricia was always entitled to wash the dishes. Slowly, she would fill the sink with water and soap, then play with the bubbles or blow them at her sister. Submerging some dishes, she would think about starting the chore. After placing some dishes in the sink, she would announce, "I have to go to the bathroom." Off she would go, leaving Teresa standing there, waiting. This was a game Patricia played to annoy her sister. She made this a regular occurrence.

There stood Teresa, waiting. Her homework and bicycle waited too.

She tried to wait patiently for her sister to return. If she showed her face in the living room, Andrea would say, "Get back in that kitchen and get those dishes done."

Understanding her mother wanted the work done, Teresa would reply, "But Patricia is in the bathroom, and I'm waiting." She quickly received 'the look' from her mother.

"Can I start washing the dishes?" she would ask.

"**No!** Patricia washes and you dry," came the aggressive response.

"But she'll be in there for a long time, and I have homework," Teresa would say. Knowing she had stepped one word over the boundary, Teresa witnessed her mother give her father 'the look.' Angered by her disturbance, Edward would glare at his daughter.

"Get in that kitchen and don't come out again until the dishes are done!" He would snarl. Not uttering another sound, Teresa would turn away and walk back into the kitchen to await the return of the honoured daughter.

Patricia's bathroom adventures lasted anywhere between twenty and thirty minutes. With a smile on her face and walking with purpose, she would come back to the kitchen, shoving her way past Teresa.

"Hurry up and start the dishes. I have homework to do," Teresa would say to her.

"Tough!" Patricia replied, as she would flick soap bubbles in Teresa's face. Teresa remained quiet. Wanting to cause trouble for her sister, Patricia would flick water at her. With water on the floor and her hair wet, Teresa ended up with soap in her eyes. Her eyes burned, so naturally, she would rub them. With her hands over her eyes, she wasn't aware of Patricia's next move. Slowly, she began winding up the soaking wet dishcloth. Suddenly, out of nowhere, SNAP! The hot wet rag snapped across her face. Shocked and in pain, Teresa screamed.

"Ouch!" she screamed.

"Shut up, stupid," Patricia would remark.

"No," Teresa would say back. "My face hurts, and you got soap in my eyes, again."

"Tough," came the reply back from Patricia.

"Just wash the dishes. I have homework to do, and it's already 6:30pm," Teresa would say.

"I don't have anything to do," Patricia would respond with a smugness that said 'too bad' to her sister. She continued to take what seemed an eternity to wash one glass.

One thing at a time, with lots of time in between, the washing of the dishes progressed.

"Hurry up!" Teresa yelled at her sister out of frustration.

Snap! Once again, the wet dishcloth made a sharp, snapping sound as it connected with Teresa's cheek.

"Ouch! Stop it!" she yelled, in hopes her father would hear that something was going wrong in the kitchen, and he would come to her rescue.

"What the hell is going on in there!" roared the loud, gruff voice of Edward.

"Teresa won't dry the dishes I put in the tray," Patricia would yell back, as she immediately jumped into action and stacked several items in the tray.

"Teresa!" boomed her father's voice. **"Dry those dishes! If I have to come in there, you are going to be in big trouble,"** Edward bellowed from his chair in the living room.

Teresa, with anger in her eyes, glared at her sister. Patricia was standing there with her hands in the dishwater laughing. She was actually proud of her actions.

"You bitch!" Teresa said, regretting it immediately, as Patricia's hand came out of the dishwater and slapped the younger girl across the face.

The slap was hard, wet, and stung Teresa's cheek. She began to cry and held the towel against her face. Patricia just stood there a laughed, quietly.

"Fat little bitch," she said to her sister. **"You are going to get it now."** And she was right. Suddenly, Teresa heard the footrest of Edward's recliner chair slam back into its base.

"TERESA! What are you doing, again," roared Edward as he staggered into the kitchen. His words were slurred, and Teresa could tell this would be brutal.

Before her father entered the kitchen, Patricia quickly turned back to the sink full of dishes.

Edward stormed in the kitchen and grabbed his youngest daughter by the arm. **"What are you doing, now?"** he demanded. His breath smelled like a case of beer.

"Nothing Daddy!" she wailed. Tears started to form in her eyes as she blurted out, "I'm waiting for her to wash the dishes, but she slapped me with the rag and then her hand."

In that short amount of time, Patricia had filled the drain board with cups, glasses, and some dishes. Edward looked at the stack of dishes and then back at his youngest daughter.

"You're lying again!" he said. "That drain board is full of dishes." Teresa could see the anger growing in his eyes. It was an anger she didn't understand, but had experienced many times in the past. "Why?" was all she could think.

She did not have time to think very long. Edward pulled her arm as he dragged her in the hallway.

She screamed. **"NO! Not that again, Daddy. NO!"**

"You stand right there and don't move a muscle," he sneered. He turned and walked into the wall as he aimed for the basement steps.

Patricia quickly finished the rest of the dishes and put them on the rack to dry and ran to her room. Her objective complete, she didn't need to stay.

Teresa heard her father's footsteps on the basement steps. She heard the cold-cellar room door open and close. She knew from that sound that her father was in there having another beer, then she heard someone pounding with a hammer. The thoughts of what he was doing terrified her. She knew her father was drunk, and when he was like this, his punishments were harsh.

Ten minutes later, Edward stumbled his way back up the basement steps. When he walked back into the hallway, where Teresa was standing, he bumped into the doorframe. Teresa could tell her father was very drunk. The fear that rose in the girl was greater than any feeling she had felt before. She had a feeling this would be a punishment she was never going to forget.

Edward had a 12 x 12 x 1" thick board in his hand, not the type of board used for spanking a bad child. When he turned it over and laid it down on the floor in front of the mirror, where Teresa normally served her punishments on the register, Teresa saw what her torture was going to be. Looking up at her father in total horror she said, ***"Daddy, No!"***

"Bad girls like you need to be punished," he said. **"You WILL learn, one way or another."**

Edward was oblivious to his daughter, by this point. It could have been his wife he was punishing. He really didn't care. He felt rage, anger, and a strong urge to punish something. He didn't care what or who.

"Pull up your pant legs and kneel down!" he said to Teresa.

"But Daddy," Teresa said, **"there are beer caps on that board. They will cut my knees."** Tears formed in her eyes as she stood there, trying desperately to understand the cruelty that was about to be her world. **"WHY?"**

When she looked down at the torture device again, Edward had nailed over a dozen beer bottle caps, with the pointed sides up, onto this piece of plywood.

The girl began to cry. "How can my daddy be so cruel?" she thought.

"Do what I told you, now!" Edward barked at her.

Teresa bent down and began rolling up her pant legs. **"Kneel down and don't you dare slouch,"** he said to her. **"If I catch you slouching, you are going to get my belt across your ass!"**

Teresa, crying harder now, felt the first of the sharp points of the bottle cap dig into her kneecaps. "Daddy, **it hurts!**" she cried.

"I don't care!" He replied. **"You are going to learn to do your chores without being a brat.** I'm sick and tired of having to tell you to do your work."

Teresa gingerly knelt down onto the bottle caps. The pain was horrible. She thought, for sure, the points were going to break the skin on her knees and that she was going to bleed to death, and no one in this house was going to care. This is the worst thing that had happened to her, or so she thought.

It took a couple of minutes, but eventually, she found the strength deep inside her, and she rose up on her knees. Even though the pain was horrible, she did not want to give her father any reason to make this torture worse or last too long.

"You are going to stay there for at least half an hour," Edward slurred the words as he stumbled back to the kitchen, where he cracked open another beer. On his way past, he gave Teresa one final look and then said, "If you slouch, you get the belt." With that, Edward disappeared into the living room and Teresa heard him sit in "his" chair.

There she was, all alone, once again, being brutally punished, and all the time, asking herself why? Teresa was beginning to understand that it did not matter what she did or did not do, she was going to be guilty for something or anything. Was everyone trying to tell her that she was bad, imperfect, and stupid? Did she really deserve these punishments? "I must," she thought. "They always tell me I'm so bad."

When she looked up in the mirror in front of her, she began to hate the person staring back at her. "You are stupid, ugly, and bad!" she would say to this image. "No one wants you or loves you."

Through the tears that filled her eyes and rolled down her face onto her top, Teresa began to hate herself. "You are worthless, and everyone would be so much better if you were not here," she said to the image.

Those words slapped the little girl across the face, and suddenly, she jerked out of her trance. Along with the jerking motion came the reality of what she was kneeling on and, with the movement, came excruciating pain. She cried out in pain and could no longer hold the upright kneeling position. Teresa slouched.

"Dad, she's slouching," Patricia yelled as she peeked around the corner.

Teresa, crying, was so startled, she bolted upright, causing another round of searing pain in her knees.

Then she heard the recliner again. She knew what was coming next. Holding her breath, she waited. She did not have to wait long for the answer. Edward came staggering into the hallway, with his belt in his hand. "I told you not to slouch," he slurred.

Teresa braced herself for what was coming. She hoped that, by holding her breath and keeping rigid, she would not feel the full impact of the belt across her backside.

Whack! She cried out in pain as the first blow came. **"Daddy!"** she screamed.

"Shut up!" Whack! Again, the belt came down across her behind.

It hurt so much! With each connection, she felt the searing pain in her skin. With each crack, she would move slightly, causing more pain in her knees. Teresa desperately wanted this night to end. She wished she no longer had to be in this body or this family and house. If only she could leave. Then she would not have to feel...anything! She hated living in this house with these people. Right now, all she had to do was survive this night.

After three hits with the belt, Edward said to her, **"Get up and go to bed. I don't want to see or hear from you for the rest of the night."**

Teresa was in so much pain she could not answer her father.

*"**Did you hear me**?"* he yelled.

"Yes," Teresa replied with her face drenched from tears, and sweat.

"Then get," Edward said, and he walked away and went back to his chair.

Teresa found it a bit difficult to get off the board. Her back hurt from the position she was in; her bottom throbbed and was painful to the touch, and then there were her knees. She found she had to bend down over the board and slowly, one at a time, remove each knee. Little droplets of blood escaped each hole in her knee. She was unable to stand up, and of course, she could not sit, so she dragged herself to her bedroom. Luckily, the torture sessions always took place in the hallway, just outside of her bedroom door, so she did not have far to go.

Once in her room, she closed the door gently, so no one would hear. Then she pulled herself up onto her bed. She lay on her side, gently rubbing her knees and cried. As her hands moved down over her knees, she felt the imprints of the beer caps. When she removed her hands, she noticed blood all over her fingers. She tried rolling onto her back to straighten her legs, but the pain from her bottom told her that she would be sleeping on her sides for the next few nights.

Teresa turned out her light, and placing a small pillow between her knees, curled into a little ball. She cradled her sore knees and cried. Her soul cried out in pain, as did her heart. Would she ever understand why this was happening to her? She had her doubts that she would ever be free.

Hours later, Teresa finally fell asleep. She thought, in her sleep, she would be alone and safe. She thought her dreams would be a safe place for her to be free. It was not to be. Every night, her dreams were haunted. Her sister's cruelty, tormenting laughter and the words, "Ugly," "Fat", and "Stupid," came to her repeatedly. Patricia tormented her during the day in person and tortured her at night in her dreams.

The insecurity in Teresa was growing, as was her hatred for her family.

During her younger years, Teresa was the victim of countless beatings and torture sessions at the hands of her parents and her sister. The anger in her was growing so large she found she was having difficulty containing it. Many times, after a negative interaction with Patricia, Teresa would storm into her bedroom and slam her door closed.

She was so upset and angered; it felt like there was a raging beast growing inside her. It was at these moments when this beast would surface. Teresa did not find beating her pillow enough of a release. It did nothing to release the anger she felt. She did find some satisfaction in beating the wall on the inside of her closet. She would punch at the wall with her fists, until the anger would subside. At times, she would use the back of her wooden bedroom door. She found anything in her room that was solid made a good punching bag.

Eventually, Teresa discovered sports as a method of releasing her anger. Doing sports was a great physical outlet for her. She found that physical activity actually allowed her to work out the anger she had been storing inside.

Finding Solace in Sports

Teresa discovered she had a gift for athleticism. She excelled in gymnastics, which was a challenge, considering she was 5 foot 7 inches at 10 years old. She was tall, but she was not thin. Most of her friends were short and tiny. Teresa stood out, because of her height, but when she played basketball or volleyball, she was in her element. She played centre for her school basketball team. She loved the game, and she excelled. Her physical education teacher took an interest in her and spent much time after school, working with her to perfect her abilities. Teresa was a force of nature on the basketball court. It was here she was nicknamed, "Wilt," after the great Wilt Chamberlain. It made her laugh when she heard it.

Teresa also excelled at volleyball and baseball. Her coach spent many hours after school in the gym, showing Teresa how to be the best on the volleyball court by jumping straight up and down at the net, each time, trying to jump a bit higher. Her coach also noticed Teresa could use her left and right hands almost equally. While playing baseball, her coach taught her how to bat and catch from either her right or left side, and throw using either hand. This way, the competition never knew what to expect. She had so much fun with this.

Track and Field was another sport Teresa loved. She enjoyed doing high jump and was close to jumping her own height in grade 8. Because of Teresa's athletic nature and strong build, she had developed a great love for physical education classes and track and field activities. Her teacher always encouraged and motivated Teresa; allowing her the freedom to practice the sport of her choice. The chosen activity was always shot put. Her teacher spent many hours working with her to teach her the proper techniques and stance to succeed in the sport. Teresa found she enjoyed having someone take an interest in her and the teacher always made her feel special. Other than her Papa, Teresa's physical education teacher was a gift from Heaven.

Teresa won many awards for her athleticism during her school years. She played countless games of basketball, volleyball, and baseball, and lost count of the number of hours she spent on track and field events. She never missed a game for any reason. The only thing that could have made this time better for her was if her parents would have watched her participate, at least once. It was difficult for Teresa, because she knew her friend's parents were always there for them. Teresa found herself jealous of her friends, sometimes. "They have parents that love and care for them," she thought.

There was one sport, however, where Teresa did have the attention of her family: cycling. Belgians are very avid cycling fans, and Teresa's family was no different. It was through this sport that Teresa found the first love of her life.

During this phase of her life Teresa experienced an event that left her questioning for most of her life. When she was ten years old, she woke up through the middle of the night with stomach cramps. Bad cramps. Maybe, I've been doing too much sports, she thought to herself, but the pain she felt washed away any attempt at logic. She was in such horrible pain. It was nothing she had ever experienced before, and the severity of it, blocked out any fear she may have felt as she approached her parents for comfort for the first time in her memory. She was terrified to ask about getting into bed with them, but all she wanted was comfort. To her surprise, she was actually cuddled by her parents. Then suddenly, she felt another horrible pain. She had never felt or imagined it's equal. Her fear was now amplified and she needed to escape.

"I want to go back to my own bed," she whimpered to them.

"Then get out," her father roared at her, as if she had done something wrong.

Teresa ran to her own bed as fast as she could. Her stomach and her bottom hurt badly. Later, when she went to the bathroom, she noticed the toilet was full of blood. Scared, she looked at her underwear. It was full of blood too. "What is happening?" she cried to herself.

She cleaned herself up and crawled back into her own bed. The next day, she approached her mother, because the bleeding hadn't stopped. Her mother tossed a pad and belt at her and said, "Hmmm looks like you've got your period."

"But I'm only ten years old, Mommy!" Teresa yelled.

"I guess you have it early for some reason," her mother barked and left the room.

Teresa knew exactly why her period had started. "I'm not stupid," she screamed out loud as her mother left the room. It felt good to yell, and because her mother was deaf, she knew she was safe and no one would ever hear her cries. Over the new few weeks, the bleeding stopped. She didn't have another period for one year, when it became regular. She knew what her father had done, but who could she tell? She would have to just lock this away and bury it deep inside. This was a secret she believed she would take to the grave, until she found the courage much later in life.

From that point forward, Teresa never felt comfortable with her father around her. Never!

For the Love of Cycling

"A friend forever on and off the bike. May you once again experience the joy of riding and showing the world who is the best!"
Teresa Syms, for my departed friend, Jocelyn Lovell

Andrea and Edward decided to become members of the local St. John's Ambulance. As part of their duties, they were responsible for attending many cycling events. Edward enjoyed this activity and it matched perfectly with his side job as ambulance attendant for the town. The ambulances were owned by the local funeral homes.

Not wanting to pay a babysitter, the girls were forced to attend.

Watching the speed and athleticism of the cyclists fascinated Teresa to her core. She loved this sport and was destined to be part of it.

Teresa was unaware that her aunt (Edward's sister, Danielle), owned a bike shop in London. When her grandparents learned how crazy she was about the sport, a beautiful emerald green ten-speed arrived just in time for her eleventh birthday. Her large brown eyes lit up with joy and her heart burst with happiness. Her brand-new bike came complete with toe clips and water bottle. She had never received such a beautiful gift. This gift represented a new-found freedom.

Jumping onto the saddle and clipping in her toes he roared off down the street. She felt exhilarated. No one could touch her here...they couldn't catch her. She was free.

Each day she ventured further from home, mapping out her best training routes and learning the landscape outside of the town.

Delhi was a town filled with Europeans who loved their cycling. It was here they decided to build a velodrome in the arena.

This indoor wooden short track soon became the most exciting sporting venue in South Western Ontario. Word soon traveled the countryside challenging all cyclists to test their skills. As word spread, the small track attracted riders from all over North America and even Europe. All summer, the town hosted cyclists hoping to hone their skills in time-trialing, the Madison, and individual and team pursuit racing. What the little track became famous for was the Six Day Bike Races.

Once again, feeling the need to help everyone else but their own children, Edward and Andrea stood guard for the St. John Ambulance.

Teresa stood mesmerized by the electrified air that engulfed the track. She stood wide-eyed like a doe caught in headlights.

On one particular race day, Alphonse decided to join his granddaughter. Having witnessed this type of cycling in Belgium when he was a young man, Alphonse relived his youth and love of cycling through this little girl's excitement.

He learned over to Teresa and whispered, "Do you want to try it?"

She turned to look at her Papa. "Oh yes," she said. "More than anything! Can I?"

"I'll talk to your father," Alphonse replied.

With that single comment, Teresa's hopes were dashed. At the mention of her father, a knife went through her. "It will never happen," she thought to herself. She fell silent as her heart broke.

The following week, Alphonse went with Teresa again to watch the races.

As she walked into the building holding her Papa's hand, he said to her, "Look over there," as he pointed towards the one wall.

Leaning against the wall was a brilliant white track bike. It was the most beautiful thing she had seen. "Someone is lucky," she thought. The bike was completely decked out.

Hanging off the handle bars was a soft back and white striped helmet.

"Go try it on," he whispered to her.

She stared at the kindly old man unsure of what he meant.

"It's yours," he said.

Teresa burst into tears. She hugged her Papa tight and refused to let go. She didn't want to break the spell.

"Thank you, Papa," she said as she kissed him on the cheek.

He gave her a kiss back and said, "Get going. The lessons are going to start soon."

She grabbed the helmet and carefully picked up the lightweight bike. With enormous pride Teresa walked over the track and down into the centre area. Here she found her favourite sport in the world.

Track bikes are a single gear bike without brakes. Therefore, special training was provided to learn the 'ropes' of handling the bike both on and off the track.

Each rider needed to become one with their machine. A challenge which the young girl dove into completely.

Luckily, Delhi was home to a veteran cyclist from England. His experience was instrumental in teaching the young riders the ins and outs of the sport.

Now, with her helmet on and her feet clamped tightly in the clips, Teresa was given instructions on how to approach the track, how to handle the different banking and very importantly, how to stop and dismount...always keeping in mind: NEVER SUDDENLY STOP PEDALING!

The excitement was building. Teresa rode around the bottom of the track getting a feel for her new bike. As she rode, the instructor followed beside, always gently talking and explaining in fine detail what to expect and how to handle each situation.

"On the next time around," he said to her, "I want you to weave up onto the track and come back down. Remember, don't steer the bike," he warned.

Smiling with confidence and determination, Teresa mounted the track and the dismounted. "What fun!" she thought to herself.

"One more time around," Jim said. "Next time, build up your speed and go up; stay up and do some laps. I want you to get a feel for the banking, the corners and your ability," he told her.

The thrill she felt in her heart was indescribable! She knew she had the power in her legs to succeed. On the next time around, she increased her speed and launched herself onto the track. Into the corners she went, easily mastering the technique. *"I'm flying,"* she thought. "This is so much fun!"

Alphonse stood on the side watching his granddaughter with pride. His face lit up as he watched her expression of pure bliss. With each lap she conquered, his chest expanded with pride. He knew her determination and her courage. He marveled at watching his granddaughter conquer yet another obstacle in her life. Thinking back, it was difficult for him to believe this girl had been handed to him as an infant with casts on both legs up to her hips. He loved her spirit.

After three times around, the coach called out, "on the next lap, I want you to come down. Watch your speed and use your legs to slow up."

"Ok," Teresa called back out to him. She remembered every word he had said to her and she executed everything perfectly. After she dismounted the track, a roar of applause flooded her ears. She made it! All of the other cyclists and trainers ran over to congratulate her. Teresa has never been happier in her life.

"Oh my God, I did it!" she said to herself. The smile that erupted on her face was something her Papa had never seen from her before. He was so proud of her.

After placing her bike in the rack, she ran to her Papa and hugged him. Tears of joy blossomed from her eyes. "Thank you, Papa," she whispered to him.

"You are welcome," he replied.

This first track ride was the beginning of a lifetime love of cycling. She loved this sport and it gave her such freedom and joy. Something she had never had before.

By the age of eleven, Teresa was extremely physically fit and strong. She was gaining respect for her fitness and skill in sports, but still, she could not catch the notice of her parents.

When Andrea was in the arena watching the track races, and Teresa was scheduled to take part, Andrea immediately left the building. Someone would have to go outside to let her know Teresa was down off the track. Then she would return.

The lack of interest from her parents, broke her heart. Teresa played on basketball, volleyball, track and field, baseball teams and raced bicycles on road and track. Her parents never attended to watch or cheer her on. Usually she had to find her own rides to and from the events, or walk.

After a while, Teresa learned not to care. Sports became her life and the freedom she so desperately needed.

Teresa developed a friendship with a cyclist from Toronto. He was a funny yet quirky sort of character, but a powerful magician on the bike. Jocelyn Lovell was ten years Teresa's senior but neither cared. They liked each other and a friendship grew. Jocelyn taught her a great deal about road and track racing. He was a master at his craft and she always inspired watching his race. His instruction was great and she was an eager student.

As Jocelyn travelled around the country entering and winning countless races. He became her mentor on the bike and a lifetime friend off the bike.

A brilliant cyclist in his own rite Jocelyn won more than 35 national titles both on and off the velodrome, in every distance. As Teresa followed his career, she kept clippings of his wins. He was a three-time Olympian, won four gold Commonwealth Games medals, a World Championship silver medal and achieved further success by winning gold medals in two Pan Am Games.

This young man, her friend, set the standard for Canadian cycling. He inspired her and many other young cyclists throughout the country. Teresa liked his sharp wit and sarcastic humour. He made her laugh.

But like everything in the young girl's life, sports came with a price. She wasn't sure as she was able to survive the fee.

The Price of Freedom is Hidden Behind the Door

Patricia was now thirteen years old and at the age where learning to work in tobacco was important. Unfortunately for Teresa, she was forced to go along and help. As a young girl, she wanted to spend her summer with her grandparents, but Andrea demanded Teresa's working career begin at ten years old.

When harvest started in August, Teresa was ordered to spend her days between her mother and sister on the tying machine. It was torture.

Andrea cut a deal with the farmer to bring on both inexperienced girls for one wage. In 1970 each girl earned $9 per day for strenuous, filthy work that lasted anywhere from 7:00 a.m. until sometimes 9:00 p.m., or later.

Because Teresa was so physically fit, her parents assumed hard physical labour would be easier for her than Patricia. Patricia was thin and always appeared weak. She just didn't want to do the heavy lifting the job usually demanded.

The three females stood at the tying machine for hours on end. They lived in the confined space in the order of, Patricia, Teresa and Andrea. Being under the watchful eye of her mother on one side and her main source of torment on the other; most days was unbearable.

Patricia could criticize, torment and harass her younger sister to her heart's content and their mother never heard one word.

Both girls soon adapted to their new roles. Patricia laid down three-quarters of the bottom layer of the stick on the machine; Teresa filled the rest, placed the stick on and added one-quarter of the top. This was all done as the tying machine (massive sewing machine) moved along and sewed the top layer to the bottom. The completed, sewed stick of tobacco then travelled up a conveyor to the kiln-hanger for hanging in the kiln.

Each girl was responsible for moving and untying their own baskets filled with tobacco and ensuring their workspace was tidy. Teresa had the extra step of adding the stick and replacing the bundles of sticks (50 in a bunch) constantly. This took coordination, speed and timing. Provided her sister would let her pass by to get out. Sometimes Patricia thought it was funny to hip-check her sister into the machine. It was a definite balancing act for Teresa to accomplish her role without missing a beat on the tying machine.

Once harvest began there were few reasons to stop working. Every day you woke up to prepare yourself to be on the farm and ready to start by 7:00 a.m. Harvesting continued rain or shine, cold or hot. It made no difference.

Many of the priming help were workers from Quebec. Some spoke English, but many didn't and relied on translations.

They lived on the farm in a bunkhouse, worked, slept, ate and drank together. At times this was a volatile combination especially after fatigue from weeks of working set in.

The farmer Andrea chose to work for was a difficult and unpleasant man.

At times the language barrier initiated his inner demon to surface, causing him to verbally abuse the migrant workers. The only part of the human equation he cared about was how fast they could get his crop off. The more he abused his workers, the slower they became. Some days were painfully slow and long. Frequently, the primers stopped working altogether as a means of protest. This action sent the farmer into a frenzy of cursing, swearing and unbelievable outbursts of rage.

The table gang (consisting of Andrea, her daughters, and the kiln-hanger), could see the primers in the field. Sometimes there were mechanical issues but those were quickly solved and rarely was this the reason for hours between loads.

Andrea said to her daughters, "when the load is finished, stack the baskets for the driver to collect, go in the kiln and pick up any fallen leaves and get ready for the next load."

Some days you could actually fall asleep between loads. The heat of the summer would wear you out fast. On the cold rainy days of the fall there was nothing you could do to keep warm. Your hands and finger tips would ache from the cold rain and almost freezing temperatures.

No matter the temperature or weather conditions you worked until 1200 to 1500 sticks were sewn up and hung in the kiln to dry.

On many occasions Edward would bring dinner out to the farm for his family; and on very rare occasions, the farmer's wife would bring out sandwiches and a shot of whiskey for everyone.

These long days of working prevented Teresa from being on her bike. She was exhausted, frustrated and sore from the long, hard labour.

If the temperatures dipped towards freezing, and frost was a threat, the farmer would panic and demand everyone go out in the fields, after finishing the kiln yard work and hand prime the precious leaves and stack them into large bundles in the rows. This meant hours of walking, bending, priming, carrying arm-loads of tobacco and stacking. Frost is a serious threat to tobacco farmers.

On these particular days, Teresa didn't get to bed until after 10 or 11 pm. She fell into bed exhausted to the bone and frustrated because she couldn't ride her bike. She needed the bike desperately to recharge her spirit.

Even at ten years old, Teresa was much stronger than her sister who was three years older. When a heavy basket needed lifting, Andrea would demand Teresa pick it up, saving Patricia from the task. Sometimes the baskets weighed 100-120 pounds. An enormous weight for a young girl of any age to lift off the ground and place on a table waist height. At times, Teresa was given no choice and was expected to lift like this several times per day. "Your sister can't lift those heavy baskets," her mother would say. "You do it." Patricia played up the thin and frail routine often.

Teresa grew stronger both physically and emotionally with every basket she lifted.

On some occasions, the constant heavy weight lifting was more than she could endure. She came home with bruises down the front of her thighs from attempting the clean-and-jerk technique used in weight lifting. It was the only way she could lift the baskets. She could manage easily to get it to thigh height, but at times as she strained to lift the rest of the way, it felt as though her back would explode from the strain.

It was on one of these long hard days Edward came out to see what was going on. Andrea immediately noticed the alcohol fumes on his breath. She went silent, secretly waiting and plotting her attack on her husband.

The drive home was treacherous as Edward swerved all over the road.

No one spoke for fear of igniting the time bomb that was waiting to detonate.

Once home both girls ran for their rooms for safety. Teresa, began changing her clothes and hoped that soon there would be dinner to eat. Having seen this from her mother before, she knew what was about to happen. Terror stuck in her throat and caused pain in her stomach. "Maybe if I hide, they will forget I'm here," she thought. "It would be safer that way."

Suddenly she heard the argument start. Doors slammed, dishes smashed as the voices grew louder. The terror inside Teresa grew rapidly. It felt like the monster growing inside her was trying to claw its way up to escape. She knew that outside of her bedroom door was not safe tonight. There would be no dinner.

"I must be quiet," she thought. "I can't attract attention to myself." No amount of hunger pain could make her touch that door handle.

The battle raged on until late in the evening. Teresa then heard, what sounded like someone falling down the basement steps.

A loud noise erupted from the laundry room. She didn't have to wait long for the noise to be repeated.

Crash! Smash!

"Those are dad's beer bottles," she thought. "What's going on?" she wondered. But terror kept her a prisoner in her room.

Crash! Smash!

Now Teresa knew exactly what was happening. She could hear everything perfectly. Her bedroom was just above the laundry room where the battle between her parents was raging. Her mother was losing her grip on sanity.

Crash! Smash! Again more bottles landed in the cement laundry tub. One after another, Andrea smashed Edward's supply of beer. The fumes rose up through the floor and consumed Teresa's nose and throat. The smell was nauseating. Given the argument, screaming and shattering of glass, it was easy to envision what her mother was doing. She had seen her mother and father lose control before.

Through the din of breaking glass and screaming she heard her father's voice erupted and filled her head and heart with terror.

The little girl heard a struggle begin. ***"What the hell do you think you are doing you stupid woman!"*** he bellowed at Andrea.

"I've had enough of your drinking," came her mother's voice in a shrieking tone never heard before.

Crash! Smash! Another bottle smashed into the cement tub.

Smash!

Teresa heard a scream. She knew her mother was in danger, but her own fear left her paralyzed.

Edward came staggering up the basement steps, uncapped a beer in the kitchen and headed for his chair in the living room. The television went on and even with the noise from the television, an eerie silence fell over the house.

Hungry, filthy and with pain in her back, Teresa hid herself between her bed and the wall. It was here she woke up the next morning to a pounding fist on her bedroom door. Her father was yelling at her.

"Get up! Be out here in ten minutes," Edward bellowed.

"Yes dad," was all she was able to say in reply.

Quickly she changed her shirt, tied her hair back in a kerchief and stepped outside her door dreading the day to come.

If she was well-behaved and didn't cause trouble today, maybe they would let her go out on her bike and once again experience freedom.

This was how Teresa lived for the next few years. She lived under the threat of abuse and torment. Never understanding why. Family life didn't improve at all, but somehow she managed to cope as long as she could spend time with her bike. This was her only outlet to release the anger and aggression that was growing within her. She loved the feel of the wind blowing through her hair as each time she tried to improve her speed. Her legs burned from the exertion at times, but it felt good. It was as if each pedal stroke released another beating or painful insult. It was the only way she could survive.

Her Papa watched his granddaughter develop her love of cycling. He must have understood why she spent so much time in the saddle, but he never said one word.

One day he surprised her again. He had made a set of training rollers for her to ride her track bike on during the winter in the basement.

"Thank you Papa," she said to the man. "It's the best present!" she exclaimed.

"Your welcome, my little liefje (sweetheart)," he replied as he gave her a kiss on her forehead.

Teresa's love of cycling exploded into a passion. She spent time with Pan-Am Gold medalists, Olympic athletes and professional cyclists from Europe.

On one special Six Day Bike race in town, her family housed the professional racers from Belgium. She was in heaven the day they asked her to go out and ride with them. They were kind and kept down to her speed, but it was the best day of her life! It was HER happy and special memory, and no one could ever take that away from her.

Change is Coming

By the time Teresa turned 14 years old, she was 5' 9" tall. She was physically powerful walking on muscular legs from cycling. She carried a thick mane of coarse sandy blonde hair. Her eyes were dark chocolate brown, bright and slightly tilted up on the outside edges like a cat. The one feature that seemed to stand out more than any other was her tiny nose. Her nose was such a small button it didn't seem to fit the rest of her. She was not a raving beauty, nor was she ugly. However, when she looked in the mirror, all she saw was **UGLY!** ***"You are fat, ugly and horrible!"*** she would comment to the mirror. She had heard these words from her sister constantly since she was a little girl. Her sister made sure she knew exactly what each hurtful word meant and how deeply each word cut. Teresa had heard these words so often that she believed them.

Adding the words of torment and to her feelings of being unloved; Teresa lacked self-image . She not only hated her image, she loathed herself as a person.

Her sister, looked completely opposite to Teresa. They were matched in height, but the similarities ended there.

Patricia had very dark, almost black hair. She was skinny with very little muscle tone, like Andrea. She looked anorexic. Her facial features were sharp. Her nose was large, sporting a big bump on the bridge. Patricia was extremely embarrassed because her teeth overlapped each other. She suffered from extreme self-esteem issues caused by her teeth and unattractive facial features which drove her to be shy and timid.

These self-image problems caused Patricia to brutally attack Teresa. After 14 years of hearing how ugly and fat she was, Teresa believed it and tried desperately to close off her heart again wishing to feel nothing. She let no one but her Papa in her heart.

By the time Patricia was 17 years old no boys had shown any interest in her. Teresa on the other hand found she did not lack attention from boys.

The summer of 1974 was hot and dry. Both girls spent endless hours working in tobacco with their mother for the same obnoxious farmer. Teresa hated working for this man. There was nowhere in her life she could escape abuse. She got it at home and now at work.

As Teresa grew older, her strength and determination intensified. She discovered she was now able to defend herself against her sister's attacks. Teresa also learned to hit her sister where it hurt her the most. The girl learned the art of retaliation.

"You're the ugly one with your crooked teeth," Teresa would yell at Patricia.

"You little ugly bitch!" Patricia would scream back.

"At least I do not look like a bird," Teresa would reply and giggle, knowing she had scored a direct hit.

Fuming with anger, Patricia lashed out with her fist. The power behind the blow caused Teresa to fall down and hit her face against a chair. She made no sound but tears began to form in her eyes. Something snapped within. "I'm not going to give you the satisfaction," she yelled at Patricia.

She summoned her courage and stood up facing her sister. Patricia was smiling her usual toothless grin of sarcasm and satisfaction. Teresa saw the laughter in her eyes.

Her rage boiled over. A dam burst inside her. Teresa was no longer responsible for her actions. Summoning her strength, she threw her right fist at her sister. One punch was all it took. Her fist connected with her sister's stomach and quickly Patricia fell to the floor in a heap. Teresa had knocked her out cold.

Suddenly fear and terror rose up in her throat. The realization of what she had done hit her in the face harder than her sister had hit her. *"They're going to kill me,"* she thought in agonized horror.

She knew it didn't matter to her parents who took the first swing; all that mattered was Patricia was hurt and it was Teresa's fault.

Unable to swallow the fear and panic that began to choke her, Teresa ran to her room and closed the door. Sitting with her back against the door, she tried to prevent anyone from entering. She waited.

A while later she heard Patricia in the kitchen getting things ready for dinner. Cautiously, Teresa opened the door and walked into the kitchen.

"You little bitch! You are going to really get it this time," Patricia sneered at her.

"You hit me first," Teresa said in her own defense.

"So!" was the last reply that came from Patricia.

"They're going to kill me," was Teresa's last thought before shock set in as her parents walked in the door.

Immediately Patricia told them her story of how Teresa refused to do her chores when ordered. They glared at the girl. Then came the 'moment de vérité,' (moment of truth), when she said Teresa hit her.

"TERESA! GET OUT HERE! NOW!" came Edward's roaring voice.

Feeling lower than dirt, Teresa guardedly left the kitchen to face her punishment.

"You hit your sister!" Andrea screamed at her.

"She hit me first," Teresa cried as she tried to defend herself.

The injustice of the situation hit home and tears sprang forth in Teresa's eyes. They hurt her face as they rolled over her bruised cheek.

"I don't care who hit who first. You are always doing something wrong. Why can you not be a better girl?" Andrea shrieked at her.

A warning alarm went off in Teresa's head. "She's losing control of herself again," she thought as she watched her mother.

"Edward, take off your belt and fix her," Andrea ordered her husband.

For the first time, Teresa saw something different in her father's eyes. It was almost a glimmer of understanding. He had to do it though, to keep his wife quiet.

Teresa flinched but refused to step away as she saw her father remove his leather belt.

Snap! One swing of the belt was all it took. As Edward whipped his daughter across the buttocks with the belt, he also caught her hand as she tried to shield herself from the blow. That made matters worse for her. She let out a scream the entire neighbourhood should have heard. But no one came to her rescue.

"Shut up or you'll get another one," her mother shouted.

Tears flowed freely from Teresa's eyes. She was unable to stop herself.

"*AGAIN*," Andrea demanded.

Edward wound up for another swing. What happened next shocked her parents to the core.

When the belt landed on Teresa's flesh a second time, she didn't cry out. Instead, she grabbed the belt in her hand and pulled. She pulled so hard, her father lost his grip on the belt. With a look of shock and fear, he stared at the strong, angry girl who now held his belt in her hand.

Never before had she taken control but something had snapped deep inside her. She felt invincible as she raised the belt in her clenched fist to her parents. She shook the belt at both of them, shouting, **"DON'T YOU EVER HIT ME AGAIN!"**

Feeling her most powerful state ever, Teresa threw the belt on the floor and walked out of the room leaving her parents both open-mouthed and stunned. She knew the tides had turned and took great comfort in knowing that they would never abuse her again.

"I won!" she said to herself as she walked out of the house, jumped on her bike, and rode herself to her own gold medal as a champion. It was liberating!

The Heart's Desire

Teresa's ground breaking stance against the brutality in her life, left her sister completely dumbfounded. With her sister's internal strength now evident, Patricia knew the gauntlet had been dropped. Teresa no longer feared her.

Fortunately, Patricia was somewhat absorbed and occupied, because finally, at seventeen years old a boy was showing interest in her. She was captivated by him but still very conscious of her appearance and deathly afraid the boy would notice her younger sister before she had him hooked.

Teresa always seemed to attract boys. Her sister on the other hand was usually ignored, until this summer. Four friends made a habit of driving their hot rods up and down the street to gain the girls attention. The girls caught the attention of Michael, a short stocky blonde haired guy. His Chevy Nova had a finely-tuned engine that shook the houses when he drove by. A second fellow, much taller with dark hair, hazel eyes and adorable dimples drove a mid-night blue Impala.

All that summer the boys drove circuits around the girls' house. They left long tracks of rubber down the street on their way passed. Both girls, infatuated with these boys would run to the window just to wave. It became a game. Later the girls noticed Michael's family had moved into a house on the corner of their street.

Once the four had actually talked, they were consumed by attraction. Michael, disappointed to learn that Teresa was only fourteen, now set his sights on Patricia.

Maks, the tall cute boy, was 16 years old and very shy. He and Teresa made eye contact several times during the conversation. It was destiny they had to get to know each other.

Much to the relief of Edward and Andrea, Patricia and Michael began dating.

Edward had a drinking partner and Andrea was thrilled that someone wanted her daughter. They would soon learn the truth behind their odd relationship.

Late one Friday night Andrea sent Teresa downstairs to their recreation room. She desperately wanted to know what was happening between Patricia and Michael. Patricia didn't hear her sister approach. The guilty look on all their faces, as the lights went on, spoke volumes.

"Oh my God, they are having sex," Teresa thought.

In a mad scramble, they covered themselves with what they could. Teresa was going to enjoy this. Her perfect sister was caught. "There is no escaping this one," she said to herself with a slight chuckle.

Teresa was very aware of what had happened. She was no stranger to sex.

Her parents read novels by Xavier Hollander, who was a well-known Dutch prostitute at the time.

They left them laying around the house, not caring if the girls picked them up and read them. Teresa found the books both fascinating and shocking, so when she found her sister and Michael downstairs having sex she was not shocked with what had transpired.

Now standing there staring at her sister with all-knowing eyes, she relished in Patricia's humiliation.

"Don't tell," she whispered to Teresa once she had her clothes back on.

"Why shouldn't I?" Teresa remarked back. "They want to know."

"Please!" Patricia begged her sister.

As she turned to walk upstairs, she said to Patricia, "We'll see."

Patricia was petrified with fear.

When Teresa walked into the living room her mother pounced.

"Well!" she demanded. "What's going on down there?"

"Nothing much," Teresa answered.

Trusting in her eldest daughter's innocence, Andrea was satisfied with the response.

Nothing more was said.

On Friday, September 13, 1974, Teresa went on her first date with Maks. Both teenagers were so nervous and shy. They drove to Simcoe to have a bite to eat, then spent the rest of the evening driving around talking and listening to Frankie Valli and the Four Seasons on eight-track. Suddenly, Maks asked Teresa if she would sit beside him while he drove. Bucket seats made it challenging, but he had a blanket rolled up to create an extra seat. Excited and nervous she slid over beside him. The sides of their legs touched and Teresa was lit up by the feeling of him.

Then he asked her a very odd question.

"Can you spell my last name?" he asked. He had an Eastern European name and thought it was a difficult one to spell. Thinking this an odd request, Teresa played along. Carefully she spelled his name. A bright smile lit up his face. "Thanks," he said, "you are the first to be able to spell it." She smiled back.

As they looked into each other's eyes; Frankie Valli was singing, "My Eyes Adored You." Looking as if they had found a missing piece of their soul, their stare deepened. They knew they were meant for each other.

Maks gently placed his arm around Teresa. He leaned in and kissed her. "Oh my goodness! My very first kiss!" she thought, and then she stopped thinking. A beautiful feeling flooded her body. It felt like an angel was wrapping their wings around her in protection. "Is this what it feels like to be loved," she wondered.

Breaking the kiss, they looked deep into each other's soul. They kissed again.

After what seemed an eternity but what was more the blink of an eye, he said, "I think I had better get you home."

She didn't want this magic moment to end. "Will I lose the feeling when he goes home?" she wondered. "Will I see him again?" " Does he like me?" So many thoughts floated through her mind.

Coming back to reality, she replied, "Ok, I do have to work tomorrow."

She didn't want to be parted from him. He made her feel alive! Her heart was being drawn to his like a magnet. This night would be burned into her memory for eternity. Never before had she felt such gentleness, kindness and love.

After the car pulled in the driveway, Maks turned off the car engine and lights. It was late and he didn't want to disturb the neighbours. He leaned over to Teresa and hugged her tightly. Having his loving arms locked around her felt so right. It was something she had longed for. They shared many more magical kisses that night.

One final kiss and Teresa got out of the car and walked towards the house. She realized she was in love!

Tears of happiness flowed over her heart.

The Relationship Grows

Teresa and Maks became inseparable and dated exclusively within months of their first date. Every morning he would pick her up before school; they had lunch together then he drove her home after school. The more time they spent together, the deeper their relationship grew.

After school and on weekends, Maks worked part time at a small garage pumping gas. During the summer holidays from school the young couple spent almost every waking minute together. They even worked on the same tobacco farm during harvest.

Several months after they started dating the young couple made love for the first time. It was special and for Teresa, a strong bond of trust had been formed between them.

Life was beautiful for a couple of years. Until Teresa's entire world came crashing down around her. Her heart fell into the bottom of a deep black well.

"I just want to see other people," Maks said to her with his head down unable to look at the pain he was causing.

"I don't understand," she said to him and tears rolled down her face. What had she done wrong?

"Why?" Teresa managed to whisper through her sobs. *"What have I done wrong?"* she asked.

"Nothing, I just want some space," Maks answered.

He had just ripped her heart from her chest. She actually felt physical pain of love lost. After what seemed an eternity, she gathered up her courage and got out of his vehicle. Somehow she found her way to the door through blinding tears. Never in her life had she felt pain like this before.

Nothing on this earth had prepared her for this. Physical pain she could handle, but this! Now completely alone again, she had no one to turn to. She had given up and lost all of her friends to be with him. Loneliness was consuming her and she fell into a pit of depression. Soon she lost all hope in life and happiness. She was back to the misery she had known before.

Teresa would soon discover this new pain was just the tip of the iceberg.

One hot summer day down at the beach, Teresa spotted Maks' vehicle driving down the street. Her heart leaped with excitement and joy at the thought of seeing him again. She noticed other people in his vehicle. Carefully she watched as the car approached. What she saw caused her heart to break all over again. His passenger was a girl.

Sitting beside him was a young girl with beautiful long blonde hair. She was shorter than Teresa, thinner and prettier. **"How can he do this to me?"** she said aloud. **"I love him!"**

This vision was more than Teresa could cope with. She quickly gathered up her belongings and got into her car.

She drove home almost blinded from the tears in her eyes. Her guardian angel must have kept her safe that day. She arrived at home, with no idea how she got there. As soon as she walked in the house, Andrea saw the state of her youngest daughter. Teresa looked to her mother for some form of comfort. What she received was an angry glare.

"What's your problem!" she snapped. Andrea had turned very mean.

"Nothing," Teresa replied.

Her mother was completely unapproachable since the discovery that Patricia was pregnant.

Teresa realized the night she walked in on her sister having sex was the beginning of Patricia's own nightmare. "Now she will get what she deserves," Teresa thought.

Michael was forced to marry Patricia to "do the right thing." In January of 1975 they were married. Less than six months later their daughter was born.

Things didn't go well for the newly married couple. Patricia was forced to sever all ties with her family. Now living in her own nightmare , she was learning just how being abused feels, she walked away from her family.

Avoiding contact was difficult as they all lived in the same small town. Patricia had to do her best to avoid her family, but Andrea did everything in her power to see her daughter and granddaughter. Andrea was out of her mind with grief. One Friday evening after seeing Patricia in the grocery store, Edward and Andrea were suffering from the rejection of their favourite daughter. Angry and devastated they turned on their youngest daughter. Andrea was screaming and Edward had been drinking. He raised his fist at Teresa and said, ***"DON'T YOU make the same damn mistake your sister did!"***

Teresa had been a great deal smarter than her sister, Patricia. Before she did anything sexual with Maks, she had gone to the doctor to get birth control pills. However, Teresa didn't realize what was involved with this request. Her mother forced her to submit to a physical exam from their family doctor. As the exam began, Andrea left the room leaving the young girl completely exposed to this older man, in many ways. Teresa felt vulnerable and terror rose in her throat. "I don't understand," she thought to herself.

During the exam the doctor was asking rather peculiar questions. "Does this feel good? Tell me when you want me to stop," he would say.

"WHY is he asking me those questions?" she wondered. She kept herself quiet during the exam. She didn't understand until much later that he was using her in his own twisted way.

"I can't talk to anyone about this," she realized. Once again, she found herself completely alone and filled with shame.

Teresa's life was a tortured hell without her love. She became moody and very depressed. Her life truly had no meaning and she began to slip back into the hole that had consumed her when she was young. Down in the bowels of the black pit, she allowed herself to 'feel' nothing. As each day passed, she tried her best to go through the motions of life without living and feeling.

After a few months of separation, Teresa and Maks got back together. Her heart was revived. She felt alive again.

Every now and then, he would look at her and say, "have you ever thought of letting your hair grow longer?"

"Why," she asked him. Her hair was down past her shoulder blades. No matter how she tried, it wouldn't grow any farther.

"Well," he replied sheepishly. "I like girls with long hair."

The horrible reality of the situation slapped Teresa hard across the face. "I'm not good enough the way I am," she thought. Suddenly she remembered the girl she saw him with that day at the beach. Teresa remembered how the girl's long blonde hair was blowing in the breeze as they drove down the street together. Her hair was down to her waist. The truth of the situation sent her back down again. "I can't live up to his fantasy girl," she believed.

"I have never really lived up to anyone's expectations," she finally understood.

So many times throughout her life she had tried to change to please the people around her. No matter how she changed or what she did, she was never good enough. Someone always said she should be better. She was beginning to lose track of herself and why she was here.

"Am I really such a disgusting person that no one truly wants ME," she screamed into her pillow that night as she came very close to losing her grip on reality.

Over the next few weeks, Teresa's depression increased tenfold. Now believing she would never be good enough for anyone to love, she gave up everything that once gave her joy.

She would walk past her bike hanging up in the basement by the rollers. There was no flicker of happiness anymore and she kept on walking. That month she sold her beloved track bike back to her aunt's store. Her passion to ride the bike had been killed along with most of her heart.

Later that summer after a particularly nasty argument with Maks, Teresa stormed into the house and headed for the whiskey bottle. For years she had seen her father drown himself and his pain in beer; maybe this was worth a try.

As always, her mother sat in the living room oblivious to anything around her except what was on television and who was doing what outside that she could gossip about. She was trapped in her own misery and solitude brought on by her deafness and years of self-pity.

In the kitchen, Teresa took a glass from the cupboard and poured it half full of whiskey. Not wanting her mother to detect the aroma, she filled the glass up with orange juice. She had no idea what she was doing. Everything else left her mind except she had a desperate need to numb the pain. Her life had become so meaningless and pain filled. It was unbearable!

Drinking to drown the misery of her life, seemed like the answer. It had worked for her father and other members of their extended family. "Maybe this is how you do it?" she thought.

Nothing mattered anymore. Her depression had grown to a very alarming state. No one in the house noticed. No one ever took the time to ask "How are you doing?" "Do you want to talk?" "Can I help?" It was obvious to her no one cared.

Her once happy life imploded in a black hole. She was definitely in a crisis. Picking up the glass of whiskey she walked into the living room and sat on the couch.

Her mother made brief eye contact with her but then resumed her crocheting. She was oblivious and ignorant to what her daughter was doing and feeling.

Sip after sip, Teresa drank the numbing potion. Each time the glass was empty, she would return for a refill. Once her mother asked her, "Why are you drinking so much?"

"I'm thirsty," she replied and the conversation was dropped.

Not finding the pain relief she sought, Teresa kept pouring eight-ounce glasses.

"Maybe this one will do the trick," she hoped. After about an hour of refills, she discovered she felt very little effects of the whiskey. She stood up and walked into her bedroom. She was on a mission and soon found her treasure. "You will help me," she said aloud to the bottle of tranquillizers. Once again her mother had insisted the doctor 'fix' her daughter. He had prescribed the pills for her 'depression.'

Quickly reaching the point or no return, she opened the bottle and started with one pill. She tossed back the pill with whiskey and orange juice.

She waited. "I don't want to feel anything. I don't want to be here! **I HATE IT HERE!**" she screamed inside her head as she sat down in the living room ten feet from where her mother sat. At the tender age of sixteen, Teresa had reached the point of no return.

The Guardian Angel

Oblivion didn't happen that easily for Teresa. She wasn't able to close off the anguish she felt inside. Her 'depression' was out of control and she no longer cared what happened to her.

Over the next couple of years, Teresa continued to drink heavily. She partied, smoked and kept her bottle of pills with her at all times.

"I just want numb," she said as she prayed at night.

During the day she worked hard, at night, she drank hard and played hard.

Even though she hated going to the family doctor for prescription refills, she knew it was one of those necessary evils. The visits to him were traumatic for her. His touch disgusted her beyond belief but she realized it was the only way to acquire the birth control and tranquillizers she needed. Teresa forced herself to expose her body to him, there was no option.

At every visit he insisted he 'check' her. Believing he was the medical professional and he knew what was best, she submitted thinking this was normal practice. Deep in her gut she knew something wasn't right, but who could she tell!

After each 'examination,' she left with her prescriptions hoping that the pills would help her weather the storms of her life and to quiet the hurricanes that tormented her mind.

Taking the tranquillizers helped her not feel. Experimenting with various combinations Teresa found that combining the tranquilizers with lots of alcohol helped her lose herself in a feeling of not caring for anything...including herself.

She tried to numb the pain completely with the pills and alcohol, and on many occasions, she did just that. She tried so many ways to stop the pain she was feeling and one night, she almost stopped herself...for good.

One Saturday evening Teresa was feeling particularly low. Earlier that afternoon she began drinking. Sitting in the living room watching television, she poured herself drink after drink. Her mother, sitting ten feet away was lost in her own world and showed absolutely no concern for her daughter.

At dinner time, Teresa told her parents, "I'm not hungry. I have a headache so I'm going to lay down for a while." Both Andrea and Edward seemed unconcerned.

Teresa went to her room and pulled out a bottle of whiskey she had stashed away in her closet. Turning on her record player she listened to the music that brought back so many memories for her. Lost in the music and the voice of Frankie Valli, Teresa didn't realize she was fighting a losing battle.

Now alone, she began fighting with the demons that lived within. "No one loves me," she thought. "I hate living here, I hate these people, **I don't want to live this life anymore!"**

Her mood sank fast. Wishing and praying she had someone to talk with, she realized she was completely alone.

She had given up her friends for Maks. "He's gone now too," she said to the stuffed rabbit on her bed — another memory of him.

Unable to live with the pain, she grabbed for her bottle of tranquillizers. Removing two from the bottle she quickly swallowed them down with a big pull from the bottle of whiskey. She hated the taste but it was better than going out in the house and being around them. "They don't care for me anyway," she told herself.

An hour later Teresa was feeling agitated and caged. She had to get out of this house. "This is the toxic environment I grew up in," she thought. "I have to escape somehow."

Leaving her room, she said to her parents, "I'm going out for a drive. I need some fresh air."

"I can come along for the ride," Andrea said to her.

Terror struck. **"You are the last person on this earth I want with me,"** Teresa thought. "No," she replied. "I would rather be alone."

Getting in behind the wheel of Edward's Pontiac, she sat and contemplated this 'life' she had. Making her decision, she started the car. Before pulling it into gear, she grabbed her bottle of pills and popped two more into her mouth and swallowed them dry. The pills stuck half way down in her throat. She had no fluid with her. Swallowing several more times, she finally was successful in getting the pills down.

Now she backed out of the driveway and drove through the town streets.

As she drove out of town, a plan came to her mind. Suddenly, she knew exactly where to go.

On one of her favourite cycling training routes, she remembered a massive maple tree that stood as a sentinel and marker for her training. The tree was massive, at least six feet in diameter and 100 feet tall. "It's perfect!" she thought.

Teresa had cycled down this road numerous times. She had always admired the majestic splendor of the gigantic maple. It was a truly beautiful tree. A wonderful gift from God.

Just as she left the town behind, tears exploded from her eyes. Suddenly and forcefully all the trauma, pain and torture she had endured throughout her life came flooding back. Teresa almost doubled over from the physical pain she felt. It was like taking a direct hard punch to the heart.

"What is wrong with me?" she screamed out. Her voice echoed inside the car. She waited to hear a reply, but there was only silence.

Her uncontrollable crying continued. The night was dark and with the absence of streetlights, Teresa found it difficult to see. She knew the road by heart, but her heart was not helping her right now.

She stopped the car on her side of the road. There was no traffic to be seen in any direction. With her foot on the brake pedal, holding the heavy vehicle in place, she screamed up to the heavens, "**Why? What have I done wrong?**"

She covered her beautiful brown eyes with her hands and bowed her head. Teresa sobbed uncontrollably. There was so much pain, so little love and such great burdens placed on her, she found the weight was killing her.

"I don't want to live," she said as she cried into her hands. "No one loves me or wants me."

Teresa suddenly jumped from shock. She thought she felt someone put their hand on her shoulder. Terrified, thinking she was alone in the car, she quickly turned her head around to see who had touched her.

She couldn't see anyone. Switching on the interior lights of the car, she saw nothing.

"What is going on here," she said. "I'm going crazy, just like her!" she screamed. "I'm turning into my mother!"

Turning off the lights, and grabbing the steering wheel with both hands, she knew what she had to do.

With tears streaming down her face, she looked out the windshield and off in the distance she saw her tree.

"I can't live like this anymore," she yelled. **"Enough!"** She said a quick prayer to God, praying for forgiveness, and slammed her foot down on the gas pedal.

The big Pontiac roared into life and sped off towards its target.

Teresa could barely see; she was so blinded by her tears.

Pressing her foot to the floor, the car raced towards the tree.

"Oh God," she pleaded with her maker, **"Help me! I can't do this life anymore!"**

The tree was fast approaching and Teresa was happy that all feeling was about to leave her for good.

Ten feet from the tree, she was completely at peace. She held on to the steering wheel with a tight grip. "Yes," she thought. "Soon."

She had given up. They had all won. After all the torment, torture, abuse and pain, she simply gave up.

Out of nowhere came the words, *"You aren't finished here yet."*

She heard them in the car, she heard them in her heart and head. *"You aren't finished here yet."*

Just before impact, she felt the steering wheel jerk from her grip. Someone was pulling the wheel away from the tree and back onto the road.

Teresa fought hard against the pull. Whoever was doing this was much stronger than she was.

The car missed the tree as it went back onto the road. Hitting the brake pedal with her foot and stopping the car in the middle of the road, Teresa looked around the inside of the car.

Once again, it was empty.

"What is going on here?" she hollered out in frustration.

It was then she felt a pair of strong arms surround her entire being. She was held in an embrace that said everything she had ever wanted to hear. "I love you! You are wanted! You are needed! You are a good person! You have meaning!"

Then Teresa heard the words again, ***"You aren't finished here yet."***

She felt the love and warmth of the embrace. Her heart no longer ached with torment. It was a beautiful feeling. One she had never felt before.

"You are my Guardian Angel," she said. "I've met you before."

Teresa's heart was filled with love and courage. She knew that someone was there to help her.

She understood she was being protected. She stayed sitting there wrapped in the arms of her angel for what seemed an eternity.

Finally, armed with strength and courage, she felt the arms let go. "Thank you," she whispered to the air. "Thank you!"

In Recovery Mode

"One day, she realized that she could never please everyone, so she gave up trying and decided to be herself. Whether people liked her or not was none of her business."

Anna Grace Taylor

Feeling more brave than she had in a long time, Teresa found the courage to turn her life around. The shocking results of her attempted suicide hit her hard across the face. "What was I thinking," she said to herself. "If it wasn't for my Guardian Angel's protection, I would be gone."

At her lowest, Teresa thought suicide was her best and only option to end her torment; but no more.

Recovering, she made a serious promise to herself to change.

She believed her relationship with Maks had come to an end, but neither acknowledged the idea. He now lived two hours away so they rarely saw each other. He had changed. His partying and drug use had altered his personality. The once destined high school sweethearts had turned away from each other, each living in their own personal hell.

Teresa began taking courses to finish her education. She went off to hairdressing school in London. All her life she loved doing hair. It was one of her dreams to get her license.

Now living in London while attending school, she was away from her parents and home. School was enjoyable and she excelled being one of the top in her class. She made many friends but something was still missing in her life.

After completing her government exam, she had succeeded and achieved her goal. Moving back to her parents house, Teresa now worked as a hairstylist in a popular salon. Unfortunately, she soon discovered she was being used by the owner and refused to stay. With a tainted view of the hair styling industry, she changed tactics.

Taking a business refresher course, Teresa landed a job doing accounting work and payroll for a local manufacturer of tobacco equipment.

The company originated in North Carolina, but their Canadian operation was very profitable.

Teresa loved the job. She worked hard and learned quickly.

Working full time, Teresa had enough money saved to buy her own car. On August 7, 1979, the day 3 tornados touched down in Southwestern Ontario leaving a path of devastation and destruction in its wake, Teresa purchased her first car; a 1979 Camaro. As she stood and watched the sky blacken, she felt her lungs struggle to breathe as the heavy air thickened with the impending annihilation of the tornado. Terrified of the sky and the fate awaited the area, she quickly drove her beautiful silver Camaro home.

The next day at work was a nightmare. The tornado had levelled tobacco farms, demolished buildings and destroyed everything families had worked their entire lives to build.

Most farmers had insurance and were able to order new bulk kilns and other equipment. The company profited from the destruction caused by Mother Nature.

On September 13th, 1979, five years after their first date, Teresa waited for word from Maks. Not expecting to hear from him and believing their relationship had died, she made other plans. She had given up on him. "He doesn't want me anymore," she said to herself.

One hour before her new date was to arrive, the phone rang. It was Maks.

"Are we going out tonight?" he asked.

Teresa was upset at the bold arrogance of him. "I don't hear from you in months and you expect me to drop everything now," she said. "I have other plans tonight. I can't see you anymore." Her heart was shot by a lightning bolt as she hung up the phone. "I can't do this anymore," she whispered as she held her hand on to receiver. Unable to let go, she held it for a moment. This was her last connection with him. Five years we have been on this rollercoaster. "I need to get off this ride."

It took all her strength, but she tore her hand from the phone. "Good bye my love," she whispered.

She left the house and went on her date. Over the next few months Teresa survived the grief. During the day she worked and on weekends she went out to clubs with friends. She met so many new people.

Teresa realized that one part of her heart would always be kept locked away for Maks. That bond was unbreakable.

Trying Hard to Make A Life

Teresa continued to work hard at her new job. Her skills and confidence were growing daily. She met a handsome young man who worked in the factory. Their attraction was strong and soon they were a couple.

He shared his past with her; telling her about his father's death when he was a young boy and about his fiancé. Drew was destroyed when his fiancé left him. "She just walked out on me," he told Teresa. "We had everything booked and all our plans made." Then to her surprise, Drew showed Teresa the engagement ring the girl returned to him. "It's lovely," she said, really not sure why he was showing it to her.

Teresa knew he was heartbroken. She also knew that part of Drew's heart was reserved for someone else.

As time passed their bond grew. They loved dancing and spent many evenings at dance clubs having a great time.

Teresa was invited into Drew's home and enjoyed family gatherings. His mother, Edith, had remarried a divorced man who had three children. His eldest son was newly married; his second son, Michael lived off and on with them, and his young daughter lived with her mother. This was an odd blended family.

Trouble was always brewing within the home. Drew's mother was an alcoholic and tried desperately to hide her condition from her husband. The children were more than aware of her problem.

Michael tried to prove to his father what a drunk his wife was. Even though he had proof, the man sided with his wife, at the expense of his son.

The strain of living with Edith and her illness became too much for Michael. At seventeen years old, he packed his belongings and left his home for adventures in Marcela. The step-mother was relieved he was gone. She no longer had his eyes watching her every move.

During family gatherings, Teresa became friends with Drew's other step-brother, Dennis. He and his wife had been married for a year. From the discussions he had with Teresa, Dennis was unhappy with his marriage. He already suspected his wife of cheating but had no proof. The two grew to be friends and chatted together often.

Christmas that year became a stressful event. Teresa found herself being tugged in many directions between her family and Drew and his extended family. It was a juggling act. As his gift to her, Teresa received an absolutely stunning pearl necklace. "Such a stunning piece," she said to Drew as she thanked him for the gift. She gifted him a birthstone ring.

It was just into the new year when Teresa began hearing that Drew's ex-fiancé had reentered his life. With his mother's encouragement, the young girl began spending time at their house.

Three months later Teresa and Drew's relationship ended. He had gone back to his fiancé. Once again Teresa's heart had been ripped out of her chest and kicked around.

Since they worked at the same place, rumors began to fly and Teresa withdrew behind her brick wall of protection. It was difficult for her to see Drew every day and maintain a respectful distance. "Everyone knows," she said to him one afternoon as he collected his pay.

"I can't help it," he replied. "It's the way things have to be."

Teresa thought she could possibly find some peace at home; but Andrea had other ideas. Her constant questions and comments about Drew and their relationship began to wear thin. "Leave me alone," Teresa would ask her mother, but the woman refused.

"Why did he leave? What's wrong with him? What's the matter with you?" she would say to her daughter.

Teresa tried to explain to silence her mother, but she soon learned silence was impossible. Not able to bare the badgering from her mother and constant stares and whispers at work, Teresa withdrew even farther.

Drew's stepbrother, Dennis, worked at the same factory, and he was aware of the growing sadness in Teresa. He took her out for lunch and together they talked and eased their own burdens.

"It's nice to have someone to talk with," she said to Dennis.

"It is," he replied. "You always make me feel better."

The two grew as friends. Then he found proof of his wife's infidelity. "Last week I had to take her to emergency," he said to Teresa. "Apparently she suffered a miscarriage. I didn't even know she was pregnant!"

Shocked and full of compassion for her friend, she let him continue.

"When I asked her about the pregnancy, she told me it didn't matter because it wasn't mine anyway!" The man had been betrayed by his wife. Teresa offered him as much compassion and comfort as she could. To her surprise, she began to develop strong feelings for Dennis.

The two were pulled together by loss, and felt comfort in each other. Something they both needed desperately.

"But he's a married man!" her mother screeched at her.

"He's left her and getting a divorce," Teresa snapped at her mother. "Mind your business! I'm old enough to make up my own mind."

"I'm moving out of here!" she told her mother. "We are getting an apartment together."

"You'll be sorry," her mother screamed. "I'm co-signer on your car loan," she yelled, desperately trying to get her daughter's attention. "I'll call in the loan."

"Go ahead," Teresa replied. "I'll stop paying and you will be stuck with the debt." She smiled as her arrow made a direct hit. The air was let out of her mother's attitude. "I've finally won!" Teresa thought.

The next week she packed her belongings and moved out of her parent's house for good.

A massive weight lifted from her heart. ***"You will never win over me again,"*** she said as she walked away from the house that held her ghosts captive.

Is the Grass Greener on the Other Side of the Fence

Teresa was thrilled and excited at the prospect of being with Dennis. Together they made plans and spent hours talking, walking on beaches and sharing.

"I have to get free of her, and I want to marry you," he told Teresa.

"I know and I'll help," she replied.

Quickly they set up their apartment. Teresa bought furniture and other necessary items to create a home. Dennis' contribution to their home was one small brass picture and his car. He gave his soon to be ex-wife everything else. "If I give her everything, then maybe she'll go away easier," he said to Teresa.

Blinded by what she believed was love, Teresa accepted him as is.

They worked hard at building a life for themselves. Teresa left her present job to manage an office for a company that expanded from Toronto. She could help build this location from the ground up. It was exciting. Dennis worked endless hours a day doing service work. Together the couple worked hard and managed to pay his wife support and hire a lawyer.

Late that summer Teresa discovered she was pregnant. One Saturday evening while visiting friends, Teresa was told about a great gynecologist. He had delivered her three children and Angie trusted him. Teresa made an appointment the following week.

A month later they visited their friends again. Dennis and Sam were soon heavily into an alcoholic adventure. Sam made his own moonshine and was eager to share with Dennis.

Teresa had been feeling unwell most of the day and by 11 pm she had a splitting headache. Angie told Dennis to take Teresa home. By this time, he had drunk so much he appeared sober.

Getting into his precious hot rod, Teresa kept with window down for fresh air. She was nauseated and she felt as though someone was taking a hammer to her head.

Half way home she became violently ill. "Pull over," she screamed at Dennis.

"What?" he asked.

"Pull over NOW! I'm going to be sick!" she screamed.

"Just wait," was his reply.

She couldn't wait. Hanging her head out the window, Teresa vomited. He knew what she was doing, but still didn't stop the car. Bringing her head back in and sitting down, Teresa laid her head back.

"Thanks," she said. He didn't respond.

Late that night while he lay snoring, Teresa sat on the couch in their living room crying. She was bleeding heavily and knew in her heart she had lost her first child. "How can he sleep?" she wondered. "Doesn't he care?"

She curled up on the couch and cried herself to sleep.

The next morning, she was awakened by Dennis. "Did you know you threw up all down the side of the car?" he screamed at her. "It dried on and it could ruin the paint job."

With a blank stare, she looked at him. "I lost the baby," she whispered as tears were hanging on the edge of her eye lids and threatened to spill over.

"Sorry, but I have to go wash the car." He walked outside and she didn't see him again for hours.

"Obviously he doesn't care about the baby or me," she said to the vacant room. "Maybe I'm being oversensitive about it."

After visiting with her doctor and having the usual D & C performed, Teresa tried to carry on with life. Her job was horrible and she hated the place. The owner's wife was angry at Teresa, she had wanted the job but her husband refused. Several months into the job, Teresa would have gladly given the wife the job. It was boring and she didn't like the owner.

Teresa and Dennis decided to move out of the apartment and into the country. They rented an old farm house with a dirt cellar that gave her nightmares. She went in the room once and quickly ran back up the old swaying steps. Teresa envisioned this room as a prison. Thoughts of going into the cellar scared her to the point where she wasn't able to breathe. She always kept the door bolted. Late at night she could hear scratching on the wooden door. She liked the rest of the house, but that room terrified her. When Dennis had to go away on business, she would leave the lights on in that area, in an effort to ward off any evil spirits.

While Dennis was on a business trip the following summer, Teresa heard the scratching coming from the cellar door area. Then she noticed a hole in the door sill. "Something is trying to get out!" she told a friend.

"It's probably just a rat," she said. That terrified her even more.

Teresa had quit her office job and reverted back to the back-breaking work of tobacco. She was 20 years old and stronger than she had ever been. "I can do tobacco," she told her grandmother one day on a visit.

After talking to the farmer one afternoon, he gave her some poison to try to kill whatever was trying to get through the floor. She had no idea what she was doing, but Dennis was gone and she had to try. She soaked a piece of meat in the chemical for 24 hours. Later that night before going to bed, she placed the piece of meat, now white, on the edge of the hole. The next morning the meat was gone, and to her joy, she never heard the scratching again.

Happy that Dennis was to return the following week, they planned a barbecue for his crew of service men. The day of the barbecue, Teresa worked like a slave scrubbing, cooking and making sure everything was perfect for their guests.

It was a beautiful summer day, with a warm breeze blowing across the fields around their house. The big willow tree in back shaded the harvest and main kitchens, which helped to keep these two rooms cooler. As their best friend Eddie arrived, they noticed he brought a date with him. She seemed like a nice young girl but something about her didn't sit well with Teresa.

Dennis was out back working on his car and the barbecue, and this is where Eddie's date ended up. "I'll take him out a beer," the girl offered.

"Thanks," Teresa replied.

Teresa and Eddie chatted away in the kitchen while she made last minute food preparations. "Oh, I forgot salad dressing!" Teresa announced. "I'm going to run into town and get some, Eddie," she said. "I'll be right back."

"I'll keep an eye on things," he told her.

Twenty minutes later when she returned to the house, Eddie was outside in the back maintaining the charcoal for the barbecue. "What's going on?" Teresa asked as she got out of her car.

"Don't go in just yet," Eddie said.

"Why?" she asked, as alarm bells went off in her head. "What's going on in there?"

"Oh, nothing," he replied, trying to be casual about the situation. "Just don't go in yet."

Now very alarmed, Teresa marched past Eddie into the house. She stormed through the back harvest kitchen and as she stepped into the main kitchen she froze in terror. There sat her man on a kitchen chair and on his lap was Eddie's date. The two were in an embrace and he was kissing her shoulder.

"What is going on in here!" Teresa screamed. Surprised, the girl jumped off Dennis' lap and dashed outside. **"What are you doing?"** she asked her fiancé.

"She was upset about something and I was comforting her," was his reply.

"I saw what you were doing," she shrieked.

"Pull yourself together," he said. "We have people arriving." With that said, Dennis stood up and walked outside to meet his friends.

Not wanting to cause a scene, Teresa grabbed a drink and walked outside. She went directly to Eddie and said, "Why didn't you tell me?"

He lowered his eyes and said to his friend, "I couldn't."

Immediately after dinner, the young girl requested to be taken home. While saying goodbye to her guests, Teresa found the girl was unable to meet her gaze. "Don't ever come back here!" Teresa told her, then turned to give Eddie a hug goodbye.

"She won't come back," Eddie assured Teresa. "We're finished."

Later that night after everyone had gone home and she had cleaned up the mess she approached Dennis. He sat in the living room watching television and recovering from the party. "What were you doing with her?" Teresa asked demanding an answer.

"Nothing," came the reply.

Teresa stormed into the bedroom, slamming the door behind herself. Obviously he didn't want to answer her. Inside she fought with herself not to keep after him to extract an answer. It's what she'd seen her mother do all her life. Her own anger flared. Leaving the bedroom, she once again faced him.

As she stood and challenged him, she was unaware that his own anger was building. When she did see it, it was too late. She ran into the bedroom and slammed the door. He burst into the room and grabbed her roughly by the arm. Refusing to acknowledge the pain she felt, she reverted back into herself. She stood behind her inner emotional wall that she immediately built during these types of situations, in order to protect herself. He continued to yell at her as he shook her arm.

"It's none of your business what I was doing," he sneered at her. Then he threw Teresa across the room. She fell over the bed and onto the floor on the other side of the bed. She let out one scream as her spine collided with the door handle from her own dresser. Unable to move for a moment she sat trying to recover. Dennis walked away leaving her there on the floor; alone.

Sometime later Teresa crawled back onto the bed. She tried to stretch out to help her back from seizing up. She had to work the next day on the tying machine and needed to get some sleep. After a while, emotional exhaustion too over and she was able to finally sleep.

Many times she thought about leaving him. "And go where?" she wondered. "I won't go back home and I don't have any money left after paying for his divorce lawyer. I'm trapped. I'll just have to learn to make the best of it. "

That winter they decided to set their wedding date. They gave themselves ten months to make arrangements. "Hopefully she will have signed the divorce papers by then," he told her. As time approached, Teresa was busy working in tobacco again, planning the wedding and packing up their belongings. Dennis decided with his father's help that they should move closer to him. That way the two could have more time to work on a business venture together.

Teresa dreaded the idea of moving away from the town she'd grown up in. Over time she had discovered how possessive and demanding his father could be and knew his children when ordered to 'jump,' did so, on demand.

Her voice was unheard by her fiancé and she didn't have the energy to fight him right now. During harvest, she packed, planned and worked long hot days. Her few relaxing moments were in the six-foot-long claw foot tub she soaked her aching body in every day after work. Teresa had a terrifying moment one afternoon when she relaxed too much and fell asleep in the tub. Startled awake suddenly, she found herself underwater. Frantically she surfaced and started breathing again. "No one would have found me," she thought. Dennis was away again on service work. That frightening moment was one she would always remember.

With their wedding date soon approaching, at the end of September, a moving date of September 1st and working, they both were running on little energy.

After the harvest was over, and they had successfully moved, the farmer gave a party in celebration and thanks to his people for a job well done. Teresa and Dennis attended the dinner and sat around with her co-workers and enjoyed a few beers after the delicious European meal. Everyone was having a great time. Moods were happy and talk was great. Teresa was enjoying a very much needed break from stress. She was relaxed and happy. Then she spotted her fiancé passed out cold in the corner. Embarrassment struck her hard. The others were laughing and teasing her. Completely ashamed that he would get that drunk in the first place, Teresa quietly asked two of the large boys to help carry him to the car. Dennis was a big man and it wasn't going to be easy. It took three of them to get him into the passenger side of the car. Wishing her well on getting him out once they got home, her friends bid her good night.

Teresa was struggling to control her temper. As she drove off she nudged him. He woke and asked what she wanted. "How could you embarrass me like that?" she asked. Dennis mumbled something incoherent and turned towards the window.

"I asked you a question," she said louder.

"Shut up!" he yelled back at her.

"No!" she said sternly. "This is twice you've embarrassed me because of your drinking."

"I said, SHUT UP!" he repeated. Before she could answer, something hit her across the face. Slamming on the brakes of her Camaro, she froze. He had just back-handed her across the face! She was blinded by pain as his hand smashed into the bridge of her nose. It felt as though she had been hit by lightening. Her face hurt and it took a few minutes for her vision to return. Tears poured out of her eyes as much from the hit as from the hurt in her heart.

"How could you do that?" she asked when she could speak.

"Just shut up and drive home," he snarled at her.

Teresa was glad it was dark out. No one could see what happened or her shame. Quickly she put her car back into gear and drove home.

Once there she turned off the car and walked into the house. "He can stay out there for all I care right now," she said to the empty house.

But he didn't stay in the car. Slowly he walked into the house and up the steps into the kitchen. Teresa was pouring a glass of water. She wanted a drink and an ice pack for her face. The throbbing of her nose was one thing but a massive headache was building.

He stormed up behind her and grabbed her spinning Teresa around. Their argument continued. It ended with Dennis throwing his right fist directly at her face. Her reflexes were sharper than his and she ducked as his fist connected with the plywood cupboard door. Afraid of him now, Teresa ran to the other side of the room. The cupboard door bounced off its hinges and crashed into the sink with a noise like thunder. There he stood holding his hand dumbfounded at his own stupidity.

Terrified of being in the same room, Teresa ran to the bedroom and locked the door. He made no attempt to get to her. Three hours later he knocked on the door and timidly asked her to come out. "I need your help," he begged.

Emerging from the bedroom, Teresa saw him sitting in the living room with his hand buried deep in an ice pack. "I'm so sorry," he said to her. "Can you drive me to the hospital? I think I broke my hand."

She felt bad believing she had played a part in this mess.

Getting back into the car she drove him the 10 miles to the hospital. She desperately needed her nose taken care of but was too afraid to ask for help. Teresa remained quiet and the verdict returned that Dennis had broken his hand and they would need to cast it.

"Now what?" she asked him when they returned home. "Fifteen days before our wedding and this happens."

Knowing she truly had no where else to go and no one to turn to, Teresa resigned herself to marry him. They almost didn't get married though, he still was not divorced.

One week before their wedding date, Dennis' lawyer laid pressure on the ex-wife to sign the paperwork. Her lawyer pushed as well, and finally she signed. "I'm free of her," Dennis said. "Now we can get married," he said to Teresa. It wasn't going to be that simple. Dennis' mother, who had remained silent all this time, now spoke. She didn't want this marriage to happen.

Returning home one afternoon, Teresa found her fiancé and his mother sitting in the house. It was obvious by their stern faces and the silence that the two had been having a heated discussion.

After his mother left, Dennis said to Teresa, "She was trying to talk me out of marrying you."

"What? Why?" Teresa asked as her tone of voice increased.

"She doesn't think you're good enough for me," he commented. "But I don't care," he continued. "I told her to mind her own business."

Teresa's heart sank. "What did I ever do to her?" she asked, not expecting a reply. "Is this what I'm walking into?" Unable to sleep that night, Teresa began wondering at his words, "She doesn't think you're good enough for me." She wondered if that statement had something to do with the horribly embarrassing stories about her family. "Is this to do with the incest stories? Will I ever be able to escape that cloud?"

She cried herself to sleep at the injustice of her life.

The Wedding Day

The day of the wedding had finally arrived. Teresa had spent the night at her parent's home, in an effort to follow some sort of tradition. The downside to this was the two step-grandchildren her soon to be father-in-law forced on her as attendants. Edith insisted her grandchildren participate in the wedding party, which meant when Dennis was instructed by his father, Teresa had no choice. She didn't care to fight with them anymore.

Early that morning, Teresa and Andrea went to the hairstylist, which luckily was next door. Now with that out of the way she could take her time to apply her makeup, have lunch and get dressed. Despite her mother's nagging, Teresa attempted to enjoy the day. Her best friend had returned home the day before to be her matron of honour. They hadn't seen each other in about two years, and the two girls got lost in conversation and laughs.

Soon it was time to leave for the church, the church that shouldn't have been. Teresa and Dennis had decided they wanted to be married outside on his father's lawn. All of the wedding plans were made accordingly. The night before the wedding it had rained, so his father deemed, "the wedding cannot take place outside."

Teresa was furious. All their plans were made, she had the train of her dress lined with a soft plastic to avoid grass stains, but when the two tried to stand their ground, his father refused to allow the wedding on his property. "He's had this planned the entire time," Teresa thought to herself.

Luckily there was a quaint little church in the village where they lived. The ministers who were set to perform the service outside for the couple, quickly changed the venue.

"It's supposed to be **our** day," she said to Dennis showing her great disappointment. "What gives him the right to dictate our day?"

"He's just trying to help," Dennis responded. By the way he talked, Teresa knew she was walking on delicate ground. This wasn't the first time his father and Edith had interfered in their wedding plans. Edith ran wild with ideas during her drinking bouts. Then she would convince her husband that her ideas were sound. At night, he would call Dennis on the phone and demand an audience, usually managing to convince his son to see things "his way."

The ceremony turned out well despite the interference. They all delighted in the traditional Hungarian dinner that was served afterward consisting of chicken soup, breaded chicken and schnitzel, salad and potatoes. Later that evening at the hall where the reception was held, they greeted their guests separately. Some found it odd how the newlyweds stayed apart. Teresa was tired of fielding questions about the cast on Dennis' hand. "Oh he had an accident," she would say. "But how? What happened," people would ask her repeatedly, teasing her and demanding the truth. Finally, sick of lying she said, "He punched the cupboard door." Instantly the person asking the question stopped speaking. They didn't know what to say after that. Now silenced, Teresa would turn to chat with another guest.

The evening continued and the dancing began. Teresa loved to dance and was kept busy for quite some time. Finally, in desperate need of a drink, she excused herself and went to the bar and ordered a glass of wine. Spotting her new husband in the throws of a deep and serious conversation with his father, she thought she would go over and rescue him. Walking silently up behind the two men, she took a drink of wine soothing her parched throat. What she heard almost caused her to choke. The words she heard from her new father-in-law speak alarmed her and sent a chill down her spine.

"Now that you've married her, take everything out of her name and don't give her any money," she heard him say. "It's what I did to Edith," he said. "I give her an allowance every week and she gets nothing extra if she runs out."

Devastated by his words and not wishing to cause a scene on her own wedding day, Teresa turned and walked away feeling as if her heart had been ripped out of her chest. Walking over to the table where her close friend, Fred, sat with his wife, Teresa pulled out a chair and dropped down on it, causing her wedding gown to billow out as she dropped.

"What's wrong T?" he asked her using the nickname he always called her.

After Teresa told him what she had overheard, she looked at her friend and fought back the tears that threatened. "He didn't even defend himself or me," Teresa said. "It looked as if Dennis thought it was a good idea!" she said while trying to hold herself together. "Is this what its going to be like?" she asked, not expecting an answer.

Her friend tried to console her. Fred felt bad for her. He knew Dennis and his family and had heard stories that the old man was overbearing, always demanding the respect of everyone even though it was never deserved. Fred knew of the struggles Teresa had tolerated with Dennis up to this point and had always done his best to support his friend.

"Chin up sweetie," he said.

"I know," she replied. "It's too late now, but I have a feeling that I'm going to have a fight on my hands if his father doesn't stay out of our lives."

Teresa wasn't aware at the time of how this statement would haunt her future and almost destroy her marriage.

The Situation as it Stands After the Wedding

The newlywed couple went on a short vacation before resuming their lives as married people. Two months later they received news that Dennis' grandparents were involved in a severe motor crash while driving to their home in the southern United States.

"Your grandfather was killed instantly and your grandmother is fighting for her life in a hospital," his father told Dennis. "We are flying down to take care of her."

Dennis was broadsided by the news. Two weeks earlier, he and Teresa went to dinner with the grandparents and wished them a good winter. For years they spent every winter in the south as many older Canadians did.

Unable to speak after receiving the news, Dennis sat in a daze. Nothing Teresa said could penetrate his armor. He idolized his grandfather and now the man he admired and loved deeply was gone forever. Teresa also felt the sting of mourning. She had grown very fond of the older couple.

With his grandfather gone, Dennis floundered with his grief. It was obvious to Teresa that he was ill-equipped to deal with it. He withdrew from everyone.

Going through the motions of existence, Dennis attended his beloved grandfather's funeral. Teresa tried her best to support her husband through the difficult time.

Several weeks after the funeral Teresa sat with Dennis after dinner and said to him, "I'm pregnant."

Stunned, he sat and stared at her.

She repeated, "I'm pregnant."

Finally, the words penetrated and he smiled. "I bet it's a boy," he said with a touch of arrogance.

"Why do you say that?" she asked.

"Because of my grandfather," he replied. "I think when one prominent family member dies; another comes along to take his place."

Teresa thought this made sense. "The timing is perfect," she replied. Then she thought to herself, "obviously the news has helped him with his grief, so let him believe what he wants."

Time passed and both families were excited about the baby news. Dennis' grandmother had returned back to Canada and now lay in the hospital recovering. She had been so seriously injured, she had not been expected to live. However, this was one strong woman. After several reconstructive surgeries to her legs and one arm, she was able to walk out of the hospital later that spring.

The summer was hot and Teresa was suffering from the heat. Very heavy with child, she cleaned the house, cooked, canned and grew a huge vegetable garden. She was determined to make all of her own baby food for her child, wishing to give her child the best possible start to life.

Now making do with only one income, the couple began to struggle slightly. Trying her best to help out, Teresa cleaned up her old sewing machine and made most of her own maternity clothes. She enjoyed sewing and felt the satisfaction of a job well done.

Dennis worked countless hours still doing the service work that took him all over North America. Left at home with all the responsibilities, Teresa continued to cut the three-quarter acre property on a run-down old riding lawnmower Dennis' father had sold them. Teresa hated the machine. "It's a piece of junk," she told her husband. "Every time I change gear; the drive belt falls off."

"Come outside and I'll show you how to fix it," was his answer to her.

Now angry with him, she went outside and learned to put the belt back on. "Just lift up the mower and stand it on its end," he told her as he demonstrated. "Here's where the belt goes back. Then you just set the machine back down on the four wheels.

"Thanks," she snarled at him and walked back into the house.

They began taking prenatal classes in preparation for the birth. "This is stupid," he said to her. After four classes he refused to go again.

"Thanks again," she said to him.

One month before her delivery date, Teresa decided they should wash the windows in the house. Together they began the task. The young couple was having a good day together. No one was around to bother them, so they turned up the stereo and danced along to their favourite music as they scrubbed.

It was a blistering hot day but the breeze blowing through the house made it tolerable. For the first time in a while they were happy again and together they had accomplished half of the windows in the house.

Then the phone rang.

"Don't answer it," she begged. Earlier she had a premonition his father would interrupt them by calling court into session. When his father, the king of the family called, her husband jumped. Everything else took a back seat to this man. "Please," she begged again.

But he walked over and picked up the receiver. Her hopes of a great day crashed and burned. Then she heard the common phrase from her husband: "I'll be right there."

Teresa knew their day together was over. "What does he want?" she asked.

"He just wants to talk over some things with me," Dennis replied. "I should be back in an hour. I'll help you finish then."

Taking the only car she could easily drive, he drove off to his father's home.

Teresa was angry. These calls from his father was becoming a weekly habit. He always called at the worst possible times, and her husband seemed incapable of speaking up to the man. Two hours later he still hadn't returned. Now boiling mad, Teresa used her anger to finish washing the windows. Then she cleaned the house and washed and waxed the kitchen floor. By the time she finished her husband still wasn't home. She tried calling her father-in-law's house but the line was busy.

Steaming, she grabbed the keys to his precious hot rod. She hated driving the beast. He had the clutch set so tight even his leg trembled at a stoplight. It didn't matter. Teresa was determined to go over and demand her husband return home.

Only laying a bit of rubber on the road, more out of spite than incompetence, she rolled into the old man's driveway. Climbing out of the car, she took a couple of minutes to stretch out her back. It had been causing her some trouble lately. Turning to walk towards the house she saw the two men sitting on the back deck; their feet on the railing and a beer in their hands.

"What are you doing here?" her father-in-law asked her.

"I've come to ask your son to help finish the job we started earlier today," she replied back with full sarcasm.

"He'll be there when we are done," came the older man's comment.

She noticed her husband kept silent. Defying her father-in-law, Teresa pulled her very pregnant body onto the deck and said, "I'm tired. I think I'll wait here until he is ready and he can drive the beast home." Her husband looked at her in shame but her father-in-law's glare shot daggers at her. She knew no one ever spoke up to him; however, she wasn't about to comply.

Shortly after she sat down, his father decided their 'meeting' had come to an end. Now as darkness was about to fall, the young couple finally returned home.

"What did he want?" she asked almost losing her patience with her husband.

"Nothing really," she replied. "He just wanted to talk."

"He just wanted to talk, and you left me with all that work!" she said raising her voice to him. ***"I struggle because I'm carrying your child and he just wanted to talk!"*** she yelled. ***"That WAS more important than ME right now! How could you,"*** she said before falling silent for the rest of the night.

Beyond angry with him, she found she was unable to speak. "It's probably safer that way" she thought to herself. Day by day she was slowly losing respect for her husband. He appeared to be timid as a little boy unable to speak up to his father. "Maybe if he spent more time watching over his drunken wife, he wouldn't have so much spare time to bother us," she believed.

Without looking at her husband, she got out of the vehicle and walked into the house.

He had nothing to say. The shame that washed over him spoke volumes.

The Special Delivery

Teresa was past her due date and found the sixty pounds she had gained during her pregnancy very draining. She went to bed late one night and struggled to find rest. The baby was large and the movements hurt.

Suddenly just after 1:00 a.m., Teresa snapped awake and felt something pop. Moving with the grace of a panther, she leapt from the bed and ran to the bathroom. Her water broke. Luckily she managed to get to the bathroom before she lost any water.

Now sitting there wondering when the water would stop, she cried out for her husband. **"Dennis, help!"** she screamed. ***"My water broke."*** His response to her was loud snoring.

Teresa sat there for quite a while waiting for the strong flow to slow. After about twenty minutes she stood up and pulled a bath towel between her legs. She noticed she had passed the plug when her water broke and knew she needed to get to the hospital.

Still unable to rouse her husband she walked to the kitchen and called the hospital. "I'll be there in about thirty minutes," she told the maternity department.

Back in the bedroom, she tried again to wake him. "Dennis, get up!" she said sternly. "My water broke and we have to get to the hospital NOW!"

He grunted at her and rolled over. Suddenly grabbed by her first labour pain, Teresa doubled over onto the bed. The stabbing pain in her low back migrated and wrapped around her lower abdomen. It took a few minutes for her to catch her breath. She tried again. **"Dennis!"** she yelled as she forcibly smacked him on the behind. ***"GET UP! I need you!"***

This time he woke up. "What's going on?" he asked.

"I have to get to the hospital," she told him urgently. "My water broke about half an hour ago."

Finally he understood and got up. Quickly dressing and grabbing her suitcase they went out to the car. "We have to take the hot rod," he said.

"I've brought an extra towel to sit on," she said. She knew his car was precious to him. At times it appeared the car meant more to him than she did.

"Never mind the towel," he told her. "I've brought a garbage bag for you to sit on. I don't want you getting the seats dirty. If you mess on them, I would have to have the upholstery cleaned."

Staring at him in disbelief, she walked around to her side of the car and placed the garbage bag and the towel on the seat. Positioning herself carefully on the seat Teresa prepared herself for the long journey she was about to face.

Once she arrived at the hospital, Teresa was taken to her room and connected to the usual equipment. The nurses were taking good care of her.

"Do you want the epidural?" they asked.

"No," she replied. "I want to try without."

Several hours later her doctor came in to see her. He always made her smile with some joke or smart comment. "Things aren't moving along as well as I'd hoped," he told her. "Your pains are close together, but you aren't dilating enough. I'm going to insert a lead onto the baby. It will tell us if the baby can handle a long labour," he explained. "I won't let you have a dry delivery," he said. "Also I'm going to begin an I.V. drip to induce you."

"Thanks, Dr. Lawrence," Teresa said.

"Let us know if you want the epidural," Dr. Lawrence said before he left. "Try to get some rest, honey."

She smiled at him.

Dennis left the room to call his work to let them know he wouldn't be there that day. When he came back he sat in the chair watching his wife. He was angry because the chair wasn't made for a tall man and he was unable to get comfortable to sleep.

Teresa did her best to focus during her contractions without the support of her spouse. She utilized the breathing techniques she had learned but the pains were very intense and long. As she laid in the bed working through the horrible pains of labour, she remembered the other couples from their pre-natal classes. The other men showed genuine concern for their wives as they rubbed their backs or arms and spoke soothingly to their wives. The kindness they showed for their partners impacted Teresa greatly. "Why won't he help me?" she wondered.

Her pain was intensifying and after fifteen hours of intense labour, she lost her control of her focus and asked for the epidural.

As the doctor came in to perform the procedure, Dennis took the opportunity to once again complain he was tired and couldn't get comfortable. Dr. Lawrence looked at him in disgust and said, "I think you should concentrate on helping your wife." That comment silenced Dennis.

Having already been awake for thirty-nine hours with an unknown number to go; fatigue owned her. The relief Teresa felt with the epidural allowed her to finally sleep. She succumbed to several cat naps. Each time she fell asleep a technician or nurse would come in and check on her, waking her up. "Please," she begged. "I'm exhausted."

Dr. Lawrence kept a close eye on Teresa. He knew the history of her mother and the stillbirths she had suffered. He assured Teresa she and her baby would be fine. After examining her twenty hours into her labour, he said to her, "You still aren't dilating well." "I will let you go to twenty-four hours and then I insist on a caesarian section."

"What? Why?" she asked. They hadn't talked about this before.

"Something may be preventing the baby from delivering vaginally," he explained. "I won't run the risk of anything happening to the baby."

"If that's what you think is best," she said to him, trusting his judgement.

"A C-section will be fine," he told her. "But now that I've said that, I'm confident you will deliver sooner." He patted her hand and gave her his best smile. "Get some rest now," he said, and he left the room.

Exhaustion washed over her and she slept.

Twenty-two hours into her labour Dr. Lawrence returned. Smiling and winking at Teresa he said, "Are you still here?", he joked.

She laughed and replied, "Yes, they won't let me get up. They have me wired for sound," she commented. "I bet I could dial in a radio station," she said as she giggled indicating all the wires that were attached to her.

The doctor checked over the printouts from the various monitors and smiled at her again. "Everything looks fine. Shouldn't be too much longer. Sometimes the babies decide to show up rather suddenly."

"I hope so," she replied.

A very short time later the doctor and his team entered Teresa's room. "You're ready," he said to her. "We will be taking you into the delivery room now." Then he turned to Dennis and said, "If you are coming in with her you need to suit up." A nurse took Dennis to the change room where he put on the sterile clothing and scrubbed his hands.

Now laying in the freezing cold delivery room Teresa absorbed every detail of the room. The nurses draped her, lifted her legs into the stirrups and made her as comfortable as possible. Dennis walked in the room with Dr. Lawrence. "Sit over there behind your wife and help her," the doctor ordered. Now in an unfamiliar domain, Dennis quickly obeyed and assumed his position at his wife's head.

Dr. Lawrence stood beside Teresa and said to her, "When I tell you to push, I want you to push as hard as you possibly can. It will feel odd because of the epidural, but you still have to do the work. Ok? Are you ready to go, girl?" he asked as his eyes lit up with a smile.

"Ready," Teresa said.

Dr. Lawrence took up his position and began his commands. Everyone took their orders and performed their tasks to perfection.

He lifted his eyes to Teresa and said, "Ok honey, **PUSH!**"

Teresa pushed as hard as she could.

"AGAIN!" he ordered.

Teresa put all her energy into this push. Then she heard, "Good girl. Wait, just breathe."

Resting for a moment she waited for her next instruction.

"Good girl," the doctor said to her as he patted her leg. "You have a baby boy! Congratulations!"

Tears flooded her eyes as the words sunk in. A boy...she had so desperately wanted a girl. She wanted the girl for herself and to prove Dennis wrong. He and her father had a bet going over the sex of the baby. Dennis insisted it would be a boy, because, "We only know how to make boys in my family," he told Edward. Now with the news of his son's birth, his father-in-law owed Dennis a case of beer.

Coming back down into the moment, Teresa was ordered to push again. The young woman gave up her last bit of strength. "Everything is good now," Dr. Lawrence said to her. "Stop now!"

Teresa felt so many emotions welling to the surface. She truly didn't know how to feel. All her life she'd heard motherhood and giving birth was such a beautiful event. Teresa found it painful, and brutal on her body.

Then she heard, "time of birth: 12:30 a.m." Twenty-three hours after her labour started she delivered her first child.

Cleaned up and back in her room, she had the pleasure of holding her baby for the first time. She cuddled him and gently kissed his forehead. Her heart felt an immediate connection to this little boy. "I love you," she whispered.

Dennis was off making the necessary phone calls to their parents. When he came back to see his wife he said, "Since we haven't eaten in a couple of days, I've ordered pizza for us, the nurses and doctor."

"I'm starving," Teresa said. She had not eaten in over two days.

The pizza arrived and everyone enjoyed the meal. Teresa had two bites of her piece and was unable to finish. "I can't eat," she told the nurse. "I just want to sleep."

During the night, the nurses woke her periodically to check on her pain levels. Teresa was unaware of most of what was said.

Early the next morning, the nurses arrived demanding she get up and go to the bathroom. Teresa sat up on the edge of the bed and passed out. When she regained consciousness, the nurse demanded again that she get up. Determined, Teresa, with the nurse's assistance, managed to get to the bathroom. The minute she sat, she screamed out in pain. "What's the matter," the nurse asked rather impatiently.

"My bottom hurts," Teresa told her.

"That's normal," the nurse replied sarcastically. "You just had a baby." Then she walked away leaving Teresa alone.

Suddenly Teresa felt the energy draining out of her body. "I'm passing out again," she thought. Luckily she had the call button with her. She managed to press it before she lost consciousness.

Two nurses helped her get to bed. "My bottom hurts!" Teresa said again.

"You just had a baby, and you have some stitches. That's why you hurt," the nurse repeated.

Knowing it was more than that Teresa held her tongue for the moment. The pain she was feeling was more than just from childbirth.

Later that morning Dr. Lawrence arrived and sat on the bed beside her. "I can't sit," she told him. "My bottom hurts so much!" Tears were threatening to spill out of her eyes.

After examining Teresa, the doctor said, "It's no wonder you can't sit. Your tail bone is broken."

"How does that happen?" she asked.

"Your uterus is heart-shaped," he began. "It doesn't have enough force to push the baby out. When he decided he'd had enough, the baby came with such force that your tail bone snapped."

"Can it be fixed?" she inquired.

"Time is the only thing that will help," he told her. "You'll be ok but it will take a long time to heal and you will probably feel it for the rest of your life," he said to her before he left.

At least she had an answer.

Being unable to sit made it difficult for Teresa to nurse her baby. With help from the professionals, she managed to have some success.

Teresa began to regain her confidence. Until one afternoon when Dennis' family came to visit the new baby. Teresa and Dennis walked down the hall to meet them. "I thought you already had the baby," his step-mother said.

"You look like you're still pregnant!" she said laughing.

Completely crushed, Teresa turned around and walked away. After a few minutes her husband followed her.

"What's your problem?" he asked.

She had tears in her eyes when she looked at him. **"I'm still fat!"** she yelled. "I look horrible with the weight I gained, and I don't need her saying things like that."

"Well, Dad was upset that you left like that," he replied. "They came all this way to see you and you run off."

"I'm tired," she said. "I need to sleep." Teresa turned over cautiously and refused to speak to him. She had always had images issues. Always being told by others, "you're fat, you're big-boned, you're husky, you're a solid girl, you're ugly," was their way of saying she was large. Every time she heard this, the torturous words from her sister slapped her in the face.

"I at least thought my own husband would support me," she thought. "I guess I was wrong."

Teresa knew there was a pecking order in his family according to her husband, and Dennis was a strong believer in the order of things. His father was on the top, followed in order of importance, by his wife, Dennis' sister, his mother, his brother, Dennis himself, the new baby, and somewhere down on the bottom of the list was Teresa.

As Teresa lay on her hospital bed completely crushed by her step-mother-in-law's comments and her husband's lack of a backbone, she knew she was in for trouble. At this moment she wasn't aware of just how much trouble was heading her way; who would cause the trouble and who would stand up for her. The 'happy' moments that a new baby brings to a family would soon be crushed.

Battle Lines Drawn in the Sand

They named their infant son Douglas. He was a large, and healthy baby weighing over 8 pounds and measured over twenty-one inches in length. Their new pediatrician, Dr. Atkinson checked Douglas over completely before Teresa and Dennis could take him home.

Dr. Atkinson said to Teresa, "Your baby was born with Infant Torticollis. I believe the baby was too large for you and he didn't have enough room. This can cause the baby's Sternocleidomastoid muscle, which runs from his ear to collar bone, to tighten and develop little knots in the muscle."

Dumbfounded by this news, Teresa stared at the doctor. "What can we do?" she asked.

"I'll show you some stretches and exercises you must do every day," he said. "Through massage and stretching and the application of moist heat, you should be able to stretch out the muscle." He showed Teresa what to do. Together they worked through a routine. Dr. Atkinson explained what could happen to her son if his neck didn't straighten. This news made Teresa all the more determined to help her baby.

On Saturday, she said goodbye to the hospital staff as they took their little boy home. "Here is a number you can call if you need any help," the nurse offered.

Thankful for the support, Teresa gingerly got into the car. It was an extremely painful ride home for her. Because she was nursing, she was not allowed anything for pain. Her broken tailbone was going to make life VERY difficult.

Walking into her home made her feel better. She attempted to sit on each chair in the house, but sitting was impossible. Dennis bought her a small inner tube to sit on but again, the pressure was unbearable.

"Go lay down while I make dinner," he told her. "Your parents are on their way over."

"Why?" she asked.

"Your mother is going to stay for a week and help you," he told her.

"What!" Teresa asked stunned by his comments.

"I have to go away early Monday morning for a week," he replied. "I have to go out East for a service call."

"But you were supposed to take a week off to help me," she said. "We just brought the baby home!" Teresa yelled. "My tail bone is broken and you promised you would help!"

"I can't help it," he replied. "They asked if I would go and I said yes."

"You had the choice!" she screamed.

"I need to go and do this," Dennis replied lowering his eyes.

"Your place is here with me," she told him sternly. "But I know where I stand."

Her parents soon arrived and were introduced to their grandson. Edward's dreams of holding his own son never came to pass, but through his daughter, he could have his dreams fulfilled.

Everyone ate their dinner at the table, except Teresa. She laid down on the living room and ate her spaghetti dinner. It was impossible for her to sit or stand for very long. Teresa was still able to breastfeed her son by laying down on the bed with him. It was quality time the two spent alone. She demanded no one be in the room with her, not even her husband.

Edward went home and Dennis left for his trip. Teresa was beside herself with anger that he had made this choice.

She felt strong enough to get through this week with her mother's help, if everyone else kept their distance.

Soon Teresa and her little one had developed a routine. Andrea was there to help with cooking, laundry and cleaning if needed. "She's actually being a great help to me," Teresa thought with great surprise.

After a couple of days, Teresa was gaining in confidence as a new mother. Then Wednesday afternoon she had an uninvited guest.

Teresa was in her bedroom with her baby, nursing. The door was closed as was her routine when feeding. Suddenly to her surprise the door burst open and there stood her step-mother-in-law. She stood there watching Teresa. The look on her face told the younger woman she had been into her bottle already. Then the smell drifted over towards Teresa and she cringed.

"What do you want Edith," Teresa asked.

"Nothing," came the slurred response.

"Then will you please go out and let me finish," Teresa asked. Dennis had warned her to be nice to the woman, because his father expected it.

Edith refused to leave. "I'm fine," she said. "I'll just watch."

"Please don't," Teresa said in a stronger tone. "I always feed him in private."

"I don't mind," Edith replied.

Now the baby started to fuss and stopped feeding.

"Oh, let me hold him," Edith said as she stumbled towards the bed.

"NO! I don't think so," Teresa remarked. "I would prefer it if you left now."

"But I'm here to help," she repeated.

"If I need anything I will call you," Teresa commented. "My mother is here and that is all the help I want."

Still not understanding the statement through her drunken haze, Edith remained in the bedroom. Finally, tired of the woman, Teresa left her son on the big bed and stood up. She promptly ushered the woman out of the house. "If I need anything I will call you," she said sharply to Edith.

Thinking that was the end of her visits, Teresa went back to her son. She was upset and frustrated with the drunken woman. Her father-in-law was not at home this week, so Teresa knew Edith would be drunk most of the week.

The next day the same situation occurred. Edith showed up unannounced and demanded to hold the baby. "No," Teresa told her again. "You've been drinking."

Paying no attention, she once again attempted to remain in the house. Again, Teresa demanded she leave. "I'll call you if I need you for anything, Edith," she said closing the door on the woman.

Now noticeably upset and shaking with frustration, Teresa tried to be with her son. She bathed him, cuddled him and attempted to feed him. He wouldn't nurse. Teresa made another attempt an hour later. Again, he wouldn't feed. This continued on for a few hours. The baby was crying, and Teresa did her best, but nothing would stop his crying.

Finally, giving up she called the number the nurse had given her. "Try giving him a little water," she said. Then she went on to offer suggestions if the baby had gas.   Nothing worked.   Although he did sleep periodically, Teresa was a mass of tension.

When she tried to relax, Edith would call, causing upset again. "Why can't she just leave me alone!" Teresa said to Andrea.

The next day, Edith walked in the house again. Teresa wasn't aware Edith had a key. "What do you want?" Teresa demanded.

"Nothing," she said. "Just checking in."

Losing her patience completely with Edith, Teresa demanded her key and escorted her out of the door demanding she not return again.

"I'm his grandmother too," she said.

"NO, you are not!" Teresa yelled. **"You will never be his grandmother!"**

Returning to the kitchen, Teresa took a drink of water. She was shaking from frustration.

She spent a sleepless night with the baby. He still wasn't nursing and was only taking a bit of water. Once again she called the hospital for help. "I think you should take the baby to the doctor right away," the nurse told her. "He needs to be checked."

Teresa told Andrea what the nurse had said. "How am I supposed to get him there?" she asked. "I can't sit! Yes, I have the car, but you don't drive."

Determined as a mother lion to care for her infant, she bundled Douglas up and put him in the car. Andrea sat in the back seat with the baby and Teresa attempted to sit in the driver's seat. The pain she felt was beyond measure. It was like white-hot lightening going off in her brain. Ignoring the pain for now, she drove the twenty minutes to the doctor.

They were waiting for her and promptly showed her into the examination room. Soon their kindly old doctor entered the room. He examined the baby and said to Teresa, **"Your son is starving to death."**

"What!" she said, now in total shock.

"He must be placed on formula immediately," he said. "What's been happening?"

Teresa explained what had been going on since the baby's birth. Tears filled her eyes as she felt like a complete failure as a mother.

The doctor reassured her it wasn't her fault. "The woman should have stayed away. It was the stress that stopped the flow for you," he said. "I'll give you something to dry up and something for the tail bone pain.

He also gave her a case of formula. "You are in no shape to go out shopping," the doctor commented. "You look like you need some sleep."

Quickly Teresa went home where she Andrea mixed up the formula for the baby. Laying down beside her baby she offered him the bottle. He latched onto it greedily. She kissed his little forehead and cheek and said, "I'm so sorry little one. This isn't how it was supposed to be."

After the baby was content and put into his crib for a nap, Teresa went out into the living room. Sitting there with a smile on her face was Edith. Andrea was agitated by the woman's presence but remain silent.

"What are **you** doing here again?" Teresa said demanding an answer.

"On my way home and thought I would stop in," she said in her usual slurring, drunken tone.

"You are not welcome here!" Teresa said. "Go home and sleep it off Edith, and don't come back!"

Edith stood up and staggered to the door. She left in silence.

Teresa sat sideways on the couch and cried.

Two days later her husband arrived back on the doorstep. She was happy and relieved to see him, but also hoped he would understand what had happened.

As he ate lunch she told him everything that had occurred. Andrea verified every detail. "He believes me," Teresa thought with relief. "Maybe now things will change."

Then the phone rang.

"Yes," he answered. "I'll be right there."

Teresa knew it was his father calling. She had seen his pickup truck pull in his driveway two hours earlier. The call was inevitable.

"Why are you going?" she asked. "You just got home! Can't you spend any time with us?"

"I want to see what he has to say," Dennis replied.

Teresa paced the house and stood on pins and needles for two hours after he left. "What is going on over there?" she asked Andrea. "I don't trust them."

"I was here the entire time," her mother said. "I was witness to everything."

Feeling a bit calmer, Teresa tried to relax. "He will believe the truth," she said.

Three hours later Dennis returned to their house. His expression spoke volumes. He stood in front of his wife and said, "You were rude to Edith. She was only trying to help you."

"Pardon?" Teresa asked. "I didn't want her here and I asked politely the first few times."

"Dad told her to come every day and check up on you," he replied. "She said you were very rude to her and refused to let her hold the baby."

"What gave your father the right to do that?" Teresa yelled. "Why didn't he tell me? Why would I let a drunk woman who can't even stand hold my baby!"

"I know she drinks, but you should have been nicer to her," he said to his wife.

"You believe a drunk over your own wife!" Teresa said as she leveled her voice. ***"I have a witness!"***

"No one believes Andrea's word because she doesn't hear," was his response. "She could have made everything up in her mind."

"So you don't believe me?" she questioned.

"I think she was just trying to help and **you** should have been nicer to her," he shot back.

"What is going on here!" Teresa screamed. **"You hate the woman yourself, and now you are taking their side. You and the old man weren't even home!"**

This was the last straw for Teresa. A knife went into her chest and carved away some of the love she used to feel for her husband. What remained was a dead spot. Her father-in-law and his wife had interfered in her life enough. "They won't do that to my son!" she promised.

Then he dropped another bomb. "Dad wants us to go over and talk," he said. "He wants to see the baby and help you understand."

"I'll go, but she will not touch my baby!" Teresa threatened. "You cannot convince me this was my fault."

That evening she walked into her father-in-law's house. He looked at his grandson and smiled at the sleeping baby.

"I will put him in the living room where he can be left undisturbed," Teresa said, looking directly at Edith.

For the next two hours they badgered Teresa to conform to their version of the story. Even her husband had taken their side. Furious at all of them, Teresa demanded the car keys from her husband. "I'm taking my son home," she said. "I'm finished here." He refused to give them to her.

She walked into the living room and there sat her one-time boyfriend Mike (now her step-brother-in-law), playing with her son. He had heard everything.

"Drew," she said, "Will you please take us home. I really need to get out of here." Tears were starting to roll down her cheeks and she did the best to hide it.

"Yes, of course I will," he said.

Teresa collected her belongings, her baby and left the house.

Sometime later her husband arrived home. "That was very rude," he said to her.

"You need to decide who you are married to," Teresa said with determination in her voice. ***"THEM OR ME!* Make your decision now!"** she said and went into the bedroom and locked the door behind her. She and her baby cuddled together on the bed. "I'll protect you," she said to the sleeping baby. "I promise. I love you."

In Survival Mode

"We live in a world where most people still subscribe to the belief that shame is a good tool for keeping people in line. Not only is this wrong, but it's dangerous. Shame is highly correlated with addiction, violence, aggression, depression, eating disorders, and bullying."

Brené Brown,

The battle lines were now drawn in the sand. Teresa realized that Dennis didn't believe her. She was devastated that he would believe his drunken step-mother over his own wife. Teresa was losing respect and trust in her husband and she found with each incident, she lost a little more love for him too.

Reality was beginning to settle in. "I can't live here anymore," she said to him. "I have to get away from your family."

"What are you going to do?" he asked dumbfounded by her comments.

"I'm going to Delhi tomorrow and talk to grandma. Maybe she will help me," Teresa replied.

After Teresa had confided in Aline of the events since her marriage, the older woman looked at her granddaughter and said, "I told you not to marry him."

"I need your help grandma," Teresa asked again.

"I can buy a house here in Delhi," she told Teresa. "You can pick it out and if we agree, I'll buy it. You and your family can live in it and pay rent to me."

Teresa stood up and hugged her grandmother tightly. "I love you! Thank you!"

The plan was set in motion. They would have to scramble to find money.

One week after Dennis returned from his trip, he was laid off. His job suddenly ended. Teresa was unable to work and was panicking about their future.

Luckily his uncle was growing tobacco. He offered to hire Dennis to work in the strip room baling tobacco. He worked all winter for his uncle. In March of 1983 Teresa and her family moved into their new home in Delhi. It was a lovely three-bedroom home with a large backyard for Douglas to play in.

Dennis' father was furious that his daughter-in-law had out-maneuvered him. He wanted his son close. It was easier to manipulate him that way.

Life was good in their new home. Teresa scrubbed, painted, cleaned and cut the grass. She was more content than she had been in a while. Dennis returned to his service job and things were looking up for them.

That spring, Teresa decided to work in tobacco. She easily got a job working for a friend. She pulled plants in the morning, planted tobacco in the afternoon, came home, cooked, cleaned and took care of her son.

Suddenly they had a surprise house guest. Dennis' brother, Michael had arrived back from out west. He refused to stay with his father and Edith; his own mother shunned him because, "he is always a problem," so his brother, Dennis offered his house.

He had a loud and forceful personality and he carried on his shoulders, years of pain caused by the rejection of his parents.

Teresa and Dennis gave him their spare room, with the understanding that if he stayed he had to pay rent and buy food. He agreed.

Michael had a kind heart and played for endless hours with his nephew. They drove little cars across the floor, played with building blocks and read books together. Douglas was in love with his uncle. At eleven months old, a playful uncle was exactly what Douglas needed.

After planting time Teresa became ill. It was nothing she could put her finger on but she was feverish and lost all her strength. She slept all the time. Michael was quite concerned for her. The two spent a lot of time together around the house and developed a good friendship. It was a friendship built on true understanding of the pain each one carried in their heart, acceptance of their similar personalities and the love and respect they held for each other.

One evening, Michael made dinner for the family. He barbecued some steak and presented his hosts with a feast.

Teresa looked at the food and felt nothing. She'd had no appetite for days and was losing weight rapidly. Trying to eat, she took a few bites of meat but suffered excruciating pain when swallowing. The next day, her brother-in-law took Teresa to her doctor.

"You have a massive abscess on your tonsils," the Doctor told her. "We don't see this very often. It's called a Peritonsillar Abscess. It's an infection of the tonsils and creates a puss-filled pocket that can, if left untreated, block off your swallowing and breathing."

Overnight, Teresa had lost her voice, so she now wrote a note to the doctor. She handed the doctor the note which said, "My father had that when he was twenty-one. His burst."

"I will give you an injection of antibiotics now. Do you know a nurse?" he asked. Teresa nodded. "I will give you a kit to take to her. She must give you an injection every twelve hours."

Again Teresa nodded and accepted the kit.

For the next two days her friend Tammy gave her the required injections. It wasn't helping. Michael returned his sister-in-law to the doctor and demanded something be done. Teresa was now unable to move her jaw to open her mouth. The doctor gave her a freezie for her to suck on in hopes the cold would help take the swelling down. He looked at the young woman who could barely sit up anymore. "I'm putting you in the hospital," he commanded.

With Michael's help, she walked over to the hospital and was admitted. Immediately she was hooked to an I.V. The nurses came in with freezer packs to wrap around her throat and they pumped in the fluids. Teresa was very dehydrated. Tears ran down her cheek and onto the pillow. Her brother-in-law sat and held her hand. "It's ok T," he said. "You'll be fine."

Unable to even smile, she blinked her eyes at him in thanks.

The following day was Teresa's birthday. Michael brought her in a lovely birthday card. He was being so kind and was aware of his brother's lack of interest in his wife. Work mattered more to Dennis than his wife, and Michael grew angry with him. Dennis was beginning to act just like their father.

The nurses surprised Teresa with a small birthday cake. Tears spilled from her eyes at the beautiful gift. Still she was unable to eat, so she asked Michael to share it with the nurses.

Later than night, Teresa was in trauma. She rang the bell for the nurses. As they entered the room she immediately handed them a note that said, "*I CAN'T BREATHE!!!*"

Jumping into action they gave her an injection to help relax her. "Try to breathe slowly," they said as they placed ice packs around her throat. The doctor walked in the room. "Increase the drip of antibiotic," he commanded. "You are at a point where the abscess will either burst and shrink. Try your best to relax. We are here."

Terrified but trying her best, Teresa actually went to sleep. They had obviously given her something.

The next day when she woke, she felt better. Now able to move her jaw, she smiled at the nurses and whispered, "Thank you," to them. They smiled.

The abscess did not burst, spilling its poison throughout her system. It just merely shrank back into non-existence.

The next day she was allowed to go home. Once again, Dennis was too busy for her, so Michael came and picked up his sister-in-law and delivered her home. Douglas, still a toddler, was very excited to see his mommy. She had missed her little boy terribly.

Teresa grew stronger and soon was back at the usual; cooking, cleaning, caring and working routine her life had become. At the end of July harvest started. Back into the kiln-yard she went. She did her best but now she realized how much strength she had lost to her illness. Still not feeling 100%, she carried on.

As the harvest dragged on, the farmer's wife was chatting with Teresa one afternoon at lunch. She said to Teresa, "You don't look very well. Are you alright?"

"I'm just bone tired and very warm," she replied.

"You don't look very well. I think you should go to your doctor," her friend commented. "Go now," she said. "I'll finish the day for you."

"Thank you," Teresa replied and left for home.

As she took her bath to prepare for her doctor's appointment, Teresa noticed a large abscess on her left breast. "Where did that come from?" she asked herself.

After showing the lump to her doctor he said to her, "I'm going to call a specialist. You are to go to the emergency department at the hospital right now! That abscess needs to be drained."

Teresa didn't understand any of this. Yes, she felt unwell but she hadn't noticed the lump before. Then her doctor said in a stern voice, "You must have had a high fever at some point recently. **Didn't you know you were sick?"**

"I felt tired and warm," she replied. "But I've had so much to do with the baby, working, the house and yard. I thought I was just tired."

"It's about time your husband helped you," he said angrily. Teresa hung her head in shame. She knew he would never help.

Now the specialist was giving her the same comments she had received from her doctor. She was being chastised! "I have to lance it," he said. "It's an abscess in the milk duct. Obviously when you stopped nursing, you didn't dry up enough." He continued, "the milk sits in the duct, ferments and infection begins. Hopefully by draining it, things will settle down."

Alone, again, while facing another terrifying event, Teresa grabbed onto the bed rails in the E.R. The nurse came up to her and said, "It's alright Teresa. Let your grip go, you're white-knuckled." Releasing her grip slightly, she held her breath while the doctor injected freezing around her nipple. White pain shot into her brain and she gasped while trying not to move. Her hands were white from the grip, not just her knuckles.

"Ok," the surgeon said. "We'll wait a few minutes for the freezing to take hold and then we will start. As I said, I have to lance it and drain the infection. I will clean it out, but you must come back here every day for two weeks, weekends included, so we can remove the packing and clean out the wound."

"Alright," Teresa said. "What about working?" she asked.

"DO NOT GO BACK TO WORK!" he yelled at her. "You are not to lift anything, and you must keep this clean. I'm going to start now."

He turned back with the scalpel in his hands and began cutting.

"Oh my God!" Teresa screamed out.

"Hold still!" he shouted. **"I'm almost done. *DON'T MOVE!"***

The nurse came up beside Teresa and made eye contact. "Slow your breathing," she said. "It's almost over." She wiped the sweat from Teresa's forehead, which gave the young woman comfort.

"Ok, now we are going to drain the abscess and pack it," the doctor said.

After enduring twenty more minutes of torture, Teresa was a wreck. They packed the wound with gauze, covered it with more gauze and then proceeded to use white tape to hold the bandages in place. She had tape from her collar bone to her bottom rib; from her sternum to her mid-back.

"I don't react well to tape," she told the nurse. "Why did it hurt so much when I thought he froze the area?" Teresa asked.

"What the doctor didn't tell you was freezing doesn't usually take when there is serious infection," the nurse whispered.

Shocked and wide-eyed and what she just heard, Teresa replied, "He should have just told me the truth in the beginning."

"Sorry," the nurse said. "I'll see you tomorrow."

Completely numb emotionally from the events of the day, Teresa gingerly got behind the wheel of her car and drove herself home. Thank goodness Andrea was watching the baby.

When Dennis arrived home she showed and told him about her day. He seemed unconcerned. "You'll be fine," he said and went into the living room to watch television.

Teresa went to bed and cried herself to sleep. With every event, he was showing her he didn't love her.

For the next two weeks she drove back to the hospital for dressing changes. The pain was all consuming, as each time they pulled the puss-encrusted gauze out from the hole in her breast. Her entire left side was throbbing with pain. The gauze was one aspect but the white tape was another. Her skin was reacting poorly to the adhesive. She was welted everywhere. The nurses felt so bad, they tried soaking the tape before removing it, but nothing helped.

After two and a half weeks of torture, Teresa was able to go with a smaller gauze bandage. She was relieved and went home and laid ice packs on her bruised and beaten skin.

Believing this nightmare was over she returned to her life as a mother; but she was unsure about the wife part.

Each time there was interaction with Dennis' family she withdrew more. When they arrived home after these visits the emotional and psychological abuse would start. For hours she would hear, "Why did you say that?" or "Why don't you talk to Edith?" but the ones he repeated, and had often for many years, were, "Why can't you be more like the women in my family?" "You're my wife now, start acting like it."

Teresa heard these insulting comments; she heard them from his lips, she heard them during the day, she heard them in her sleep.

She began asking herself, **"What's wrong with me? Why is he always trying to turn me into someone I'm not?"** Then the epiphany happened. **"He doesn't love me...he's just using me."**

"I'M TRAPPED IN THIS MARRIAGE! I HAVE NO WHERE TO GO!" Faced with the cold realization of the truth, she began building the brick wall she used when her heart needed to be protected. Each time he turned his back on her, another brick was added. Soon she had built a massive wall around her heart; the only door in the wall was left open for her son.

Trying To Find Happiness in this World

"No Experience is wasted...Everything in life is happening to grow you up, to fill you up, to help you to become more of who you were created to be."

Oprah

In order to fill the void in her life, Teresa busied herself with being a mom and took pride in her clean home. When her husband came home from work, everything was cleaned, and his meal was always on the table waiting for him.

Her son was thriving and was a happy baby. Soon Teresa discovered Douglas would have a sibling. Dr. Lawrence confirmed her pregnancy and warned her not to overwork herself.

Teresa thought, as do some women, that another child will help fix her marriage. Dennis was pleased with the news and things did improve between them.

Then came the sudden miscarriage. The bleeding started the same as it did for her first miscarriage and during her pregnancy with Douglas. When the bleeding didn't stop, she went to her doctor.

"You've lost it," he said to her with great compassion in his voice. "We need to do a D.& C."

Deeply saddened, Teresa bravely went home and told Dennis. "Oh well," he said to her. "We can always try again."

"How can you be so cold?" she asked him.

"I can't fix it!" he said. "It's done." He refused to speak of it again. In ignoring the facts of the loss, he also failed to see his wife was grieving.

When she tried to speak of the loss, he would chastise her. There was no comfort to be found with him now at all. Her loneliness and despair was growing and she didn't know where to turn for help.

She did find temporary comfort in the arms of a friend. When Dennis found out he was furious and extremely possessive. It was now that he showed interest in his wife, but not of a loving and caring nature.

Teresa knew she needed to make changes in her life but lacked the courage to act. They argued and fought. He threatened to take her son away from her, calling her horrible and degrading names. For two nights she slept on the floor in the hallway outside Douglas' bedroom. She had to prevent him from stealing her son away through the night.

When he saw she could not be manipulated this time, he decided he should move out temporarily. He believed she would be unable to take care of herself and then beg him to return.

Another line was drawn in the sand when he took shelter with her parents. Three weeks later they mutually decided he could come home. She made it clear she would not be treated like yesterday's garbage.

Life had it's progression and soon spring came and it was time to go back planting tobacco. Teresa worked seven days a week in planting, then hoeing and cultivating. Driving the tractor for nine hours a day in the hot sun was draining but there just was no escaping the sun. The skin on her back felt like she was being attacked by 1,000 bees. It hurt, burned and itched. When she scratched it the pain was horrible.

After taking a cool bath that night she asked Dennis to apply some cooling lotion.

"You have blisters all over your back!" he yelled. "You're burned."

"It will be better tomorrow," she replied. "Please apply the lotion." As he did, some of the blisters exploded and fluid oozed down her back.

"You need to go to the doctor," he said. "I'll call the farmer and tell him you'll be late in the morning."

The doctor looked at her body and said, "You have second degree burns. You can't go back out into the sun."

"But I have to work," she said.

"Then wear a hat, light coloured, long clothing and have the farmer's wife rub baby oil into your skin four times per day."

She agreed.

At lunch the next day, the farmer's wife attempted to rub oil onto her back. It was like having rough sandpaper rubbed over an open wound. Blisters popped as she gently applied the oil.

"Teresa," the woman said to her. "You need to go home. You can't work like this."

Fighting to control her emotions, Teresa thanked her friend and drove home without touching her back to the car seat.

Eventually all the blisters burst. It was a relief. Teresa was tired of working in the fields. She wanted to go back into an office and be clean. She accepted a job for a family-owned company from Ireland who had recently opened a local manufacturing plant. Now managing the office, Teresa worked as their bookkeeper, receptionist and did the company payroll.

The pay was reasonable and she was out of the elements.

Five months after starting the job winter set in. Teresa also discovered she was again pregnant. The office washrooms were located in the plant and were unheated. The owner's wife refused to turn on the heat because, "Teresa went and got herself pregnant," she snapped. "What do you want?" the woman asked her. "A velvet toilet seat cover!"

Each time Teresa used the washroom she developed severe stomach cramps. She was now four and a half months pregnant and prayed the cramps would pass.

Too ill to go to work one day, Teresa rested at home. Her mother had Douglas at her home, so Teresa could get some rest. Suffering several massive abdominal pains and thinking she was going to be violently ill, she went to the washroom. Here, alone, with no witnesses present, Teresa had her third miscarriage. Falling to the floor, she picked up the tiny fetus and gently wrapped it in a cloth. Unable to move from shock, she sat on the floor and stared at her hands. "I'm sorry," she whispered to the little body. She was numb.

Eventually she gathered her strength and called Dennis. "I've lost the baby just now," she told him. "I need to get to the gynecologist now."

"I can't leave work right now," he told her.

"I drive right by your work. Can't you take an hour and come with me?" she begged. But as always, work was more important to him.

Teresa drove herself to the hospital and met her doctor there. "I'm sorry," he said to her. "It truly was not meant to be. I will admit you and tomorrow we will do another D & C."

Teresa called Dennis and told him what was happening. He met her after she left recovery the next day. He drove her home and her father, whom he brought along, drove Teresa's car home.

When she regained her strength, she said goodbye to that office position and reverted back to tobacco. This would be her last attempt. Months later Teresa developed the abscess on her breast again. The surgeon said to her, "We have to remove the duct. It's the same one as the last time. Have you been pregnant recently?" She related the last pregnancy to him.

"We must remove it," he said. "Be here tomorrow and I will do the surgery. Make sure you have someone here with you. You can't be alone."

Once again her husband was a disappointment to her. "I can't get time off," he complained. By now he had switched jobs and was manager of his own department. She believed he could take the time; he just chose not to.

Patricia, Teresa's sibling had come back into her life. Teresa was still unsure if this was a good idea. She asked Patricia to take her to the hospital. To her surprise, her sister agreed.

With surgery complete; a duct removed the doctor approached her. "NO lifting for two weeks!" he ordered. "No housework and you must come back to have the dressings changed." Teresa agreed.

Day after day she went for dressing changes. Not once did her husband offer to help.

Recovering slowly, Teresa decided to make a change. "I want to go to school and upgrade my education." Luckily for her there was a government program that assisted women trying to reenter the workforce. She applied and was accepted.

"I'm going back to school to learn computers," she told her friend one afternoon. Life is looking up for me. If I'm going to get anywhere, I have to do it myself. I can't depend on anyone." Lesson learned.

School, Computers, Tragedy and a Job Offer

"All misfortune is but a stepping stone to fortune."
Henry David Thoreau

Teresa buried her grief deep. Unable to trust anyone, she faced her grief alone. The one person who she wanted help from desperately was her husband, but he ignored her pain. Her mother, who had lived through a worse nightmare when she was young, grew more and more emotionally unstable.

The college course she dove into showed her a new way out of tobacco work. Now in her element, Teresa excelled and approached top ranking in her class.

In mid-June she applied for a job as a school secretary. The ironic part was, this was the school she attended as a child. After her interview, she walked down the main hallway and glanced at all the graduation pictures. There she was! Instantly she was snapped back to a time she loved and hated. It seemed an eternity ago. In her senior years she fought with her teachers constantly, was star player on the basketball, volleyball and track and field teams, raced her bicycle and did all this on one meal a day.

Snapping back into reality, she headed for home. "This would be the perfect job," she thought to herself.

"Three blocks from home, and Douglas can go to school here when he's ready." She was armed with motivation and determination. "I can work the school year and have summer's off with my son."

One week later while finishing up her college diploma, Teresa received a call at college. "We want to offer you the job with our school," the principal told her.

"I accept," she replied happily.

Thrilled beyond belief, she went back into class and announced her great news. Everyone was happy for her. "We're on a roll, ladies," the professor said. "We have our first hire!"

Life was moving in her direction for a change. She signed the necessary documents and agreed to be the school secretary for twenty-six teaching staff, the principal and 350 elementary students.

The last week in August, she began her new career. It was a good choice. Andrea agreed to babysit Douglas which made life uncomplicated for Teresa.

Early that September they received word that Dennis' father was in the hospital. He had been battling cancer for a couple of years now, but their presence was requested at his bedside.

In a rush, Dennis and Teresa drove to see his dad. Teresa had made peace with the man and said her good-bye before leaving the room. A few minutes later, her husband emerged. His dad was gone. His loss was great but he stood like a stone statue; unyielding for eternity.

Later that evening Dennis called his brother out west to tell him about the death. They had no idea the lengths the young man would go to, to pay his respects to a man who turned him away all his life.

Still refusing the talk about his father, Dennis returned to work the next day. That evening after dinner, his world came crashing down around him.

The phone rang and Dennis answered it. He dropped into a chair beside the phone. His head fell into his free hand as he listened. "Thank you," he said as he ended the call.

"What's going on?" Teresa asked. She could tell he news was bad.

"Michael was killed last night in a car accident!" he said. Teresa tried to hug her husband but he stopped her cold. He continued. "That was the police. Michael's girlfriend Gloria just identified his body. He will be flown back to Ontario tomorrow."

Heartbroken at the loss of her brother-in-law she began to cry. Once again she tried to give her husband comfort, but he refused her.

"What happened?" she asked choking back her sobs.

"He had completed his shift on the rigs and borrowed a friend's sports car to drive to the airport. He was coming home for dad's funeral. The police believe he fell asleep at the wheel and hit a dump truck head-on. He was almost decapitated," he said as he now brought both hands to his face.

Not knowing what to do, Teresa asked him, "What can I do to help?"

"Nothing," came his reply. "I have to go tell Mom."

Teresa went with him for support, but she definitely was the outsider. She felt horrible pain for the family. The next afternoon was the first visitation for his father. It was here he announced to the rest of his family that Michael had been killed. Older family members passed out from shock and others stood rigid with disbelief. "So young," they all said.

Teresa knew her husband was drowning in grief, but she couldn't reach him. Then he announced,

"Michael's girlfriend is flying in to attend his funeral. She is staying with us."

Surprised by the announcement of his offer to Gloria, Teresa did feel however that the girl did have a place at the funeral. She had loved Michael.

To Teresa's astonishment, Dennis drove to Toronto to collect the girlfriend. Gloria was a nice person and the three bonded over their memories of Michael. Then something amazing happened. Teresa witnessed her husband sharing his grief with this total stranger. He avoided his wife and child, but he chose this woman to grow close to in grief.

The days were a blur. One day melded into the next. All filled with visitations, prayers, church and funerals.

As the family approached the cemetery to lay his brother to rest, Teresa tried to hold Dennis' arm. He pulled away from her and walked on with Gloria, leaving his wife standing alone. Their friends came up and urged Teresa along.

Tears streamed down her face at all the heartbreak and loss. Now she realized, she had completely lost her husband. ***"Why won't he talk to me?"*** she asked her friends. "He is suffering and he won't let me help!" Then she finally admitted, ***"I need him too!"***

Her friends understood and carried her through the rest of the day. They watched as Dennis clung to Gloria in grief.

Things deteriorated at home. Teresa cooked, cleaned and took care of her son, while Dennis and Gloria grew closer. They talked for hours late into the nights learning about each other and sharing stories.

On several occasions when Teresa unexpectedly entered the living room, the two separated with guilty looks on their faces.

Teresa was tolerant of this woman in her home but not for much longer. Approaching Gloria one afternoon, Teresa said, "You can't have both brothers. It's time you left and went back to your children." Gloria returned an expression of understanding.

Two days later she was gone, never to return.

The relationship between Teresa and Dennis had suffered a dramatic blow. She didn't know if the damage could be repaired.

Later that fall her doctor confirmed she was once again pregnant. "This is the last try, I hope," Dr. Lawrence said to her.

"Yes," she said. "I don't think our marriage is going to last."

Just after Christmas 1985, Teresa began to bleed again. Frantic she made an appointment with her doctor.

"Your blood is incompatible with your husband, and probably the baby," Dr. Lawrence told her. "Your body is rejecting the baby. We will need to give you injections of Rh immune globulins. These injections contain antibodies that will help prevent your body from rejecting the fetus."

At a loss for words but determined to save her pregnancy, Teresa began the injections.

She worked a full day, picked up Douglas and drove to St. Thomas to have her injections. She noticed Douglas appeared sick. On her way back home she stopped at her doctor's office to have him looked at. "I'm admitting him to the hospital right away," the doctor said. "He has pneumonia."

"What!" she exclaimed. "All he's had is a cough."

It was late that night when she finally arrived home. She was emotionally and physically exhausted. One of her children was in the hospital sick and the other she was desperately trying to carry through to full term.

Feeling like a complete failure as a wife and mother, Teresa almost lost hope. "I have to fight for my children," she promised herself. But the constant work, driving, housework, hospitals and doctor appointments were wearing her down. Luckily for Teresa, her parents helped her where her husband wouldn't. His age-old excuse of, "I can't take time off work," was growing thin with her.

Douglas recovered and continued on being the happy child he had always been. Teresa loved her little boy and his love for his mother was evident.

One afternoon while sitting cuddling together, Teresa hugged her son tightly and said, "Very soon Mommy will be home for a while. Then we can play Lego and transformers together." His chubby little face lit up with joy.

"I love you," she said to him.

A Very Special and Complicated Delivery

"A baby is something you carry inside you for nine months, in your arms for three years, and in your heart until the day you die."

Mary Mason

In mid-April Teresa left her job and began maternity leave. In 1986, the best a woman could hope for was 16 weeks of benefits. Since Teresa normally had 8 weeks off during the summer, she actually only received 8 weeks of maternity leave, she had to return to work the last week in August as always.

With her due date being Victoria Day, May 24th, she knew some time was needed to recover her strength and energy before the delivery.

This time she gained 40 pounds with all the weight in front of her. The extreme burden pulled her forward and at times caused her to lose her balance, dropping Teresa onto her knees.

The principal she worked with teased her about her 'orb.' She knew it was in good fun.

For the last few months Teresa said to Dennis, "I'm being kicked in the behind all the time." He laughed thinking it all quite funny. "I'm serious," she said. "With Douglas the kicking was all over, but this time it's all on the bottom."

Early in April, she attended her regular checkup with Dr. Lawrence. She told him about the odd location of the kicking and after his examination he told her, "I want you to drive over to the hospital after you leave here. I'm going to order an ultrasound. I want a better look at what this baby is doing."

"Alright," Teresa replied. She had a premonition something was happening before she left home that day. Her suitcase was already in the car.

Dr. Lawrence also added, "You are already three centimeters dilated, so things are starting to happen."

"But I'm not due until May 24th," she replied.

"Go on over and let's have a look at what's happening," he told her confidently.

During the ultrasound, Teresa was able to see her baby. "Beautiful!" she commented. "The baby is so big!"

Dr. Lawrence walked into the room and took charge. "According to the measurements, the baby is full term. Are you sure you had your dates right?"

"Yes," she replied.

"Well," he said. "Since you appear to be full-term and you are dilating and you're here, I'm admitting you."

Once labour starts we really need to have you close."

"Why?" she asked.

"Teresa, your baby is breech."

"What!" she asked. "What can you do?"

"Well, the baby is a footling breech. If you go into labour I want you here to ensure a safe delivery," Dr. Lawrence told her. "I am not sure I can deliver the baby vaginally. A footling breech means the baby is bum down with one foot up and one down. If we try to delivery vaginally, we may break its hips."

"Oh my God!" Teresa said. "What are you going to do?"

"We are going to keep you here and watch you closely. When labour starts we may try to delivery or I may do a Cesarean section. If I do a section, the baby's hips won't be hurt."

Weighing the options, Teresa agreed with the Cesarean. "Do what you have to," she told her doctor. "I trust you."

Later once she was settled, she called her husband and explained what was happening. "I'll see you tomorrow night," he said before hanging up.

Again her husband's lack of love and compassion for his wife and unborn child hit her head on. She was beginning to believe he truly was cold-hearted.

Teresa was allowed to leave the hospital for short day trips within close proximity. Dennis took her out one very hot afternoon. They went to the park. She enjoyed sitting on the swings and relaxing away from the sterile environment. Soon the heat of the day overwhelmed her and she asked to go back. She had strict instructions from the doctor should labour begin. "You are to lay down right where you are. Don't move and call an ambulance," he told her seriously.

Teresa was afraid for her baby. Now waiting for nature to take its course, she remained bored to tears in the hospital for five days.

"Now you are at seven centimeters," Dr. Lawrence told her. "I will give you two more days," he said. "If nothing further has happened we are going to do a C-section."

"Will I be awake?" she asked

"Yes," he replied. "I've give you an epidural. I also think your husband **needs** to be there with you."

She tried to control her impatience while spending her days walking the hallways. Her husband had agreed to be in the delivery room with her. "If it's a

337

boy," he said. "Your father owes me another case of beer."

"I hope it's a girl," Teresa replied out of spite.

The day had arrived finally. "Let's do this," Dr. Lawrence said to her.

"I'm ready!" she replied with a smile.

Once the epidural had taken effect she was transferred to the operating room. The room was crowded with doctors, technicians and nurses.

The doctor in charge of her vital signs and epidural had a lovely Scottish accent which Teresa found soothing to listen to. He was a kind man and showed great concern for her.

Dennis sat on the other side of her head taking in the surroundings. Laughingly he said to Dr. Lawrence, "Why don't you tie her tubes while you're in there. Then she won't have to do it later."

Dr. Lawrence's demeanor changed immediately. Anger and disgust was evident on his face. "Your wife has been through enough over the years in trying to give you children. It's time you stepped up and became a man and handled the situation yourself," he snarled at Dennis.

Chastised and embarrassed by the doctor's words, Dennis became quiet.

"Ok dear," Dr. Lawrence said to Teresa. "We are going to start now. We just broke your water."

Suddenly **Teresa was unable to breathe**. She couldn't speak! There was no way to let the doctor know. Frantically she moved her head back and forth to get the doctor's attention.

The Scottish doctor said, "My dear, you are turning red. Are you alright?"

Shaking her head violently, the doctor yelled out. **"Tilt the table. She can't breathe!"**

The sound of a large splash filled the room. Teresa lifted her head and gazed at the doctor. "It's ok," he said. When we broke your water, it slammed up against your diaphragm. You'll be ok now."

Tears began to slip out of her eyes. Her husband just sat behind her watching the procedure, with no concern for his wife.

Again, Teresa found she was unable to breathe. She tried desperately not to panic and let fear control her. Dr. Lawrence must have sensed her terror, for he suddenly looked up and said to her over the screen, "This baby doesn't want to come out yet." His eyes lit up with a reassuring smile.

To Teresa's surprise a little cry pierced the room. She lifted her head but was unable to see anything. ***"It's a boy!"*** Dr. Lawrence told her. Powerless to hide her emotion any longer Teresa began to weep. "My last chance for a girl," she thought.

Dr. Atkinson brought her baby to her. "You can hold him for a minute," he said.

Instantly she fell in love with this little boy. She smiled down at him but was incapable of speech. All of a sudden Dr. Atkinson took the baby from his mother's arms and left the room with two nurses.

"It's alright," Dr. Lawrence told her. "They're just going to clean him up for you."

Now that her procedure was complete she felt as if her life-force had been drained from her. "I feel so weak," she thought.

After returning to her room, Dr. Lawrence and Dr. Atkinson came in to see her. "What's wrong?" she asked.

"You had a very big baby," Dr. Atkinson told her. He weighed almost nine pounds and is close to twenty-two inches long. It was his size that led us to believe he was full term, but he isn't. His lungs are slightly underdeveloped.

He just has a bit of trouble breathing on his own," Dr. Atkinson said. "According to all the testing and my calculations, I believe your son is one month premature. He will need to stay in an incubator for a few days, possibly one week. I'm positive he will be fine after that."

"We will allow you to stay here with him," Dr. Lawrence said. "I don't want you driving that distance every day to see him and I know if I let you out, you won't get any rest. This way we can keep an eye on you too."

Later that afternoon, Edward and Andrea brought Douglas to see his mommy. Teresa was prepared for this visit. She had purchased a small action figure that her son loved and gift wrapped it and stored it in her suitcase.

Without the strength to walk, Dennis pushed her in a wheelchair to the waiting room.

"Mommy!" shouted Douglas, as he ran to his mother. She hugged him tight and kissed him. "I love you," she whispered to him. With her son sitting gently on her lap, Teresa told him about his new baby brother. "Look," she said to him. "He brought you a present." Quickly the little boy unwrapped the small gift. His eyes lit up with joy as he saw his favourite Transformer. He hugged his mother tight. "Tell the baby thank you," he whispered to her.

"I will." she promised.

Glancing up and noticing the other people present, Teresa saw several people wipe tears from their eyes. One older lady said to her, "That was beautiful."

For the next seven days Teresa wandered the hallways of the hospital while her baby lay in an incubator with wires attached to his scalp and I.V.'s in his body. The only way she could touch her son was through the hand spaces in the side of the unit. She touched him through gloves. Other mothers were bringing their babies into the room and celebrating their births, something Teresa was unable to experience. As she watched the other mother's with their infants, Teresa's depression grew. After a few days, things became so bad for her, she couldn't bear to go into the nursery. "Look but don't touch," she heard in her head. "I **Need** to hold you and **Love** you," she said to the baby behind glass. "Please forgive me." Turning away from the nursery, she slowly walked back to her room. She fought to hold back the tears and pain she felt in her heart.

The night before she left the hospital, she was allowed to feed her son for the first time. Nursing was not an option for her. She was warned against it after the abscess and duct removal. So her doctor had given her a shot immediately after the birth to dry up the milk supply, then the nurses bound her chest tightly with a corset-type garment.

Teresa sat in a rocking chair in the nursery that evening with her little boy in her arms for the first time since his birth. She gently rocked him back and forth, she kissed his little forehead and told him how much she loved him. It was surreal for her. "I feel like I've missed so much of you already," she whispered to him.

The bonding time for a mother with her infant is crucial within the first few hours. She knew this was her baby, but at the same time, he felt like a stranger.

Eleven days after entering the hospital, Teresa was allowed to bring her baby home. That morning her staples were removed and Dr. Lawrence warned her to take things easy at home. "No lifting, sweeping, bending or pulling," he said. "In other words, NO housework and make sure your husband helps you with the baby."

Teresa was thrilled to be going home, but something inside her wasn't right.

She had heard the words 'Post-Partum Depression' before, but truly had no idea what it was or that she was living it. Out of fear, Teresa told no one how she felt and she believed no one cared.

Trials and Tribulations of a Working Mother

Life at home with the new baby was improving and everyone soon settled into a routine. Teresa was able to bond with her son. They gave him the name Kevin. He was growing rapidly and became a very satisfied baby.

As with her first son, Kevin began sleeping through the night at one month old. This pleased his tired mother a great deal. One week after arriving home with her new baby Teresa had already lost thirty pounds. She was glad to have the weight off but the sudden drop was difficult on her system. She found herself lightheaded a great deal.

Douglas enjoyed having a baby brother in the house and carried the little transformer his brother gave him everywhere he went. Douglas took an active role in helping his mom care for the newborn. He helped his mommy fold blankets, locate the soother when his brother cried and happily produced soap and wash cloths for the baby's baths.

When the baby cried, Douglas would announce to his mother as he covered his ears, "He's loud, Mommy."

"He certainly can be," she replied with a smile.

Summer time came and Teresa began her usual routine of canning and freezing fruits and vegetables. She was proud that through making her own baby food for her children, they had a great start in life. It was a proud 'Mom moment' when her pediatrician complimented her on the excellent care her children were getting.

On one visit, Teresa and the doctor discussed circumcision. "Because he was a preemie, we should wait a couple of months before doing that procedure," he replied. Then Dr. Atkinson said to Teresa, "Do you have diabetes?"

"No," she replied. "Why?"

"Given the size and prematurity of the baby, had he gone full term, he could have weighed over ten pounds."

Completely surprised, Teresa began asking questions of him. "What does all of this mean?"

"I think you are a prime candidate for gestational diabetes," he told her. "It is a condition where women without a previous diagnoses of diabetesexhibit high blood glucose levels during pregnancy. Usually during their third trimester."

"I've never heard of that before," she replied shocked.

"I want you to go for testing," he said to her. "If you didn't turn diabetic through this pregnancy, the chanced are high that you will for the next. The baby birth weight could go up to twelve or fourteen pounds next time."

Teresa starred at him with disbelief. "I don't plan on having any more children," she commented.

"I will order the testing, but you will need to have it retested for the rest of your life," he said to her.

"Thank you," she said to the doctor.

After the six hour glucose tolerance testing, Teresa's results came back normal. "I'm not diabetic," she told her husband.

"That's good," he answered back.

Two months later the circumcision was performed. "Everything is fine," Dr. Atkinson told Teresa and Dennis.

"Dr. Atkinson," Teresa said, "Kevin vomits a great deal."

"He's a solid, healthy baby," he replied. "Tell me what's been going on."

"Every time we feed him, lay him down for his nap, pick him up from his bed, or really just anytime, he vomits," she told him. "He doesn't just do the usual 'spit up,' it's projectile vomiting."

"He doesn't seem to be losing weight," the doctor commented. "Sometimes this happens with premature babies. Let's give it a few months. Cover yourself and your furniture, and just deal with it the best you can for now."

At six months old, Kevin's vomiting problem had not stopped. He was still growing and gaining weight, but, "You can just look at him and he'll throw up on you," Teresa told her friend one afternoon. "This is crazy the amount of laundry I have to do."

After another trip to the pediatrician, Teresa learned why her baby was vomiting so much. "A lot of preemies do that because they aren't fully developed," he told her. "It's also more common in boys. I am sure this will all stop by the time he is one year old."

"We have to deal with this until he's one?" Teresa asked in shock. "I've had everything in my house covered for so long now. People won't come near the baby because he vomits on them."

"There is a surgery we can perform," he told her. "I don't like to take that action until the child is at least one year old. The valve on the top part of the stomach is the problem," he continued. "It's underdeveloped so it doesn't always stay closed. When it opens, the child vomits. I will run some tests on Kevin just to make sure," he told her.

The tests proved Dr. Atkinson was right. So they just had to keep everything covered and wait. However, Kevin was not the same happy baby when he returned. He screamed all the time. There was no amount of love or attention that soothed him. Teresa tried her best. She had to keep working and send her children to a babysitter. She didn't want Andrea to take care of her children anymore. Her mother's interference was wearing thin and everyone knew her words were intended to constantly demean Teresa as a mother. Instead of helping, her mother would sit in Teresa's home and say, "Put that baby down! All you're doing is spoiling him."

"How?" Teresa would ask. "By showing him I love him?"

But her mother didn't understand.

At work, Teresa began helping some new students from other countries with their English. Every day, she would take the three boys into the library of the school and teach them new words. She enjoyed helping the students. After school, she coached the girls' volleyball and basketball teams as well as co-coached the co-ed volleyball team. Keeping up her love of sports with the students kept her alive. For her own fitness, Teresa participated twice per week in aerobics classes. She was strong and in good shape.

However, in April she began feeling physically drained. She had been experiencing severe migraines at least once per week. They were debilitating and knocked Teresa down hard. Staying in a blacked-out room, with absolutely no sound, for fear her head would explode, Teresa found life quite challenging. She began missing a few days of work because of the headaches. In order to have solitude, she would drive her children to day care, then return home and rest for the day, only to pick her children up at the allotted time. Her husband refused to take them or collect them, even though he drove right passed the day care on his way to work.

On Mother's Day, Teresa was sitting on the patio enjoying a day with her sons. By two in the afternoon, a severe migraine began thundering inside her head. To her surprise, she began experiencing sharp pain running up her spine. No one could touch her skin. If they did, she felt millions of razor blades slicing into her. "What on earth is happening?" she said to her husband.

Then to her dismay, her parents arrived. "You don't look well," they said to her.

"I have to go to bed," she said. Her migraine medication was ineffective and she began vomiting. It felt like her head was imploding from pressure.

At 4:00 o'clock, Dennis came in and checked on her. She rolled on the bed in agony and begged him to take her to the hospital. ***"Please!"*** she said. ***"I can't stand the pain in my head! Please!"***

Holding her fists to her temples, she staggered out to the car. She left her house equipped with a garbage bag just in case she lost more of her stomach contents.

Immediately she was rushed onto a bed at the emergency unit. Crying and writhing on the bed from pain, she tried to explain to the nurses what had happened that day. Unable to finish, Dennis continued the explanation.

"PLEASE!" Teresa screamed. ***"Give me something for this headache! I can't stand the pain!"***

"We can't give you anything until we do some blood work," the nurse replied.

Once the blood was extracted, Teresa lay in excruciating pain for what seemed like hours. The next time she opened her eyes, she was unprepared for what she saw. There in front of her was a doctor and three nurses. That was not unusual.

"Why are you wearing masks?" she asked them.

"Teresa," the doctor began. "We will have to take more blood work from you. The other thing we will need to do is a spinal tap immediately."

"What? Why?" she asked in disbelief. "All I have is a migraine."

"Your blood work came back suspicious," the doctor replied to her. "I believe you have meningitis."

Unable to comprehend what was happening she screamed out, **"When will you give me something for the pain in my head?"**

"After we have drawn the spinal fluid," the doctor told her.

"Then hurry up and do it!" she shrieked. "I can't stand this pain much longer."

The torturous pain was evident. Her hands clenched into fists and jaw clenched tight from horrendous pain, Teresa lay there waiting for a spinal tap.

A Mother's Desperate Gift for Her Son

"God is working on your behalf today. Heaven is holding conversations about you. Angels have been assigned to you. Just breathe, and be at peace."

Unknown

The doctor and nurses returned to Teresa's bedside. "You have to turn on your side and curl into a ball," the nurse told her soothingly. "That way," she continued, "your spine will spread and the doctor will be able to insert the needle to drain the fluid."

Crying now from pain, Teresa turned on her side and did as directed.

"You **must** lay still," the nurse said to her. "Don't move!"

"I can't stand the pain in my head," Teresa cried out.

"Once we have the results we'll be able to give you a shot. Now lay quiet," the nurse replied. "Relax, Teresa," the nurse said again. "Trust him, he's done this many time before."

That comment did nothing to sooth Teresa's already destroyed nerves. She fought back a scream as she felt the needle slide into her spine. Suddenly she received a massive electric shock down her left leg and she jumped slightly.

"Hold her still," the doctor said.

"My leg went numb," Teresa screamed at him.

"We're almost done," he snapped. "Hold still."

Even though they had drained fluid from her spine, it was still another hour before she received an injection for the crushing migraine she had now had for over six hours.

Then she saw the doctor walking towards her bed. A nurse followed with a needle. This time they were missing their masks.

"I've prescribed morphine for your headache," the doctor said to Teresa. "We've tested your spinal fluid for meningitis, but the tests are inconclusive," he continued. "I'm sending you to a London hospital by ambulance. There is a neurologist there who will take over your case." Once this news was delivered, the doctor exited the cubicle and was not seen again.

The nurses prepared Teresa for her ride. With the medication now working, the stabbing ice pick in her brain finally stopped chipping away at her. Finding it difficult to lay on the stretcher from back pain, she was however, able to sleep for a short time in the ambulance. Now totally exhausted, she gave up caring what happened to her.

The neurologist met her in the emergency department at South Street Campus. "I'm Dr. Hahn," she said kindly to Teresa. "We will get you settled for the night, and tomorrow we will chat about some testing."

Teresa liked the doctor. She had a caring manner about her.

"How are you doing now, Teresa?" the doctor asked.

"My head hurts terribly," the young woman replied. "The headache was getting better but its back."

"I'll give you something to help that," she replied. "Try to get some rest and we will talk tomorrow."

Teresa had a horrible night. Her head wouldn't stop pounding. "Thor must be in my head with his mythical hammer," she thought. "It would take a hammer that size to cause this headache."

The next day, Teresa met with Dr. Hahn again.

"You do NOT have meningitis," she said.

Teresa was relieved. "What's wrong then?" she asked. "Why can't I get rid of this headache?" she questioned the doctor.

"I'm not sure completely what is happening yet," the doctor commented. "I want to run more tests. You seem to have slow reflexes on your left side and according to my tests so far, it appears you have lost strength on that side."

Then she said to Teresa, "I may have to take more spinal fluid, to run more tests."

"Please NO!" Teresa cried. After explaining her experience with the spinal tap of the day before, Dr. Hahn replied, "Let me see. If there is enough fluid left from the first test, I won't take any more."

"Thank you," Teresa said to the kind woman. Tears began to slip down her cheeks. "My head hurts horribly," she said. "Can you help me."

"I will order something for you," Dr. Hahn said. "Just try to rest. It will be best."

Later that morning Dr. Hahn returned. "I've ordered several tests to be done," she informed Teresa. "I want a muscle enzyme test, an MRI, an ECG and more blood work.

"Alright," Teresa said still fighting her horrible head pain. "Thursday is my little boys' first birthday. "I want to be home for him that day."

"I don't think that will be possible, Teresa," the doctor replied.

"You don't understand," Teresa said with as much fight as she could manage. "I *MUST* be home for him.

I will not have my child celebrate a birthday without me being there!"

"We will see how the week goes," Dr. Hahn said. "Maybe I can give you a pass to go home for a few hours."

Teresa had very little rest that week. The hospital staff was very kind and compassionate towards her. She submitted to all the testing and on Wednesday morning she welcomed a visit from her doctor.

"I have no answers," the doctor told Teresa. "There is some evidence to support you had a stroke, but it is inconclusive. Your muscles show they are in a weakened condition and you are deficient in some vitamins."

"Why won't my headache go away?" Teresa asked.

"It is a delicate balance when performing a spinal tap. I believe the doctor removed too much fluid at the time. That will cause massive headaches. It will pass in time," she answered the young woman.

"Anything else?" Teresa asked the doctor.

"I have noticed that your cells are not producing enough oxygen. Over a few days, I thought that would change, but the last tests show that as each new cell is generated, you are not receiving enough oxygen."

"What on earth does that mean?" Teresa asked. She was not really certain she understood all of this.

"You will fatigue quicker," Dr. Hahn replied. "Hopefully in time things will change or you will need to learn new ways to adapt."

"My baby's birthday is tomorrow," Teresa said sternly. "I want to be there for him."

"You are very ill, my dear," the doctor said. "I want you to stay in the hospital for at least one full week. However, I see you are determined to go. If I give you a pass tonight, will you promise to come back tomorrow afternoon?"

"I promise," Teresa said.

"If you have any difficulties overnight or in the morning, **GET BACK TO THE HOSPITAL IMMEDIATELY!**" Dr. Hahn said sternly.

"I will," Teresa promised her.

Later that evening, Teresa left the hospital and went home to see her children. When she saw her boys, her heart immediately lit up. After many hugs, kisses and cuddles, Teresa began to relax. The boys began to tire, so Teresa walked Douglas to bed. Together, they read a story book. Douglas sat snuggled up in his mother's arms as she read to him. When the story was finished, she kissed him repeatedly on the cheeks and forehead and said, "I love you Snuggle Bug."

"I love you too, Mommy," he said. He then closed his eyes and went to sleep.

Teresa returned to the living room to collect her baby. "Come on big boy," she said to him. "You need to go to sleep. It's your first birthday tomorrow and you need your rest. It's a big deal turning one." She smiled at Kevin. He threw his arms around her neck and nuzzled her cheek.

The two of them sat in the big comfortable chair in Kevin's room. They were surrounded by Mickey Mouse, and many other Walt Disney characters Teresa has drawn as decoration for her son. She read him a story and her little one fell asleep in her arms before she was finished.

Lifting the heavy baby into his crib was a chore in her weakened condition. Once she had him in bed, she covered her son and gently kissed his forehead. "Good night Birthday Boy," she said as she switched off the light and closed the door.

With the desperate need to make her little boy's birthday special, Teresa went into the kitchen and started baking a cake. All she was able to do with limited energy was make a single layer vanilla cake. By the time this was done, she staggered to bed exhausted.

At 4:00 in the morning, she woke up from severe pain in her head. She woke Dennis and said, "My head hurts so badly, please take me back to the hospital now."

"Are you sure?" he asked.

Clutching her head between her hands, she replied, **"I can't stand the pain in my head!** I might as well beat my head against the wall. It would all be the same. **PLEASE!"** she cried.

With no further questions, he took her back to the hospital where she remained for one week. Over time, the headache lessened but it took weeks before it went away.

"I'll never forgive myself for missing Kevin's first birthday," Teresa said to herself. **"Never!"**

Life and the Pursuit of What?

Teresa returned home from the hospital weakened but determined to get on with her life. There were no medical answers to what had happened to her. "I am going to send all of your information and samples to the Forensic Lab in Toronto. Hopefully in time they will uncover what went on," Dr. Hahn told her.

Teresa continued to have debilitating migraines. Dr. Hahn connected her with a specialist who began a drug protocol in an effort to give the young woman back her life. Teresa had just turned twenty-seven years old; she was the mother of two young children; a wife and working woman. Somedays she could tolerate the thunder storm in her head; other days she was forced to visit her doctor or hospital for an injection of morphine to deaden the pain.

Even after receiving the shots, she was unable to rest. Her husband still refused to pick up the children from day care and school. Most days he was very little help to her. He rarely cooked, cleaned or did the laundry. What he always *made* time for were his friends.

Thinking she could have help from him after receiving an injection for a migraine, Teresa would go to bed with an ice pack covering her head. Dennis' friend would come knocking asking for help or offering a beer, and like a fish to water, he would leave her with the two small children in the house. Her husband always helped everyone else, but rarely his wife.

The only thing he didn't realize, was by leaving home all the time, he was not being a 'present' father. On countless occasions her boys would come to her crying. "Why won't daddy spend time with us? Doesn't he love us? Why won't he play with us?"

Her heart broke for her boys. "I don't know honey," she would say. "He's busy."

"He's always busy with Joe!" Douglas would cry out as he wept on his mother's shoulder.

Teresa's anger for her husband grew. She could tolerate his absence but it was affecting their sons and she refused to let him hurt them.

The young woman fought on to make a better life for herself and her boys.

She continued to work at the school. Taking on the extra job of noon-hour supervisor, she earned enough money to afford her babysitter, but had no time to eat during the day.

After a long conversation with a principal one afternoon, it was strongly suggested to Teresa that she organize the non-teaching staff of the board. Compared to the teaching staff, the rest of the school board employees were not respected properly or paid fairly. The Secretaries, Custodians, Speech Pathologists and Psychometrists were just as important to the daily functioning of the schools as the teachers were. However, Teresa's group was not protected by a powerful union.

Teresa met with two friends who were also secretaries and the idea was launched. Recognizing Teresa's leadership skills, the other two women let her take the lead.

Teresa organized meetings and with the full cooperation of the dozens of secretaries, they began their work towards respect, a raise in pay, pay equity and the right to be heard.

The women researched neighbouring school boards, worked on job descriptions and talked over their plans. Teresa met with representatives from various unions and school boards to ensure her plan of attack had a solid foundation. Some members were afraid of standing up and rocking the boat, but Teresa encouraged them to believe in themselves and to have faith in their decision.

Months of preparation went into their first meeting with the school board representatives and trustees. With Teresa as Chief Negotiator and her team of two amazing assistants with her, they took up their place across the table from the school board negotiators. Teresa was demanding pay equity with their various counterparts throughout the region. They asked for retroactive pay back to a time when the discrepancy began and the women felt it was within their rights to have equal benefit packages to what the teachers were enjoying.

At their next meeting, Teresa stood up and announced to her group, ***"We've won! We won our first negotiations!"*** Teresa was beside herself with joy. "I've made a difference," she thought.

The retroactive pay was a God-send. Teresa purchased a used swimming pool for her children to enjoy their summers in. The family never went on vacation, because her husband always found some excuse to be needed at work and away from his family. His business was busier during the summer months, but he never asked for time off.

Teresa and her boys had a great time with the swimming pool. When she was young Teresa loved swimming. She even took some diving lessons at the local pool. Her boys refused to take swimming lessons, so she taught both of her sons to swim.

As the new school year approached Teresa connected with her negotiating team and began working towards their new contract. For three years they were successful in achieving their goals. Then suddenly, the school board tried to put an end to the women. They refused to negotiate with the group again.

Swiftly moving into action, Teresa called a meeting. Much to her surprise other non-teaching staff, who originally opted out of their bargaining unit, asked if they could join. There was a common bond and a common goal. Everyone was welcome to participate.

The new group voted unanimously that Teresa champion their cause. She accepted the challenge. Teresa was beginning to feel recharged. In her professional life she now found a purpose, a cause, and she was respected.

She met with several union leaders and decided that OSSTF (Ontario Secondary School Teachers Federation), was the best choice for her group. One representative worked side by side with Teresa setting up contracts, outlines and formalizing the necessary paperwork to certify their collective bargaining unit.

Finally, everything was in place and the day for the Labour Board hearing for bargaining unit certification was upon them.

Teresa and another team member travelled to Toronto. They enjoyed a lovely dinner with the president of OSSTF. Teresa was in her element.

The next day their team was introduced to the Labour Board representatives.

When everyone took their place at the table, Teresa found herself on equal ground with the Chairman of the School Board and their lawyers, the President of OSSTF, the Chief Negotiators and lawyers and at the end of the large rectangular table, the four members of the Labour Board.

"I'm making history here," she thought to herself. "This is because I had a dream and people believed in me."

Each side presented their case and at the end of the day the ruling was handed down. "Congratulations Teresa," said the President of OSSTF. "You've done it! Your group is now a certified collective bargaining unit."

Teresa's smile lit up her face. She was proud of her accomplishments and felt like superwoman! Her group celebrated over dinner at a local restaurant. It was such a happy time. After dinner, the president of the chapter approached Teresa. "I would like you to come and work for me at the head office," he said. "I like the work you've done and I believe you could have a good future here."

Astounded by this offer, Teresa received his business card and asked to take some time to think over his offer.

"It's a big decision and please take your time, but I really want you as part of my team," he said.

Returning home, Teresa was on such a high. She was now ready to face the school board across the negotiating table armed with, Sylvia, the Chief Negotiator of O.S.S.T.F.

Sylvia said to Teresa, "I will take the lead on these negotiations. I want you to observe and learn." With that said, Teresa absorbed every detail she could. The new bargaining unit was very successful in their endeavours. They were successful on every item on their list of demands except one. Teresa wanted long-term disability coverage. All other units, and teacher unions have this coverage. "We just want equality," she told Sylvia.

"Include this in your next set of negotiations," Sylvia told Teresa.

"Thank you," Teresa said as she shook hands with the woman. "You've been an immense help."

Walking with her feet in the clouds and feeling very empowered, Teresa returned to her unit and gave them the great news. "We were successful again," she told them. The group of employees were pleased.

It was strongly suggested by the union that Teresa remain as Chief Negotiating Officer. Her group wanted her as President of the local chapter, but these two positions could not be held by the same person. Teresa gladly accepted Chief Negotiating Officer and Vice-President of the Local Chapter.

Finally, she felt fulfilled in her career.

After her success, she returned home and told her husband of her good news. He was happy for her. She had invested countless hours of time and effort into this cause.

Then Teresa said, "I've been asked to go to Toronto and work at the head office of OSSTF." The silence that fell over the room was deafening. Dennis' facial expressions changed from happiness for his wife's accomplishments to something that resembled anger and jealousy all at once.

"You can't go!" he said. **"I'm not moving to Toronto!"**

"No one said we had to move to Toronto," Teresa commented. "We could move closer and I could take the train in. I really want to do this," she said. "This could be a huge salary and our problems would be solved."

"No!" he said. *"You have to turn it down."*

Deep in her heart Teresa knew that if she tried to take the job, he would block her somehow. If she went on her own with her children, he would take them away from her. She was trapped and there was no way out.

With her hopes and dreams of a brilliant career smashed, Teresa turned down the job offer. She was devastated. The life had been drained from her...again.

She went back to work at the school but now it held no joy for her. She stopped coaching the sports teams but did help out during the track and field meets. Her area of specialty was shot put. When she was young, Teresa set school records for shot put. Her gym teacher mentored her on the art of 'putting the shot.' This was an event Teresa was passionate about.

Now feeling like she was going through the motions of life, Teresa lost interest in most things. One activity she did enjoy was playing volleyball with her teacher friends. Every other Friday evening the group congregated at the school and played volleyball for two hours. Every couple had a turn hosting a social afterwards. It was a time of fun, exercise and discussing school board happenings and politics.

Volleyball was becoming her only avenue for releasing her anger towards her husband.

Soon, Teresa would be fighting another battle. The constant interference of her mother was causing discord in her house. Dennis was furious because her mother was always 'there.' He disliked Andrea and her strange ways and was preparing to dig in his heels.

But another event took place before the war began.

Teresa received a call at work one afternoon from her father. "Get over here immediately," he said. "Douglas has broken his arm and needs to go to the hospital."

Before she left school, Teresa called Dennis to tell him the news. "I can't get time off," he said yet again.

"I'll be driving right by your work," she yelled at him.

"I can't get away," he repeated.

"I will never forgive you for this," she snapped at him and slammed down the receiver. As adrenaline rushed through her veins, she ran out of the school and drove to her parents' house to help her son.

An Incident, An Accident or Neglect

"You have to love your children unselfishly. That is hard. But it is the only way."
    Barbara Bush, Former First Lady of the United States

With her heart in her throat, Teresa drove into her parents' driveway. It was a cold November afternoon and her breath was visible as she ran to the door.

Bursting into the house, Teresa realized she needed to control her emotions. She must remain calm and not upset her son. Luckily Kevin was sleeping in the bedroom when she went in. He didn't need to see his brother right now.

Walking over to where Douglas sat, Teresa leaned down and gave him a big kiss on the forehead. "Hi sweetie," she said lovingly. "How are you doing?"

"My arm hurts Mommy," he said.

"Just hold your arm still," she said as she touched his cheek tenderly. "We will go see the doctor in a minute."

Teresa turned to her mother. "What happened?" she asked.

"He was outside playing around the clothesline pole," Andrea said. "Earlier I was out with him, I was sitting on a lawn chair watching him play. Everything was fine, so I came in the house. The next thing I knew your father heard him screaming. We ran outside to see what was wrong and found Douglas laying on the ground below the pole. The lawn chair was turned upside down laying a few feet away."

"Where you watching him at all?" Teresa screamed at her mother. "How could you let him do that? Never mind," Teresa said. "I have to get him to the hospital."

Andrea gathered Douglas' coat and to Teresa's horror attempted to straighten his arm. She was going to put his arm in the sleeve.

Douglas shrieked. **"What are you doing!"** Teresa screamed at Andrea. "With all your first aid training! You should know better! Get out of my way!"

Taking control of the situation to protect her child, Teresa folded her son's broken arm over his chest and wrapped his coat around him. She zipped up his coat hoping the coat would act as a splint for his arm.

Carefully sitting her boy in the car, she drove off to the hospital. Eventually her husband arrived.

"I want Douglas sent to London," Teresa said to him. "I don't trust these people."

"You have to trust them some time," Dennis replied. "Everything will be fine."

After the initial examination and x-rays being taken, the doctor approached the couple.

"Your son broke his elbow," the doctor said. "It's a serious break and we will have to put him to sleep to fix it."

Teresa was on high alert now. "What all is involved?"

"Once Douglas is asleep we will try to replace the cap of his elbow. That is the part that broke. I want to warn you both. Sometimes we aren't always successful in keeping the cap in place once it is put back. In some cases, it will need to be pinned," the doctor explained.

"Try to fix it first," Teresa said. "I want to know if it was successful before you do anything else."

"I will come and tell you personally," the doctor assured them both.

Teresa felt like a caged lioness. Her cub was hurt and she didn't trust the people taking care of him. She paced the floor for what seemed an eternity. Hours passed and there was no word. Dennis thought she was being ridiculous.

Now later in the evening, they approach a nurse walking by. "Where is our little boy," they begged. "He went into surgery hours ago to fix a broken arm and we haven't heard any news."

The nurse went to inquire about Douglas.

She returned twenty minutes later. "They were unable to fix his arm. The break was bad enough that the cap would not stay on," she told them.

"Why didn't the doctor talk to us? Where is he?" Teresa demanded.

"He left for the evening," the nurse replied.

"Unbelievable!" Teresa shouted. **"Now what?"** she asked. *"Where is my son?"*

"The doctor wants to pin your son's elbow," the nurse said. "It's the only way to keep the bone in place."

"WHERE IS MY SON!" Teresa said as her voice level increased with each question.

"That is the problem," the nurse commented as she lowered her head in shame. "We can't find him."

"WHAT DO YOU MEAN YOU CAN'T FIND MY SON! THIS IS A HOSPITAL!!!" Teresa shrieked at the woman. *"HOW CAN YOU LOSE A CHILD?"*

"We are looking everywhere," the nurse replied. "We are trying to find him."

Anger at the stupidity of the hospital staff, Teresa said, "Let me look for my son."

"I'm sorry, but we cannot allow that," the nurse said to her. "Please, just be patient. We will find him."

Teresa turned to her husband. ***"I WILL NOT HAVE MY SON'S ARM FIXED IN THIS HOSPITAL! I WANT HIM TO GO TO LONDON TO A SPECIALIST!"***

"You need to trust the people here," he said.

"I tried and look what they've done. NO!" she said.

Thirty minutes later a different nurse approached the couple. "We found your son," she said shyly.

"Where is he?" Teresa demanded.

"He is safe and asleep in the operating room. When the procedure was complete, they left him sleeping on the table and turned out the lights. No one thought to look in there for him," the nurse said.

"How stupid!" Teresa said. "How incompetent can they be! I want a referral to a London hospital. My son will NOT be treated in this hospital."

Later that night, Teresa and Dennis went home with their son and a referral to an orthopedic surgeon in London. Their appointment was the next day.

"We fix this type of break all the time," Dr. Willis told Teresa and Dennis. "We have two options. Once we put your son to sleep we will assess the damage. The first option is trying to pop the cap back onto the joint. If we feel the cap will not stay then option two is, to pin it in place. That is the more intense choice. This option involves surgery, but once the bone is back and set, it will be permanent."

"Will you tell us what you have done?" Teresa asked. Then she related the story of their previous hospital visit.

"Absolutely," he replied. "I will come and talk to you myself. Douglas is scheduled for early tomorrow morning. One of you is welcome to stay the night if you wish. We have a room set aside for parents from out of town."

"Thank you, Dr. Willis," Teresa replied. She wanted desperately to stay the night and wait for the results of her son's surgery the next morning.

Dennis refused to allow it. "He's not a momma's boy," he snapped at her. "He will be fine."

"I want to be here before he goes in and when he wakes up," she snapped at him.

"I'm going home now. You either come or you wait until tomorrow night when I come back up," he said sarcastically at her. "Douglas has to learn to face these things on his own."

"How cruel can you be!" she screamed at him. **"He's only five years old!"**

"He will be fine," he said.

"Ok, we go home tonight but be back up here before he goes into surgery tomorrow morning," she said as she tried to reason with him again.

"No," he replied. "I have to work tomorrow."

She knew she had lost the fight with him and vowed to never forgive him for this. Teresa kissed her son goodnight.

"Mommy, will you stay with me?" he begged.

"No sweetie, I can't. Daddy wants to go home. I'll see you tomorrow when you wake up," she said to her son. "I love you!"

She burst into tears as she left his room. "How can you be so unfeeling?" she said to Dennis. "He's all alone!"

He refused to answer and she was unable to say another word to him for days.

Teresa tried going to work the next day. Trying desperately to concentrate, she found she was unable to take her mind off her little boy. Her work suffered that day and she made mistake after mistake. The principal was very understanding.

That evening they returned to the hospital. Douglas was very happy to see his mommy. Teresa hugged her son gently and kissed his cheeks. "I'm so happy to see you," she said to him.

Dr. Willis walked in the room to check on Douglas.

He explained to Teresa and Dennis that he had to surgically replace the cap of Douglas' elbow and pin it. "The one side stayed in. However, the second side refused to stay in place," he told them. "That is the reason for the large splint. He's a very healthy young man and should heal quickly," he said as he smiled down at the boy. "I want him to have physiotherapy. It will help him regain his strength and mobility. Your family doctor can make the arrangements locally for you." Before he left the room, he turned to Douglas and said, "See you later big guy!" The boy smiled at him and waved with his good arm.

Eight weeks after surgery, Teresa took her son back up to see the surgeon. "Everything healed well," he said. "I'm very pleased. Have your family doctor arrange for physio now," he told Teresa.

She thanked him. "I appreciate everything you have done for my son," she said as she shook hands with the surgeon.

They left the hospital thinking everything would be fine. It wasn't. Their family doctor didn't think physiotherapy was necessary. "He's an active boy," the doctor said to Teresa. "Playing should give him enough exercise."

Teresa tried to argue her point but the doctor flatly refused to listen.

Upset with the situation, she said to her son on the way home. "Would you like mommy to help you with your arm?"

"Yes," he said and promised to do his exercises with her every day.

True to his word, Douglas did exactly what his mother told him. Together they developed their own physiotherapy program and the two enjoyed the bonding time every day. Douglas' strength and mobility returned. Soon he was able to use both his hands and arms equally as he had done before the accident.

When Andrea babysat Teresa's children, she never again left them unsupervised. Teresa thought the problems with her mother would calm down now. She had no idea she was about to walk into the eye of a hurricane...Hurricane Andrea.

Protecting Her Children and Breaking the First Cycle

"I did then what I knew how to do. Now that I know better, I do better."

Maya Angelou

Growing up as Teresa did, the youngest child, in a home where her sister was the favoured child, she was concerned that history would repeat itself with Andrea babysitting her children. She had always assumed that age would have mellowed her parents, which it did with Edward, but Andrea, Teresa was unsure about.

Her parents were devoted to Douglas as a baby and young boy. He was their first grandson and the first grandchild they were allowed to see. Patricia had not returned to the family which left a large gap in her parents' hearts.

Teresa always wondered how Andrea would cope having a second child under her care. She was about to get her answer.

One Friday afternoon, Teresa left work early. She'd had a terrible headache all day and knew she just needed to go home and rest. With her father at work, there was no point in calling her parent's house.

Andrea was completely deaf by now and had given up wearing any type of hearing aid years earlier.

Unlocking the back door of her parent's home, she heard her mother's voice raised in anger. "Maybe Edward was home and that's who she is yelling at," she thought. Walking through the kitchen, Teresa soon realized her mother's angry voice was coming from the bedroom. Stopping just outside the bedroom door, Teresa listened to what her mother was saying.

"I hate your guts, you little brat!" she yelled. "Why can't you be more like your brother? He's a good boy and does what I tell him. You never do what you're told! I hate you!" his grandmother yelled at him.

Armed with enough ammunition to sink a battle ship, Teresa stepped into the room. There was her 18 month old son Kevin, standing in his crib. His little hands gripped the railing of the bed as he stood wide-eyed staring at his grandmother as she berated him. His beautiful little face was tear stained and agonized with trauma.

Teresa made the move to rescue her son. As she stepped between her mother and child, Andrea snapped back to reality.

"What on earth do you think you are doing?" Teresa screamed at her mother. "You do not speak to him like that."

"He wouldn't lay down for his nap," Andrea said.

"Well, he certainly won't now," Teresa retorted. Hugging her little boy to her, Kevin soon stopped crying. "Why would you talk to him like that?" she demanded from her mother.

"He just won't do what I say," Andrea replied. "Douglas was always such a good boy, but this one isn't."

"You are finished!" Teresa shouted at her mother. "I'm taking my son home now. I will be back in one hour to collect the rest of their belongings. Make sure it's all ready. My sons will never step foot in this house again." She turned and left the house.

Furious with what she had witnessed she began wondering how long her mother had been treating Kevin this way. "History is repeating itself," she thought. "I will not have her do to my children what she did to me."

One hour later, Teresa returned to the house. This time she went in the front door. Her mother sat in her chair in the living room window waiting. As Teresa entered the house, her father met her in the hallway. "What went on here?" he asked her. "Your mother is very upset."

"She should be," Teresa replied. After relating the events she had witnessed an hour earlier, Teresa said to Edward. "You are welcome to come to the house to see the boys, **but do *NOT* bring her**. Not until she gets help!"

Walking out the door, Teresa felt energized. She was protecting her children from her own abusers. No one was going to harm her children. Not while she was alive!

A few weeks passed and she had no contact with her parents. Realizing part of this was her own fault, for not stepping up sooner to remove her parents from her life, Teresa tried desperately not to let her own guilt consume her. "Am I a bad mother for putting my children in harm's way?" she wondered. She tried her best. With very little information or positive role models in her life, Teresa did her best, but deep in her heart, she was capable of so much more.

One day after school, Douglas said to Teresa, "Mommy, I saw grandma at school today. She talked to me at lunch time."

"What?" Teresa asked her son. Working within the school system, Teresa knew **no one** was allowed to approach the children outside. "Tell me what happened," she said to Douglas.

"I was out playing and she walked up to the playground and called me over," he said. "She said she missed me and wanted to see me."

"Alright sweetie," Teresa replied to her son. "Your grandmother is not supposed to do that. She is breaking the rules. I would prefer you not talk to her again. I will take care of everything."

"Ok mommy," Douglas said, then ran off to go play.

For the next week, Teresa went out on yard duty. She watched and waited for her mother to appear. Then to her surprise Andrea walked up to the playground. Teresa came around the building and approached her. "What are you doing here?" she asked.

"I'm here to see Douglas," Andrea replied.

"As someone who has been warned to stay away from a child, you should not be doing this. I can easily call the police and have you arrested for approaching a child on school grounds," Teresa told her.

Andrea stared at her.

"I am warning you for the last time. Stay away from my children until you can prove to me that you have sought help for your mental problems," Teresa warned.

Andrea stared at her daughter. "I'll do what I want," she sneered.

"Not where my children are concerned you won't," Teresa snapped and walked away leaving her mother standing.

Teresa knew her mother would not give up. The woman was mentally ill and needed help. "I am not going to wait until you kidnap my child," Teresa thought.

The next day Teresa went to a lawyer. He drafted a letter of warning to Andrea and Edward to never approach Teresa or her children again. If they did not comply with the letter a restraining order would follow.

The weight of a mountain had been removed from Teresa's shoulders. She had taken the first step in breaking the cycle of abuse in her family. "No one is going to harm my children," she vowed. Armed with the feeling of empowerment, she felt confident her life would change. "I'm strong and I can survive!"

A Woman In Desperate Need of Her Husband

"The truth that many people never understand is that the more you try to avoid suffering, the more you suffer, because smaller and more insignificant things begin to torture you, in proportion to your fear of being hurt. "

Thomas Merton

Marching on with life Teresa continued to work at the school, began preparations for the next round of union negotiations and to be a mom. When at home she cooked, cleaned, did the yard work, and looked after her children. She gave up going to aerobics classes; she just didn't have the extra time or energy.

Teresa was experiencing migraines every day now to some degree. Her specialist had her tracking everything she ate, everything she did, her sleeping habits, etc. He was trying to get a picture of what was causing the debilitating headaches.

Originally she wouldn't have a severe headache until Friday, but things had deteriorated. Now it was Wednesday and she found her head was about to split.

Driving herself to her doctor to receive an injection she was told to go straight home. "I can't," she told the doctor. "You know he won't pick up the kids. So I have to go get them."

"You must have rest," the doctor ordered her. "You can't rest with little kids at home."

"They are actually very good," she said. "They cuddle up with me on the couch and watch a Disney movie while I sleep," she explained.

"Your husband should help you more," the doctor snapped.

"I know but he won't," Teresa said. "He's too busy helping everyone else."

It was true. Every Saturday, Dennis would help out the neighbours or the friends in the club he belonged to. At times Teresa's migraines were so bad, she would beg him, "Please stay home and watch the kids for me. My headache is so bad I can't focus my eyes," she would say with tears streaming down her face. But in the end, her pleas fell on deaf ears. He would walk out the door leaving her with the two boys and a massive migraine.

This was not the only problem she faced. Her boys were beginning to notice their father's lack of family time. "Why does daddy always leave?" Douglas would ask her. "Doesn't he like us? Why won't he ever play with us, mommy?"

Teresa's heart broke for her children in so many ways. "I'll play with you, sweetie," she would say. Fighting the effects of the injection she would play Lego or transformers with her boys.

What little love and respect she still had for her husband was wearing thin. "He's never here for us," she thought.

Teresa kept her home and yard spotless and took great pride her accomplishments. She was a perfectionist. Her efforts were not appreciated. Dennis would actually complain that the house was too clean, telling their neighbour one afternoon that, "I could really eat off the floor." Most men would be pleased to come home to a clean house but Teresa was realizing she would never be appreciated by her husband, no matter what she did.

Her loneliness grew as did her stress levels. She fought every day to keep up the work, the kids, the house and yard. There was never any time for her.

An old shoulder and neck injury Teresa suffered as a child was beginning to resurface. When she was seven years old she went to her neighbour's house to play alone in the backyard. She had a great rapport with the elderly woman and visited her frequently. This hot afternoon Teresa didn't want to be home with Patricia so she went to climb the massive old willow tree. It was a cranky old tree whose foliage covered most of the back yard.

Teresa loved climbing trees. She was quite the outdoor little girl or "Tomboy" as active girls used to be called. On this occasion she was hanging upside down about five feet off the ground on a large horizontal limb. Having done this a million times off trees and clothesline poles, she was confident in her abilities. It was fun hanging upside down.

On this day, something spooked her. Suddenly her legs let go of their grip on the branch and she fell. The top of her head connected with the hard-packed ground. Landing with her body straight up and down it was the impact that caused her body to collapse in the end. Teresa felt her neck give way and her body folded down over top of her. Fear struck her as she lay on the ground, unable to move. "If they see what I did, I'm going to get in trouble for falling," she thought. Struggling to sit up a horrible wave of nausea washed over her and she vomited. "I have to get home," she said out loud. It took her three attempts to stand.

Finally, on her feet she staggered next door to her house.

"If I tell them I fell, I'm going to get beaten," she knew. "I just won't say anything," she decided. After laying down for a while on her bed, claiming an upset stomach, Teresa pretended nothing had happened. She never told anyone she had fallen.

Over the years as she grew, her neck caused her some discomfort. Since her marriage, her neck grew worse and her chronic headaches began. Now unable to control the migraines with medication, her doctor suggested a different mode of treatment.

"I know of a great physiotherapist in London," he told her. "I want you to go see her."

Adding to her stress, Teresa now drove to London once a week after work for her treatments. She met with the owner of the physiotherapy clinic and immediately felt a connection to the woman.

Gloria is brilliant. She helped Teresa understand what her body was telling her. "Learn to read the signals and take control of the situation. You can, in time, keep the pain under control by being proactive," Gloria told her. "The muscles in your neck and shoulders have been tense for a long time. The top of your shoulder feels like a rock," Gloria commented. "I will do some trigger point work on you to help release the knots in the muscles, and I will teach you how to stretch properly, and help you to recognize the signals your body is sending when trauma is occurring. That will be your best ammunition. But the most important thing you can do for yourself is to learn to not be under so much stress. Can you get any help at home?" she asked.

"My husband doesn't help with anything at home," Teresa replied. "I've asked and I've begged, but it's no use. I'm on my own with this. I don't matter to him."

After a two-hour treatment in the clinic, Teresa felt battered and bruised. Then she would have to drive over an hour to collect her children, go home and make dinner for her family. Many times she would follow her husband's vehicle down the road towards home. "He could have picked up the kids, but just doesn't want to," she said to herself. Seeing this created anger in her which set off the tension in her neck and shoulders again. At this point in her life, Teresa didn't know how to deal with stress. She had lived with it as a friend all her life.

The physiotherapy appointments continued for months. Teresa was learning a great deal about fitness and muscular health. Gloria also believed Teresa was suffering from Fibromyalgia.

Teresa's next trip to London was to University Hospital. There she was seen by Dr. Mc Cain who specialized in Fibromyalgia and Chronic Pain Disorders.

The doctor was shocked at how exhausted Teresa was. After lengthy testing he said to her, "You are suffering from severe Fibromyalgia and Chronic Pain. Fibromyalgia is a disorder that we characterize by widespread musculoskeletal pain. It is almost always accompanied by extreme fatigue, sleep, memory and often mood issues. This disorder can also affect the way in which your brain processes pain signals."

"What do you suggest I do to help myself?" Teresa asked.

"I run an intake clinic here at the hospital. I want to you be part of the program. Here you will learn everything you need to know to help you live a productive life; to keep your pain levels low and to be proactive in the treatment and prevention of flare ups. The program is four weeks long, and you must stay on campus during the week. You can go home on weekends."

"I don't think my husband will like that," Teresa said.

"Never mind what he thinks," the doctor said. "You need to be in this program."

Later that evening Teresa told her husband what the doctor had said.

"No," Dennis said. "You can't be away from here for all that time. What would I do with the kids?"

"I need the help," Teresa said to him. "I'm so exhausted all the time and I can't live with the headaches anymore." Beginning to cry, Teresa said to him, "I can't live like this much longer."

"You can't go!" he said. "See if the doctor can help you in another way."

Returning to the specialist, Teresa told him her husband refused to support her through the treatment program. "He won't allow me to be away from home that long, and he refuses to help or support me. He doesn't think there is anything wrong with me," she told the doctor. "He thinks it's all in my head."

The specialist was furious. ***"Chronic Pain is not in a person's head.*** It is real and people need to be educated about it. Given your level of exhaustion and pain, I recommend, and will help you apply for a disability pension. If you don't stop working now, you will ruin your body and your life," Dr. Mc Cain said to her.

Staring at him in disbelief, Teresa said, "But I have to work. I can't afford to sit at home and he won't like it." Knowing in her heart her body was beaten down physically, she knew she couldn't push herself much more. She also knew Dennis would not understand and she was afraid to tell him.

Before she left the specialists office, he had the paperwork for the disability benefits completed. "Fill out the rest and send it away. It is your only option to help you recover. My clinic would have taught you how to prepare yourself and give you the tools to help life with and management the chronic pain. I am sorry you won't be part of the group. I hope you will reconsider," he said.

"Thank you Dr. Mc Cain," Teresa said. She left the office knowing she would have to face this battle alone...like always. "How on earth am I going to do this," she thought. "I'm so tired and my head hurts so much, I have no fight left in me."

Teresa was ready to give up. Her constant migraines made life unbearable. Any noise aggravated the headaches. The injections only took the peak of the pain away. It did nothing to squash the rest of the headaches. As time went on her headaches got worse. At times it felt as if someone was beating her head with a sledgehammer. It would have hurt less if she had beaten her own head against a wall. On top of the pain, she began vomiting during the headache. Half laying on the bathroom floor, propped up on the side of the toilet with her fists clenched against her head, Teresa spent hours vomiting and trying to recover. At times she was unable to help her children with their needs and her guilt was compounded. "Some mother I am," she thought.

Over the last several months, Kevin refused to sleep at night. Something had scared him and he would sit in his room and scream. In desperate need for sleep, Teresa tried brining him into their bed so she could rest.

"Get him out of here!" Dennis demanded. **"He can sleep in his own bed!"**

"He won't sleep!" she screamed. "Something has scared him and he just needs comfort. I need the sleep too."

"No!" Dennis snapped. "Put him in his own room and close the door. He will cry himself to sleep."

"He doesn't," she yelled at him. "You sleep through it all because it isn't important to you! I can't sleep because I'm his mother and I hear every noise he makes. Bringing him in here for a couple of nights is the only way I will get sleep. **I NEED SLEEP TOO!"**

"NO!" he bellowed. "I won't allow it."

"You are so selfish," Teresa declared. "How can you be so heartless?"

Knowing the only way she could sleep was to go into her son's room and sit by him. He wanted her close and just sitting in a chair in his room was insufficient. He wanted physical contact with his mother. Sitting on his bed holding his hand would cause Teresa to relax and she would fall asleep. She also fell over. So as a compromise, she sat on the floor beside his bed with her hands on him. Her little boy was comforted enough that he finally fell asleep. Teresa laid her head down on her arms and fell into a fitful sleep.

In the morning she woke up stiff and very sore, but her son had slept. Her son was all that mattered to her.

Dennis argued with her and demanded she not baby the boy. "You're just going to spoil him," he announced.

"What does it matter to you," she snapped back. "I'm the one here for them; not you."

For weeks Teresa defied Dennis' wishes and spent the night on the floor beside her young son. Eventually her son was able to find his happy place and sleep on his own again.

"You're crazy!" he yelled at her.

"My main priority is my children," she stated to him. "I will do anything for my children!"

Teresa desperately wanted to give her children the love and understanding of a good home. Something she had always wanted and needed; something her parents were not able to provide.

The End of an Era

"You may encounter many defeats, but you must not be defeated. In fact, it may be necessary to encounter the defeats, so you can know who you are, what you can rise from, how you can still come out of it."
Maya Angelou

By end of the school year of 1991, Teresa was physically drained. She devoted all her time to her children, her work, her job and the collective bargaining unit she represented.

After learning from Gloria about chronic pain and Fibromyalgia, she believed she could cope. She had learned how to recognize the warning signs and understood what to do but did not have the luxury of time on her side.

After her day at work was done, she had either meetings, phone calls or planning to do for the upcoming negotiations of her bargaining unit. Teresa threw herself, heart and soul into everything she did. Half-way was not an option for her. She was a perfectionist.

In September, she went back to work at the school. Kevin developed chicken pox and had to be kept out of school and away from the babysitters. Teresa turned to the only person she had left as family: her grandmother, Aline.

Aline opened her doors to Kevin and enjoyed the little boys company. They became great friends as Kevin filled an empty spot in Aline's life.

Now with contract negotiations over Teresa was completely drained. She had absolutely nothing left to give. Hoping the contract would include long term disability, she was very upset when the item was voted down. "Now what do I do?" she thought to herself. "I am the one that needed it!"

After the Christmas holidays when the new school year began, Teresa knew she had nothing left. Upset, unable to continue and admitting defeat, she knew the doctor was right.

"There is just too much right now," she told her specialist. "I can't keep going." Teresa completed the application for Disability Benefits, expecting that with some time off, proper treatments and training, she would one day soon return to work. She believed this road would only be temporary.

Immediately Dennis' first comment was about the money. "Of course everything is more important than I am," she thought.

As it turned out, Teresa's disability payments were close to what she had been making at the school. However, her husband continued to complain. She did her best to ignore him and focus on her own health.

Learning how to care for herself made her a better mother. Definitely she was under less stress and she had more time to spend with her boys. They enjoyed having their mom at home. Every day she walked them to and from school. She went on class trips with them and was always there whenever they needed her. She was not an absent mother.

Teresa practiced her routine of exercise and stretching every day. She walked to the store or library and actually stopped to smell roses. Developing a love for flowers, Teresa added gardening to her list of exercises. Their yard was transformed into a beautiful oasis. People would stop and talk about her plants and admire her designs. Teresa felt better than she had in a long time. She had the understanding that her condition would never disappear, but it was manageable.

Even though her income wasn't great, she was still contributing to the income. Dennis didn't see it that way. Teresa had enough of his complaining and after one year at home applied to Fanshawe College to their two-year Developmental Service Worker Program. Not necessarily wanting to work hand-in-hand with the clients, Teresa believe if she had a good working background knowledge, she could apply her experience in business and develop a good career for herself.

That was her goal and she was excited about it. Into her first semester her marks were great. She attended school during the day and did homework in the evening. Teresa had gained knowledge in anatomy, training programs, abnormal psychology and learning disabilities. Life was good.

Then her family began complaining. "You're always studying. You never have time for us. Why isn't dinner on the table at 5:30?" The complaints were often and sometimes harsh. She supported them in everything they did, but her husband and children were incapable of helping her.

Even though her grades were good, Teresa found the added pressure from her family too much. Her stress levels went through the roof and the headaches that had been absent for almost eight months returned.

"How can you be so selfish?" she asked her husband.

"You just don't need to be there," he replied.

Teresa now began to wonder if her husband was behind the complaints from her children. "Was it sabotage?" she thought.

Admitting defeat again, Teresa gave up on school. "I will never forgive him for his lack of understanding," she thought.

Two months later, stunned and angry at her husband, she sat and listened as he told her he wanted to take courses in business from Fanshawe College.

A heated argument ensued and Teresa refused to speak to him until she was able to calm down. She made no concessions for his school work and took no pity on him.

Late one spring night, Teresa received a call from her grandmother Aline.

Panic rose in Teresa's throat. It was 12:30 in the morning, and Teresa was aware her grandmother retired at 9:00pm every day.

"Hello," Teresa said into the phone.

"Teresa, helppp meeee," the weak voice replied.

"Grandma!" Teresa said. "What's wrong. What happened?"

"Please come to the house," the older woman said before the phone went dead.

Teresa and Dennis rushed over to Aline's house. As she walked in her grandmother's home, a shroud of panic washed over her. Teresa immediately knew there was something seriously wrong here.

Teresa found her grandmother laying on the floor in the dining room beside the phone. The eighty-year-old woman was unconscious. Quickly placing the receiver back on the phone, Teresa ordered her husband to call the ambulance. Running to the bedroom, she grabbed a blanket and returned to her grandmother and covered her gently.

"Grandma," she whispered. "Grandma," she tried again, a bit louder. She received no response.

Laying her hand, a bit heavier on her grandmother's shoulder, Teresa called her again. This time, the older woman stirred.

"Don't move," Teresa ordered. "We have help on the way."

Aline began to cry. No one had ever seen her in a weakened condition and she was ashamed.

Teresa got a cool cloth and sat beside her grandmother on the floor. "Don't move please," Teresa urged as she wiped the older woman's forehead. "Everything will be fine."

Aline reached up and grabbed her granddaughter's hand. The woman was shaking.

"It's ok Grandma," Teresa said soothingly. "I'm here. Just be patient."

Her grandmother squeezed her hand as tight as she could.

"Do you want to tell me what happened," Teresa asked.

Tears started to form again in the old woman's eyes. "I had to get up through the night," she began. "I went back to bed and when I turned around to sit on the bed to take off my slippers, my leg gave out." Aline began to cry harder.

"Shhh," Teresa whispered. "It's ok."

"I hit my hand on the bedside table when I fell. I was trying to stop myself from falling," Aline continued.

"But grandma!" Teresa exclaimed. "Your bedroom is thirty feet away. How did you get to the phone?"

"I tried to get up," Aline continued. "My leg wouldn't work, so I crawled here."

Teresa knew her grandmother was a strong woman, but she now witnessed how strong her grandmother's survival instincts were.

"Teresa," Aline said. "You have to clean the carpet. I think I left blood from the cut on my hand."

"Ok, Grandma," Teresa replied. "I'll take care of it."

Suddenly a knock on the door pulled the two women from their conversation. Dennis went to the door to admit the ambulance attendants.

Aline whispered to her granddaughter, "Come with me, please," she begged as she refused to let go of Teresa's hand.

"I will grandma," Teresa promised. "You won't be alone. I love you!" Teresa had never said those words to her grandmother before. They felt odd yet comfortable. Aline squeezed Teresa's hand and refused to let go.

Once the older woman was placed on the stretcher, the attendant turned to Teresa and said, "Looks like she broke her hip."

"Can I come with her?" Teresa asked. Her grandmother still had not released her hand.

With permission, Teresa climbed into the back of the ambulance with her grandmother. "I'm right here grandma," she said reassuringly. "I won't let anything happen to you."

Aline relaxed and allowed the technician to do his job.

Teresa and Aline were inseparable. "I'm here, Grandma," she said repeatedly in assurance to her grandmother.

"Stay with me," Aline said as the doctor walked in.

"Aline," the doctor began. "Looks as though you broke your hip. Your bones are extremely thin," he commented. Holding up the x-ray, he showed Teresa how Aline's bones barely showed on the image. I have to operate to repair her hip," he told them.

Aline panicked, she knew afraid she was going to die. A few hours later, the proper paperwork was signed and Aline gave her granddaughter a kiss. "What blood type are you?" she asked Teresa

"I'm O negative, grandma. Why?" Teresa asked.

"I am the same blood type," Aline replied. "If I need blood during the operation, I want it directly from you."

Surprised at her grandmother's words, Teresa replied, "Grandma, I don't think they do things that way anymore."

Aline became agitate and had a look of desperation in her eyes. Teresa looked into the aged eyes of her grandmother/Godmother and replied, "I'll talk to the doctor. I will see you after your surgery."

Aline relaxed and allowed the nurses to step in beside her.

Her surgery was successful. The surgeon told Teresa, "I did the best I could. Her bones are very weak so I'm not certain the implant will hold."

"What do I need to do to help her?" she asked.

"She will need physiotherapy and homecare. I will arrange for those from here," he told Teresa. "Keep an eye on her as best you can."

"I will check on her every day," Teresa replied.

Aline was a strong and invincible woman. In a matter of months, she was up walking and asking Teresa to take her out for a piece of lemon meringue pie, which was her favourite dessert.

Teresa enjoyed the time with her grandmother. The two were developing a deep bond. Neither woman knew just how much in common they shared.

Several months after her hip surgery, Teresa went to Aline's house to check on her. She found the older woman sitting in the living room with her head in her hands. "Grandma!" she said. "What's the matter?

The old woman looked up at her and said, "I've had a bad headache for a couple of weeks now, but today I can't clear my eyes. Can you take me to the doctor?"

"Yes, of course," Teresa said. She helped her grandmother change her clothes and walk out to the car. "She really can't see well," Teresa thought to herself.

The doctor examined Aline's eyes. "I want you to take her to the ophthalmologist right away," Aline's doctor said to Teresa. "Something is happening with her eyes, but the specialist is better equipped to give you an answer."

Quickly driving her grandmother to Simcoe, they were ushered into the doctor's office. A long eye examination ensued. Teresa watched her grandmother. She could see Aline was nervous by the way she rubbed her fingers together.

When the exam was complete, the doctor approached the women.

"Aline has suffered Retinal Detachment," the doctor announced.

Teresa stared blankly at the doctor. "What does that mean?" she asked.

"This is a condition when the light-sensitive layer of tissue inside the eye detaches itself from its normal position. If it remains detached, the optic nerve will stop sending messages to the brain," he explained. "There is a great deal of blood pooling up behind her eyes, so I can't tell the full extent of the damage yet. We will just have to wait until I can get a better idea on what damage has been done," he said.

"What will happen to my grandmother's eyesight?" Teresa asked.

"Depending on how much damage has been done, I don't believe Aline's eyesight will recover. If I had seen her as soon as it happened, the chances would have been better," he stated.

Teresa looked at her grandmother. The older woman's chin quivered, but she held her composure.

"Come back next week," the doctor said. "Hopefully by then I will be able to give you a better answer."

Aline was very quiet on the drive home.

Teresa reached over and took her grandmother's hand, "I'll help you in any way I can grandma," she said. Aline squeezed Teresa's hand in reply but remained silent.

The prognosis was not good. "Unfortunately the damage was extensive," the eye specialist told them the following week. "The best you can hope for is peripheral vision," he told the women.

"What can we do?" Teresa asked him.

"Register your grandmother with the Canadian National Institute for the Blind," he replied. "They have programs that can help with setting up her home and assist in other aspects for her everyday living." "Aline," the doctor said. "You also have cataracts. I would like to remove them, if you are agreeable. With the cataracts gone, you may have more light entering your eyes. That can help."

Aline agreed to the cataract surgery. Unfortunately for her, it didn't improve her vision at all. Aline was almost completely blind. The struggles she faced seemed a twist of fate. At eighty-one years of age, she lived independently, drove her own vehicle and cared for herself completely, as she had done for the past thirty-five years since Marcel's death. Now for the first time in her life, she was forced to depend on another person.

Aline was a strong woman who had survived the adversity of her young years. Now she trustingly placed her life in her granddaughter's hands. Teresa hugged her grandmother tightly. "I'm here for you, grandma. Always," she said to the older woman. She had developed a deep love and admiration for her grandmother. "Come and live with me," Teresa said to her.

Tears rolled down Aline's cheeks. "Do you have room for me?" she asked.

"I will make room for you," Teresa replied. "I will take care of you."

Aline began to weep. She let her granddaughter hold her as she cried.

"I love you, grandma," Teresa whispered.

"I love you too," the older woman replied.

Aline's sense of independence would not allow her to accept her granddaughter's invitation. She wanted to stay in her home; a home she had built with her husband.

Teresa knew this was a bad decision, but her grandmother was a stubborn woman. "It will have to be her own idea," Teresa said to her husband one evening. "I can't force her."

Everyday Teresa went to check on Aline. She knew the woman was struggling. Aline was a gifted knitter and did exceptional embroidery and needlepoint work. She used to fill her days visiting her friends for coffee, shopping at the local stores, reading or working her magic with her hands. Now, she sat and listened to the television and radio.

Teresa helped the woman as much as possible. A lady cleaned for Aline, while Teresa prepared her meals. Douglas and Kevin read stories to their great-grandmother which allowed for wonderful quality time.

Through the help of the C.N.I.B., Teresa connected Aline with talking books. Together they marked the recorder to indicate the start and stop buttons for ease of use. Aline enjoyed the books. She did not, however, enjoy being a 'burden,' on people.

The once strong, vibrant woman, now depended on Teresa for every aspect of her life. Teresa bathed her grandmother, which the older woman felt very ashamed about. Teresa enjoyed setting her grandmother's hair every week and spent hours talking about their lives. This was a new experience for both women. Sixty-five years in age difference disappeared when they talked. Aline was beginning to trust and Teresa's admiration for the woman grew. They really enjoyed their time in the kitchen baking together.

A system was developed between the two women. Aline made Teresa her primary care-giver legally and signed over power of attorney for both medical and financial care.

When news of this made its way to Edward and Danielle, the war began. Her children, who had maintained their distance from their mother for years now decided they should be entitled to her fortune.

Aline felt she was at the end of her life and usefulness. If she couldn't see, she wanted to die. Smelling the end and money in the air, her children circled like vultures.

Opening the Heart and Home for the Love of Family

"Love begins at home, and it is not how much we do...but how much love we put in that action."
Mother Teresa

Aline didn't want to leave her home yet. She and Marcel had built this house for their retirement in 1968. Despite not being ready, another link was added to the heavy chain of burden Aline bore just after she turned 80 years old.

While she stayed in her home, Aline once again fell and her repaired hip broke again. "I cannot replace her hip in this hospital," the emergency room physician said to Teresa. "She will have to go to London."

Aline lay in her hospital room crying. "One thing after another is going wrong," she said to Teresa.

"Am I being punished? Why is this all happening to me? I just want to die!"

"I don't know grandma," Teresa answered as she sat beside Aline. "I'll be here with you always," she whispered.

The next day Aline was transported to London. Teresa followed the ambulance and never left her grandmother's side. The women met with the surgeon and gained a good understanding of what would be happening. Aline needed a complete hip replacement.

"It will be challenging," the surgeon told Teresa. "Her bones are so thin. I'm not sure the femoral stem will cement properly into the femur. Over time the stem may move around inside the bone, which can cause pain and discomfort."

"I'm sure you will do your best for my grandmother," Teresa said, trusting the surgeon.

Aline's surgery went well. One week later she was walking around with the aid of a walker. The embarrassment of using an assistive device was evident on her face. "It's ok grandma," Teresa said to her. "We all need help some time."

After being released from the hospital, Aline lived in Teresa's house. Kevin offered his bedroom to his great-grandma, which made the elderly lady's heart sing with joy.

Now with five people living in the house, the walls began to close in. Dennis had always talked about building a house, but Teresa felt their property was large enough for an addition. Dennis refused.

"I've always dreamed of owning a farm," he said. "Let's buy a farm and build a house. It's my dream!"

Plans were made to sell their home and a vacant 100-acre farm just outside of town was purchased. Excavation began on the large home. In April, Teresa and Dennis' home sold.

"Now what?" she said to him. "Where do we go?"

Aline replied, "We can all move into my house. When you get farther along with building, we can list my house and then move onto the farm."

It was a good idea. Teresa packed up her house, cared for her grandmother and children and planned the new home. The new 3,400 square foot home sat central to the front of the farm. Two acres of land had been designated for the large stone home to sit on. It truly was a beautiful location.

As construction began, Teresa and Dennis worked side by side with the builder. "It will save us money if we do a lot of the work ourselves," Dennis said casually, just expecting his wife to fall into place.

Already exhausted from caring for her family, two houses, packing, moving and her grandmother's constant care, Teresa became numb. She turned into a robot that went through the motions of living without feeling.

Aline's nurse stopped coming to the house after one week. Before leaving, she gave Teresa full instructions on changing her dressing; extra bandages and sterile tweezers to remove the staples out of her grandmother's leg three weeks' post-surgery.

Her time spent with her grandmother was precious. Aline confided in Teresa about her finances, her will and parts of her life. Teresa cared for her grandmother with love and compassion. During the day, Teresa delivered her children to school, cooked, cleaned and made many trips to the farm.

With the structure up, the extra work began. Dennis and Teresa ran electrical wiring throughout the house. It was a good thing Teresa was handy with tools. Her training beside her papa, Alphonse, came into play. She installed the electrical boxes, split the wires and made the proper connections. Then it was time for insulation.

The boys helped when their schoolwork allowed. Douglas stepped up and helped his mother insulate the basement. It was horrible work in the summer heat, but together they had a job well-done.

Dennis hired his friend to do the plumbing and another friend to install the furnace; all reputable tradesmen in their own rights. He also hired a company to do the drywall work. Teresa was relieved. The sheets of drywall were too heavy and awkward for her to handle.

Teresa had to take some time away from the construction site while the drywall installers worked. It was a good thing she did.

One afternoon while talking with Aline, Teresa noticed her grandmother's face went blank and she hunched over in her chair. Rushing to her side immediately, Teresa was able to rouse the older woman.

"Grandma!" Teresa exclaimed. "What happened? Are you alright?"

Aline was breathing but was unable to speak. Teresa tried hard not to panic. She sat with her grandmother and held her hand and talked to her about random topics. She was trying to distract herself as much as her grandmother.

Twenty minutes later, Aline was back to normal; normal in every way. She refused to see a doctor. Teresa kept a close eye on the woman after this episode. Douglas and Kevin watched their great-grandmother in the evening when Teresa and Dennis went out to work on the house.

The ceramic tile in the mudroom, kitchen, powder room and front foyer needed to be installed. Dennis believed himself and expert, having watched and talked about how to install ceramic tile. They had driven to Hamilton and bought a lovely granite-type tile. Teresa believed it was perfect for high traffic-areas on a farm where sand from the fields was everywhere.

Night after night they worked like beasts of burden. Extra plywood was put down to make the floor sturdy. Teresa went behind Dennis and sunk a screw every two inches around each plywood sheet. Then came the wire mesh, which was stapled down. Finally, they were ready to start laying tile.

On hands and knees they worked applying scratch-coat, then tile, and spacers. Completely exhausted they would arrive home after 11:00p.m.; fall into a deep sleep, only to get up and start over again. They had seven hundred square feet of tile to lay.

Dennis went to work during the day, which left Teresa to ensure everyone was taken care of before going to the farm to work.

The builders were now installing the custom trim. Teresa had to stain and seal the trim. The installer refused to let her stain the trim prior to installation. "The joins will show. I'll put plastic behind the trim, then you can stain it when it's up; after the nail holes are filled," he told Teresa.

It made sense but it would be a lot more work for her.

Teresa became creative. She used on of the boys' skateboards to sit on and traveled around the house staining baseboards. The skateboard made life a great deal easier for her.

The living room window faced south on the farm. It was a large set of French doors with a transom above. It provided a beautiful view of the farm and 20-acre bush lot. The stone mason who was creating their enormous field stone fireplace left his scaffolding behind for Teresa to use to stain the window trim. She appreciated the kindness.

When their kitchen and bathroom cabinets were installed, Teresa had the fun job of staining those as well. Each night she went home with permanently stained hands, and very stiff back and a body pushed beyond its limits. "I'm too busy working to work," she thought. "He's forgotten why I'm home."

Aline began having spells which left her temporarily paralyzed and speechless. After several of these episodes, Teresa said, "Grandma, I'm taking you to the doctor. We are going to find out what is happening. This isn't normal."

Aline fought her granddaughter as much as she could, but the younger woman was very determined. "Just let me die," she told Teresa.

"No!" Teresa yelled at the older woman. "You aren't ready to go yet. He doesn't want you yet."

Aline consented to see the doctor. As much as Teresa disliked her grandmother's doctor, she thought he was a real quack, her grandmother's spells needed to be dealt with.

After the examination the doctor took Teresa aside and said, "Your grandmother is full of cancer. She is dying. We just need to make her remaining time more comfortable."

Staring at him in disbelief, Teresa said, "What are we going to do?"

"I'll prescribe her some medication. It will keep her sedated. She should stay in bed from now on," he said as he handed Teresa a prescription.

Teresa knew her grandmother was suffering. Deep in her heart she didn't believe the doctor but thought she should put her feelings aside and do what was best for her grandma.

The medication was strong painkillers and they knocked Aline flat. She truly became bedridden. Teresa became her full-time nurse. Aline wouldn't allow anyone else to help.

On top of caring for her children and the building of the house, Teresa made time to care for the woman she had grown to love. She fed her grandmother, changed her diapers, bathed her and most importantly, sat with her and talked. Teresa learned a great deal about the soft-hearted, kind woman.

Aline gave Teresa instructions about her funeral, how she wanted the grave-site cared for, and made Teresa promise that Edward and Danielle would not take control of her estate. "You know them," she said to Teresa. "You know what they are capable of. Protect yourself."

"I will, grandma," Teresa replied. "But you aren't going anywhere."

Teresa spent most of her summer with Aline bedridden and working on the house. Aline saw how exhausted her granddaughter was becoming. "Put me into a respite home for a couple weeks," Aline said. "You need some rest. You are ready to fall down."

Teresa refused her grandmother twice. After the third attempt, Teresa stopped fighting and made the arrangements.

Aline was placed in respite care for two weeks. Teresa didn't really have a rest, she just had more time to work on the farm and around her grandmother's house.

Her grandmother's home was surrounded by massive pine trees which wreaked havoc on her roof and yard. Every month the eaves troughs had to be cleaned out and the yard needed to be raked each time before cutting the grass. If you forgot, and ran over the pine cones, they became nasty projectiles that could put holes in windows and large dents in cars.

One very hot summer afternoon, Teresa was out front raking the yard before cutting the grass. Douglas called out to her. "Mom, telephone. It's aunt Patricia."

Teresa and her sister had tried to make their piece with each other over the last couple of years. It was the second such attempt. Patricia had asked her sister's help in escaping her first brutal marriage, which Teresa did. She gladly helped her move, find a lawyer and make sure her sister was safe with their parents.

Patricia had a new boyfriend, which Teresa liked. He was kind to her sister.

"Hello," Teresa said, answering the phone and trying to catch her breath at the same time.

"What the hell do you think you are doing?" Patricia demanded.

"Pardon?" Teresa asked.

"You did it! You're finally in grandma's house. Then you put her away somewhere and are taking all her money. You sneaky bitch!" Patricia shouted.

"What are you talking about?" Teresa demanded.

"You just want her money," Patricia announced with her voice full of malice. "You won't get away with it."

"I have no idea what you are talking about," Teresa said. "You are more than welcome to come here and help me do grandma's yard work," she commented sarcastically.

But her words fell on deaf ears. Her sister had hung up the phone.

Later that evening when Teresa was visiting Aline, she explained to her grandmother about the call. "Patricia isn't thinking right," Aline said. "I'll fix her."

Just as she finished speaking, Patricia and her boyfriend came walking in the room. She was on a mission. Her posture was one of authority and she was going to lay down the law.

Teresa bid her grandmother goodnight and left. She was finished with Patricia. "I wipe my hands of her for the last time," she told her husband that night.

But, it wasn't over. Patricia accused Teresa of stealing Aline's money and throwing the old woman out. All of Patricia's scheming and attempts at manipulation got her nowhere. Aline didn't like Patricia. She never had, believing she was just like Andrea, and it was true.

The good part about Aline's stay in the respite home was a new doctor took on her case. "She is severely over medicated," the new doctor told Teresa. "There is no evidence of stomach cancer or any type of cancer. I'm going to switch most of her medication and I'm sure in a few weeks she will be her normal self again."

One week later, Aline came home a new woman. She was walking without using her cane and was once again enjoying her life with her family. Douglas and Kevin enjoyed their great-grandmother, and she spoiled them with love. For their birthdays, she bought them each a new bicycle. The boys loved her and they took turns sitting with her and changing the tapes for her talking books. They had fun with Aline. Teresa's sons were tall and they enjoyed teasing Aline about her short stature. When they hugged her it always made her laugh as their arms wrapped around the top of her head. Teasingly they would say, "Grandma, where did you go?"

Later that fall, Aline's house sold. Now in a panic because the farm house was not finished, they had to push the contractor. The closing date on Aline's house was extended to the first middle of December, which was a blessing.

Aline decided she would call in her two children, one at a time, to let them take one or two items from her home. "That's all they get from me," she told Teresa.

"Grandma, are you sure you want them here?" Teresa asked. "I know how much they have hurt you in the past."

"Yes," Aline said. "It will be finished after that. They will only get what I give them."

That afternoon, Aline made the call to her son, Edward and her daughter, Danielle. She mentally prepared herself for what was to come.

The Vultures Swoop in for the Kill

"Earth provides enough to satisfy every man's needs, but not every man's greed."

Mahatma Gandhi

On the appointed day, Teresa left the house to go work on the construction. She worried the entire day about her grandmother. Knowing better than anyone what her family was capable of, she distrusted all of them. Teresa prayed her grandmother was strong enough to deal with the deceit and lies of her children and oldest granddaughter.

Aline admitted Edward into her home. "You can have two things from the house," she directed him. "Provided I agree with your choices," she strategically added.

Edward walked through the home as if shopping for treasures. His first choices were denied by his mother. Finally, he chose a cabinet she had brought back years earlier from one of her stays in Europe. His second choice item was a small figurine. Aline agreed and their meeting ended.

The next day, leaving the house once again to avoid any unpleasantness, Teresa went back out to the farm to work on the house.

Aline admitted Patricia into her home. This in itself was unusual as Aline had never spent much time with Patricia, and really didn't care for her. However, Aline was attempting to do right by her granddaughter.

Despite her best efforts to talk her grandmother out of moving in with Teresa, Patricia realized her efforts were in vain. "Your sister is the only one of my family who is helping me," Aline commented to Patricia sarcastically. "She is always here for me so don't say anything against her!"

"Patricia, I would like to give you this gold necklace and earrings," Aline announced. She gave Patricia no further opportunity to speak against Teresa.

Patricia accepted the necklace and said, "Thank you." Like the rest of those who were swooping in, she expected more...much more.

Teresa and Aline sat in the living room after dinner enjoying a cup of coffee and chatting about their day.

"What do you want out of the house?" Aline asked Teresa.

"The only thing I have ever truly loved in your house is your Swiss clock on the wall," Teresa answered honestly. "That is the only thing I would ever ask you for, grandma."

"It's yours then," Aline announced. "I know Danielle would like to have it, but then she wants everything in the house. I promise the clock is yours."

Teresa reached over and held her grandmother's hand. "Thank you grandma. That means the world to me. I have admired that clock all my life. I remember when you carried it back from Switzerland. It's beautiful. I will treasure it always."

"I know you will take care of it," Aline replied as she squeezed Teresa's hand. "Danielle is coming tomorrow." As soon as the words were spoken, Teresa felt Aline's hand tense.

"Do you want me to be here with you?"

"No," she replied. "I will handle her on my own."

Teresa's worries were set aside. "Do what want you want grandma. Not what they tell you to do." She smiled at the older woman. Teresa turned on the television and together they sat and watched Aline's favourite soap opera.

Danielle was as transparent as glass. She tried every form of manipulation available to her and even yelled at her mother, but her tirade went unanswered. Aline knew her daughter well. She was not about to play her daughter's game.

"You may take two things from the house; provided I agree with your choices," Aline instructed.

Danielle went straight for the Swiss clock. "No," Aline told her. "That is for Teresa."

Now hating the young woman who had once been her favourite niece, Danielle vowed revenge. She chose the two items from Aline's home she wanted and left. She was angry at her mother. She wanted to control her.

After years of treating her mother with disrespect and loathing, Danielle had always kept her eye on the bigger picture...Aline's estate. Now she felt threatened by Teresa and despised the younger woman.

With the visits now over, life as they knew it could once again settle down to a routine.

Aline announced to Teresa later in the week, "Everything that is left in the house is yours," she said.

Teresa looked at her grandmother in shock. "Grandma," she replied. "As long as you are with me, these things belong to you. I will just take care of them for you."

Aline smiled.

Teresa and Dennis continued to work on the farm house. The boys went back to school and Aline continued to listen to her books and learn to live her life without her full eyesight. She also continued to have mini strokes and kept her medication with her at all times; the spells were mostly kept under control.

The massive push began when the closing date for Aline's house drew nearer. The furnace was not completely installed in the new house and the company to install the carpets was delayed.

"We will just have to move in the way it is," Dennis snapped at her one day.

"How can you expect me to take my children and an old woman into a house with no heat in winter!" she screamed.

"The gas fireplace in the living room works. Just turn on the ceiling fan and it will distribute the heat," he replied sarcastically.

"You and the boys are gone during the day," Teresa declared. "Grandma and I are stuck in that house with no heat! What are you thinking?"

"Wrap her up in blankets and set her by the fire," was his answer. Teresa was stunned speechless by his lack of concern for her and Aline.

When she found her voice again, she said to Dennis, "You had better push the contractor to get that furnace in here as fast as possible. Make it happen," she warned.

As the first of December drew nearer, Teresa began packing up her grandmother's house. There was so much to pack and organize. They had enlisted the help of several of their friends, who over the years, as couples, always helped each other out. Aline helped Teresa with the packing as much as she was able, but Dennis was always busy somewhere else.

Teresa had called Edward the week before the move to ask if Aline could spend a week with them. She explained the furnace in the house wasn't ready. Andrea spoke up and shouted over the phone, **"She**

can only stay the day you move. After that YOU deal with her." Edward greeted Teresa and Aline at the door on moving day. Teresa kissed her grandma on the cheek and said, "I'll see you later, ok?"

"Ok," the older woman said as she kissed Teresa on her cheek and winked at her. "See you later."

Trusting Edward that he would care for his mother, Teresa left.

Arriving back at Aline's house, she walked into the kitchen, and greeted several male friends who were having coffee. "Where are your wives?" Teresa asked with concern. "I understood they were going to be helping me today."

"They can't make it," came all the replies. Teresa smiled at them and said, "Well, I'm glad you are here, we really appreciate your help." She excused herself and went to the bathroom on the far end of the house. She closed the door, sat on the edge of the bathtub and cried. "I've always helped them, no matter what," she cried. "I need help today!"

When her friends moved, Teresa did everything she could to help. She unpacked their kitchens, brought food over for their first meal and never thought twice about it. Now when she needed the help in return, no one was there. "It's just like always," she said to herself. "They always want my help, but no one is ever there for me. I cannot depend on anyone but myself. *I trust NO ONE!*"

Standing up she walked to the sink. Washing her face and drying it on her shirt, she pulled up her courage and went to work.

The Move from Hell

"We have no right to ask when sorrow comes, 'Why did this happen to me?' unless we ask the same question for every moment of happiness that comes our way."

Author Unknown

All day long the men moved furniture and boxes. It was chaos but organized chaos. Teresa had labelled every box with a location and content list. "Please do your best to ensure the boxes end up where they are supposed to be," she told the men.

Several pickup trucks and a couple of trailers moved the contents from one location to the final destination several kilometres away.

Now stationed at the farm house, Teresa directed traffic inside as she attempted to unpack some kitchen items. "They are going to want to eat when they are done," she thought. "I will have to come up with something."

The inside of the house was freezing. With no working furnace and the door constantly opening and closing, Teresa kept her coat on. She visibly saw her breath while moving about unpacking.

Teresa was tired and began to lose focus. She had been moving non-stop since 6:00 a.m. that morning. One of the wives stopped by at lunch with a bucket of chicken. Unable to eat from stress, Teresa thanked her friend, but kept on working. Her friend, not wanting to help, left after talking with her husband. There was no offer of help. The man looked at Teresa after his wife left and lowered his eyes in shame. Not a word was said.

By 5:00 p.m., Teresa received a phone call from Edward. "It's time you come and got your grandmother," he said. "She's been here long enough."

"You said you would keep her there until I was finished," Teresa shouted.

"Your mother wants her out now," Edward replied. "Come and get her now."

Putting aside what she was unpacking, Teresa climbed into her van and drove into town to pick up Aline.

Once at the house, Aline walked out the door to meet Teresa on the front steps. "I'm so glad you're here," Aline said. "Your mother is horrible!" she announced when they were driving away.

"She's not my mother!" Teresa replied. "I know she isn't right."

Back at the farm, Teresa had Aline's favourite chair and blanket set by the fireplace. She ensured Aline was warm, and comfortable before she returned to her tasks.

Now, with Aline here, Teresa felt it was a major priority to set up the older woman's bedroom. Her bed and dressers had been delivered earlier that day. Aline's sofa and television were placed in the sitting room that adjoined her bedroom.

Working like a woman-possessed, Teresa made up her grandmother's bed and unpacked her clothing. By

7:00 p.m. that evening Aline's room was complete, minus the pictures being hung on the walls.

Aline was completely exhausted and wanted to go to bed. Most of the helpers had left leaving Teresa and her family trapped in a house that looked like a disaster zone.

Teresa was proud of her sons. They were each given control over their own bedrooms and both had their beds ready for a place to sleep. "It's cold in our rooms, Mom," they announced.

"I know, guys," she replied. "Take extra blankets and some sleeping bags and pile them on your beds for the night. Do the best you can to keep warm. If it gets too cold, come down into the living room and camp out."

Teresa was beginning to feel ill. She felt faint and her entire body was shaking. When she tried to speak, her words were slurred from her jaw chattering. "I have to go lay down," she said to Dennis. She staggered into the living room and collapsed on the one sofa. "I'm cold," she said. Her boys jumped into action and each brought a blanket for their mom. Ten minutes later, Teresa repeated as her body continued to vibrate, "I'm so cold. Please get me another blanket."

Dennis left to make another trip back to Aline's house. They still had a few days before the closing date, but he felt it was important at that time to leave.

One hour later, Teresa was shaking more than before. She could no longer control her body movements. She lay on the sofa in terror and fear. Never experiencing this before, she had no idea what was happening to her.

This episode lasted over three hours. When it finally subsided, Teresa felt like she had been run over by a road grader. Sitting up caused dizziness to occur, but she had to get up. What if grandma needed her? "I still have to go make our bed ready," she thought. ***"Where***

in the world is HE?" It was now past 10:00 p.m. and her husband had not returned. Even though she had experienced his abandonment frequently throughout their lives, it still made her angry. Now, with no energy of her own left, she used her anger to propel her body into action. She went upstairs and made the bed. Climbing in between the freezing cold sheets, she waited for sleep to overtake her.

Later that night, Dennis woke Teresa up from a sound sleep. "Where have you been," she asked.

"The builder stopped by the house when I was there so we had a beer together," he replied in a challenging sort of way.

Needing the sleep more than arguing, Teresa turned back over and went to sleep.

Over the next week she worked like a wild-woman to get her home in order. The living room carpet was still not installed and would not be, she later discovered, until after Christmas. The installer was ill and unable to do the job.

Not wishing to let plywood floors ruin their Christmas, Dennis and the boys went out a cut down a massive eleven foot Christmas tree. It sat majestically in the corner of the living room that was open to the main level and bedroom level of the house. "It's a good thing it's open there," Teresa commented to her grandmother, when they stood the tree up. "I'm going to have to use the upper hallway to decorate the top half of the tree." The two women laughed and joked and enjoyed their afternoon cup of coffee together.

Everyone shared in the decorating of the tree. It was a family event that they each looked forward to every year. Aline even participated by hanging some of the ornaments on the tree. It was a happy time.

Over the years, Teresa spoiled her family with extra special meals at this time of year. This particular

Christmas Eve, she made roasted butternut squash soup, broiled salmon steaks, Brussel sprouts sautéed in onions and bacon and cooked carrots. For dessert, she had purchased a Hungarian Walnut Torte, from her old neighbour in town. The lady belonged to a Hungarian Church in the area, and for Christmas, the older congregation made the walnut tortes, poppy seed, walnut rolls and traditional Hungarian sausages as a fundraiser. The meal was outstanding.

After the dishes from dinner were cleaned up, Teresa started making a cherry tea ring for Christmas morning breakfast. It was the first time she attempted this recipe and was up long into the night letting the dough proof in order to be perfect.

Christmas morning, the aroma from the cherry tea ring filled the house. The boys woke up early and were excited to share Christmas in their new home with their great-grandmother.

Aline, happily allowed Douglas and Kevin to escort her to her chair in the living room so they could begin sharing Christmas. Teresa had never seen her grandmother laugh so much. She walked over to her grandmother's chair by the fireplace and sat down beside her. "I'm so glad you're here with us, grandma," she said.

"Me too," said the older woman as she broke out in laughter at the actions of her great-grandsons.

Once the packages had been unwrapped and everyone had eaten their share of the cherry tea ring, Teresa went back into the kitchen and began the preparations to stuff and cook a 20-pound turkey. Everyone loved her stuffing and mouths began to water as the heavenly aroma began to waft through the house.

At dinner, the family collectively raised their wine glasses and shared a toast of cheer and good will to all.

It was a beautifully memorable day. One Teresa would never forget. She experienced and shared a new beginning with Aline. Each day the bond between the women grew stronger and the trust grew deeper.

The next day, Teresa was once again slave to the kitchen. Dennis' mother, his sister and her family were coming for dinner. This time, Teresa prepared a beautiful ham for dinner. Spending hours in the kitchen seemed her lot in life lately. Forging ahead as always, Teresa knew this meal would be the last of the massive dinners until Easter.

At dinner, the baked ham was served with fresh homemade apple sauce, green beans sautéed with onions and bacon, a green lettuce salad and whipped potatoes. For dessert, Teresa began a tradition of making homemade pies from scratch. Kevin's favourite was Dutch apple pie; Douglas's all-time favourite was pumpkin pie and Dennis enjoyed minced meat pie. Everyone had something they could enjoy. On separate occasions, Teresa made lemon meringue pie which was Aline's absolute favourite pie.

After the Christmas season had ended, the carpet in the living room and main hallway was installed. The house was turning into an inviting home. In its place of honour between the kitchen and living room, where everyone walked by, hung Teresa's favourite clock. "The wall was made for the clock, Grandma," Teresa commented to Aline one day with pride in her voice. "It's beautiful there."

The clock was a showpiece, Teresa had admired since she was a little girl. It was a beautiful Swiss clock made of perfect dark wood. On the top of the piece stood the six-inch tall gold figure of Atlas, standing as always, carrying the weight of the world on his shoulders. As a small girl, Teresa would stand in front of the clock and stare up at the golden figure. She always wondered what his face looked like. Now older and much taller, she was able to discern his beautiful facial features.

Once per week the clock would need to be set. Aline demonstrated to her granddaughter how to carefully pull the golden chains, which pulled the five-pound tear-dropped golden weights back up into place, and how to make sure the proper time was displayed.

"Grandma, it is a beautiful piece," Teresa commented as she placed her arm around her grandmother. "Thank you so much."

The older woman looked up at her granddaughter and smiled. "You're welcome," she replied back as she squeezed Teresa around her waist. Then Aline grabbed Teresa around the middle again. Pinching her sides, she announced, "You're getting fat."

Teresa's heart sank through the floor. All her life she had struggled with image issues. Since early childhood she endured the horrendous comments from her sister about her size and how ugly she was. Thinking she had finally freed herself from the torture of her past, she had been trying desperately to put any weight issues behind her and rebuild her self-esteem. Now, hearing this statement from someone who claimed they loved her, brought all those years of abuse at her sister's hands right back in her face.

Teresa dropped her arm from her grandmother's shoulder and walked away. "Even her!" she thought.

Walking up to her bedroom, she closed the door and sat in her chair. Rivers of tears escaped her eyes and her chest hurt from the pain she felt in her heart. With her vision blurred by tears, Teresa was unable to see a herd of deer walking across her lawn. She was missing the beauty of her home and surroundings.

Her heart was such a delicate object. "Why do people have to be so critical of me?" she wondered. She sank into a deep depression. There was no one she trusted to talk to about how she felt. Especially her husband. He was just as critical about her.

Down Teresa fell into the black pit of depression. Right now, she didn't care where she ended up.

Changing Currents

"Parents are the ultimate role models for children. Every word, movement and action has an effect. No other person or outside force has a greater influence on a child than the parent. "

Dennis Keeshan

In April 1996, Teresa received news that her other grandmother, Elvira had passed away. "This woman helped raise me," Teresa told Aline. "She and papa were everything to me. They were the only safe place I had in the world." Teresa's darkness grew.

Her beloved boys were growing up and needed her less and less now. Her husband was still an outsider to her. She had tried desperately over the years to talk with Dennis about their problems. They were married; she only intended to marry once in her life, because Teresa didn't believe in divorce. As long as there was a glimmer of hope, she kept trying.

Teresa knew she wasn't the easiest person in the world to live with. The skeletons in her closet and the abuse and trauma she had suffered had affected her. At times, when triggered, her anger exploded from her. At times she felt like she was living in a vortex. Her husband made no attempt to understand her.

Every time Teresa fought her way back to a good place, something would come along and kick her back down. But she would fight. Her life was full of fighting and she was exhausted by it.

Teresa attended her grandmother's funeral. Her heart was ripped apart as she prayed over her Elvira.

Teresa had not seen her grandmother for two years. During her worst time, when her children were small and Andrea was constantly interfering, Elvira had sold her home and rented an apartment in town. Teresa and Andrea scrubbed the entire place from top to bottom. Actually washing the walls, ceilings and floors. After Elvira's furniture was delivered, the two women embarked on the large task of unpacking. Teresa worked on the kitchen, made lunch for everyone, vacuumed furniture and made Elvira's beds. During the entire process, Kevin was constantly crying and misbehaving. The child was bored and didn't want to be trapped in an apartment with not much to occupy him.

Teresa was at her emotional end by the time everything was finished. She loved her grandmother dearly and would do anything for her. Until later that day, when Elvira looked her granddaughter in the eyes and said, ***"You are a terrible mother! You need to read books and magazines. It will help you be a better mother."***

Horrified by these words, Teresa was speechless. "How could she be so cruel?" Finding her voice, she said to her grandmother, ***"I'm doing the best I can, considering my role models."***

Teresa collected her children and their toys and walked out. She never returned to her grandmother's apartment.

Douglas and Kevin were still desperately needing their father. They repeatedly asked their mother, "Why is dad always gone? Why won't he spend time with us? Why doesn't dad ever come to my baseball games?" The questions went on and Teresa was unable to answer. She tried her best to fill the void. She had told her sons for years, "Talking is the best way to solve problems. If you have a problem, I'm here, let's talk. I don't care what has happened or what you've done; let's talk about it." Those were the words she lived by.

It didn't matter what time of day or night, if her child needed her, she was there. She would sit in their bedrooms on the floor with them for hours and just talk. She let them pour their hearts out to her. Teresa tried never to be judgmental or patronizing. Each boy took their turn spending time with their mom. It didn't matter what they wanted. They talked, played guitar or drums, or video games. She was there, fully engaged and willing to give.

Dennis became jealous. One particular evening, Teresa was asked by Douglas to come to his room. They lost track of time. Three hours later a knock came on the door. "What are you doing in here?" Dennis asked as he opened the door.

"We're just talking," Teresa and Douglas both responded.

Dennis glared at his wife. "He wanted to talk to me," she commented.

"Well, he can talk to me," Dennis snapped.

"I don't want to," Douglas replied. "Mom is always here to talk to and she doesn't lecture."

Dennis's face turned sour. He knew he was not gifted with conversation. When he spoke to his wife or children, it was always a lecture, and they hated it. Teresa had learned to ignore it.

Later that evening, he confronted Teresa. "Why don't they talk to me?" he snapped. "Why is it always you?"

"He's jealous!" she thought. "It was his choice," she said to her husband. "They don't like being lectured to when they come for help. I would rather they talk to one of us rather than neither of us," she commented. "I'm always here for them."

Angry now, he began attacking Teresa verbally. After suffering three broken noses and undergoing a Septoplasty to correct the damage done to her nose, Dennis no longer raised a hand to her. The physical evidence of his abuse was a documented fact. No longer using physical violence against his wife, he verbally and psychologically battered her now.

Teresa had escaped his battering and went to bed. She lay on her side with her hand resting on her cheek. This position was the only way to keep the breathing passages open on the one side.

Dennis walked in the room and got into bed. He continued his verbal barrage. **"Look at you,"** he yelled. *"You're such a coward!* You have to hide behind your hands all the time."

She ignored him, but his attack continued. Tears streamed down Teresa's face but she refused to turn towards him. He would have enjoyed seeing her weakness.

Eventually he gave up and went to sleep. She wondered how things could ever improve between them. Over the years, she had asked, begged and even written letters to him. Each times she bared her soul to her husband and asked for him to get help. "We need help as a couple," she said many times. He ignored her every time.

The following spring, 1997, Teresa received a phone call from Roger, a neighbour from when she was a child. She knew the people still lived beside her parents, but there had been no contact for many years.

"Teresa," Roger said. "I was instructed by your mother not to call you, but my wife and I discussed it and we felt we had to."

"What's happened?" she asked.

"Your father died this afternoon," he said. With no response, he continued. "He had a heart attack at lunchtime today. He was in the kitchen when he collapsed and his belt caught on the cupboard door. His limp body was hanging there when your mother walked in the room. She cut his belt with a knife, laid your father on the floor and then came to our house for help. We called the ambulance immediately."

"I understand," Teresa said.

"He wasn't gone by that point," Roger replied. "He was alive in the ambulance, but on the way to the hospital, he suffered a massive heart attack and died immediately. We thought it was important you know. We know your grandmother lives with you. I'm sorry you will have to break the news to her."

"Thank you for telling me, Roger," Teresa said. "I've always appreciated your kindness."

Teresa put the phone down and went to her grandmother's room.

"Grandma," she said as she sat down beside Aline on her couch. "I just had a call from Edward's neighbour."

Aline looked at Teresa with a surprised expression.

"They called to tell me that Edward has passed away from a massive heart attack this morning." Teresa hated causing her grandmother pain. She now saw the suffering in the woman's eyes. Leaning over, Teresa enveloped her grandmother in her arms and let the woman cry. Her son had just died. "Aren't the parents supposed to go first," she whispered. "Why can't it be me?" she snapped.

"Because, grandma, He doesn't want you there yet," Teresa answered. "You aren't finished here yet."

Teresa let Aline cry silently on her shoulder. Not one tear escaped Teresa's eyes. She felt nothing. "I have to be strong for grandma," Teresa thought. "This will be so hard for her."

Aline suddenly looked up at Teresa. "Why didn't your mother say something?" she asked.

"I'm sorry grandma, but the neighbour said she didn't want us to know," Teresa replied.

"Oh, she's crazy!" Aline announced.

Teresa and Dennis took Aline to the funeral home. They walked to the casket. Teresa helped Aline kneel down and then took the same position. They each said their prayers for the soul of this man. Aline gently laid her hand on her son. Tears began to escape her eyes but Teresa was the only person who witnessed the escape. "Good bye," Aline whispered.

Helping Aline stand, Teresa asked if she wanted to speak to Andrea. "No," she replied immediately. "I have nothing to say to her." With that said, they left the funeral home to attend the grave-site service.

Standing with a smile on her face, Andrea looked all around her. "She's acting like a crazy woman," Aline commented to Teresa. Andrea spoke out at odd places during the service leaving everyone thinking grief was occupying her mind.

Teresa knew her mother was glad her husband was gone. For years, she complained to Teresa about Edward and his mother and how she hated them all. "I should have left him years ago," she would scream in her tirades. "I just couldn't hear, so I stayed. I had no choice."

Teresa didn't believe her mother's stories. She was tired of hearing her make excuse after excuse and never take any action to make things better for herself, even with her disability. "She just didn't have the strength,"

Teresa thought. "Or she just didn't want her freedom bad enough."

After the funeral, Danielle approached her mother. Teresa refused to leave. She needed to protect her grandmother. "Ma, I want to see you," Danielle said to her mother.

"I live with Teresa," Aline replied.

"I know," Danielle snapped sarcastically. She did not have the courage to face her niece. She tried a different approach to get to her mother, but each time she tried, Aline ended the attempts.

Finally giving up, Danielle said, "I'll see you another time, Ma." She turned and left the cemetery.

Teresa hugged her grandmother. "I'm proud of you grandma," she said. "No one has the right to tell you what to do. You are a smart lady and you've worked hard for everything you have. Enjoy it."

Aline smiled at her granddaughter. Together they walked away from Edward's final resting place. On the way home, Teresa said to Aline. "You know grandma, you are all I have left."

The older woman turned to Teresa and said, "You and the boys mean the world to me." She fell silent after that. Deep in thought. The reason she had been forced to marry Marcel for seventy years earlier was now gone. Her son was dead.

Visions of Grandeur

Living on a farm and owning 100 acres wasn't enough for Dennis. For the past few years Teresa and Dennis had rented out the tillable fifty acres of land to farmers for such crops as corn, soy beans and vegetables. The rent was nice but the only thing it did was pay for insurance and property taxes. The land had yet to produce an income.

Dennis' dream of being a farmer himself, kept creeping up and causing problems within the family. "We can farm it ourselves," he would say to Teresa. "You're home anyway," he would add. "You can run the operation and I can do the rest when I get home and weekends."

Neither Teresa nor the boys wanted anything to do with 'his dream'. For them, they knew what it meant. They would do all the work and Dennis would be not available to help. The boys were young teenagers now and were looking for a means for extra cash for their hobbies and spending money.

Teresa and her sons came up with a couple ideas. They wanted to use the front small section of land, which was not being rented out, to grow fruit crops. They wanted crops like, raspberries, blackberries, currants, elderberries, grapes and strawberries. On another section beside this field, Teresa wanted to grow

Christmas trees. It was a perfect idea that would mean a yearly income for her and extra for the boys. Another idea Teresa had was to grow gladiolus. It was an easy crop to grow and there was always a demand for fresh flowers. These were solid ideas that Teresa and her sons were eager to dive into.

All of Teresa's idea were verbally destroyed by Dennis and discarded as useless. "I want to grow garlic," he announced. There is big money in it and we can do all the work ourselves."

He was adamant about his idea. "Farming is all I've ever wanted to do," he would say to his wife. "It's been a life time dream."

"But that is a very labour intensive crop," Teresa replied. "Who's going to do all the work, while you're gone to work every day?"

"It's not that bad," he told her. "We can do it as a family."

Dennis approached Aline with his idea. "All it would take to set up, is $6,000," he explained to her. "Can you loan me the money?"

They struck a business deal and Dennis scurried off to buy his seed stock and old corn planter he would modify to plant garlic.

Teresa was furious with him when he put 'his' garlic crop in the field location where she wanted her ideas to go. He was ensuring she could not use the field for anything.

Late that November, Dennis took one week off work for planting garlic. "I have to drive the tractor to operate the equipment," he instructed Teresa. "You can walk behind the planter to make sure everything is working fine."

"I'm very capable of driving the tractor," Teresa argued. With her left foot being fused and causing all sorts of problems, the last thing she needed was to be walking for hours on uneven soil, but her arguments fell on deaf ears. For one week solid in freezing cold, Ontario, November temperatures, Teresa walked behind the planter watching the garlic cloves fall through the hopper into the furrow below. All sorts of problems occurred with the planter. At time twenty or thirty cloves fell at once, other times the unit clogged up and planting had to stop. It was a cold nightmare.

After the planting season, Dennis and a friend began redesigning the unit. They adapted the unit to work perfectly for garlic. Dennis was an intelligent man in this area. His designs worked well and was paid a small design fee. The machine would have worked equally as well for gladiolus.

The next spring came spraying and the borrowing of a sprayer from a friend who was growing vegetables on the farm. The crop seemed to be fairly simple so far.

In June the garlic plants went into flower. "We must cut the flower stocks off," Dennis told Teresa. Garlic is like any bulb plant that grows. Once it flowers, you must cut the flower stock off in order to have exceptional bulb development and growth. All of this was a new experience for the family.

The next day, armed with a pair of gardening sheers, Teresa walked the rows of garlic in the usual bent over fashion. There were thousands of plants growing in the small field. It was her job. How she got stuck with it she wasn't sure.

Eight hours later, barely able to stand up, Teresa had only completed one and one half rows of the twenty-five row field.

"I have to have help," she announced at the dinner table that night. "It's too much for me to do alone."

"I'm at work all day," Dennis announced. "Boys, you will have to help your mother," he commanded.

Both boys were in school full time and had part time jobs. They were not thrilled with their father's demands. They did help but only when they had spare time.

"This isn't working," Teresa snapped at Dennis one evening. ***"This was your brilliant idea; HELP!"***

His idea of help was to have the boys ask their friends if they would like to earn some extra money by helping cut scapes. With the help of a few extra bodies, the job was complete.

Two months later came the harvest. Dennis had borrowed a potato digger from a friend. "Alright," he said with authority. "I'll drive the tractor and the three of you walk behind the digger and pick up the garlic bulbs and put them in the baskets." The boys began in unison. "Why do we have to walk all the time, and you drive the tractor?"

"Because I can handle the digger and you can't," came his reply.

"You could show us all how to work it," Teresa said rather fed up with his schemes.

"You'll never be able to handle it," he said.

"So we're not smart enough for you to teach how to use the equipment is what you are saying," Teresa commented. "Only you are smart enough to know what to do. Is that right?" she asked.

"Yes, I am the only one who knows how to use the equipment," he said again.

"That can't be true Dennis," Teresa challenged. "I've driven tractors with mowers, cultivator, planters and wagons on them. I think you're lying."

Getting his back up, he said, "This is the way we are going to do it. Understand."

"No!" she said, "and because of this attitude of yours, the boys don't want to be here to help. They have taken summer jobs elsewhere so there will be no one here to help."

"Oh, you don't know what you're talking about," he replied with a smirk on his face.

Teresa was right. The boys became tired of their father always taking the easy way out while they and their mother worked like filthy dogs in the fields. With the aid of one student, the crop was finally harvested.

"I want you to go back over the fields and search for any bulbs of garlic we might have missed," Dennis announced.

"Are you crazy?" Teresa replied. "Why should we do that?"

"I think we lost a lot of bulbs with the potato digger and they got reburied."

"We would have to go on our hands and knees through the debris in order to find anything."

"You and the boys can do it," was Dennis' reply.

The next morning Teresa, Douglas, Kevin and some friends of Kevin's were back out in the field. Crawling along in the dirt to find missing bulbs of garlic was a disgusting job and it got worse for Teresa when a snake came out of the debris in front of her. Teresa has a severe fear of snakes. She screamed and ran back several paces. The snake followed. She ran farther. Finally, the snake went off in a different direction. The boys where are laughing at her. "It's just a garter snake mom," they teased. "What a baby."

Teresa had dealt with a lot of wildlife on the farm. Most of it didn't bother her; but snakes...that's where she drew the line. When the filthy group of people were done gleaning the field they had found only about a bushel basket of garlic they had missed during harvest.

Now the garlic needed to be dried slowly but not completely. Dennis made a deal with the neighbour to use one of his bulk kilns, normally used for curing tobacco. It worked well and the bulbs were perfect. They harvested about 1500 pounds of 3 inch in diameter garlic bulbs. It was lovely hard-neck garlic.

Shortly after this, Dennis had an idea for grading garlic. He believed an old converted tobacco tying machine would serve well as the foundation for the grading machine. The belt was replaced with wire mesh of different size openings. The two inch bulbs fell through into the two inch holes and three inch bulbs went into three inch holes. It was fine but suddenly they couldn't find help to work on the farm. Most of the kids they had hired in the past all had summer jobs, like Douglas and Kevin did. They didn't want to work on the farm for their dad, because the pay was terrible. The boys decided they could get summer jobs off the farm and make more money. So help was scarce.

When the grading was finished they kept the largest bulbs to sell and made a nice profit. The smaller bulbs had to be cracked for next years' seed stock. This work was done in their garage. They stored the garlic in large wooden bins that apple growers used. The boxes were about four feet square and three feet deep. It was a lot of garlic. During the day, Teresa worked in the garage by herself. She would place the choice, cleaned, bulbs into onion bags and when ready hung them from a scale to be weighed. They did three different sized bags. There was a 10-pound bag; a twenty-five-pound bag and a 50-pound bag. Teresa was getting very strong from all the intense farm work again. The seed stock bags were 100-pound bags. She easily lifted them over her shoulders and set them aside. There was no alternative for her. The work had to be done and it was apparent she had to do each job on her own during the day; then cook, clean and other household duties at night. There was no one else to depend on.

At night, Teresa, Douglas and Kevin would go in the garage, provided they didn't have to work, and crack garlic for seed stock. They each had a bucket of bulbs, a bucket for garbage and a bucket for seed. When their seed bucket was full, it would get dumped into the orange seed bags and weighed. The seed bags were heavy and large.

With the date for planting fast approaching, Teresa hired two of the boy's friends to come and help. They all sat on lawn chairs in the garage and cracked garlic, talked a lot and laughed constantly.

In early December, the planting process started all over again. Once again Teresa was forced to walk behind the tractor even though she had surgery on her left foot earlier that fall. It was another repair to her fused ankle. Dennis didn't care. She was just slave labour to him. He had made that message very clear.

For four years they grew garlic. Each year, more and more of the work fell onto Teresa's shoulders. The boys both went to school full time and had part time, year-round jobs. They didn't have time to do what their father wouldn't. They had each told their father they no longer wanted any part of his garlic operation. Dennis couldn't understand what their problem was.

The last year that Teresa and Dennis grew garlic, they grew 6 acres. It was beautifully sized garlic. Each bulb was the size of a beef steak tomato. The cloves from the monster bulbs were about the size of tulips bulbs. They were massive and very flavourful.

Teresa was now working in the fields, cleaning the garlic, bagging it and delivering orders to stores and people's homes. Her end of the business was going well. She did however think it was ironic that she never saw any of the profits. Teresa always wondered what Dennis was doing with the money.

For this last year they decided to sell the seed stock after they kept the garlic they wanted for personal use and some they sold to their friends. Teresa now looked at all the apple bins she had to clean. She knew she wasn't going to get much if any help in cleaning the 8,000 pounds of garlic. She became very proficient at breaking the garlic into cloves. It was a hard job on her hands. Because the garlic was dry and still had some sand on it, your skin became severely dried out. Teresa had deep crevasses worn into her thumbs and first two fingers. She would tape them before the start of every day to prevent the cracks from getting worse. Each night she would rub liniment into aching, arthritic hands; being careful not to let the liniment into the cuts.

"I want to keep growing garlic," Dennis announced to his family.

"Then you do it ALL by yourself," they all told him.

"We don't have time with school and working," the boys said. Teresa glared at him. "I'm tired of doing all the work by myself," she snapped.

So ended the garlic adventure. Dennis still refused to let Teresa try her hand at fruit crops, Christmas trees or flowers.

"It's his way or no way," Aline said to Teresa. "That isn't fair."

"I know grandma," Teresa replied. "don't worry. One of these days, he will get what he deserves."

"I hope so," Aline replied.

The time had come and Aline felt like she had infringed on the family enough. She asked Teresa to take her to the nursing home/retirement home in town. Her name was placed on a list.

"Why grandma?" Teresa asked her. "I like having you here."

"It's just time I was out of his hair," she said. "I don't think he likes having me here."

Upset by this, Teresa responded, *"I don't care what he likes. You are a member of this family and you live here."*

But Aline's mind could not be changed. Teresa began to wonder if there had been harsh words between Dennis and Aline. Every time Dennis would come in the room, Aline would get up and claim she was tired and go into her own room to watch television. "Something had happened or someone had said something," Teresa thought to herself. "This is odd behaviour."

In November, Aline moved out into the retirement home. Here she could be around people her age and have visitors. Teresa finally understood why Aline chose this route. "You want to see Danielle," Teresa said to her.

"She has been asking to see me and won't come to the house," Aline replied.

"That's too bad," Teresa said. "If she had been nicer to both of us, she would have been welcome in my home."

When she moved into the retirement home, Aline left most of her furniture behind. "That's all for you," she said to Teresa. "That is your share from my house."

"It doesn't belong to me grandma. These items will always belong to you. I'm just going to take care of them for you as long as you are alive," Teresa replied to Aline.

One afternoon, a few weeks later, Teresa went to visit Aline. The older woman was quiet and upset. When Teresa asked what was wrong, she replied. "Danielle was here yesterday. She brought paperwork to have me sign everything I own over to her. She wants complete control over my money and investments." The older woman started to cry.

"Do you trust her, grandma?" Teresa asked.

"NO!" was Aline's reply. "I know how to make her go away for good though."

"What does she want from you grandma?" Teresa asked.

"She wants the Swiss clock," came the reply.

Teresa's heart sank. She loved that clock. To her it was a thing of beauty that had captured her imagination. Staring at the clock took her to distant lands where kings and queens lived in harmony and the rolling green hills of the countryside was dotted with sheep and cows. Now she was going home to take her favourite piece of furniture in the world off her wall and return it to her grandmother as a bribe to make Danielle leave Aline alone.

It was one of the saddest days for Teresa. "I'll buy you a new clock," Aline said to her when she saw the sadness in her granddaughter's face. "Thank you, grandma," Teresa replied. "But it won't be the same," she thought.

The next day, Danielle arrived at the retirement home and her usual foul mood. She greedily took the clock and walked out of Aline's life. Aline never saw her daughter again.

Dennis had now joined a group of men from their Catholic Church. He became a Knight of Columbus. It is a prestigious order of men who do great works of charity throughout their community. It's a men's club, Teresa was told, as at first the wives are excluded from the functions.

The ironic part of the whole situation was, The Knights of Columbus claim to be a family organization. All they ever did for Teresa and her sons was pull her husband and their father away from them. He went to monthly meetings, worked at bingo nights almost every week and found various other activities to be involved in order not to be at home.

Dennis also joined a fishing club in town. Every Saturday, he and a few of the guys were taking an electroshocking course. When the trout and salmon were running, they would shock the water and fish long enough to harvest the egg from the females and fertilize the eggs using the males. These eggs would then be shipped off to a conservation hatchery until the fry were of the right size to be released back into the stream.

Basically Dennis was gone a lot. When he was at home, he spoke to no one. He sat is his chair and watched television. Teresa would try to engage him in conversation, but either he didn't want to talk or if he did, every time she said something, Dennis would correct her. Or heaven forbid she said the wrong thing, he would start to laugh at her. Dennis took great pleasure in tormenting and humiliating Teresa if she spoke wrong or gave a wrong answer. He had a laugh-fest at her expense. It was cruel, but any attempt at stopping him only fell on deaf ears. Teresa learned to stop talking to him. "Why bother," she thought. "No matter what I say, I'm wrong or he just laughs at me thinking I'm stupid." Eventually, she became afraid to speak for fear of encouraging his remarks.

As the boys grew into their teenage years, they adopted their father's mentality of correcting and laughing at Teresa if she answered or spoke incorrectly. It appeared they needed their father's approval and they would get it one way or another.

Thinking he needed to go farther into the Knights, Dennis took his 4th Degree indoctrination. He had to buy himself a tuxedo, which for a man his size, was a costly endeavour. They didn't seem to ever have extra money, but for his 'wants' the money always seemed to appear. He was indoctrinated which meant he could now attend the 4ᵗʰ degree dinners once per month, and they should attend as a couple. "If you don't say something stupid or inappropriate you can go along," he would say. She hated him for those comments. Teresa had no problem speaking with other people...just her family.

A year later, Dennis was elected Grand Knight. One of the first things he said was, **"You're a Grand Knight's wife now......start acting like it."**

Teresa had a few choice words for him and said she would act like she felt; not the way she was told to. **"I'm not a child,"** she told him.

Thinking this was a family organization, Teresa and her boys found it was a 'family of men' organization. The hilarious part for them was when Teresa and Dennis' family won Family of the Year Award, on two separate occasions. **"What a joke,"** she said to him laughing. **"We are not a family. You really think you're fooling these people?"**

Teresa said to him, "If you got some help, we could maybe become a family, but not until then."

"Yes, I have problems and issues to deal with; and I try my best," she said, "but no one else in this house ever tries to change their behaviour. **Dennis, YOU need help!"** These statements infuriated Dennis. He believed that everything that was wrong with their family life and marriage was Teresa's fault. He was the perfect man, just like his father had been.

"I don't need help," he snapped at her.

"That's what you think," she commented back. "You are in desperate need of help. Only you can save our marriage."

"There is nothing wrong with our marriage!" he shouted.

"YOU need to open your eyes; and soon, or you will miss it! A good counsellor can help you with that," she said. **"It's almost too late,"** as she walked away from him.

Coming to the Close

"We must believe that we are gifted for something, and that this thing, at whatever cost, must be attained."

Marie Curie

Their marriage was deteriorating, and after 23 years, neither person respected the other. Teresa was tired of being used, abused and taken for granted and ignored by her family. For years her income was absorbed into the family accounts and in return she was given $200 weekly to purchase groceries for a family of five. With the money she had left over from her allowance, she purchased gas for her van. Whatever was left was hers...usually nothing. Realizing now that what Dennis' father had told him on their wedding day had actually come to fruition. "Take everything out of her name and only give her so much money a week." Stunned that this was what was happening, she approached Dennis about the money.

Discussing finances were always nasty events that caused major battles. Dennis belittled Teresa and told her she was stupid. Teresa eventually gave up listening to him and deciding the battle wasn't worth fighting.

"Why bother," she thought. "He does what he wants anyway."

Teresa was at a turning point in her life. Once again she asked her husband to get help to deal with the grief of losing three important men in his family. "You can go on your own, or we can go together," she offered. Again he felt he was not part of the problem. He believed **SHE** was the problem. His only attempt at therapy was sex therapy, which did nothing to improve their relationship. Dennis could not see in his heart that a marriage was built on two people working together. His solution to the problem was for Teresa to seek help, because she was the broken one in the marriage.

With her boys growing up and in their late teen years now, she was definitely not needed as much. "There is no purpose for my life," she thought. Silently she would pray, "You said, *'I'm not finished here yet'*, but I don't know what I'm supposed to do. Help me! Show me!"

Teresa was alone. At night Dennis sat in his chair and watched television. He rarely talked to her. The boys were either working, playing music in their bands or off with girlfriends. She was miserable and begged her husband to help make their marriage work. "I'm going to leave," she threatened.

He replied to her, "Who would want you! Look at you! No one would want you!" He said these words to her so often, she began believing it was the truth.

One afternoon, Teresa went and sat in her church. The serene peace she felt enveloped her like a warm and familiar blanket on a cold winter's night. She sat in thought while holding Aline's rosary. Such a beautiful rosary of white beads, each uniquely shaped. In the base of the crucifix was a tiny vial that once contained holy water that Aline brought from Lourdes in France. Teresa was honoured when Aline gave her this gift. She now sat in the church thinking, rubbing the rosary beads and staring up at the statue of Mary and Christ on the cross.

"What is my purpose?" she asked. "Please tell me." Tears started to escape her eyes as she stared up. She saw something unusual happening to one of the statues. Teresa blinked her eyes hard and looked again. It happened again! As she stared at the statue of Jesus on the cross, the face turned and looked directly at her. The look filled Teresa's heart with pure love. As the love filled her, she felt the warmth radiating throughout her body. It was filling her entire being with strength. A smile appeared on Teresa's face as tears of joy ran down her cheeks. "Thank you!" she whispered. As she uttered these words, the face of Mary turned towards her and smiled. It was beautiful and a look of pure love and faith.

Wiping her eyes and leaving the church, she felt empowered and better than she had felt in years. She knew what she had to do. That summer she connected with the Ontario March of Dimes and enrolled as a student. Come September she would start a course designed to update her accounting skills and teach her how to use a computer for business. Teresa was excited. "I'll make my own way," she thought.

One evening she announced to Dennis she would be attending school in the hopes of returning to the workforce as a contributing member of society. He didn't care about the school. "What about your pension?" he asked. "Will you lose it?" He was only worried about the money. There was no concern or excitement for her.

Teresa stated, "Douglas is heading off for university in the fall, and Kevin is busy with his own life and school. That leaves you and me here; alone. Are you going to be part of this life and come along with me or are you going to stay here with the television? Make your decision?"

He laughed. "You won't go anywhere," he said sarcastically. "You have nothing."

"We will see," she answered as she walked away. He had made his choice.

Late in August they drove Douglas to University. It was his first time away from home and Teresa felt the knife jabbing in her heart. "My first child," she thought. "How you've grown from a tiny baby to a big strong grown man." Her heart softened a great deal that day as they helped Douglas unpack his belongings. They had lunch and walked around the beautiful grounds of the school. When the time came for the farewell, tears were brimming in Teresa's eyes. She stepped towards her son to hug him. He stood his ground and looked at his mother and sternly said in a nasty tone of voice, "MOM, DON'T YOU DARE CRY!"

Shocked that her son would say such a thing, she looked at him. "I won't see you until Christmas," she said to him. "I will miss you."

He gave her a brief hug and stepped away from her.

"I love you," she said as she turned and walked back to their vehicle. Tears escaped her eyes at the pain he had just inflicted. "How could he be so cruel," she said to her husband.

Dennis didn't answer.

The long eleven hour drive home was unbearably quiet and lonely. Teresa read her book and stared at the scenery. She already missed her son terribly and she was worried. Douglas had been having serious stomach issues for the last few years that made him quite ill at times. However, she was instructed not to worry about him. "I'm not a little boy anymore, Mom," he would say. "Stop worrying."

Teresa was beginning to feel everyone in her family was turning their backs on her. "I have to do it alone," she thought. "And I will!"

Two weeks later she started school herself. Every day she drove to Brantford to school. Teresa enjoyed learning and being around other people. She had been isolated for far too long. Teresa and her instructor became fast friends. The two women had so much in common. Close in age and both finding their marriages were ending; they bonded.

Douglas would call during the school year and beg his mother to send up care packages filled with his favourite treats Teresa made. Happily, she baked his favourite cookies and snacks and sent them to her son.

At Christmas time, her son flew home. He hugged his mother tight and told her how he missed her. This Christmas Teresa did her usual traditional meals. She once again made a lovely Christmas Eve dinner, then prepared a special breakfast of freshly made Belgian waffles with warmed peaches and whipped cream. Dinner was the usual turkey feast for her family. Douglas and Kevin went to the retirement home to collect their great-grandmother. She was so happy to see them. Aline loved her great-grandsons. She was always so proud when they came to her home. Seeing the young men so neatly dressed and impressive looking made her smile. They flanked Aline as they walked her out. Each son being well over six feet tall, stood like goal posts beside the shorter five foot four inch Aline. She always laughed because she had to look up so high to them.

The family enjoyed another wonderful Christmas Day. Immediately after cleaning up, Teresa began her preparations for the large Boxing Day meal she had to prepare.

Now with the larger home, they took on the role of hosting Dennis' extended family Christmas dinner. Everyone brought something to contribute to the meal, which was greatly appreciated, but at times the contributions were useless to help her.

Teresa now cooked a twenty-four-pound turkey with all the trimmings, a ten-pound ham, complete with homemade applesauce. No one would ever want for anything at her table. Aline always enjoyed these meals but this year Teresa made it a bit better for her grandma. Aline's longtime friend, Alyce, whom she and Marcel had been friends with since they moved to the area to farm, was also invited to dinner. Aline and Alyce enjoyed a great visit, good company and a wonderful meal. That day alone, Teresa fed twenty-six people. It was a very festive day.

With Christmas over, everyone could get back to their routines. Douglas flew back to school; Kevin went back to high school, Dennis did his own thing and Teresa continued her studies.

Just after the new year, Teresa wrote her exams. She passed her course with ease. As part of the course, the students were encouraged to apply for jobs. Teresa attacked this part of the course with a vengeance. Her work was rewarded. She was offered a contract position as Senior Administrative Assistant to the CEO and Controller of a company in Brantford. A position which she gladly accepted.

No one could tell she had been out of the workforce for nine years. She wouldn't let them see any weakness.

Teresa enjoyed her time working. The job was rather boring for her but it was a good first step. She met some wonderful people and became friends with several co-workers.

It was here she met James. He worked in the computer department of the company. If she had computer or equipment issues, she was to call him. At first she didn't care for the man. Teresa found him rude and abrupt.

In talking, Teresa and James found they had a great deal in common. Soon they became close friends.

Teresa told her husband about her friends at work, but he did not seem interested until she mentioned James's name. Instantly he was jealous and pretended to be curious about what she was doing. Not being a stupid woman, Teresa saw through Dennis's jealousy. Truly she didn't care anymore. Her heart was dead to him. There was nothing left. She had given her husband every opportunity to step up during their twenty-three-year marriage. Each time something went wrong he was all too quick to point the finger of blame in her direction.

That day in the church, Teresa found her life again. By going to school, she had taken the first of many steps in making a break on her own. She refused to play the game with Dennis any longer.

"I am NOT responsible for all of this," she screamed out to the trees as she went for a walk in the bush on their farm. **"But I WILL end it!"** she said.

Don't Let Fear Dictate Who You Are

"There is only one thing that makes a dream impossible to achieve: the fear of failure."
        Paulo Coelho, The Alchemist

The plan of action was starting to take shape. Teresa's steps in bravery were emerging. First: education; second: job; third: money to make a life for herself; fourth: leave the man she had been with for twenty-five years.

Teresa knew for self-preservation she must take action now or live a miserable existence for the rest of her life. Not life! Existence.

Looking over at her husband while he watched television, she knew there was nothing left. She felt nothing inside for him. There had been too much over the years to even like this man any more. She certainly didn't love or respect him. Even though the physical abuse had stopped many years ago, she constantly felt the sharp sting of the verbal and emotional abuse that was inflicted almost daily.

Teresa's contract job ended in June so she went to work full-time looking for work. She read newspapers, searched job ads, contacted agencies and made connections 'with people who knew'. "I have to find another job right away," she told her friend Margaret one afternoon. "I have a plan and must see it through."

There was one saving grace for Teresa at this time. Her friend Don had a kind heart and was a good listener. The two talked, went for walks and shared the stories of their marriages and children. Both were married the same year, both were miserable, unappreciated and used by the partners. Their friendship grew and a bond was deepening. Teresa felt something in her soul when she was around this man. Was it his kindness? He always listened to her and was never judgmental. Was it his own personal torment that was calling her? His wife was a master manipulator and psychological tormentor. Don understood Teresa in a way that no one ever had before. They talked, supported each other and were good friends.

Teresa was called to attend an interview for a lawyer in Hamilton. She and Kevin went up for the afternoon. While his mom was interviewed, Kevin waited patiently in the car. Later the two went shopping and had a nice lunch.

"It would be a good job," she told her son. "The lawyer is from Libya and practices in contract law. He is just starting up his business here in Canada. In Libya he was a law professor and partner in his own firm. He's a lovely, gentle, man. After he moved his family to Canada, it was his intent to do the contract work for his International clients. His office would set up international buyers with Canadian products." She continued to tell him she would manage his office while the lawyer travels, perform all the research for his clients when requests come in for Canadian products and act as his private assistant during high-stakes law investigations. Kevin was happy for his mother.

One week later, Teresa received a call offering her the position at the law firm. "I accept," she replied. Excited beyond belief that her plan was falling into place, she knew everything would be fine. "I'm the only one I can depend on," she reminded herself when Dennis complained about the driving.

The job was wonderful and a good start to a new beginning. Teresa and her new employer took turns talking about their different cultures. He was Muslim and she was Catholic. Each was eager to learn about the other. Teresa was shown his beautiful prayer rug. She marveled at the emerald and jade tones and the stunning pattern that was woven into the rug.

Teresa made a plum pudding for her boss as a Christmas gift to his family. As Teresa's confidence grew, Dennis lost the iron grip of control he once held over his wife.

On Valentine's Day, Dennis and Douglas showed up at Teresa's office. Shocked, she said to them, "What are you doing here?"

"I've made reservations in Niagara Falls overnight," he announced. "Douglas is here to drive the other vehicle home."

Teresa looked at her son. She was speechless! There she stood facing two men, both well over six feet tall, and being trapped into going on a romantic get-a-way weekend with a man she despised. The two had not been intimate in over a year. "Why?" she asked.

"Because I thought I would do something nice for you," came Dennis's reply.

Now she knew he was up to something. "He's starting to feel he's losing control over me," she thought. "And he's nervous." But she was trapped. There was no way out.

Teresa closed up the office for the day and left with Dennis. "I don't have any clothes with me," she stated.

"I've packed you a suitcase," was his reply.

Never in twenty-five years had he done anything that remotely resembled what he was doing now. She was terrified of what else he had planned. Teresa knew he was testing her. He was going to manipulate and pressure her into having sex and that was the farthest thing from her desires with him.

They arrived at their hotel and checked in. It was a nice room with a stunning view of the falls. Walking into this room with him, Teresa felt a vise clamp down on her chest and throat. Slowly it was squeezing the life out of her. She was having trouble breathing. How could she get out of this? "Will I have to prostitute myself in order to survive this night?" she wondered. "I'll do what I have to," she thought. It was something she had learned to tolerate with Dennis for a few years now. Every time she submitted to him, she felt a piece of her soul being carved away.

Teresa looked around the room. Like a caged animal, she prowled to find an escape route. There wasn't one.

"We have a reservation in the dining room at 6 pm," he announced with a smile.

"Dinner," she thought. "If I drag it out, that will kill time."

Teresa took her time getting ready for dinner. The less time she had to spend caged with him the better.

It was a beautiful dining room overlooking Niagara Falls. The meal looked inviting but to Teresa, the food was tasteless. She picked at her food, ate what she thought she should and had two glasses of wine. "Maybe the wine will deaden my senses," she hoped.

After the wine she could see Dennis was eager to return to the room. She was NOT. "I think I would like dessert," she said and asked for the menu. She rarely ordered dessert and Dennis grew suspicious.

His barrage of questions began. Actually it was an interrogation. Teresa held her ground with each question. She knew what she had to do to survive this night and she was prepared. That didn't mean he had to have all of her, heart, mind, body and soul.

Dennis was beginning to attack her verbally because she wasn't in the mood for sex. He threw insult after insult. The truth of the matter was, he suspected she was having an affair, and by taking complete control over her this weekend, he would lay claims back on his property.

Teresa's marriage to Dennis was dead. She had long given up asking, begging and pleading with him to fix their relationship. She no longer loved him, if she ever did: A thought she was reexamining more and more as time went on.

In order to shut him up and stop the attacks, Teresa submitted. When it was finally over, she felt lower than dirt. The only thing that was missing in this transaction was the money left lying on the side table.

Rising from the bed, Teresa walked into the bathroom and locked the door.

For the next hour she soaked the filth away in a scalding hot bath. Unable to cleanse her soul, she left the bath and walked back into the bedroom. There he sat, smiling like the Cheshire Cat, watching television. He said something to her, but she didn't hear the words. She took her medication to help her sleep and washed it down with alcohol. Something she had done in a previous lifetime. "I don't want to feel anything," she thought. "I just want it all to go away."

The next morning, she woke and immediately said to Dennis, "I'm hungry. Let's go get breakfast."

She dressed and packed her suitcase in a matter of minutes. It was important for her to escape this room.

Teresa didn't stop long enough to put on her makeup. She was desperate to leave.

They ate breakfast in the main dining room. Again the falls made a stunning backdrop. "It would be so much more meaningful if I were here in the Honeymoon Capital, with someone I actually loved," she thought to herself.

Soon they were on the road home and she was relieved. During the long drive she kept telling herself, "I did what I had to do to survive." It was convincing, but it didn't cleanse the black mark from her soul.

Two months later, the war in the Middle East broke out and Teresa's employer told her he had to let her go. "There will be no business happening as long as things are unsettled back home," he told her. "I'm very sorry but I have to scale back business and let you go."

Teresa understood and thanked him for his kindness. "I will call you when things pick back up," he told her.

She was very sad. Teresa had enjoyed the position. She researched Canadian products for his clients. During her work she priced container loads of mozzarella cheese, Canadian grain, underwater welding equipment, fire-retardant clothing and the biggest one was a Bombardier aircraft. The plane, and other equipment were quoted for use in the Middle Eastern oil fields and the cheese was for another client in Egypt. It was fascinating work and she had made some good connections with the lawyer's law partners in Libya.

Now, her world was crashing down around her again. She frantically looked for work just to have a job. During all of this Teresa was making plans to leave, but she needed money.

In April she told Dennis she wanted a divorce. **"It's because of him isn't it!"** he yelled. **"You're a slut!"** he bellowed.

"It has nothing to do with anyone else," she replied. "I cannot stay with you anymore. There is nothing here for me. It's time to put the farm up for sale. This 'relationship' is killing me."

He was angry. His face turned red and she feared what his actions might be. "It's always all about you, isn't it?" he screamed. **"You will get nothing!"**

Teresa ignored his tirade as much as possible. "I will be contacting a lawyer and we will see who gets nothing," she replied.

"You had better go tell your grandmother before I do," he threatened. "You know she won't like what you're doing."

"You stay away from my grandmother," she warned as her voice lowered threateningly. "She doesn't like you anyway and if it wasn't for her, you wouldn't have anything! Especially this farm!"

The next day Teresa went to the bank to apply for a credit card for herself. The had one together, but it was important she have her own.

Her application came back denied. "Why?" she demanded to know.

"Because you're a female and don't have your own credit rating," they replied.

"Try again in a month," came the response.

One month later Teresa reapplied. In the meantime, she took a reception job at a tractor dealership. Her main job was reception, but she was also responsible for payroll, accounting, including month end reports and on Saturday mornings, she had to work the sales desk. It was a horrible job and she hated it. Every night she went home and smelled like diesel fuel and a machine shop.

Her life at home was deteriorating quickly. Dennis took over the master bedroom and Teresa was forced to sleep on an old sofa bed of her grandmother's in

Aline's old room. It hurt her back terribly, but it was better than pretending everything was fine.

Her sons were beginning to turn on her. After years of telling their mother to leave their father, "because he doesn't love you, and he hurts you," when she finally takes the steps, they turn their backs on her. Teresa didn't want her sons involved in the war that was raging between her and Dennis.

Then she received a call from the bank. "Your credit card application has been denied again," they said.

"What happened this time?" she inquired.

"You co-signed a loan for Douglas to buy a vehicle," the woman began. "He has missed two payments on the loan, so the credit company feels you are a bad risk."

Teresa was beyond furious now. She confronted her son with the news. "Why aren't you paying your loan?" she demanded. "You're working full time at the store. What's going on?"

What he said to his mother next rocked her very foundation. "I just didn't feel like paying it."

Teresa believed that Dennis had approached his son and suggested the default on the loan, which would cause Teresa to be responsible. With this in place, she wouldn't be able to leave.

"How could you be so irresponsible!" she stated. **"You just cost me everything!"**

Douglas seemed unconcerned. "You had better make good on that loan within the next two days, or I will take my own action," she threatened him.

He knew his mother was furious. He also knew better than to cross her when her back was against the wall. Two days later everything was cleared up.

Adding to the turmoil that was now Teresa's life, she had to push daily for Dennis to finish the work in the house that he had been putting off for years. Faced with the inevitable, he complied and finished the tiling on the hearth in the living room, doing extra work on the central vacuum unit, finishing work on the furnace and then there was the outside work. Every day after working, Teresa went out into the gravel driveway and hoed out weeds that had been taking over. She had hated the mess but didn't have the time to dedicate to the task, and Dennis refused to spray the weeds. "Get out here and help me!" she demanded. He did. The tension between the two people was as if lightning bolts had hit the ground. It was bad.

However, she was trying to be civil to him. When her hoe dulled, she asked him to sharpen it. He did willingly, but when he handed it back to her he said, "here you go...the hoe for the whore." Then he smiled.

She ignored him. His rage was growing and she was beginning to be afraid of him. She knew what his temper was like. After being thrown around their bedroom and having her nose broken three times, she knew what he was capable of. Teresa was worried. They had shot guns in the house. They were all licensed hunters and Teresa, Dennis and Douglas were licensed to carry and purchase firearms and ammunition. "I just don't know what he will do if he is pushed too far," she thought.

Soon the work was completed around the farm. The real estate agent came and placed the For Sale signs.

Aline had been having some severe health issues. She was now ninety-one years old and she was tired. The last thing Teresa wanted to do was burden her grandmother with her problems, but she needed to be told.

Visiting with her grandmother one afternoon, they shared coffee and cookies together. Aline looked at Teresa and said, "What's happened? You've gotten skinny!" It was true. Teresa ate, slept and breathed stress and anxiety lately. She had lost forty pounds. In a way it was funny. She was now thinner than her sister.

"I've been under a bit of stress lately grandma," she replied. Pulling up her courage, Teresa said, "I need to tell you that I am divorcing Dennis. I've had enough of him and his ways. I can't live like that anymore."

Teresa lowered her head thinking she had shamed her grandmother in some way. Tears started to run down her cheeks.

Aline raised her hand and laid it gently on Teresa's head. "It's ok," she said. Surprised, Teresa looked up at her grandmother. The older woman had tears in her eyes too. Then she raised her index finger to Teresa and said in a stern voice, **"I told you not to marry him!"** Teresa stared blankly at her grandmother. Aline continued. **"Don't ever do it again!"** she warned. Relieved, Teresa smiled at her grandma. She hugged the old woman tightly and said, "Thank you for understanding grandma. I love you!"

Aline hugged the younger woman and said, "I love you too." Then she said something that shocked Teresa. "Where is your sister?"

Teresa didn't understand.

"Where is your sister when *YOU* need help? Every time she needed help you were always there for her. Who is here for you?" she asked.

Understanding what Aline meant, Teresa replied. "Patricia is where she belongs, grandma. She's used me for the last time. I have no one who can or will help me. All I have in this world is you." Teresa laid her head on her grandmother's lap and enjoyed the feeling of a true mother. "You have been more of a mother to me in the last few years than Andrea ever was," Teresa said. "Thank you."

Aline stroked Teresa's head and said, "You are the daughter I always wanted. I will help you in any way I can." Then she added. "Don't let Dennis have any of my things that I gave you!"

"I won't grandma. I will fight him," Teresa replied.

Gathering up her courage and strength, Teresa left her grandmother and returned back to the hell that was her life.

United We Stand, Divided We Part

"We may encounter many defeats but we must not be defeated. "

Maya Angelou

Teresa was living in hell. She began making a list of every item in the house. Beside each item she indicated who had given the item and to whom, and of any items still in possession from before their marriage.

"We can do this on our own," Dennis said to Teresa. "We don't have to involve lawyers."

She stared at him in disbelief. "I don't trust you," she said.

Then he said to her, "I've made an appointment with a counsellor. You know him. Would you go with me for moral support?"

"We can't fix this," she replied.

"I know," he said. "I want the help and maybe if you go along, you can fill in places and answer his questions better."

"I will go to help you. **ONLY** to help you!" she said, making herself very clearly understood.

She knew this counsellor. Teresa had taken Kevin there many times for help in dealing with his anger.

As the meeting started, Teresa once again felt cornered like a rat. The counsellor initially began talking about Dennis. Then he turned everything onto Teresa's shoulders. "You see," he commented. "Dennis is trying to change and to get you to understand him. He's also trying very hard to understand how you feel."

Teresa stared at him in shock. "I said I would come to this meeting to help him, **NOT TO FIX THIS MARRIAGE.**" She declared.

"Can't you see he feels bad and wants to make this right," the counsellor continued.

"It's too little too late," Teresa replied. "I begged him for years and he refused. He's only doing this now because he knows I am entitled to half of what we have."

The counsellor looked at Dennis. "I think she is right. This cannot be fixed," he stated.

"If he wants to get help, that is great," Teresa commented. "I truly believe it will help him."

She stood up and left the room. Teresa knew Dennis would stop at nothing now.

"How dare you do that to me!" she snarled at him outside the building. **"You lied to me!"**

"I wanted your help," he said.

"I won't give it," she said and got into the van.

On the way home Dennis turned to Teresa and said, "I want my share of what your grandmother gave you."

"Those things belong to my grandmother!" she replied. "They do not belong to me."

"We will see," he said with a smile coming out on his face.

Realizing now that the gloves were off and he was going to play nasty, Teresa came up with a plan. She took her list from the house and every item that Aline had given her. Armed with the list, Teresa visited her grandmother's lawyer. "I need your help," she said and explained what was happening.

Two days later, he had drafted a document that he took to Aline for her signature. Carefully, he read the document to Aline explaining that every item she had gifted to Teresa was part of Teresa's inheritance and given to Teresa only. The document stated the at no time did Aline intend for any item to become the property of Dennis.

Aline agreed with the document and gladly signed the paper. It was witnessed by the manager of the retirement home.

That evening, Dennis walked through their home indicating which pieces of Aline's he wished to have. Teresa said to him, "I'll give you something from my family if you can show me one thing your family has given us." She had him. There was nothing in their house that Dennis's family had given them.

Teresa had outsmarted him, and his temper flared.

Her next step was to meet with her divorce lawyer. She trusted Wayne and told him the truth about her relationship with her husband. She explained about the early physical abuse and the constant emotional abuse. Then she told him about the shot guns and rifles in the house. "I don't know what he will do if pushed," she told him.

Two weeks later Teresa and her lawyer attended court and she won the case to have Dennis removed from the home. Teresa and her sons would be allowed to remain living in the house until the property was sold. The judge deemed that Teresa's safety given the prior history was most important. Consequently, a sheriff's order was drawn up and the date was set for one week from that day.

Fearing for her safety when presented with the order, the judge also commanded that the police be present to prevent Dennis from committing any acts of violence.

The day was drawing nearer and Teresa did not want her sons to be witness to anything. She suggested Douglas spend the evening at his girlfriend's house and urged Kevin to spend the night at a friend's. She explained, "There is something going to happen here tomorrow night between your father and me, and I don't want you here. It will be over soon. I promise." They hugged their mom and kissed her forehead.

The next day arriving home from work first, Teresa paced around the house. She was filled with electrified nervous energy. She was terrified of what was to come.

Thirty minutes later a car drove in their long lane way. A man got out of the car and approached the house. Teresa opened the door and he introduced himself as the Sheriff of the County. "I have the appropriate paperwork with me," he said. "We will have to await the arrival of the O.P.P. Officer."

Teresa felt a bit more at ease but her senses were all on high alert. The next vehicle down the laneway was the police cruiser. The Officer entered the home and sat on the kitchen stool waiting for the arrival of Dennis.

Suddenly Teresa spotted his truck coming down the lane way. "He's here," she announced. "I'm terrified!"

"He can't harm you," the Officer replied. "We will sit him down and explain everything to him. Then I will escort him to his room. He will be allowed fifteen minutes to pack enough items for one week and I will see him off the property."

Seeing the extra cars in the lane way, Dennis cautiously opened the back door to the house. The Sheriff and Constable greeted him, asking his name. The expression on Dennis' face was unique. He had not expected this from Teresa. He looked at her with questions in his eyes. "They will explain," she said before she left the room.

Dennis was asked to sit down. With the Sheriff on one side and the Police Officer on the other, he hung his head. The court order was shown and explained to him. A few moments later he was escorted up to 'his' bedroom. When they returned to the kitchen, Dennis turned to Teresa and said, "It didn't have to be this way." The Officer escorted him out of the house and into his vehicle.

Teresa knew this wasn't finished. Her stomach turned and she was almost sick. The Sheriff noticed her look and said to her, "You're safe. He won't be back."

"Thank you," she replied. "I wish that were true."

The next day when Douglas and Kevin found out what had happened they were furious with their mother. They knew their father had a violent temper. "How quickly they forget," Teresa thought. She remembered just over a year ago when her husband in all his height stood nose to nose in a horrible argument with their youngest son, Kevin. Both men had mean tempers and Teresa was afraid for her child. Only standing five foot nine inches she muscled her way in between the two to break up the argument. She was terrified but her mother instincts won over. Both men held tightly clenched fists.

After all the protection, guidance and love she had given her sons, they now turned their backs on her.

Kevin wasn't as angry as Douglas was. He was more understanding of what his mother was going through.

The next day after work, Douglas arrived home with a smug, arrogant grin on his face. **"You won't win,"** he announced to his mother.

"What are you talking about?" she asked.

"I went to the lawyer with dad today," he stated. "I swore an affidavit against you."

Teresa felt stabbed in the heart. When she had recovered herself, she asked her son, "Why did you do that? You should stay out of things you know nothing about."

"I swore that you are unstable and always have to be the centre of attention. If you're not, then you do stupid things like you just did to dad. He's not violent. *You're crazy!*"

Her son's words cut hard, fast and deep. "You should not have done that Douglas! You of all people! How could you!" she screamed. Tears started pouring down her face.

"I'm taking dad's side," he stated. **"You need to be stopped."**

"GET OUT!" she shrieked at her son. *"GET OUT AND GO WITH YOUR FATHER! HOW DARE YOU DO THIS!"* Teresa was completed destroyed. Her children knew what happened; they knew the abuse; the loneliness; the isolation. They just didn't believe, like their father, that Teresa would ever have the courage to take action. They were wrong.

Douglas packed his backpack and left the house, without speaking to his mother.

It took a few days for Teresa to recover from the nightmare. She was now under doctor's care for stress and anxiety. Her life was a complete disaster, but she knew in her heart she was moving in the right direction.

Her friend, Don, was a great source of support. No one else knew the nightmare she was living through. He was a great comfort to her.

One week after Dennis was removed from the house, he returned. Walking into the house he showed his dominant authority as he glared at Teresa and then smiled. Her blood froze instantly. She knew he was up to something.

He walked over to her and threw a folded document at her. "Read it," he snapped. He turned and walked up to the master bedroom.

Opening the document scared her. Her heart stopped beating as she read the court document allowing Dennis to return to his home. Included in the paperwork was Douglas's affidavit. That piece of paper cut her heart in half. Her son had hurt her in the worst way possible. Telling his mother was one thing, but actually reading his lies destroyed her.

Dennis returned to the living room and said, "We'll see who wins now."

Teresa glared at him. "You won't beat me!" she swore to herself. "NEVER!"

As if this wasn't enough, Douglas then walked back into the house. He gave his mother a look of total defiance. "What are you doing back here?" she asked.

"Well, if dad's back, then I can come back too," he responded with complete sarcasm. "Look at the court order."

Looking back at the paperwork, Teresa sat in stunned silence. Included in the return of her soon-to-be ex-husband was a statement allowing Douglas to return to the house.

Teresa had no choice. She was living in a home run by Dennis and their son. Kevin managed to stay out of the situation and Teresa greatly appreciated that.

Life was horrible. Teresa's clothing was placed in Aline's old bedroom and that was where she was forced to sleep.

Beaten down but still moving forward Teresa continued to work and exist. She hated her job. It was a job where the parameters were constantly changing based on which manager was making the decisions for the day. Nothing was clearly defined. One man decided Teresa was an easy target and was making open advances towards her. Unable to be alone in a room with this man, Teresa began looking for another job.

Late one afternoon, Teresa had to go into the basement of the warehouse to collect a part for a customer. It took her a bit of time to locate the part. Before she could get to the steps to go back up, her path was blocked by her male tormentor. Terror struck in her heart and throat and she was unable to catch her breath. Feeling the panic attack rise, she side-stepped the man as he approached her. Suddenly, the panic attack grew beyond her control and Teresa temporarily lost her eye sight. Blinded for the moment and unable to breathe, she stumbled in the direction of the steps. Once she found the railing, she knew she could escape and quickly her sight returned. Bolting up the stairs, she left the pervert alone in the basement.

During this time, her only bright spot was her daily conversations with Don. He was her strong shoulder in life and she knew he loved her and would give her the world. Teresa knew how he felt about her as they talked openly about every topic that came to their minds. She just was not ready and neither was he.

Teresa and Don mutually supported each other. "It's always easier for me to help someone else, than it is to help myself," she told him one evening. "Everyone has always come to me with their problems...but where are my friends now when I need some help?"

Don was always there for her in a way no one in her life had ever been. He didn't realize yet, how much support Teresa was going to need. Her life was about to turn a corner and head down a slope she might not return from.

Aline was ill. Very ill.

The Rise and the Fall

"There is a sacredness in tears. They are not the mark of weakness, but of power. They speak more eloquently than ten thousand tongues. They are the messengers of overwhelming grief, of deep contrition, and of unspeakable love. "

Washington Irving

One week later, Teresa was sitting in the living room enjoying the sun and the break from work. The phone rang. It was for her.

"Hello?" Teresa said into the phone.

"It's Kathy from the nursing home calling," the voice said. "You need to get down here right away. Your grandmother passed away this morning. The doctor is on his way in and he will meet you there."

Teresa dropped the phone on the floor. **"NO!"** she screamed. ***"NO!"*** she sobbed.

Dennis came running into the room. "What's wrong with you now?" he snapped. He was frustrated and angry that she had disturbed him.

Trying to get the words out, Teresa said, "Grandma just died. I have to get to the nursing home now. The doctor is going to meet me there."

"I'll go with you," he said. Immediately the smell of money came to his nose.

He sat beside her and tried to put his arm around her. She shook him off. "Don't pretend you care now. That's out of character for you," she said.

He moved off like an injured puppy who had been slapped.

"I have to get to the nursing home now! The doctor will meet me there," Teresa said.

"I'll drive. You are in no condition to be driving," he said. "The boys will come with us."

Dennis felt bad for her. He knew what Aline meant to his wife. Yes, she was her grandmother, but she had been more of a mother to his 'wife' over the last ten years. She had also been a great inspiration to their boys.

At this point, Teresa didn't care who came along. She just had to get there!

The nurse stopped her as she walked into the nursing home.

"Your Grandma died while sitting in her chair watching television," the nurse said. "She just went to sleep about an hour ago."

"Where is she?" Teresa asked.

"She is in her room. We put her in her bed for you," Kathy replied.

Teresa walked past her and entered her grandmother's room.

The silence of the room hit her hard in the chest. She couldn't breathe. It was like walking into a brick wall. The absence of sound in the room was deafening.

Everything was so still. Cautiously, she walked in a bit further. Turning her head to the left, she saw her grandmother lying on her bed. She looked peaceful, truly as if she were sleeping.

Teresa sat down beside her grandmother and took her hand.

"Grandma!" she cried. Unable to hold back, she began to weep. She hadn't realized Dennis had walked in the room too and that her sons were standing out in the doorway.

Teresa leaned down and hugged her grandmother. She was now sobbing uncontrollably. The pain of so many deaths, losses and unhappiness came rushing into her all at once. *"Don't leave me! Don't leave me alone Grandma!"*

Dennis stood there speechless. Teresa's sons felt their mother's pain, but instead of trying to comfort her, they turned and left the room.

Teresa and Aline had the same family doctor. Teresa had just been to him a few days earlier discussing her home life situation. He had given her some medication to help with anxiety and also something to help her sleep. He felt bad for her because he knew her husband and children. This man understood what her life had been like and tried to help.

When the doctor walked in the room, he looked at Dennis. "It's time you left her alone," he said. "Please leave."

The doctor found Teresa sitting on the floor beside her grandmother's bed. Her sobs were heard out in the hallway. Her body shook uncontrollably.

Teresa settled down a bit when her doctor walked in.

"Are you taking your medication?" he asked.

"Yes," she replied with a voice roughened from crying. "But it's difficult," she said. "He was at me again this morning."

He put his hand on her shoulder and said, "You certainly didn't need this on top of everything else that is going on. Let me know if I can help," he offered.

"No, I don't," she replied. She began to cry again. "I'm not sure I'm strong enough to survive all this."

"You will," he said. "You come from a very tough woman and you are just like her."

She tried to smile at him but was very unsuccessful.

Without asking Teresa to move away from Aline, the doctor pronounced the elder woman dead.

At ninety-one years old, Aline's heart gave out. She was tired.

"I want to see you in my office next week," he told her before he left. Teresa agreed.

She sat on the bed beside her grandmother. Laying her head on Aline's chest, Teresa cried, **"Grandma, please! Please don't leave me! You are all I have left."**

But her grandmother remained silent. She truly was gone and Teresa was alone. Alone in so many ways. Her grandmother's death represented the last of Teresa's family.

Teresa was grateful that Aline had her funeral planned and paid for many years before. All that remained was a prayer to be chosen, and her grandmother's wishes to be followed.

Teresa walked into the funeral home, and immediately stepped into the next role she needed to play. She welcomed interference from no one. Especially her soon to be ex-husband. Shutting down his unwelcome comments when he tried to chose the final prayer for Aline, Teresa turned an walked away from him.

A special request was made by Teresa to the funeral director. She wanted Don to meet Aline. He was a special part of her life and Teresa wanted him to be introduced to the woman she had grown so fond of in the last ten years, and Teresa wanted her grandmother to know she would be fine and that someone loves her.

The funeral home was closed to everyone and the exterior doors were locked. Instructions were left to allow no one in; especially Dennis. The stillness of the funeral surrounded Teresa as she walked to her grandmother's coffin. Breaking the silence, she introduced her grandmother to the man she cared for deeply. The overwhelming smell of roses filled the space in which they stood. Don put his arms around Teresa and held her as she wept. For the first time in her life, Teresa felt real comfort from another human being. She knew her heart and soul were safe with him. She knew she would always be safe with him.

The funeral was a terribly lonely ordeal for Teresa. A few of her close friends came but unfortunately some hostile family members attended. Beside the coffin, Teresa stood strong and tall. Dennis stood beside her followed by their sons. The tension in the room was beyond measure.

Danielle stomped into the room with an attitude no one could chip off her shoulder. After viewing her mother's body in the coffin, she glared at Teresa and sat down with the visitors. She pretended, and insisted on being a guest. She rudely made a point of refusing to stand with Teresa as part of Aline's family.

Teresa spent the entire time with the façade that she and her husband were on good terms and that he was being a great source of support, when she would rather he just left her completely alone. No one knew they would soon be divorcing.

Towards the end of the visitation, Patricia, Teresa's one-time sister and tormentor walked in. She hugged Teresa and said, "I'm not staying. I have Andrea in the car with me. I just wanted to see Grandma." Then she walked to the casket, looked down at Aline, turned and walked out the door never to be seen again.

Very near the breaking point, Teresa sat in the church contemplating her life. While sitting there before laying her grandmother to her final rest, she once again heard those familiar words from her Guardian Angel who always whispered to her in dire times, ... *"**You are not finished here yet.**"*

She knew there was more for her in this life. Always, when she was at her lowest; more times than she thought ever humanly possible, she would hear those words. The words gave her strength and courage. Those words rejuvenated her. She knew through those five little words there was a purpose for her. She **MUST** continue! Somehow she would find the strength to survive this disaster of a marriage and say her final goodbye to her grandmother.

Teresa knew in her heart and gut that her husband wasn't going to make things easy for her. She was in for a battle royal.

Before the casket was closed for the last time, Teresa went to say goodbye. As a gift to their great-grandmother, Teresa purchased two small brown teddy bears. Each little bear held a tiny red rose bud in its paws. The little bears had been placed on either side of Aline's head. They were there for her to remember the love of Douglas and Kevin for all eternity. She would never be alone.

Aline had loved stuffed bears almost as much as she had loved roses. Before the casket was closed, Teresa moved the bears down to sit on Aline's shoulders. She gently removed the rose buds and handed them to her boys. "From grandma," she said. She received no response from either son.

During the entire funeral, Danielle criticized, talked behind Teresa's back. When Teresa tried to include her aunt in the ceremony, Danielle refused and made a show to others.

"I've tried," Teresa thought.

After the mass, Teresa walked down the long church aisle following her grandmother's casket. Dennis tried to grab her arm to stabilize her, but she stiffened at his touch and pulled away. "I don't want your help now!" she whispered. Her sons, who walked two paces behind, not once offered to support their mother.

Smothered in the world of grief, Teresa stood at the gravesite beside Dennis and her sons: all of them now complete strangers.

Teresa stood strong and tall. "They won't see me crack," she thought. "If I show any weakness, he'll use it against me."

Taking a beautiful, perfect long-stemmed red rose from the floral spray Teresa had placed over her grandmother's casket in the funeral home, she walked slowly up to the casket and ever so gently, laid the rose on top. "Goodbye, Grandma," she whispered. She didn't want to take her hand off.

Out of the corner of her eye, Teresa saw Dennis approaching her. Quickly she lifted her hand and stepped back.

"I love you Grandma," she whispered.

Aline
1912-2003
May Your Soul Be At Peace

Living in Hell

"Do not shrink your beautiful light to make someone else feel more comfortable. BE WHO YOU ARE without hesitation and you will inspire others to shine, too!"

Anna Taylor

Living in your home when your home feels like a prison is not living at all. Teresa had just completed most of her tasks as executor of Aline's estate. Aline had left her granddaughter a small amount of money and the remains of her furniture. With this money, Teresa knew she would now be able to afford to make the break she needed to change her future and life.

Every day after work she would travel into Brantford or Paris and look at either homes or apartments. Her boys decided they didn't want to move with her, choosing to stay with their father on the farm until it sold. Kevin had explained he wanted to stay in the area to finish high school, but Douglas was another story. His anger spoke volumes to his mother.

For years her sons complained to their mother about the treatment she received from of their father. "Leave him mom." "Why do you put up with his crap," they used to say to her. If she wasn't hearing that from her sons, she would hear through anger and tears, "Why doesn't dad want anything to do with us?" "Why is he always helping everyone else but never has time for us?" These were questions Teresa could not answer but she did her best to sooth the aching hearts of her boys.

She spent time with them, coached their baseball teams, drove them to band practices, even acquired her hunting license to share that adventure with them, but mostly she loved them. Above anything else in this world, she loved them! She had sacrificed so much for them, but it was what a mother does to protect her children. She tried to do the best for them. Teresa wanted desperately to give them better than she had. At least they knew their mother loved them. That in itself was more than she had.

Her sons were now twenty-one and seventeen. Teresa believed this was as good a time as any to make the break from this marriage. Believing her sons would understand more now that they were older. She was wrong.

Douglas had surprisingly taken sides in something that was not his business. His actions had caused a rift in the once very close relationship between mother and son.

The smugness that Dennis brought back into the house after the funeral lingered for many months.

From April until December 26th they lived under the same roof. He was cruel and mean. He called her humiliating names when no one was around. He actually went as far as to copy her private journal to use against her in the divorce proceedings. She now knew that when she was not at home, he was rifling through her personal belongings.

Throughout this horrible time, Don was a rock for Teresa. He was facing the same humiliation at home from his soon to be ex-wife, but his main focus was helping Teresa. Their relationship was built on support, trust and strength.

Eventually, Teresa found herself a lovely three-bedroom town house in Brantford to rent. It was owned by a lovely Italian couple who were very kind to her. They repainted the entire inside of the house and installed new carpeting in the living room: All choices made by Teresa. The couple wanted Teresa to stay long term, so they did their best to make her feel welcome.

After they would have their large family meals, one of them would bring over plates of food and dessert for Teresa. They were very sweet people. Their kindness and generosity were appreciated very much.

Teresa moved into her new home on Boxing Day of 2003. This was the first time in her life she lived alone. It was such a great experience for her. She loved the freedom. On moving day, Don and his youngest son Alexander helped her unpack some of her things. They shared a pizza together and enjoyed each other's company.

One unfortunate part of the move was Teresa had to leave her dogs behind. She had rarely been without a dog. Now she found herself completely alone and missing the company of her pets. In time the loneliness for her pets would lessen, but never truly leave. "Just another loss," she said to herself.

Teresa was alright now. She had made a move her soon to be ex-husband said she was not capable of. She had taken the steps to a new future...one of her choosing and as she fell asleep that night she was at peace. Things were starting to turn around for her and she was happy. This was the first time she had ever been on her own in her life. It was a good experience at any age, but now at 43, Teresa was eager for a new future.

She had a man that loved her and she connected with on so many different levels. This was something she never thought possible.

Teresa knew she had made the right decision. She was about to make several more very difficult decisions on the road to, 'Her Life.'

Starting from Scratch

"I believe that one of life's greatest risks is never daring to risk."

Oprah Winfrey

Living on her own, and in her own place was completely new for Teresa. She was growing as a strong, independent woman and she enjoyed the solitude.

At 43 years old, she was given a new opportunity; a clear slate to start over. With the money she received from her grandmother, she bought herself a bedroom set and a car.

Teresa's new home was furnished mostly with her grandmother's furniture, but that was good. It was healing and therapeutic.

Because her boys had decided to stay with their father, Teresa left most of the dishes, the newer furniture, pots and pans and and main household items with them on the farm. "The boys need to have a good home," she said to Don.

The farm finally sold after Christmas so now the divorce proceedings could begin. Dennis tried every trick in the book to exert his power over Teresa. She was forced to submit to a two-hour intense discovery session generated by his lawyer, which questioned every transaction in their chequing account. Unsuccessful in his efforts to beat her down, Dennis eventually gave up and the divorce went through. Even though he tried to hide it, Dennis was pleased in the finality because he was now free to announce he had been seeing a woman for quite some time. His tactic was to constantly accuse Teresa of cheating on him in their marriage, but he was hardly blameless.

With the divorce settled and finalized, Teresa was given a monthly support amount due to their long term marriage and her physical disabilities. She hated having any ties to her EX-HUSBAND but it was worth it in for the short term.

Teresa took a few months to recuperate. Her grief for her grandmother, her children, her home and pets was evident. Her main plan of action for grief was to get on her bicycle. Like she had done a lifetime ago, she used her physical strength to fight the demons. It worked. Each day she grew stronger and stronger. She not only rode her bike, she walked miles, did Pilates and yoga. Her spirit was soaring.

One morning very early, Teresa received a phone call from her friend Lauren. They had been very close friends since Teresa attended the March of Dimes School a few years earlier. Their other friend was in trouble. The three women were very close and would do anything to help one another.

Lauren and Teresa knew that Connie struggled with mental illness. They just had no idea how bad her struggle was.

"Teresa, I got a call from the emergency unit this morning," Lauren said. "Connie has driven herself in. She attempted suicide this morning."

"Pardon?" Teresa asked, not sure she had heard correctly.

"I can't go," Lauren said. "Connie's sons are not available, so she is alone. Can you go and be with her?"

"Absolutely," Teresa replied. "I'll go right away and keep you posted."

In a mad dash, Teresa drove to the hospital. She was directed to the Psychiatric Wing. As Teresa approached the unit desk she noticed a women sitting slumped in a chair. The woman's hair was a mess, she had curlers still hanging in her hair. Her clothes were wrinkled and disheveled. Then she noticed the bandages on the woman's arms and legs. They were red with blood.

Standing at the desk Teresa waited for the administrator to acknowledge her. She didn't, but the woman with the bandages looked up at Teresa.

In that horrible instant, Teresa knew this was her friend Connie. Kneeling down beside Connie, Teresa looked into her eyes. They were blank. Unable to see any life in the eyes, Teresa said, "Connie, it's me...Teresa. I'm here for you."

Sparks snapped in the eyes and a tear rolled down one cheek. "Thank God she recognizes me," Teresa thought.

"Are you ok?" Teresa asked. "What can I do for you?"

Connie smiled at Teresa and said, "Can you stay with me?" "I scared," she said with only a fragment of the true women who was locked away inside her own head.

Holding her friends hands in her own, Teresa said, "Of course I will stay with you. Whatever you need, I'm here."

Connie smiled briefly.

The nurse approached the two women. She checked on the bandages around Connie's wrists. Turning to Teresa, the nurse stated, "Keep her talking. It will help."

"What happened today Connie?" Teresa asked. "Do you know Sweetie, you still have rollers in your hair?" Teresa removed them from her friend's hair and laid them on the desk. Connie laughed.

"Everything was going fine this morning," Connie began. "I got up, did my hair, ate and got dressed. I left the house and went to the hardware store. I needed some tape for the office. When I was standing there selecting the tape, I saw an Exacto-knife. Why it came into view, I don't know. But the knife was calling to me. I had no reason to buy the knife, I didn't need it. The thing just kept calling me. So I bought it." As she told her story to Teresa, she clung to her friend's hands and squeezed. Teresa could see life returning to her friend's eyes and saw that letting Connie talk was the best medicine for her.

"After leaving the hardware store, I went and bought myself a coffee to bring to work," she continued. "Driving to work was no problem, but then for some reason I pulled off into a parking lot. I parked and turned off the car. I took the Exacto-knife from its wrapper and looked at it. Suddenly I saw myself from above. I saw me cutting my legs. I saw myself slicing this razor-sharp blade across my thighs. I saw the blood start to form, but it was surreal." Connie took a deep breath and sighed. Tears started forming in her weary eyes. "You won't leave me will you?" she asked Teresa.

"I'm not going anywhere," Teresa replied with calming assurance. "What happened next?" she asked.

"I was sitting in my car watching the blood come onto my thighs," she continued. "Then something like a demon took over me and I started slicing the blade across my chest and stomach." Connie looked deep into her friend's eyes.

"She's waiting for my reaction of disgust," Teresa thought to herself. She held her face calm and gave her friend a look of complete support.

Connie started talking again. "I don't know what possessed me to do it, but then I took the knife to my wrists." She lifted her arms as if to show Teresa what she had done, but still refused to release Teresa's hands.

Teresa kept her eyes focused on her friends face. "Connie," she began. "Why did you come to the hospital?"

Her friend stared at her. "I have no idea. After I cut my wrists and arms, I just drove straight here."

"I'm glad you did," Teresa replied. "Lauren and I are here for you. She had to go to work at the school today, but she will be here later."

Connie smiled at Teresa. "Finally," Teresa thought. "Some life is coming back to her eyes." Teresa gave her friend a kiss on the cheek.

The nurse approached the women and said, "We have to take Connie for intake now. You will have to leave."

Connie's sudden reaction caused the nurse concern. "I want her to stay with me," Connie demanded. "If she can't stay with me I won't admit myself for treatment." That was her statement of finality, and she meant it.

The nurse agreed and Teresa walked down the very long hallway that led into the psychiatric area of the hospital. As the nurse pushed Connie in the wheelchair, Teresa walked beside her friend, not once letting go of her hand.

The process of admittance was long and very detailed. Standing by and sending love and strength to her friend, Teresa showed no sign of weakness.

Proceeding to the next phase of her hospitalization, Connie became agitated. It was the doctors turn for evaluation. Once again Teresa was asked if she would leave the room. Making an attempt to stand, Teresa was forcibly pulled back down by Connie. **"No!"** she demanded. **"I want her to stay, or I won't cooperate."**

Teresa looked at the doctor. "I will remain quiet and nothing will leave this room," she assured him.

She could stay and signed documents of confidentiality.

Teresa sat with her friend and held her hand during the lengthy intake with the doctor. Each time Teresa attempted to let her mind wander in effort to not hear her friend's statements, Connie would become agitated and squeeze Teresa's hand. The diagnosis shocked Teresa. She had known this woman for four years and not been aware that she was bipolar and schizophrenic.

After nine hours in the hospital, Connie had settled into her private room and began to relax. Of course she received medication to aid in her relaxation but soon her mood changed for the better. The brilliant, kind and loving woman that was Connie was beginning to reemerge.

Connie was exhausted but was beginning to exhibit traits of her usual self. She talked about the school where she and Lauren worked, the students and her grandson.

"Do you want me to call your sons?" Teresa asked her. "They are probably worried."

"Lauren has their phone numbers," Connie replied. "Can you ask her to call the boys?"

"Of course I will," Teresa assured her. "Don't worry. We will take care of everything."

As the hospital began to announce the end of visiting hours for the day, she suggested that her friend get into bed and rest for the night. "I will ask the nurse when I can come back tomorrow," she said.

"Yes, bed sounds like a good idea," Connie said. "Thank you for taking care of me. I'll see you tomorrow."

Teresa kissed her friend on the forehead and hugged her. "Take the time you need and get better," she said as she left the room.

Walking back down the long, sterile hallways, Teresa was hit hard with the reality of the day. "Poor Connie," she thought.

As she stepped to the locked double doors, Teresa rang the buzzer and identified herself, indicating she was leaving for the night. Walking through the security doors gave her a sense of relief and dread all at the same time. She stopped and turned. Watching the doors close and lock behind her, locking her friend in this ward, made her shiver.

When Teresa stepped outside into the fresh air of the night, she felt the breath of freedom on her face. Getting into her car, she quickly turned off the stereo. Teresa always had music on as she felt it lift her soul, but tonight, the music did nothing to soothe her. It actually irritated her. She was emotionally drained and needed to go home.

A short while later, safe in her own home, alone, she made a cup of tea and climbed into her bed. Sitting propped up against several pillows for comfort, she reached for the book she had been reading. Soon she was transported to another century. The book took her mind back in time and she now lived in the era she was reading about.

For the next week, Teresa visited Connie in the hospital. She was pleased to see her friend's personality returning.

With her friend safe, Teresa began to think about her life and the direction she wanted to go in. She began to explore her options.

School! The thought came to her suddenly one afternoon while walking by the river. "Now I can go to college and get a good education. There is no one in the house to stop me anymore!" she said to a bird that flew by at close range.

A huge smile appeared on Teresa's face and her heart skipped with joy. The next day she visited the local campus of Mohawk College of Applied Arts and Technologies.

She was no longer afraid. She felt empowered. "Imagine that," she said to Don later. "At 44 years old, I'm going to College." The excitement and happiness in her voice spoke volumes to him. Don could hear the excitement in her voice and he was happy for Teresa.

Stepping Into Life as a Student

"Sometimes the strength within you is not a big fiery flame for all to see, it is just a tiny spark that whispers ever so softly, 'You Got This,' Keep Going."
Author Unknown

Driven by a strong desire to succeed, Teresa began her new life as a student. Enrolled in the three-year Business Administration program at Mohawk College, she began her school career believing business was the right direction for her.

She soon discovered which courses she liked and which ones she loathed. Two of her favourite courses were English and Marketing. After being the first student to give a speech one day during an English class, public speaking being her nemesis, Teresa received perfect marks for her efforts. The other students and professor complimented her on her subject matter and ease of delivery. "Apparently I hid my fear well," she told the professor after class. "I have always been afraid of public speaking."

The professor praised Teresa for her accomplishments and continued encouraging her throughout the semester.

Marketing was another course that captivated Teresa's interest. As part of their marks, group projects were the norm. Being the perfectionist she was, Teresa always disliked group projects. In her experience, few people actually lived up to their parts, causing those who were driven to succeed, extra work at the last minute. The group of girls proved Teresa wrong. She was pleased. For their project, they used Teresa's business idea and developed a company, outlined a full marketing campaign complete with designs, presentations and printed materials. Their hard work was rewarded with a perfect mark.

With each great mark she was awarded, Teresa's confidence grew. She studied hard and threw herself head-long into her work. Devoting extra time and effort to the courses she disliked paid off for her in the end. Economics and Business Math were two of the courses she struggled with. Being an artistic individual, Teresa always found math to be her weakest subject. When combined with the "you are stupid," comments she received from her ex-husband and sons, when the subject of math or accounting was brought up in the house, Teresa developed what she called a lifelong 'allergy' to math. She was capable of doing math, but it made her nervous and uncomfortable, making her skin itch and her left eye twitch. "It's an allergy," she told Don. "Brought on by anxiety."

After her first semester in college, Teresa was proud of her accomplishments. Her marks were solid. The department head of Business invited Teresa to lunch with her one day in the teacher's lounge.

The two women were about the same age, so there was a great deal in common. They talked for two hours. The department head asked Teresa to switch programs from Business Administration to E-Commerce, which was her area of expertise. "Just talk to the Dean of

Business, and he will arrange everything. I've already spoken to him about you," she stated.

Surprised that she was a topic of conversation, Teresa asked several questions about the program and decided to make the switch.

The next day she entered the office of the Dean of Business. Bill was a great man and was very supportive of the students. They had a good meeting and all arrangements were made for Teresa to change program focus. "My door is always open to you," Bill told Teresa. "If you have any problems, come to me."

"Thank you," she replied.

With her program focus changed, Teresa began her second semester at college. She was awarded some exemptions because of her previous schooling and life experience. The exemptions were helpful and allowed her extra time to focus on her other courses.

The second level of marketing was a perfect course. Teresa learned, absorbed ideas and let her true personality out. Some people found her personality very dynamic and driven, others found it threatening. Succeeding in school and achieving outstanding marks for her work were her main focus.

One of her computer teachers decided to change the rules on his students. He owned a private business and was using his students to set up his business electronically, downloading tax forms and other pertinent applications that would aid his business endeavours.

Teresa found his method of teaching unprofessional and his approach to her and other younger female students inappropriate.

This professor was a man of approximately Teresa's age. His personal approach to the females in the class was sexist and demeaning, and Teresa refused to stand for it.

She approached the Dean of Business and explained the professor's behaviour and teaching methods. "I'm a lot older than the other girls in his classes. I am having difficulty with his advances at my age, so how are the younger girls coping?" she stated to Bill. "I find this very inappropriate and unwarranted," she said. Teresa asked the Dean if the curriculum being taught in the class was suitable. "He's using the class to set up his business," she told him. "Every class is involving his inventory, employees, accounting work, and payroll. I think this is wrong."

The Dean replied, "Do any of the others students feel the same way? In order to build a case, I must have more than just one complaint."

"I will talk to the other students," Teresa told him. "I know they feel the same, as we have all talked about it. I will direct them to come to you."

Now time was running out on the class. They had not been taught the correct course material and the semester was almost over. Student after student went to the Dean's office to complain about the professor. No one had learned anything of value from his teaching.

Three weeks before the semester ended, the professor was fired. "It was deemed his behaviour was incorrect and his teaching methods were sadly lacking," the Dean of Business said to the class. "You will all be asked to take an exam in order to evaluate what you have learned. There is nothing to fear about this exam. It is only formality. All of you will be given a passing grade for the course and the College apologizes for any wrong that has been done," Bill announced to the class.

Bill approached Teresa later and thanked her for helping the college set things right. "We cannot have teachers here who do not put the students' learning first and foremost," he said to her.

Taking a stand against injustice empowered Teresa in her life. Having the students come to her afterward and say 'thank you' encouraged her.

End of term was soon approaching and in February, Teresa began looking for a summer job. Her efforts paid off. Within two weeks she had scheduled five job interviews. The first one was at the Brantford Campus of Mohawk College.

Teresa's honesty was her best asset. During the interview Louise asked the question, "Given your background and work experience, why would you consider working for a low wage like $11 per hour?"

Teresa replied, "I am not after money. I believe experience in this field is much more valuable." She was hired on the spot and was introduced to the entire team.

In early May, Teresa started her summer job in the Student Summer Placement Office. It was a full time position where she helped students and employers connect for summer jobs. Teresa enjoyed her position and impressed her employer and manager. Her manager was set to retire in the next year and Teresa was a candidate for taking over the program.

In mid-July, Teresa made the decision to change programs again. She had thoroughly enjoyed Recruitment and Selection at Mohawk. Now she made the choice to switch into Human Resources. Since she knew she would eventually be moving to London with Don, she looked into Fanshawe College. They have a beautiful campus in London and the commute would be easy.

The Human Resources program was part of their Business program. The decision was made and she enrolled in the two-year program.

Meeting with the program coordinator for the signing of the necessary paperwork, Teresa discovered that her work history, life-experience and her year in the Business Administration program at Mohawk College would all play to her advantage. Her credits were transferred and it was decided that Teresa would begin in the second year of the program. She was thrilled with the new prospect.

Everything in her life since her divorce had been better than she had hoped. Her son Douglas, after 8 months of shunning his mother, had come back into her life. Each time she tried to speak to him about his actions with his father's lawyer, he backed away and refused to talk about it. Teresa said to him, "I love you, you are my son. You obviously had your reasons for what you did, and hopefully some day you will talk about it. I forgive you, but not your actions."

Their relationship began to grow again.

Then one day Douglas and Kevin came to their mother. Both her sons were visibly upset.

"What's going on," she asked.

Douglas began, "Dad is moving in with his girlfriend."

"That's none of my business," Teresa replied.

"He's selling the house in town and buying a place with her," he continued. "We have no were to go."

Teresa was assuming that the next question would be to have her sons move in with her. They were both old enough to be on their own now, and she enjoyed her privacy a great deal.

"Can't you rent the house from your father?" Teresa asked.

"No," they replied. "We've asked."

"What about the two of you buying the house from him?" she said.

"We've asked dad that too. He wants top dollar for it and won't even consider selling to us."

Teresa knew her ex-husband was selfish, and really had no consideration for his children, but her sons were visibly afraid.

"We won't have a place to live," they said again. "We've tried everything we can think of but dad won't budge," Kevin stated.

Teresa thought for a moment. "I have an idea," she said. "You know I'm Executrix to Grandma's estate and that the bulk of what was left of her money is to be divided between you two."

Both sons nodded in acknowledgment.

"I'm not supposed to give you the money until you turn 25, but there are concessions to the will and it is up to my discretion. What if I gave you the money and put a down payment on a small home where the two of you could live. You both have jobs, so you could work together to pay the mortgage," Teresa announced.

Her sons were shocked. "You can do that mom?" they asked.

"Yes," she replied. "This divorce was not your fault, and I won't see you go without a home."

Kevin said, "I would rather use the money to buy a vehicle for myself," he said. "If Douglas buys the house, I could rent from him."

"That would be your decision," Teresa commented. "Think about it and let me know soon. There would be a great deal of paperwork to do as grandma's money is still sitting in investments."

As it turned out, Douglas decided the investment of a home was his choice. Kevin wanted the vehicle and would rent from his brother.

Teresa worked to get the investments released for the purchases, and she went house shopping with her son.

They enjoyed their time together. "What are you going to do for furniture?" she asked.

"Dad says he's leaving most of it behind, as they want to buy new. He's only taking a few pieces with him," Douglas stated.

What Douglas didn't know was his father had already purchased a home with his girlfriend and he was about to move his things out leaving their sons in the house until that house sold. He was walking out on them.

With what Dennis had taken, the boys ended up with most of a house full of furniture. Suddenly that house sold and the deadline for her sons to leave was fast approaching.

Teresa pushed to get the investments closed and the money to her son for a down payment.

Every day her sons called or visited her. They were in turmoil. They were now responsible for their father's house and the new owners were pushing the boys and making all sort of demands.

"Mom, can you come down and help us pack the house?" they asked. "Dad left a mess and we can't make this work."

"You have to make sure your father gives permission for me to come into that house," she said. "I do NOT want to be around him."

"He said it's fine. We've already asked him," came the reply.

Both Teresa and Don would do anything for their children. They canceled their plans and went to help pack up the house.

All of them worked together as a team with one goal in mind. When they were finishing up, they noticed Dennis driving by the house. A few minutes later the phone rang. Douglas answered. After a brief discussion he hung up and turned to his mother. "That was dad. He wants you out of the house," Douglas said.

Thinking this rather rude, but knowing they had done all they could for the day, Teresa and Don decided to leave.

"Will you help us move?" her sons asked them.

"I can't help if your father won't let me in the house," she replied. "Get some other friends together and rent the necessary vehicles, and of course we will help. Just make sure your father stays out of the way."

Her sons agreed. They were very angry with their father. "He dragged us into town long enough to make appearances look good. Then abandons us to move in with her," they told their mother. "We don't like her at all mom. She's a snob."

"It's his choice boys," Teresa replied. "Your dad has known her for a long time. They've been taking courses together for a couple of years now."

Surprised at this news, they said nothing.

The following weekend was time to move. Teresa had managed to get the documents closed on Aline's estate and Douglas purchased himself a small home in a neighbouring town. The two boys worked together and this made Teresa's heart sing with joy. Her boys had always been complete opposites. They looked nothing alike and acting nothing alike. Their only similarities were their height and sharing a love of music that their mom had passed on to them. As they grew up, Teresa always listened to music. They enjoyed everything from Classical Rock, to Disco and Classic Masterpieces by Strauss and Bach and many other genres. Both of her sons were also gifted musicians and Teresa had spent hours taking them to lessons, listening to them play just for her in their rooms or attending their band performances. She was proud of them both.

Together with friends, Teresa and Don helped move the boys into Douglas's new house. It was a small older home, but it was perfect as a starter place.

As the men unloaded the trailer, Teresa unpacked the boxes for her sons. She loved them both so deeply and there was nothing she would not do for them.

Very late that night the move was finished. Teresa and Don returned to London to Don's house and his two sons.

Every morning they would get up early, drive the 1 ½ hours to Brantford so Teresa could change her clothes at her house. Then each went their own way to work and met up again later to return back to London. There were massive plans happening at the London house. Change was happening, and they assumed with most problems averted, life would be less complicated. However, we all know that the definition of assume is to accept something without proof.

Always Helping Others First

"I was bold in the pursuit of knowledge, never fearing to follow truth and reason to whatever results they led."

Thomas Jefferson

With September soon approaching and her second year of school about to start, Teresa realized she no longer needed to live in Brantford.

Thanking the kind couple whom she had rented from for eighteen months now, she packed up her house again and with the help of her sons and Don, she moved to London.

Since April, Teresa and Don and their sons had spent a great deal of time and energy renovating Don's house. It had been in such a gross state after his ex-wife moved out that Teresa flatly refused to live there.

They ripped up carpets chewed and soiled by mice, stripped wallpaper that was out dated, torn, taped and marked. They lifted disgusting linoleum that was impossible to clean.

The major plan was to renovate the house and then sell it. Each room was given new life through a coat of paint. "Let's paint the inside of the house a neutral colour. That way we can decorate with accents and furniture," she told Don. "It will help sell the house if we keep the interior neutral."

All the walls were painted a soft grey tone; the hardwood flooring was a beautiful unstained oak with matching solid oak treads replacing the carpet on the stairs. The ceramic tile in the kitchen, front entrance and powder room were a light marbled beige colour. The upstairs main bathroom linoleum was stripped out and replaced with eighteen inch off-white tiles. Everyone worked together. Douglas, Kyle and Don laid the hardwood flooring, while Teresa and a friend began laying new ceramic tile in the kitchen. Construction on the inside wasn't the only thing happening. Behind the house, Don had a massive back yard. In the space large enough for three tennis courts, Don had worked his magic. When his children were young, he had put a great deal of work into laying down an interlocking brick patio the full width of the house and twenty-five feet deep. This connected with a raised area where the in-ground pool was. Surrounding the welcoming cool waters of the pool, Don had built a wooden fence. On the far side of the pool he had built a gazebo large enough for a few overstuffed lounge chairs and tables. The surroundings were perfect to enjoy a swim, have a barbecue or sit and read a book in the shade of the gazebo. On the one side of the pool area, the children had a playground for climbing, hiding and playing pirates. With the boys now teenagers, this was rarely used.

During the day, the new family worked hard. After work, they shared a meal and cooled off with a swim. Both Don and Teresa were pleased that the four boys were getting along so well.

Teresa was enjoying teaching Braden about cooking from scratch, and he was an eager student. "Mom made everything from a box," Braden told Teresa. "This is much better!"

Kyle and Teresa got along well enough, but he found the transition from no rules in the home to being responsible almost too much. He loved his party lifestyle and was content to not be responsible for anything in his life.

He fought Teresa at first but soon gave up when the law was laid down hard one night.

Don and Teresa were exhausted and planned to stay in Brantford this particular night. Something made them both uncomfortable and both were unable to settle. "Let's go back to London," they said to each other. "Something is not right."

Arriving home unexpectedly they found their entire property consumed by teenagers. A massive party was going on in their home. Every room they walked in was filled with drunk, loud teenagers. Unable at first to locate his children, Don and Teresa went out back to the pool area. There, laying drunk in a lounge chair was the youngest son Braden. Furious, Teresa went back into the house and continued her search for the other son. Heading upstairs to the bedroom area was the last resort. Opening her bedroom door, she found Kyle with two girls. One girl was crying while the other girl and Kyle were trying to provide comfort. "What is going on here?" Teresa screamed.

The girls looked at her with the questioning look of, "who are you?" etched on their faces. Teresa looked around at all the empty beer bottles and plastic cups standing all over her furniture. When Don's ex-wife moved out, she took 98% of the furniture and other items. Leaving him and their children with not even the barest minimum. Teresa's belongings were turning the empty shell back into a home.

Kyle stared at Teresa in horror. "Sorry T," he said. "She had a fight with her boyfriend and we were trying to help her."

"Get out of my room!" Teresa snarled. "Get these kids out of this house! NOW!" she screamed. Storming down the stairs, Teresa was unable to find a spot anywhere not occupied by drunk teenagers.

Teresa knew of the parties Kyle and Braden held at the house before she moved in. Their mother loved partying with young kids, firmly believing she was one of those "cool" adults. All they used her for was free alcohol. She even went as far as buying their drugs. She was a desperate woman, and enjoyed having the attention of the boy's friends.

Two hours later Kyle and Braden finished cleaning up the house and yard. "If you can't act responsibly when we aren't home, then we will either get you a babysitter or you won't be allowed in until we return," their father told them.

Kyle's partying life had cost him greatly, as he failed his last year in high school. The boy had never failed at anything in his life before, but somehow he still had the delusion he would still be accepted into university.

Once everyone had calmed down, a few days later, Kyle talked with Teresa and told her of his plans for school.

"You can't get into university without grade twelve," she told him.

"I want to go to university, T," he said. "Can you help me?"

"Alright," Teresa said. "I'm going to start my last year of college in a few weeks. You go back and retake your grade twelve. We can challenge each other and work together. Let's have a contest to see who can get the better marks?" she offered. "An old woman like me, or a young smart guy like you."

The challenge was laid down and accepted by Kyle. "We will get you into university," Teresa said to him with confidence.

As the school year began Teresa found three other people from London to share the drive with. Her Human Resources program was not at the main campus but at a satellite campus forty minutes away.

New family, new house, new school year, new program, and new students. Teresa had a lot to do and the best part was learning. She was a dedicated student and completely immersed herself into school work. The new program was a good choice; one she was glad she made. She now found the age gap of her classmates wasn't as bad as it had been in Mohawk College. There was a good mixture or first time away from home students and people her own age.

The program head and main instructor was a remarkable woman. An international woman, a great teacher, entrepreneur and motivator. Teresa enjoyed learning from her. This part of her life would be very good.

Finding herself living in a family situation again with children that were not hers was difficult. Her step-sons didn't appreciate having responsibilities and chores to do. They found every way possible of getting out of doing their share of helping out.

In their past, they were given a chore to do, for example, cut the grass today. They would wait until the last minute, and then do the chore just before their father arrived home. They didn't care about the chores or requests or respect the people who set the chores. Their main focus in life was playing video games and socializing.

Being raised the way she had been, Teresa didn't understand this. Yes, chores were assigned, but no parameters were given. So the boys didn't care and they showed that at every opportunity.

By October, Kyle stopped his focus on his studies. "I can't spend the time you do on studying T," he said to Teresa. "I don't know how you do it."

"It's simple, Kyle," she replied. "If you want something bad enough, something that speaks to your soul, you will find the energy and make the time to do it, and do it well," she added.

"I just can't do it," he commented.

"Then I guess you won't be going to university, will you," she said.

Kyle stared at Teresa with hate in his eyes. She didn't care at this point. Her main goal was to get him into university. What he did with his life after that was up to him.

"Come on, Kyle," she said. "Fight for what you want."

He walked away from Teresa and went upstairs. She hoped he was going up to study.

Continuing on with her studies, Teresa was very successful. She was not the top student in the class, but she was close. It didn't matter to her who was top, she was just being driven by her own will to succeed.

Teresa enjoyed every aspect of this curriculum. She soared in her student life.

As part of the Labour Relations course work, the professor assigned the students into two groups: Union and Management. She carefully chose students for each side based on their backgrounds.

Because Teresa had negotiation experience, she was assigned to the management side of the bargaining table scenario. Each side was given a set of parameters and they needed to work their way through the negotiation process.

Every item was presented by a different student. The teams would confer and then set up again and negotiate. It was a brilliant way of doing the curriculum. Role playing, usually Teresa's least favourite thing in the world, was now her most brilliant role.

The management team worked together like a well-oiled machine. Each time they approached the Union, they became stronger and more knowledgeable. The bargaining continued on for four hours. In the end, the Union conceded and Management was successful in their negotiations. Teresa's team was elated.

After the role play was over, one of the Union members approached Teresa. They were friends and enjoyed a laugh over the day. Then the young woman said to Teresa, "I never want to meet you professionally on opposite sides of the table."

Her comments surprised Teresa. "I didn't think I was that bad," she replied.

"No!" the woman commented. "You were that good!"

"But I wasn't trying very hard," Teresa replied. "It was fun though."

The only down time Teresa took from her studies was at Christmas. She became a mom again, cooking the full turkey and ham dinner she had always done. Her sons had grown to expect such a meal, but Don and his sons were shocked at the feast that was laid before them.

Christmas was good for the family and everyone ate well, had fun and gave thanks.

The new semester brought courses Teresa didn't enjoy as much, but she fought her way through. As part of the curriculum, each student was to find a business where they could job shadow an HR person. Teresa approached several businesses in London and Brantford, as fortune would have it, she had 5 placements she had to choose from. The ones she didn't select, she offered to other students, but the main one she wanted was in London. This company manufactured light-armoured vehicles for the military. This was a place she had always admired and said when she drove by, "I want to work there some day."

With her placement set, she went into the Human Resources department and spent one week in each area, learning and experiencing how daily operations went. She thoroughly enjoyed her two months. It was suggested to Teresa that a position would soon be opening up in the Training and Development Department and she should apply. She did. It was a dream that was falling perfectly into place.

After her placement was complete, the students went back to school to discover shortly that the Teacher's were going on strike.

"Looks like it's going to be a long one," Teresa was told by a trusted staff member.

"Now what do I do?" she asked the program coordinator. "My education is being held hostage on one hand when I'm two months away from finishing and I have the opportunity of a permanent job on the other.

"Take the job," Teresa was urged.

"What about my diploma?" she asked.

"Go and talk to the principal. Explain your situation. I'm sure they will work something out."

Teresa did approach the principal. "It doesn't look like the strike will be over by the end of the school year," Teresa was told. "Take the job, and I'll give you your school year."

Completely shocked at the offer, but very pleased, Teresa grabbed the offer on the table and ran. "Thank you," she said as she shook hands with the Principal.

Teresa began work at her dream job, with her employer knowing about the strike and the deal that was made. Life was great and the job was perfect. She was actually the only person in her department that would have an actual Human Resources diploma. Teresa found that rather odd.

One month into her job, the teachers settled their dispute, the strike ended, and they went back to work.

Teresa received a call from the Principal.

"You have to come back to class," she stated or you will lose your diploma.

Teresa weighed out the options carefully. She talked to the program director and told her about the Principal's renege on the deal they made.

"Let me talk with the principal and see what can be done," the director said.

Teresa was furious. "She lied to me! If I go for the diploma, I lose a good job...if I keep the job, I'll lose my diploma," she told Don. "Why do people lie," she screamed.

As it turned out, the director made an agreement with the principal. "Because you are working, we will give you the credits for all but one course," she stated to Teresa. You must attend one class every Thursday morning until the end of school. You will be given your diploma at the end," she said.

Teresa made the arrangements with her employer and everything was set. She didn't like it but it needed to be done.

Soon, graduation pictures were taken and school ended. "Your one credit short," the principal said. "If you take it this summer; you will graduate in the fall."

"Here we go again," she thought. "Another twist added." Teresa worked all day and once per week stopped at the Fanshawe London campus and participated in the one course she was missing. Ironically it was in Training and Development.

One very good thing happened throughout this entire ordeal. Kyle had managed to work hard enough and graduated grade twelve with marks high enough to get him into university engineering. Everyone was thrilled. Everyone except his mother. He refused to tell her.

"I'm so proud of you!" Teresa said to him as she hugged the boy. "You did it!"

"We did it T," he said to her.

Teresa was happy as she had graduated with honours.

During this entire year, another special project was in the works. Don and Teresa had decided to get married.

Don was now free of the burden of his previous marriage, or 'mistake' as he referred to it. There was nothing holding them back.

Plans were made, plans were changed but the date was set for mid-June.

Teresa and Don were strong as a couple. Strong in their understanding and respect for one another. They believed their bond and love for each other could endure anything thrown at them for they already had proof their love was lasting and powerful.

As their lives fell into place and their wedding plans were being worked on, they had no idea what life held in store for them. In the very near future, they were going to be tested in the cruelest of ways. Would their love for each other survive?

Wedding Bells

Very much in love and bonded as soulmates, Teresa and Don planned to be married in June of 2006. They believed strongly that their lives had been intertwined since the beginning of time. Now, both in their forties, they were learning the value of trust, love and a true bond. God had brought them together to share this life.

The two seemed to come alive when together. He completed her and she did the same for him. They knew each other in their hearts and souls. Their souls had been together in a past life. Nothing else mattered.

At first they thought they would have a garden wedding at their home. They worked hard to landscape the yard and set up beautiful living spaces around the pool. It was inviting and colorful and peaceful when the flowers were in full bloom.

Even though they had started renovations on the inside of the house, there was too much work to be done given the state of the house. Soon they realized they wouldn't have the house ready in time for the wedding.

Making several calls to find a venue, Teresa came across a beautiful old estate not far from their home. Both fell in love with the gorgeous Spanish Colonial Revival house which was built in 1916. The main hall of the estate would serve for the ceremony and gathering areas, while the formal library was open for guests to sit and chat. People could freshen their drinks and indulge in some wine and cheese in the dining room.

Upstairs the master bedroom was for the bride and her attendants to laugh, primp and prepare for the festive day.

The men were given the other side of the upper floor to dress. Their area was originally the servant's quarters. His attendants were passing around jokes teasing Don. Always a good sport, he laughed.

Their guests would be able to wander the 68 beautiful acres of parkland that surrounded the main home. It was perfect! Together Don and Teresa signed the contract and began making plans.

Both Don and Teresa had done the formal-type wedding the first time. Neither wanted a repeat of those days. They agreed their day would be a fun event that everyone would have fond memories of.

Only the closest of friends and family would be invited. Their four sons would play an integral part in the celebration, each taking a shining role as a member of the newly united family.

The wedding day dawned with new excitement and happiness for the couple. It was going to be a beautiful summer day. Quickly, they gathered up their sons and drove to the estate to begin decorating. When they stood back to admire their work, a sense of peace fell over them.

"This really is the beginning of a new life for both of us," Don said to Teresa as he hugged her.

"Yes, it is," she replied as her smile lit up the room. He was her world. He brought her soul to life and had given her the freedom to be herself. Now she just needed to find who that was.

With hair done and flowers arranged, the couple sat with their boys and bridal party for a picnic lunch in the sunshine of what would be the best day of their lives. Everyone was in a festival mood. The laughter could be heard all over the estate.

As lunch finished, they knew they had to pay attention to last minute details.

Just before the ceremony, Teresa, her maid of honour who was her best friend, and her Goddaughter who stood as bridesmaid, climbed the beautiful staircase to get dressed. It was hot in the upper part of the house, so the girls turned up the fans and enjoyed each other's company.

Once dressed, they waited for the last guest to arrive before heading down the main staircase of the house.

As each guest entered the main doors of the estate, they were greeted and given a smooth stone by Braden. They were asked to hold the stone during the ceremony and pour their good wishes, blessing and hopes for the couple into the stone.

Finally, everyone was ready. Teresa walked down the staircase to the waiting arms of her grown sons. Her happiness lit up her face with a glow never seen before.

She took hold of her son's arms and let her maid of honour and bridesmaid take the lead.

Now that the two girls had arrived under the arbor, it was her turn. With Teresa in the middle and her tall sons on either side, the three of them barely fit side by side. It was quite an amusing vision and made everyone smile.

The biggest smile of the day came from Kaitlyn. She and Teresa had a special bond. They loving referred to each other as the Fairy Godmother and Fairy Goddaughter. This bond was one that could never be broken.

Don's best friend stood by his side as his best man, while his sons Kyle and Braden stood by their father's side as groomsmen.

This day was a gift from God. It was a sunny, brilliant and warm June day. Nothing could spoil this day. There were guards posted around the grounds of the estate to ensure Tammy, Don's ex-wife, could not follow through on her threat of ruining their day. She had threatened to make the couple's lives miserable.

The ceremony began at 6:30 pm. It was a beautiful ceremony filled with love, laughter and tears. As Don spoke his vows to his new bride, tears ran down his face. He proudly looked her in the eyes and said, "I Do." He had never been happier in his life. With a bit of a tougher exterior built up, Teresa was able to hold her tears, but it was a struggle. She replied to him, "I Do."

The tears in the room were soon broken as Don had some difficulty getting Teresa's ring on her finger. The marriage official looked at Don and smiled. She said to him, "Just twist it on." Everyone heard and roars of laughter filled the room.

As part of their ceremony, the new couple and their four sons shared a toast to their union. With the register signed and all paperwork complete, the new couple walked down the aisle towards their gathering.

Upon leaving the great hall, each guest was asked to deposit their stone in a small wooden chest, set on a side table. It was now a treasure chest of memories for the happy couple created by their friends and families.

Appetizers were served by servers in black tie and crisply ironed white shirts. Guests mingled on the beautifully landscaped lawn of the estate. They were served food and drinks while beautiful memories were captured into portraits of the newlyweds, their bridal party and family. Happy, beautiful memories captured for all time.

It was a day to remember. Teresa married the man that was put on this earth just for her. He treated her with love, respect and kindness. When they first met she poured her heart out to him about her past. He was prepared to help her heal, as she was for him. Don also had suffered the abuses and indignities of his first marriage. He was a lonely man and had been very isolated during his first marriage, constantly making excuses for Tammy's behaviour. Teresa and Don trusted one another; they loved each other deeply and their soul connection was very strong. Nothing would break this bond.

Leaving later that night for a three-day honeymoon, the couple left Douglas in charge of their home. He would take care of everything and that there would be no parties. The 'lovebirds', as they were called spent their few days of peace horseback riding, walking by the lake and watching a lightning storm that rumbled over their room one night. Finally, life was beautiful. They prayed together that it would last.

Life soon returned to normal once the returned home. Each day they went to work, and at night they worked hard on renovations. The reconstruction of the house seemed endless. Their game plan was to complete the work and sell the house. Living in a house haunted by an ex-wife and her demons was unhealthy for everyone.

Don's boys were asked to do small jobs to help out after school and during their summer vacation. Here is where the conflict began. One son was asked to do a specific task. That boy wanted to just party with his friends, so he bullied his brother into doing the job. The second brother didn't know how to do the required task, so needless to say, the work was a mess.

All this meant was the frustration level in the house increased as neither brother would tell the truth. Of all the unacceptable behaviour in the world, the one thing Teresa could not abide was lying.

Kyle was partying constantly and using drugs in the house when Teresa and Don were at work. He hooked his younger brother into his trap ensuring Braden wouldn't tell on him as he was equally guilty. Braden watched his older brother and friends drink themselves into oblivion. His mother always told him, "you should be more like Kyle!" Taking his mother's words to heart, Braden soon slid down the same slippery slope his brother fell down.

Things in the house were being stolen and destroyed, but no one would tell the truth.

The major breaking point was when each son took a turn in trying to bully their father into submission. The verbal battering that took place reminded Teresa of her life as a child. Summoning all of the courage she, stood between father and son. ***"YOU WILL NOT SPEAK TO YOUR FATHER IN THAT WAY! DO YOU HEAR ME!"*** She bellowed at the boy. ***"IF, YOU ARE GOING TO CONTINUE TO LIVE IN THIS HOUSE YOU WILL LEARN TO RESPECT YOUR FATHER!"***

She had never spoken to either teenager like this before. Her stand shocked them into silence. Kyle never spoke to his father in such tones again.

Braden on the other hand, being quite immature for his age, ran to his mother. She fed his confusion and anger with brainwashing and manipulation.

Braden's behaviour became suspicious. Suddenly at odd times he would run to his mother's with a backpack heavily burdened with "things."

When confronted one afternoon, Don and Teresa discovered Braden was stealing from them and taking the items to his mother.

"She said she didn't get what she wanted out of the divorce settlement and that she is entitled to them,"

Braden wailed at his father. "She said you didn't give her everything she was supposed get."

"Braden," his father said, "you know she received her share plus more. Why did you listen to her lies?"

"She wanted the things," Braden replied.

"But you don't steal from us," Teresa said to him. "Some of those items belonged to me." Braden glared at her.

It was apparent to Don and Teresa that they had lost the battle to try to help Braden. "The manipulation has gone on for so many years, he doesn't know what the truth is anymore," Don confided in his wife later that night.

Within a few weeks Braden began to turn on Teresa. Where they had once shared a special bond, he showed disrespect and laughed in her face. This was so hard for her. Braden, one year ago said to Teresa, "You are a *REAL* mother to me." He would hug her and say, "Thanks T."

The betrayal cut deep but she had to protect her husband from his own children.

When people talk about spousal abuse they automatically assumed the man has somehow abused the woman. Not so in every case! Some women can torment a man's mind and twist his heart completely out of his chest without batting an eyelash. There are a great deal of men who have been abused by their wives. They suffer in silence because it is humiliating for them to admit they are abused. At times, some women can cause severe emotional anguish in their partners. The man withdraws from his friends and family in order to accommodate his wife's wishes and to avoid 'those unpleasant scenes.' Eventually the man is isolated and unresponsive. Don was such a man. "In order to keep peace, I kept quiet," he told Teresa.

Her heart broke for him. "If he can't protect himself from these attacks, then I will," she thought to herself.

Braden continued his argumentative ways. He would become so enraged he would raise his fist in anger and swear at his father's face. Don tried his best to defend himself. He would not be baited by his son.

One day, tempers flared and the situation exploded out of control. Braden had been caught stealing from the house again.

"We can't trust you anymore here Braden," Don said to him. "Give me your key!" He ran and together Don and Teresa chased him to the corner store. They caught up with him in the parking lot where he waited for his mother to pick him up.

"Give us the things back, Braden," Don warned him.

Braden seemed out of his mind with rage. He swore at his father with horribly vulgar words. Black ooze spewed from his mouth as he called his father name after name.

"Enough!" Teresa screamed at him. ***"YOU WILL NOT SPEAK TO YOUR FATHER LIKE THAT AGAIN!"*** she warned him.

Even though he was close to sixteen years old he stood taller than Teresa's 5'9". His blue eyes flashed hate at her. Braden turned on her with a face full of rage. **"Get out of my face, you bitch,"** he said to her.

"How dare you speak to me like that!" she yelled. Now angry beyond words at the verbal abuse, Teresa raised her hand and slapped his face.

With a clenched jaw and tears sprouting in his eyes he spoke in a threatening tone to her. **"You'll pay for that, you bitch,"** he said.

"You go and stay with your mother," Don told him. "She wanted joint custody anyway, so go, and don't come back!"

On the way home, shaking and completely agitated, Teresa received a call from Kevin.

"Mom, I'm at Douglas's and my truck has been broken into," Kevin said.

Unable to absorb the words she just heard she asked him to repeat what he had said. Frustrated with his mother, he loudly repeated his original statement.

"Did you phone the police?" she asked.

"Yes, but can you get down here. I need you here," Kevin begged. "You have to help."

Torn between helping themselves recovered from the earlier incident and one of their sons in need, they immediately left for Tillsonburg to help their other son. They were being pulled in so many directions from their boys. Despite everything that was happening, they desperately wanted to help each son. They loved them all.

Once the situation was sorted out from the break-in, Teresa and Don headed back to London; emotionally and physically drained.

Both numb from all the trauma, they truly believed things couldn't get any worse. They were wrong.

Teresa's cell phone rang.

"Hello," she answered.

"WHAT! Pardon? All colour completely drained from her face. She felt as life draining from her body. "We are about a half hour away. Yes, we will meet you at the house," she said.

"Who was that?" Don asked.

Unable to speak at first, she stared out the window with eyes like a deer caught in headlights. Finally, able to whisper she said, "The police." "Braden and his mother called the police on me for slapping him this morning." "The police are meeting us at the house. I may be charged." Trying to hold back the tears, Teresa knew if she let go she would dissolve into a puddle on the floor of the Dodge Ram. "I tried to help them," she managed to say before she choked and was unable to speak again.

"Dam fool," Don said.

Terror and panic rose up in Teresa. What was she going to be facing when she got home? Home? His home with his children. What have I done? Had she made a mistake? By this time, she had let her townhouse in Brantford go. She had nowhere to go. Again in her life there was no escaping the torture.

The torment of her past resurfaced as the police and her future waited in London.

To Press Charges or Not to Press Charges

"You gain strength, courage, and confidence by every experience in which you really stop to look fear in the face. You must do the thing which you think you cannot do."

Eleanor Roosevelt

Teresa was terrified of what awaited her once they got home. It was like she was living in some other realm, a nightmare life that would not stop. The police were waiting for her. Her step-son, a boy she loved like her own had turned on her out of anger and with the help of his narcissistic mother involved the police.

Her entire body shook with anxiety and fear. Putting on a brave face, Teresa let the female officer in the house.

During the discussion, the officer explained why she was called and that a taxi driver had witnessed the entire scene.

"Braden doesn't want to press charges, but his mother does," the officer said.

"Can you tell me what happened to lead up to this situation," the office inquired.

Once Teresa and Don had finished telling the officer what had happened she said, "Well they didn't tell me that part. Looks as though they left out some very important details. I think the mother is just out for revenge," the officer said.

"We can't have him back in this house right now," Don said. "She wanted joint custody of the boys, so she can have him and deal with the little monster she created."

"She won't keep him," the officer said. "His mother said he made a choice to live here with you, so he can stay here. She doesn't want him."

"We can't have him in this house right now," Don said.

"I will see he stays at his mother's for the weekend," the officer stated.

Then she turned her attention to Teresa. "You will not be charged," she said. "Due to the circumstances, I would have reacted the same way. "

"Thank you," Teresa replied.

Once the officer left Teresa was like a caged animal. The rage that was building inside her was about to explode. She was angry at the world. ***"Why does this have to happen now!"*** she screamed. **"Why can't we just have a good life?"** Taking a walk outside around the pool she contemplated if she had made the right decision in taking on these other two boys.

Then things went from bad to worse.

Don no longer trusted his son. During a search of Braden's room, they found drugs, weapons and stolen merchandise from the place Braden worked part time.

What Don found very disturbing was a small bag of female clothing tucked away in his closet. Teresa also found her personal items in his room. Items that came from her dresser and jewelry box.

Thinking this was bad enough, what they found after doing a complete sweep of the room shocked and terrified them to the core. Tucked away between the wall and his bed was a hatchet. Immediately Don went to his workshop and discovered his hatchet was missing. Never having faced anything like this before, Teresa was now terrified of being in the same house with the boy. **"He is unstable,"** she told Don.

"I will not live in the same house with him!" she screamed. **"I know he is your son, but his behavior is completely off the grid now!** *Is he going to snap and kill us in our sleep?"* she yelled.

"Do you remember the story of Lizzy Borden?" she asked Don.

"Why would he have your hatchet in his bedroom anyway?!" she yelled. *"It doesn't make any sense."*

"I love you Don, but I can't live like this. I'm going to have to move back to my place in Brantford," she told him.

Don was heartbroken. His son's actions had been unpredictable over the years, and he had been in trouble many times for stealing and lying. But this! "What did she do to my boys?" he said as he hung his head in shame. "I thought she was an ok mother," he said. "She was manipulative, and a bit unstable, but maybe her heavy drinking when she was pregnant caused more damage than we knew."

Now facing the hardest decision of his life, Don sat his sixteen-year-old son down and said, "You have to go live with your mother. You are causing too much damage here and we can no longer trust you in the house. Why did you have my hatchet in your room?"

"I was sharpening it for you," he answered. As he gave his father the biggest and saddest expression he could manage, Teresa saw the smirk in his eyes. He was playing his father as he had always done. This time, however, Don was not going to accept his son's behaviour.

"You are old enough to know better," he told him. "You need to go live with your mother."

Braden knew he had pushed his father too far this time. Both boys had the gift of manipulation and had played their father many times over the years. Don had finally had his eyes opened and would no longer accept their actions.

"Go tell your mother that you are moving in with her," Don said.

Braden left dejected but still believing he would come out on top.

Later that afternoon, Braden came back to the house. "She won't let me live there," he told his dad. She said, "It would ruin her lifestyle having her son live with her."

His mother sat alone in a three bed-room town house. Turning her son away was her way of punishing him for choosing to live with his father and his "whore."

Braden was devastated. He thought his mother would always be there for him, but she just proved she wasn't. He ended up sharing a bedroom with his best friend. The boy's mother agreed to this arrangement, as Braden told her his dad would let him back in the house by the end of summer.

Over the years, Don had noticed Tammy's mental health decline. She had told him of her struggles after her father's suicide. Her life had gone from one of wealth and status to one of blaming her mother for her father's death and near poverty.

Not having faced her grief and trauma over the death, Tammy internalized everything. But in time, she began to exhibit narcissistic tendencies. Don thought in time she would improve. She began having difficulties at work, having personality conflicts with coworkers and superiors. Tammy was fired from many jobs. Now isolated, by choice, and not feeling any responsibility towards her husband and children, she spent up to eighteen hours a day playing on-line games and luring people into her trap of lies and deceit.

While absorbed in this gaming world, her interaction with her family suffered. She kept photos, detailed notes of each person she talked with, searched the internet to learn all about them and depending on who she was speaking to, her persona would change each time.

While talking with a young boy from the UK, she would become a young girl and use language she felt a girl of 14 would use. Her life was a fantasy world. She made up fantastical stories of her life and family. During one particularly long interaction, Tammy had convinced a seventeen-year-old boy from the United States, that her husband was a brute and beat her just for fun and games. She created an entire story around the fact that her marriage was falling apart and it was all "his' fault. So convincing was her story, the young boy believed she was the victim, and when she asked him to help her 'create an accident' for Don and his bitch, he was ready to take action. She wanted them both dead.

Her life was pitiful. A few times she actually tried to meet with her some players; mostly men. One guy in particular, she had made detailed arrangements with. She went to the bus stop to pick him up for their rendezvous at a local hotel. He didn't arrive. After two hours, she gave up and left. Two days later she discovered he was in jail.

Time after time, she tried to prove to herself she was not the reason her marriage collapsed. "I must prove I can have someone love me," she said as she frantically played her game, while secretly she made plans with another man she met on-line. Their entire conversation both ways were filled of promises and lies. Their plan was to meet locally and drive to his secluded cabin in Northern Ontario.

After returning from her adventure, her mood deteriorated even more. Conversations with the 'on-line' friend became strained. After he called her frigid, she dropped him from her list of playmates immediately.

Unfortunately, one very young boy stood out among the rest. Don and Teresa felt her activities needed to be stopped when they discovered she was baiting an eleven-year-old boy. The poor child had just suffered the death of his father only days before. He played this game to escape his pain and grief.

Frantically Tammy searched the internet to find the actual obituary. Printing it, she taped it into her journal for safe keeping. Now armed with information, she went on-line to talk to the boy. She laid out in detail exactly what the embalming process is before burial. The little boy didn't understand and was severely traumatized over this.

The next day, Tammy received an email from the boy's mother demanding all communication with her son stop immediately. The mother had contacted their local police. Not taking kindly to this type of luring, the police warned her and made ready to take action. Stupidly, Tammy tried to defend her actions, stating, "I was only trying to help him. I'm a medical professional and know what goes on." But once again the mother threatened her with police action. **"Stay away from my child!"** she demanded. **"You are a sick and evil woman!"**

All communication with the boy ended, but Tammy kept herself busy elsewhere. There were other people she could connect and play with.

Her life became all about this on-line world. She pretended to have sex with people; she bought fancy dresses, showered, applied makeup and nail polish, then sat at her computer to attend a pretend on-line wedding of game characters. Her real life was too painful to face, so her on-line world became her reality.

Unfortunately, her sons knew of her on-line life. She had been playing for a couple of years already and tried desperately to involve them. Suspicious of her behaviour and her non-stop computer gaming actions, Don actually tracked her conversations. What he saw in these conversations shocked him to the core. She needed help, badly! He had no idea she was this ill. It was when she shared their home address and the children's pictures, Don took charge.

Don's oldest son, Kyle said to his dad, "Take the stuff to the police dad. That's the only way she's going to be stopped."

"But she is your mother," Don said to his son.

"I don't care!" Kyle yelled. **"Someone needs to stop her! She needs help and she really needs to get a life! She does nothing around here all day except play games!"** he screamed. "She won't cook, she doesn't clean, she does nothing! *Stop her dad! Please!"*

Eventually, Don and Teresa did call the police. They had a long conversation with a constable in their dining room. They handed over copies of her conversations, her notebook and photos she had of young boys. The two hoped the police would take action. "The children need to be protected from people like this," Teresa told the officer.

"We have a special task force that specializes in these areas," the constable told them. "Thank you for reporting this."

"Hopefully she will get the help she needs and the children will be safe," Don said as he shook hands with the officer before he left. "Thank you."

Looking at each other after the officer left, they knew nothing would be done. Because it was Don's ex-wife, the police would assume it was more a domestic grudge than a real threat to society.

Don and Teresa hoped their lives would settle down now. Kyle had been accepted to a university to study engineering and enrolling in the military had given him the ability to afford school. Once finished he would emerge an Officer. He moved in with his girlfriend and life seemed to be moving in a very positive direction for him. It appeared this was one less child they needed to worry about.

Douglas and Kevin spent a great deal of time at their mother's house swimming in the pool, having a barbecue or playing guitar around the fire at night. Teresa thought it was a huge blessing that all the boys got along so well. At least it looked like they did.

Teresa and Don struggled financially for several years, spending most of their money helping their sons or paying for lawyers to fight Tammy in the courts. Both of them worked their full time jobs and part time in retail to help make ends meet. They didn't mind too much...they did what was necessary.

As part of her divorce settlement, Teresa was entitled to spousal support. Not wanting anything further to do with Dennis after she and Don were married, Teresa returned Dennis' money. She severed all ties with her ex-husband.

It was unfortunate that what they thought was a justice system, turned into a legal system. Don lost almost everything in the divorce. Even though he had the boys, Tammy's lies and manipulations had the court taking pity on her. She used every resource available to gain sympathy for her cause. She even went so far as to be trained in baiting Don to hit her. Something he never did, much to her chagrin.

Teresa was feeling added pressure because her employment contract was coming to an end. She desperately needed this job. Having graduated with honours from College in Business and Human Resources, she was thrilled to be hired to work in Training and Development with such a prestigious company. With the one-year contract end date quickly approaching she began to panic. She talked to her manager about her future, but her questions were met with a cold shoulder.

"I can't lose this job," she said to Don one evening. Tears began to flow from her eyes. "We need the money!"

"I know," he said to her. "Everything will work out. Please don't worry so much." Her two sons lived on their own, and she knew they were very strapped for money. Many evenings after working, Teresa would buy bags of food and drive the hour to give her boys groceries for the week. It was the only way she could help them right now.

Teresa found she was unable to calm the terror and panic that was taking control of her. For the first time in her life, she had felt comfortable with someone. She trusted Don and loved him beyond measure. But his sons had proved to be too much for her. Her past life traumas were beginning to rear their ugly heads, and she lived in fear, anxiety and panic all day long. There was nowhere to turn to escape it.

Still unable to get an answer from her manager, Teresa did her best to soldier on. The stress in her was mounting to a critical level. At home, they were constantly having trouble with Braden and desperate measures needed to be taken.

No longer comfortable in her own house and not trusting the boy, Don began making plans to take action with his son. Braden was no longer allowed in the house unless a parent was present; they took his keys away from him; he was to be supervised in the house at all times. They were at the point of no return with him. Something had to change.

Together they had tried their best with each of the boys. It seemed that their best efforts were not good enough. Understanding they were fighting against the 'other' parent, made their struggles even more difficult.

They thought trying to understand each son and help them through the divorce process would help. After all, these boys were not little children. They ranged from middle teens and twenties.

As time passed, they both hoped life would ease up and the boys would settle down.

"We just want a good life for ourselves and our kids," they said repeatedly to each other. Now that they had found each other after existing through a lifetime of unhappiness, they wanted to, 'Live.'

'Life,' would be their biggest hurdle. 'Life,' together was their ultimate goal.

'Life,' itself was about to be challenged.

Teresa's Guardian Angel would be paying her another visit.

A Second in Time

"Time takes it all, whether you want it to or not."
Stephen King

It's funny how one second in time can change a person's life completely. We always think that each minute of our lives is precious, and that is true, however, when you are in that split second between life and death you are faced with the brutal reality of your own existence.

Teresa faced her own existence as she headed home from work. The turmoil in the house with Braden had hit a frenzied state. Teresa feared being in the house alone with him. She was afraid for her life. Her work life was unstable as her contract was ending, with no future in sight. After a particularly difficult day with her manager, Teresa was relieved to leave the building. However, that February afternoon the weather had changed severely and as she walked towards her truck she was slapped in the face with wind, snow and ice.

Finally in her truck, she caught her breath and cleaned her glasses. The weather conditions were horrible and deteriorating by the minute. The wind was howling from the north, rocking her truck from side to side as she sat in the parking lot building her courage. With the wind came the heavy snow; blinding snow actually, and ice.

"I have to get home," she said to herself. "I'm sure I can handle driving in this. The truck is solid and 4-wheel drive. If I take my time I should be fine."

Now armed with confidence in herself and her vehicle, Teresa left the parking lot and headed for the opposite side of the city.

Usually she used one main route to and from work. That road was riddled with stoplights and considering they were icy, she decided, not to trust the other city drivers. She thought, "I need to take a different route home. One with less traffic."

With a new route in mind, she turned north. This route would take a bit longer but there were less traffic lights. "I should be fine," she believed.

Coming from a farming area, Teresa was used to driving in inclement weather. She was confident and a very capable driver. After all, what could go wrong?

As she made her first turn heading out of the city she saw the true conditions of the road. The roads were covered in a sheet of ice, then blanketed by snow. The wind whipped the snow around causing white-outs.

Thankfully there was little traffic on this road. With only two other vehicles travelling the same direction, Teresa believed she was safe. The three vehicles kept a safe distance from each other. As elephants travel in a single file, so did the three vehicles, with Teresa in the middle. They opened the distance between each vehicle to 15-20 car length. They wanted to keep each other in sight so they would not lose the tire tracks of the vehicle ahead.

After five kilometers of the line dance, all three turned left onto the road that would take them back into the city. No one changed their speed or distance. "Looks like we are all seasoned winter drivers," she chuckled to herself. But heading back towards the traffic areas, Teresa tightened her grip on the wheel and had all senses on high alert.

"I know I will be fine once I get passed the mall," she thought to herself.

Now heading west, the wind slammed into the side of her truck. She fought to keep the heavy vehicle in her lane. Road conditions were deteriorating with each passing kilometer.

As Teresa approached the outskirts of the city traffic became heavier, with most of the traffic heading out of the city. Not enjoying city life, Teresa tolerated the traffic as a necessary evil. "I just need to get passed the mall," she kept thinking.

Now approaching the first sets of stoplights, Teresa's senses went on high alert. She became hyper aware of her surroundings.

The cream coloured minivan, she had been following since leaving work, and the dark red pickup truck behind her continued to keep their distance.

Ever vigilant, she watched each car drive past her while she fought against the storm. The truck seemed to have a mind of its own as the storm raged, and soon it became a battle of wills between Teresa and her truck. Her hands began to ache from the tight grip she had on the steering wheel.

Off in the distance a blue pickup truck caught Teresa's eye. As the truck moved closer to her, she became hypnotized by the dance it was performing. Was it her Guardian Angel that was tapping on her shoulder to make her aware of oncoming danger? "He's helped me so many times before," she thought. "Keep me safe," she whispered to her protector.

As the blue truck approached, Teresa felt unable to tear her eyes away.

"I have to be careful; I need to have my wits about me; I have to be ready," she thought. Her life would depend on it.

A feeling of calm washed over her; as if everything would be alright.

In the next instance, her eyes widened in alert. The blue truck was in trouble. Something horribly wrong was happening as Teresa watched the truck weave off and on the road. Each time the wheels hit the gravel, the truck would jerk back onto the icy surface causing the truck to fishtail.

"Something is wrong," she said out loud to her Angel. "What's happening?"

Unable to remove her gaze from the on-coming vehicle, Teresa remained unaware that a split second in time would decide her fate.

The mistakes of the driver must have been caused by panic and fear. Trying to recover their vehicle, mistake after mistake was made. Another attempt was made to maintain control. Again they failed. Each time the driver forced the wheel, the truck went more out of control on the ice.

Almost mesmerized by the oncoming vehicle, Teresa stopped her truck in her lane. The van in front and the pickup behind followed suit. Everyone seemed aware of the circumstances, and was giving the blue vehicle a wide berth.

Now stopped, Teresa could feel the severe wind hammering on the passenger side of her truck. She took notice of every minute detail of her surroundings; the open field and ditch beside her on the right, the van in front, the red truck behind; the old houses on the left and just ahead was some type of office building. Oncoming traffic began to dissipate. Everyone seemed very aware of the scene that what was unfolding before them.

The silence in her truck became deafening. Her mind was screaming for some type of solution over this situation. There wasn't one. There was no way out for her. Trapped inside her truck surrounded by field, and traffic, Teresa placed her life in God's hands.

She continued to watch the driver fight to control their vehicle without success. At times the driver seemed to win but the next split second the truck went into the gravel again.

The tension in her body was out of control. She had never felt fear like this in her life. Alone in the truck she screamed out to God, ***"Is this why you wanted me here?"*** Fear and terror began to crush her chest. ***"If I'm not done here yet, why is this happening?"*** she cried.

Watching the oncoming truck continue to struggle, time began to slow down. With a death-grip on the steering wheel and her right leg stretched straight out to apply extra force to the brake pedal, Teresa waited for fate to take control.

Feeling the walls of her truck close in around her, Teresa knew there was no escape. Panic and terror rose in her throat and she found it difficult to breathe. She waited for fate to play out it's cruel hand.

Glancing to her right, Teresa noticed her cell phone lying in her purse on the passenger seat. She desperately needed to hear her husband's voice before it was too late. She had to tell him one last time how much she loved him. "Will I ever see him again?"

Still she watched and waited. Time slowed down even more; almost coming to a standstill. It was surreal. She could hear her heart beat, her lungs scream out for a breath and her own muscles shriek from pain as she tried to brace herself for impact. She went rigid with terror.

Suddenly the blue vehicle recovered out of the gravel and swerved back onto the road. They had overcompensated and now they lost control completely. The truck began to spin. As it spun, the truck connected with the van in front of Teresa. In an instant the mirror was taken off the van and flew onto the road laying there like a dead animal.

Again the truck spun on the icy road and went back into the gravel. The battle between machine and driver must have been horrible, for in the next instant the truck was spinning in circles on the road directly in front of Teresa.

"Oh my God!" she screamed as she pushed even harder onto the brake and squeezed the steering wheel, her fingers turning white. **"Will I ever talk to Don again,"** she wondered. **"Will I ever see my sons again?"** Briefly she looked at her phone before returning her eyes to look out the windshield and the heavy truck that was about to crash into her.

She gripped the steering wheel so tight she felt her hands melt into the wheel. Her gaze was frozen on the oncoming vehicle. Teresa clenched her teeth as her entire body fought the terror. Every body part screamed for release as she watched the truck spin around and head backwards for the ditch right in front of her.

Teresa prayed hard. *"Oh my God! What is going to happen?"* she heard her soul scream out from within her. *"SOMEONE PLEASE HELP ME!"* she cried. **"I don't want to be here! Am I going to die?"**

She quickly saw a vision of her husband's face in front of her eyes. "I waited 46 years for you, and all we can be married is 8 months?" she asked the face.

Then blue flashed in front of her eyes.

The blue truck went backwards into the ditch five feet in front of her truck. Every second happened so slowly but yet instantly. Teresa saw the back end of the truck spin into the gravel, and then to her horror, the front of the other vehicle came at her.

It had built up enough momentum that when the back tires grabbed the gravel, the back end of the truck stopped moving, but the front was not finished.

Completed petrified by this point, Teresa wanted to jump out of her skin. Impact was imminent now. She couldn't remember the last time she took a breath.

Absolutely beside herself in fear, Teresa turned her head slightly to the right trying to cower away from the impact. The last thing she saw was the front of the vehicle swinging towards her truck. Time froze.

Fear of the unknown is horrible. Some say that when trapped in such horror a person's life flashes before their eyes. The only image Teresa saw was her husband. She was afraid for him. What would happen to him if she died. "Who will love him?" she thought. He had felt so alone until they found each other. He was alive for the first time in his life. Life for the both of them was happy and they loved each other deeply.

Faced with death, Teresa tried desperately to hold the vision of her husband's blue eyes in her mind. But terror washed over her again and tears welled up in her eyes.

Time stopped. "I have to get out," she thought. **"I have no where to go!"** she screamed.

The sound of the blue truck slamming into her vehicle was deafening. It was like cannon fire. The hit was quick and terrible. The back end of Teresa's truck lifted a foot off the ground, then pounded back onto the icy road. Leaving her badly shaken.

Teresa had been hit in the front, towards the passenger side. Her truck's solid steel frame was pushed eight inches back; the radiator was ripped and pouring onto the ice; the engine block was moved back towards her and the lights all smashed. During the impact, Teresa noticed the cover plate for her stereo was launched into the back of the cab, her purse flipped over itself and landed on the floor, but her phone popped out and lay lifeless on the seat beside her. What she found extremely odd was that the air bags did not deploy. She had heard nightmares about the facial damage they inflict, but Teresa's air bags didn't deploy. Considering she wears glasses, she was thrilled about that.

Once her truck landed back on the ground and the blue truck had bounced back off, Teresa thought the nightmare was over.

Unable to let go of the steering wheel she cringed at the stabbing pain in her right hip and the right side of her neck. ***"I can't feel my legs,"*** she screamed. ***"I can't move!"***

She looked out her windshield at the other truck. It landed 15 feet away. The hood was up, the air bags had gone off and the she saw her own terror mirrored in the face of the woman who had hit just her.

Teresa overflowed with emotion. Anger won out. "How could she do this to me! Why didn't she stay in her own lane," she yelled.

Shocking her out of her thoughts, Teresa heard a tapping on her window. Pain shot through her neck when she tried to turn. Instead, she lowered the window and heard a kind man's voice asked if she was ok. ***"No, I'm not ok. I can't feel my legs,"*** she said to the man. He then said the worse words imaginable; **"I smell gas!"** he exclaimed. "Just a minute, I'll be right back."

Absolute terror consumed Teresa. All she could think of was, ***"Oh my God! He smells gas; I can't***

move my legs; WHAT IF THE TRUCK EXPLODES!" She began choking back sobs and gasped for air. Tears rolled down her cheeks as she watched the man run over to the other woman.

When he returned, he offered Teresa a piece of paper with his information on it. "I'll be a witness," he told her gently. "I saw the entire thing."

"Thank you," she muttered.

"I can't feel my legs," she started to say but then the woman that hit her emerged from her vehicle.

She walked over to Teresa said, "Are you hurt?"

"Yes I'm hurt," Teresa yelled.

The woman looked at Teresa and said, "I knew I should have stayed in the Chapters parking lot." With that said, she turned around and walked back to her truck.

Shock was consuming Teresa.

The horror of the event was crawling up her throat trying to escape. She was losing the battle to reign it back in.

As each woman sat in the smashed vehicles they waited for help to arrive.

Teresa was like a caged animal. Despite the pain she stretched out her arm to grab her phone. "I have to talk to Don," was all she was capable of thinking. As she reached, she felt an excruciating stabbing pain in her low back and hips. "I have to talk to Don," drove her through the pain. She had to let him know what had happened. "I have to talk to him before I lose my mind."

Shaking she hit speed dial. Fighting tears, she waited. It was now she realized her body was shaking violently.

When Teresa heard her husband's voice on the phone it was like an explosion happened inside her. She tried to remain calm, but lost control. She thought if the roads were this bad here it would be a very difficult hour drive from work for him. Suddenly she realized he would push himself beyond the limits to get to her and she couldn't have him risk his own life. That thought snapped her back. Teresa regained a bit of her composure.

She explained to him what had happened. Unable to hide the terror in her voice...he knew how badly she was shaken. The more she talked to him, the more silent tears rolled down her cheeks.

As they talked she began to feel a bit calmer, but her body continued to shake uncontrollably and her teeth chattered.

His voice soothed her and they began to discuss what needed to be done. He would call the insurance company and his son to come and get the truck and drive it home.

"I'll call you back when I know what hospital they take me to," she promised him. As soon as they stopped talking, Teresa fought to gain control. Her mind would not stop. Over and over she saw the truck, she heard the sounds and 'felt' the impact. She quickly picked up her phone and called 911.

"It's a busy day with the storm," the dispatcher told her. "Someone will be there soon."

What seemed like after a lifetime of waiting, she heard sirens in the distance. "There!" she screamed. "I see them." Finally, she would get help.

The pain in her back and neck was growing and she felt her body stiffening.

The fire truck roared onto the scene with lights flashing. They blocked the road with their truck and attendants jumped out to help the other driver first.

"She can walk!" Teresa thought. "I can't move! I need help." Suddenly someone was at her window. They asked about her injuries and while she was explaining, she fell silent as she watched the other woman climb into the cab of the fire truck.

"We'll be right back, Ma'am," he said. "The ambulance is almost on the scene."

More flashing lights and sirens broke the silence of the wind that was still howling around them.

The attendants came to Teresa first. "Finally someone is going to help me," she believed. They opened the truck door and talked for a minute or two. She retold them about her pain and the inability to feel her legs.

"Stay calm," they urged her. "We have to get some equipment from the truck."

In order to stay in control, Teresa called Don again. She knew he would be worried.

After hanging up the attendants were back beside her. They gently placed a collar around her neck and then spent the next five minutes trying to figure out how to remove her from the truck without bending her due to possibility of the back injury. Eventually they decided to pull her out sitting up rather than lying her down on the seat. "We can get you out straight then lay you on the spinal board," they told her. Teresa didn't agree with them.

"You can't pull me out sideways, she said. "You'll hit my head on the frame." But they ignored her.

It was a fiasco. She couldn't bend, and her temple was even with the door frame. "How are they going to pull me out!" she wondered. "It won't work." They assured her it would be fine.

As they pulled her out of her truck, the first thing that happened was the side of her head impacted with the door frame.

"Brilliant!" she thought, "let's just add another injury to the list." The sudden connection with the frame jarred her neck again despite the heavy, solid neck brace she was wearing.

After what seemed an eternity of maneuvering, she was free of her cage. Gently they laid her down on the board. "Remove your glasses," she was told. They quickly wrapped her in blankets and strapped her to the stretcher. Even with the warm blankets, Teresa could not stop her violent shaking.

Then came the tape. "What are you doing?" she questioned them.

"We have to tape your head to the board to keep you still. Its standard procedure with all neck injuries," the attendant said. As they taped her forehead to the board terror rose in her again. She was just freed, only to be trapped by tape.

They must have suspected shock. The attendant kept telling Teresa to take some deep breaths and to try to relax. "Right! Like I can relax after everything that has just happened!" she thought.

They lifted her into the ambulance and began preparing her for the journey. The smell of the truck made her want to vomit.

Suddenly she looked up and saw her stepson Kyle was standing in the ambulance with her. "Hey T, how are you doing?" he asked. His expression spoke volumes. "Dad called and asked me to take the truck home. So don't worry," he said. He grabbed Teresa's purse out of the truck for her and called his dad.

"They are taking her to Victoria Hospital," he told his father. He then grabbed Teresa's hand and her told he would see her later. It was the nicest and most honest gesture she ever received from him.

When the doors on the ambulance closed, Teresa felt trapped as she did so many years ago hiding in her closet in fear of her parents. She was constantly being told to calm down and breathe. Breathe. Yes, she had forgotten to do that.

"Is this day ever going to end," she asked.

"Everything will be fine," she was told.

Teresa realized that a part of her was dead and still sitting in that truck. But then she heard the all familiar words that she heard throughout her life... "**You're not finished here yet**." "There is more," she believed.

After a long and painfully bumpy ride, she was wheeled into the emergency unit of the hospital.

There stood her husband waiting for her. No longer able to hold back her emotion, Teresa began to cry. All she wanted was to be held by him. She needed to feel his arms around her to help her feel safe, loved and protected but it was impossible. Instead he leaned over and kissed her cheek. The warmth of his lips and cheek gave her comfort. She began to settle immediately.

Now she could face the truth of her injuries because she was not alone.

As they waited for a place to wheel Teresa's bed, the emergency doors opened again and to Teresa's shock the woman who was being wheeled in was the woman who hit her. "Why is she strapped down to a board?" she asked her husband. "She was running around outside after the accident!"

"We have a spot for you, Teresa," the nurse told her, breaking Teresa's train of thought.

After being taped to the board for five long hours, enduring x-rays with questionable staff Teresa grew impatient. They refused to remove the tape on her heard or let her go to the bathroom until the doctor talked to her.

"You have a severe whiplash with soft tissue damage to most of your body," the doctor told her. "There is nothing broken," he assured her. "Go home and take a couple of days off, rest and maybe have some physio," he said. "I'll give you something for the pain." That was it! The doctor walked over to the next bed to examine another accident victim. The nurse gave her an injection and other pain medication.

Even though she could barely hold her head up, they released her without a neck brace. "What kind of doctor was that?" she asked Don as they left.

Slowly she walked out to their small car for the journey home. She struggled to get into the vehicle. "I can't bend my neck or back," she told Don.

"Take your time," he told her.

The ride home was long and rough. Every slight movement of the car wrenched her neck and back. Tears poured down her face. The injection hadn't taken hold yet.

Once home, Don called Teresa's sons and told them what happened to their mother.

"Is she ok," one asked.

"She's alright now," Don told him. And that is where it ended. Neither son came up to see their mom. She could have died that night, but that didn't matter to them. Or maybe they are not able to face things. Either way, it cut Teresa deeply.

Surviving the next couple of days was difficult. Unable to brush her hair, or clean her teeth properly, or sit at the table, Teresa stayed in the house with her husband taking care of her. "Thank God I have you," she said to him.

"I'm glad I still have you," he replied.

Assuming that two days was enough rest time, Teresa attempted to return to work. But she had blinding headaches, her neck hurt and she was unable to climb the thirty steps up to her office. Two days later, she lost her job. Her contract was over...end of story.

Now seriously injured, no job and mounting bills, what was she going to do? **"I have to work,"** she told Don. "I have to help with the bills."

"Just look after yourself," he told her. "Your health is most important."

More terrified now than before the accident, Teresa was unable to relax.

She had to get up and get on with things; forget the injuries. "How can I let a simple thing like an accident stop me," she said to Don one evening.

But deep in her heart she knew this might be the battle she couldn't win. Her future had looked so bright and hopeful. "I have to come back," she thought.

Life After Tragedy

"I know God will not give me anything I can't handle. I just wish that He didn't trust me so much."
Mother Teresa

Two weeks after the accident, Teresa was offered a temporary contract position at a local hospital in recruiting. Since her specialty was interviewing, she accepted the position informing her employer about her injuries. She excelled in her work and loved every minute.

During her time in recruiting, the situation with Braden had gone past critical. "He has to leave, now!" she told Don. "I will not live like this anymore."

"Yes, he does," he agreed. "His behaviour has deteriorated since he has been seeing his mother more often. He is still stealing and we have to protect ourselves," he told his wife.

Teresa made several calls around the city and found a group home for Braden to live in; provided he follow the rules.

The stress and pain in Teresa's body was taking over her every waking minute. Three times per week, after leaving work, she went for chiropractic treatments. Unfortunately, the chiropractor left her head hanging backwards off the table, then told her to lift. She tried, thinking, "He is the doctor, he should know what is right." But it caused more damage to her already delicate neck. In a short time, she began suffering severe migraines and her entire upper body felt as if it had impacted the oncoming truck again.

Every day she went to work, life became harder and more painful. Before lunch she would sit at her desk crying from the pain. Unable to continue with the job she loved, she talked with her manager. "It's more than I can bare," she told the woman.

"I see that you are in pain," her manager replied with compassion. "Things are slowing down now for us, so don't worry. You go home and recover," the woman said.

Now, just after her 48th birthday, Teresa left her job and admitted defeat.

Before they could get Braden in a group home, he made one last major mistake. He was holding a part time job, but was caught stealing and smoking a joint in the back kitchen of the restaurant.

With the last straw broken, Braden had 24 hours to find accommodations for himself. His mother refused him again, citing he would cramp her lifestyle. So her two spare, furnished bedrooms remained unused as her son was about to end up on the streets. She claimed to Don, "He's your problem. You and your whore."

Fortunately for Braden, his friend's mother agreed to take him in, temporarily. He moved in with his friend, thinking by the end of summer his dad would cave and let him back. "Dad always gives in to me," Braden told Teresa sarcastically. But Braden forgot who he was dealing with now.

"You will not manipulate your father anymore," she told him as a warning. He smiled.

Once summer ended, so too did Braden's welcome with his friend. Now threatened with being kicked to the curb, Braden approached his father. "No!" Don told him. "Absolutely Not! You can ask your mother."

Faced with the harsh reality of his actions, Braden returned to his dad and said, "She won't allow me to live with her."

"You can go to the group home then," his father replied. "It's all set." We have made the arrangements for you. That is were Braden went.

After four months, Teresa received a call from the coordinator of the group home. She went to meet with him.

"Braden has broken several rules of the house," he told her. "He was caught drinking alcohol in his room and has been selling drugs from the house. He has to leave."

"I understand," Teresa replied. "He has to face the consequences of his actions."

Braden returned to his mother, only to be refused one more time. He asked his brother and his girlfriend for a place to live. They allowed him to sleep on their couch for two weeks. Soon, he had worn out his welcome here too. His habits and behaviour were intolerable.

It appeared the young man was not welcome anywhere. "He needs to grow up and face his own actions," Teresa said to Don. "We can't fix their problems all the time! It isn't healthy for them. They'll never learn."

Braden found lodging with another friend, which ironically stole from him. Shocked at his friend's actions, he soon moved out and shared a small house with four other friends.

Now in a party-house and needing money, Braden used his smooth-talking entrepreneurial skills to purchase a keg of beer. He then sold tickets to his party. The guest paid $10 admission which purchased a beer cup and a great time.

After several events, the Police were called in to calm the multitudes of party-goers. Their last big event proved dangerous. The house caught on fire.

Braden had rented a room in the basement and after the firetrucks had finished dousing the blaze, everything Braden owned was either smoke covered or soaked in water. He was not allowed back in the burned out house for a week. When Braden was allowed in, he found most of his possessions ruined. Armed with a new-found sense maturity and a lot less arrogance, he once again moved in with a friend. Learning a lesson from his struggles, he went to work. He worked as a general labourer, and he soon learned the rewards of hard work.

It appeared their youngest son was maturing. "Sometimes tough-love is exactly what they need," Teresa commented to Don.

However, Braden was not the only child to have problems. Unable to stop his partying habits, Kyle soon found himself failing out of university. He said he had tried his best, but after three years, he found his school career had ended. He hadn't even completed his first year courses. Because the Military had paid for his tuition, he immediately owed the full amount back. He was now substantially in debt. He was feeling full-blown reality slap him against the head. In the meantime, his girlfriend had cheated on him and left; his friends were all graduating university and moving on; Kyle had his drinking and drugs to keep him company, and not much else.

Adding fuel to the fire, Kyle's mother sunk her claws in. Having been absent from his life for a few years, she took full advantage of his bruised ego. She bent and twisted his ear with her poisonous words. She blamed Don and Teresa for his plight and convinced him of their guilt. Kyle was more than happy to place the blame anywhere but on his own shoulders.

Through the mother's manipulative, narcissistic behaviour, both boys walked away from their father and Teresa to live a life controlled, once again, by their mother.

With pain in their hearts and exhausted from trying to provide structure for the boys, Teresa and Don admitted defeat. "They are adults and hopefully in time they will learn and grow up," Don said to her.

"I hope so," she replied. "I love them like they are my own, but I can't live with their behaviour."

In the meantime, Teresa's life was filled with medical appointments, tests, exams and exercises. She thought her insurance would cover her loss of income, as the agent told them. However, due to the roll of red tape she was now wrapped in, her income replacement was held up for two years. Slowly, she began losing her savings. This is a tact taken by insurance companies to force injured people back to work and have them sign away their insurance claims. "If you can work, you don't need their money."

With each appointment and new examiner, she had to endure her life being laid on the table for all the world to see.

During one of the 'professional medical exams,' by a physiotherapist, Teresa came out more injured than when she entered. Unable to accept the answer Teresa couldn't move her hips and low back in certain directions, the examiner forced the issue, causing excruciating pain to her right hip that still haunts her today. While lying on her back the examiner lifted Teresa's right leg and forced it over her left. Teresa screamed out in pain, but the examiner refused to stop.

She forced the leg farther, causing an explosion of pain in Teresa's hip and low back. Refusing to submit to further exploration by this practitioner, Teresa left the building. Severely limping, and armed with detailed notes of every question and action taken, Teresa went home and wrote detailed notes for the exam for her lawyer.

Then came the invasion of her privacy. Teresa discovered she was under surveillance. She felt like a prisoner, trapped in her own home. The insurance company had placed cameras outside her home and had people follow her.

Now afraid to leave the house, she began losing her nerve to drive. She found a psychologist who was extremely helpful. Teresa chatted openly about her accident and past issues. Each time she tried to relay the accident details, she began to panic and tremble with fear. At times, she couldn't speak.

"You are suffering from PTSD," the doctor told Teresa.

"What is that?" Teresa asked the psychologist.

"Post-traumatic stress disorder is a form of mental illness. It involves having been exposed to trauma involving either death or the threat of death, serious injury, or sexual violence," the doctor told her.

Now armed with a better understanding of what she was feeling and facing, Teresa slowly began to rebuild her life.

She worked with her former physiotherapist, Gloria, who now specialized in Chronic Pain and brain injury.

"You have to listen to what your body is telling you and take the right action to help it," Gloria would tell her. "Stretch to the point of pain, but do not go beyond," these were statements she taught Teresa. As she learned to care for her body, she was unaware of a silent threat. Concussion. Whiplash causes concussion to the brain. The brain is shaken violently inside the skull, causing trauma.

Teresa began having severe balance issues. One day while standing at the top of the stairs she moved her eyes to look at the railing before grabbing it in her descent. A nauseating wave of dizziness washed over her.

Before she knew what was happening, her feet were out from under her. She felt her left side impact each step as she fought to stop herself. After thirteen hits, she found herself lying on the floor at the bottom of the steps.

"DJ," she screamed. Don came running into the house. He had heard the pounding.

"Are you alright? What happened?" he asked.

She relayed the events to him and as the shock wore off she slowly got to her feet. Bruised and very sore she went outside and sat by the pool, not really sure why she was still dizzy.

Teresa took six more trips down the stairs over the next couple of years. "I don't understand any of this," she thought to herself. "If I turn my head or move my eyes I'm immediately nauseated and lose my balance."

As part of her checkup routine, Teresa visited her dentist.

"You have ten fractured teeth," the dentist told her. "What on earth has happened to you?"

She told him of the accident and how she was clenching her jaw. "This type of damage was caused by the impact," he told her. "I can rebuild your teeth with crowns."

Always terrified of dentists, Teresa was resisted but knew the teeth had to be fixed. This man was very gentle towards her and she began trusting him. Her face ached after one grueling six hour session in his chair. He rebuilt three of her molars in one day. After many appointments and what seemed like endless hours, her teeth were shiny and new. He was a brilliant dentist. One step complete.

With Gloria's help, Teresa tried many different modalities to help with the pain. She used massage therapy weekly, physiotherapy, acupuncture, and an infusion treatment (using intravenous with Lidocaine to block pain receptors). She submitted to acupressure, Reiki and hot stone massage. The pain continued. Teresa attended exercise classes in a warm pool; she had a Pilates and yoga instructor; she walked as often as her damaged feet would allow.

The pain was one aspect of her life she hoped to overcome, but the inability of her family and friends to understand what she had suffered, and why she was now changed, hurt her deeply.

"I'm sick to death of people telling me I'm fine, there's nothing wrong with me," she told Gloria. "Everyone says it's all in my head because I look fine." The lack of understanding, compassion and love from her own children made her heart ache. Her sons still refused to admit their mother was injured.

"They just can't face it," Don said to her one night as he held her while she wept. "They've always seen you as a strong, physically capable woman," he told her. "They can't show their emotions."

"Maybe not," she replied. "But they always expect me to be there the minute they have a problem. I could use their help now," she struggled to get out between sobs. "They don't even care about me." They still had not even acknowledged their mother was in an accident and could have been killed.

For five years, Teresa had to endure medical examinations, lawyer appointments, and was constantly being pressured by her insurance company to settle her law suit. She refused.

Now, almost bankrupt, she had to take out a loan against her settlement in order to survive. Don was forced to support his ex-wife financially while she claimed depression as the main reason she couldn't work, while the woman he loved fought hard every day to move and walk.

Five years after the accident, she was awarded a disability pension. It was a small amount compared to her salary, but she clung to it. Life was a struggle and she questioned it always. As time went by, the 29% interest on the loan became a mountain.

Then after some major testing, Teresa had proof that she had suffered a brain injury during the accident. Her center of balance was now eight inches to the left of centre. "That's why you lose your balance and fall down the stairs," the specialist told her.

"That makes sense," she thought. She could now simply hold her head still, move her eyes slightly, and cause waves of nausea to flow over her. Added to this was memory loss. ***"What else can go wrong!"*** she screamed up to the sky. ***"Is this why you left me here?"*** *She received no answer.*

Her love of reading and writing helped her keep her brain active. She began doing brain games hoping to repair the damage. Taking an active role in her own health care and rehabilitation was paying off. "I know what the signals are, I know when to take action and what to do. I can help myself," she told Don. "I can't sit back and wait for someone to fix this for me. I have to try," she said to him.

Armed with a bit more confidence, she was about to face her biggest challenge yet; lawyers and the insurance company.

"The insurance company will try to get you to agree to a settlement," her lawyer told her. "They are trying to figure out what your life is worth and place a dollar value on it."

The insurance company dragged Teresa and her life through the mud. They tried every trick at their disposal to prove she wasn't deserving a settlement. "I'm the victim here," she said to her lawyer. "She hit me! I didn't ask for this!" During a seven-hour discovery (interrogation), her entire medical history was used against her. They needed to prove a pre-existing condition. That would lessen the settlement value. They were brutal and ignorant in how they treated her. It was humiliating. She was forced to see a psychiatrist, whose first question floored Teresa. He wanted to know about orgasms. Shamed and embarrassed, Teresa refused to answer.

"Why do they force victims to go through this?" she asked her lawyer.

"They are trying to prove you are lying so they won't have to pay you," he replied.

"This is HUMILIATING AND UNFAIR!" she yelled. ***"I was hit!"*** she told her lawyer. ***"I was almost killed!" "I didn't hit her!"***

"This is how they work," she was told. "It isn't fair and maybe in time, you can help change things for others."

Now she braced for a fight. Her heart broke for her husband who was an innocent bystander in this war. "This isn't what he wanted," she thought. "Maybe it would have been better for him if I had been killed."

Their lives were supposed to be better once they found each other, but the mountain of struggles seemed too high to climb.

"God, why did you spare my life that day?" she begged. Suffering in anguish, she was losing the one thing that had kept her alive all these years...her will.

More Hidden Secrets

"What one hides is worth neither more nor less than what one finds. And what one hides from oneself is worth neither more nor less than what one allows others to find."

Andre Breton

For many years, Teresa played with her passion for writing. She dabbled in writing poetry and short stories for fun. Rarely did she show anyone, but it gave her a release she so desperately desired.

Several years earlier, Teresa made the first casual attempt of writing about the journey of her Grandmother, Aline. She felt compelled to share the injustice and brutality that was her grandmother's and her own life.

While relaxing in her gardens one afternoon after a difficult physio treatment, she received a suspicious email. The author of the email asked for private family details that only a close relative would know. They asked about her aunt Danielle, and if she was from Delhi. Immediately suspicious and with senses on high alert, she pondered over the request for days. Then her curiosity got the better of her so she responded.

"No one else could know about these things," she said to her husband. "Maybe this has something to do with the child Danielle was forced to give up."

"Are you sure you will be ok with this?" Don asked her with great concern.

"I need to know the truth," she replied. "I have been lied to all my life. I need the truth!"

Responding to the original email, Teresa asked some very pointed and cautious questions.

Several emails later, the sender asked to meet with Teresa. The email said, "Will you have coffee with my wife? I think you should talk to her. She has some questions that need to be answered and you are the only one that can answer them for her."

"This must be the daughter I was told Danielle had to abandon at birth," Teresa told Don excited at the prospect of new family. "Are you sure, Teresa?" Don asked.

"I really need to know. Trust me," she replied.

After several more emails, Teresa agreed to meet the woman, but insisted Don would be with her.

They set the date, time and restaurant for the meeting. She waited with nervous anticipation for the day to arrive.

With her stomach in knots and hands shaking, Teresa and Don walked into the restaurant. As the hostess led them towards the waiting couple, Teresa's feet froze in place. She looked at the two people sitting at the table. She had been led to believe she was there to meet the woman; her new cousin. Turning towards Don she whispered, "It's not her, it's HIM!" she whispered in a shocked tone.

"What?" he asked.

"It's not her. It's him!" Teresa repeated.

As she looked at the man who sat at the table, she saw her great-grandfather Henry. "The likeness is incredible!" she said to Don.

Shock, excitement and caution ran through her. As they approached the table the man stood. He offered his hand to Teresa and said, "My name is Martin, and this is my wife," he said.

Almost stunned into silence at the strong family resemblance, Teresa and Don introduced themselves, then they sat down.

The two couples enjoyed an exciting and pleasant conversation. They talked of family history as Martin asked questions and Teresa did her best to answer. Still erring on the side of caution, Teresa was hesitant. Seeing her need for proof, Martin brought forth his adoption papers. Now she realized there was no point in denying the truth. Pleased that this man was her first cousin, Teresa also felt her heart being stabbed yet again. Once again she was being forced to face the fact her family had lied to her all of her life...another lie. The lies were mounting with each passing day. "How many more lies will I find?" she wondered.

After having a great conversation over dinner both Teresa and Martin were pleased they had met.

"I just needed to know where I came from," he told her.

"I'm so thrilled you found me," she replied with honest joy in her heart.

When Teresa and Don returned home, she began to reflect over all the stories she had been told. "How many more of them are lies," she said to Don. Suddenly she realized the irony of the meeting. "His name is Martin; my parents named their one stillborn son Martin. What were these people thinking!" she screamed.

Over the next couple of years, Martin and Teresa developed a bond. They talked often, met when able and each appreciated the relationship. The two were finding answers to so many unanswered questions. Together, they still had more questions, but who was still alive to answer them?

"I have been given a beautiful gift," she said to Don. "A miracle. Now together, we can find answers."

Most of the older family members had died and Teresa wasn't sure they would have the answers she was searching for. One of Aline's friends lived nearby. Teresa told Martin, "I'm going to go talk to Claire, she knew grandma very well. Maybe she can help us."

"Let me know what you find out Kiddo," he replied.

Claire was the daughter of one of Aline's friend. She had always treated Aline with kindness, love and the respect she deserved. In return, Aline loved Claire like a daughter. Their bond was precious.

Teresa had known Claire for many years too, taking her grandmother to her friend's birthday parties while she lived with Teresa's family. "Hopefully she can help us," she said to Don as they drove to Claire's house for a visit.

Teresa adored this woman. She understood her grandmother's feelings towards her. As an avid horticulturalist, Claire's gardens were stunning. Her love of plants and soil was evident and she shared her plants with the couple, helping them create beautiful gardens around their home.

After unearthing some unique plants to take home for their gardens, they sat and enjoyed their coffee, dessert and chocolate.

Teresa discussed the idea of writing a book about her grandmother's life. Claire thought the book would be a lovely tribute to her friend Aline. She also noticed Teresa had been struggling with some of the lies and secrets of her family. Feeling compassion for the younger woman, Claire decided to divulge the truth.

Claire looked up from her cup of coffee and said to Teresa, "What do you know about the story of your grandma?"

Looking at her friend, Teresa conveyed the stories of her family shame she had grown up with. When she finished, she waited in anticipation to learn what Claire knew about Aline's life. As it turned out; she knew a great deal. Teresa was astounded to learn that Aline had unburdened her heart to Claire over the years. As she began exposing the truth behind the lies to the younger woman, Teresa was happy to hear the truth, but at the same time, she now knew she had been lied to for 54 years. Her parents, and grandparents lived and fed the lies causing shame and humiliation to be eaten for breakfast.

"My entire life and family history is a lie!" she exclaimed to Don on the drive home. "Who am I really? Why didn't they tell the truth? They forced me to live with their shame!"

Thankful that Claire loved her enough to communicate the truth, Teresa was now armed with enough ammunition to write the truth. She desperately needed to tell the world, she was not a product of incest. The truth did set her free. It liberated her passion for the truth. She began her journey with more determination than she had ever experienced in her life.

In telling the truth about the injustices of her family and the horrors of her past, "I can help other people who may have felt the same sting of humiliation and abuse," she told her husband. "I know grandma suffered because of her life, and I need to set her soul free," she said. "She deserves to rest in peace."

"And?" her husband asked her.

"Yes," she replied. "I need to heal myself and my own soul. "

During the writing of this book, Teresa faced many more obstacles. She toiled with the idea of having her personal and private life exposed. Her mission to expose the truth was greater than her shame could ever be. "I can't keep it hidden any longer. There are more generations of this family that need to know the truth," she told a friend. "If I keep silent, the lies, secrets and shame grow. I have to kill the lies now and break the cycle. Especially the cycle of abuse."

This book was no just longer her passion...it became her mission. She hoped that by sharing, others who read this will have faith. "You can overcome anything, if you have faith......in yourself," Teresa thought.

"Is this why *I'm not finished here yet?*" she asked one afternoon while praying for the first time in months. "Is this how I am to put the demons of my past life to rest?"

Unfortunately as Teresa began her new journey, she was faced with another health scare. As she was aging the earlier abuse and hard work was beginning to take its toll.

In two years she faced sudden high blood pressure, a possible heart attack, menopause, skin cancer and thyroid tumors.

"Honestly, how many more problems do I have to deal with?" she asked her maker as she raised her fists to the sky in anger. "I finally know why I'm here...help me to succeed."

Suddenly a peace flowed over her.

"You are not finished here," was the response she heard whispered to her. Trusting in her journey and mission, Teresa no longer asks why.

Let's Get Out of Here

"There are things that we never want to let go of, people we never want to leave behind. But keep in mind that letting go isn't the end of the world, it's the beginning of a new life."

Unknown

After having her life laid bare by lawyers and insurance companies Teresa was emotionally destroyed. She wanted out of the city. She despised the house they were in. The accident had put an end to the renovations and used up all of their savings. Teresa watched her husband struggle in his attempt to finish the work in the house. After driving over three hours and working all day, he pushed himself to the point of exhaustion. At night and every weekend, he attempted to complete the renovations.

"I should be taking care of you," Don would say to his wife.

"I'm fine," she would reply trying to ease his anguish. "I want to help," she said to him. "This was a team project. Now that none of the boys will help, it's up to us."

"You have to protect yourself," he said to her.

"But I've never stopped before," she snapped in anger. "I hate that woman for taking my life away!" she screamed as once again tears poured down her face. **"I've worked so hard to rebuild my life!** In one split second, she destroyed everything!" "This isn't why I fought so hard to get away from the old life."

Over the many months, rehabilitation treatments continued, and together they did their best to rebuild their lives. Teresa eventually grew stronger and her fighting spirit returned. She realized there was nothing that could possibly repair the damage done to her body, but she needed to try.

They decided to put their house up for sale. It was part of the original plan when starting all the repair work.

The long wearisome drive to and from work was slowly destroying Don. He had also been the victim of two car accidents. Twice he was on the receiving end of a hit-and-run accident. Now faced with his own neck and shoulder injuries, they desperately wanted to leave this city and move closer to his work.

Work for Teresa no longer mattered as she faced with the harsh reality of her injuries and truly believed her working career was finished. She gave up on that aspect of her life.

While attending an appointment with an orthopedic specialist, he told Teresa, "You will never work again. You need to face facts and just plan on doing the best you can for the rest of your life. Your condition will only deteriorate as you age."

"I can't give up now!" she said. *"I've fought too hard for too long!"*

Trying to make the best of her life she and Don worked magic in the house. Together they finished the painting, installed new trim in the house, cleaned carpets and finished landscaping. Friends were shocked at the beautiful transformation.

Her days were filled with treatments, exercise, renovations and another passion of hers: cooking and baking. She kept her brain working with simple tasks like reading and following a recipe. She was retraining her brain and it was working. Her new practice of yoga and meditation accelerated her emotional healing.

Finally, the reconstruction on the house was complete around the same time as the law suit was finally settled. Teresa had won a settlement but after paying her lawyer, the expensive income replacement loan and catching up on Don's support payments there was little left. The greatest injustice they found was being forced to pay his ex-wife spousal support for the rest of her life. She raped Don during the divorce and was set financially but her hate and manipulation won over the judge. Once again their funds were limited. However, that didn't stop the children from asking her for money.

Their plans were set to leave, and they would soon be free and clear of the city she despised. In January of 2012, they found a stunning old home in a near-by city, that was originally built in 1880. The stately home built in the Italianate style and lovingly maintained throughout the century called to both of them immediately. "This is your home," it whispered. "Welcome." Within minutes they both fell in love with the house. The day the viewed it, was the day they placed an offer. Twenty-four hours later they bought their first home together.

"Light Haven," as Teresa and Don refer to it, was purchased on Don's birthday. **"Happy Birthday!"** she said lovingly to her husband; her hero; the man she adored. As they signed the paperwork their excitement grew. Finally we can start our life together free of the ghosts of the past. As an additional birthday present, Teresa gifted Don with three decorative lady bugs to hang on the wall in their new sunroom.

For the first time in several years, the couple knew true bliss. Life was finally good.

With April as their moving date, they packed, planned and arranged for movers. All four boys decided they wouldn't help with the move. "You're furniture is too heavy," they said repeatedly.

April 2nd, Don and Teresa took possession of their new home. They started moving truck loads of items on their own as Teresa spent her days at the new house cleaning and waiting for appliance deliveries. Early one morning on their drive with a full load, their truck broke down. The insurance company had salvaged the Ram after the accident but it was never the same sturdy and dependable truck.

Faced with expensive repairs and left at the new house without a vehicle, Teresa received news that her oldest son was hospitalized with a severe intestinal disease. His wife messaged Teresa to inform her about the tests being done. Unable to get to the hospital, Teresa kept in touch with her daughter-in-law and received regular updates.

Later that day as she struggled with worry over her son and trying to coordinate movers and deliveries, Teresa received a call from her son. "Why didn't you come?" he demanded of his mother.

"I don't have a vehicle!" she replied. Nothing she said mattered to him. He refused to understand and just assumed his mother should be there for him no matter what her situation. He was scared and she knew it, but it was out of her hands.

Both Don and Teresa were pulled to the end of their ropes. Exhausted, worried and frustrated, they eventually moved and then came the days of unpacking everything.

"We have too much stuff," she told Don.

"Where?" he asked. Teresa smiled at him and replied, "Everywhere."

They loved their home and she felt free here. It was warm and inviting. The couple were very aware of the two spirits that occupied the home. One on the upper floor was kind and compassionate. She prevented Teresa from falling down the huge flight of stairs one morning. The second entity occupied the old cellar. His energy wasn't always so positive. Eventually they understood each other and the house became a home to all. Even Buddha their Pekingese, learned to respect the "pretty lady," upstairs. Every morning on their way downstairs, Teresa would always tell Buddha, "Say hi to the pretty lady." As if knowing, he would stare in the direction of the spare bedroom, and then saunter downstairs.

Later that fall Teresa and Don flew to Jamaica for a week of relaxation. They needed to get away. The two of them relaxed, soaked up the sun and enjoyed each other's company and enjoyed the soothing water.

The trip was planned because in March of 2013, Teresa was undergoing another round of reconstructive surgeries on her left foot.

She needed another joint fused in her mid-foot. The original triple joint fusion of 1978 had not held together over the years. Refusing to give up playing volleyball and baseball, the fusions were unable withstand the pressure. Now she needed her big toe scraped clean from arthritis and four other toes straightened. The work was necessary as age, time and arthritis was causing her severe pain.

After the surgery she was well cared for by Don. He moved a bed into their sunroom and rented a wheelchair for her. She was unable to stand on the foot for six weeks which normally was not a problem. However, a large cyst had developed under the knee cap on her right leg (caused by her knee impacting the dash during the accident). Her knee swelled to triple its size. Teresa was unable to stand. She needed help.

Don was home with her for the first week. His attention to his wife was a beautiful gift to her and one she could never repay.

The problems began when Don had to return to work. Still unable to stand and highly medicated, Teresa was unable to cook for herself or do simple things like reach for a glass of water or take the dog out. She was frustrated and angry.

Her surgeon suggested she contact a local government service agency who assist people during convalescing.

"Oh, you are too young to need help. We only help old people," she was told.

"Pardon?" she asked. "What about young people that can't help themselves?" Teresa questioned. "Who helps them?" She received no reply.

Another agency told her, "have your family help." That wasn't possible. Her children would never raise a finger to help her.

Teresa asked one agency, "How am I supposed to take a bath?"

The woman replied, "take a sponge bath for six weeks, you don't need to get in the water."

Teresa's anger was now at the boiling point. The pain from bone reconstruction was brutal. "Don't we pay taxes to have your organizations in place?" she snapped as she lashed out at the one woman.

"You and your husband make too much money. We don't help people who can afford private help," Teresa was told.

"We can't afford it!" she screamed at the woman. *"We are paying an ex-wife! And I don't work!"*

Then the final blow came. A family member said to Teresa, "well you have a loving husband at home, and he makes good money, hire someone."

Appalled and stunned by the statement, Teresa lost her self-control. She cried harder than she had after her near death experience. "Why is it when I need help, no one will help me?" She asked her husband. "When those kids of mine need help, I've always been there for them. Never their father...me!"

Douglas took offense to his mother's comments and struck back.

As she sat in her wheelchair crying from frustration and pain, the phone rang.

"Mom," he snapped at her. **"You just need to stop complaining and get off your fat ass and go get a job!"** he blasted out. "Then you wouldn't have time to worry about all these things and feel sorry for yourself."

"What gives you the right to speak to me that way?" she demanded.

"Oh Mom, you're just whining like you always do. Get over it, not everything is about you."

"I've never asked you for help before Douglas, and the one time I need help from my family, you do this to me! *How dare you! You truly are a spoiled brat!* I helped you buy the house you're living in; I've bought you food when you couldn't afford to eat; we've moved you and your brother countless times; I've co-signed two loans for you; loaned you my vehicle for hunting and *this is the thanks I get from you! I CAN'T TALK TO YOU ANYMORE!"* And with that she hit the off button and threw the phone across the room in anger. Several emotions ran rampant in her heart and head. She felt rage, rejection, disgust and abandonment all at once. Once again she saw the true nature of her son and how he felt for his mother.

She had been living to give her children a better life than she had. She starved herself when the kids were young and they couldn't afford to buy groceries. For days she went without eating.

"This is how they show me they love me?" she said to Don as she completely lost control of her emotions.

Later, after she calmed down, she said to her husband, "I don't think I can ever forgive him this time."

Teresa now saw with her eyes completely opened. Her kids didn't love or respect her. They just used her as their father had always done. "They learned well from him," she thought.

The only thing she wanted in life was a family that loved one another. A happy family.

"Is that so difficult to have," she asked God. She sat in her wheelchair, a pathetic , broken woman. Those that could hurt her the worst, just did.

She was dead inside.

Throughout her life she had overcome so many horrible obstacles. The pain her children now inflicted on her heart was a new experience. This could be the one thing she never recovers from.

Determination in the Face of A Broken Heart

"Some of the biggest challenges in relationships come from the fact that most people enter a relationship in order to get something: they're trying to find someone who's going to make them feel good. In reality, the only way a relationship will last is if you see your relationship as a place that you go to give, and not a place that you go to take. "

Anthony Robbins

The joy and life had been knocked out of Teresa. Her son, through his words and actions cut her heart so deeply, she wasn't sure she would ever be whole again.

She struggled in her wheelchair to fend for herself during the day. Her foot was a disgusting mess with blood oozing from the four pins sticking out the ends of her toes. The hospital had sent her home before the bleeding had stopped. Before she left they handed her some gauze and said, "stuff this down inside the cast to stop the blood from leaking out."

When guests came to the house, Teresa covered her foot with a towel or sock. It was a horrible sight, especially with the pins sticking out of four toes and a cast encrusted with blood.

Determined to have a bath, Teresa crawled her way
backwards up the flight of stairs. She used all her
strength to lower herself in and out of the tub while
keeping her left foot elevated. Her husband watched
his wife struggle but knew he was unable to help.

"I've done this before when I was 18 years old, surely
I can do it now at 53," she told him.

He smiled and tried to remain brave as he watched
his wife's balancing act in and out of the tub. He knew
her heart was broken. She had barricaded herself
behind her brick wall; a place where she went when she
was unable to cope with the pain life threw at her. He
knew she was fighting with the will to survive, but he
couldn't break through the wall she had built .

Throughout her life, when someone hurt her, Teresa
would withdraw behind her emotional brick wall. It
was the only way to protect her heart and prevent
herself from feeling the pain of heartbreak and grief.
The wall would not come down until she felt safe and
strong again. Sometimes this lasted many months.
Teresa would close herself off from the world and those
who hurt her.

Sometimes the pain and devastation was worse than
others. The pain her own children caused her cut deep
and left lasting scars.

A few months after recovering from one surgery and
learning to walk again, Teresa had to undergo another
operation. This time to fuse a joint and straighten the
second toe on her left foot. She needed this done. The
toe was causing great difficulty in walking. Later that
month, her youngest son was looking for a new place to
live and wanted to save some money. "Can I live with
you for a while?" he asked his mother. It went against
her better judgement, but it was one of their children,
so, Teresa and Don opened their home to him. He
moved in with all of his clothes, some furniture and his

menagerie of lizards. The one cage was massive and took up part of one room. This young man had disrupted their lives and their home and apologized for nothing.

He rarely asked his mother if he could help her around the house or with meals. He ate, slept, and ignored the pain and struggle his mother was living with.

Part of the arrangement with Kevin was for him to pay them a small amount of rent money each month. He had agreed, but each month Teresa found she had to chase him down to collect. He avoided being home around rent day, spending time with his girlfriend.

He took their generosity for granted and treated them both with disdain.

After Christmas, Kevin's foul moods hung in the house with smothering effects on everyone. Soon harsh words were spoken between he and his mother.

Don hated the way his wife was being treated but had always remained silent. This was the final straw. Kevin's treatment of his mother was appalling and for the first time, Don spoke out.

Angry and stunned that his step-father would speak to him in such a manner, Kevin, collected his coat and wallet and stormed out of the house to celebrate Christmas with his father. Not returning for three days.

The day he returned to his mother's house the tension he brought with him electrified the rooms. Teresa gathered up her determination and said to her son, "Kevin you need to find another place to live, soon! This is not working. It isn't a healthy environment for any of us."

When she looked into her son's steely blue eyes, she saw the anger building. She knew exactly how he was feeling. Teresa had witnessed the look, and the anger that followed, many times throughout his life.

Within a month Kevin had found a place to live. He definitely made his mother aware that this wasn't *his* choice of apartments, but, "it's the best I can do on such short notice," he told her.

His friends helped him move but he left several of his delicate plants and his lizards behind. "It's too cold to move them now, Mom," he told her. "Look after them for me and I'll get them when it's warmer outside."

Teresa agreed seeing no cause for concern. However, her son left no money behind for food for his creatures. He snapped at his mother, "they don't need to be fed very often."

After consulting a local expert on the lizards, the couple soon learned Kevin was wrong. Unable to see any living thing suffer, they bought food for the creatures. "Why should the lizards suffer for his ways," Teresa said to Don. The lizards thrived under their care and they actually bonded with them.

In April, Kevin returned to claim his pets. He ranted at his mother claiming she had fed them too often and caused them stress.

Several days later Teresa called Kevin. "How are the pets doing?" she asked.

"One died," he replied. "They probably had too much stress at your house," he snapped sarcastically at her.

She couldn't believe what he said. Teresa was sad to learn the one lizard had died. She and Don had taken special care of it and watched the creature flourish.

"Well, I wasn't going to starve them," she replied back.

Teresa found Mother's Day to be very difficult. She knew enough not to expect Douglas and his family, but when Kevin called and said he was going to his father's house, she was shocked beyond belief.

"Pardon," she asked her son.

"I'm going to dads for Mother's Day," he said. "We are visiting with Grandma."

Completely destroyed now, Teresa hung up the phone.

"Why did I have children," she asked looking up to the heavens. "I don't understand. Is this payback?" she screamed. She knew Kevin was still angry and holding a grudge about the past few months, but she had never expected this.

Several more bricks were added to the brick wall she had built around her heart.

To soldier on, Teresa tried to concentrate on regaining the use of her foot. Her birthday was the following month, which she was dreading. Since giving birth to her boys, she had never been separated from her boys like this before. With her courage fading and her heart almost destroyed she wondered what her birthday would bring. It had never been much of an occasion all her life. She had her first birthday party and cake at 40 years old. It had been a nice event and a lovely surprise when people began arriving at the farm. It was the one thing Dennis had done for her that actually made her feel special.

The day started out with trepidation. She did hope Kevin would drive the 30 minutes to spend some time with her, even though he always made excuses and complained because he had to drive to see his mother.

The best gift in the world would be a kiss on the cheek from her boys.

Suddenly the phone rang.

"Hi Mom, Happy Birthday," Kevin said.

"Thanks," she replied. "Are you coming up today? Don picked up a cake," she said.

"No, I can't. I'm going to my aunt's today. Her birthday was two days ago and Dad's having a barbecue for her," Kevin declared with a hint of sarcasm in his voice.

"Pardon?" Teresa asked, unbelieving what she had just heard. "You've never celebrated your aunt's birthday before!" she said.

"Well, Dad is having a barbecue," he replied.

"You're going to your aunt's on your mother's birthday?" she questioned him again, still in shock at what she had just heard.

"Yup, I'm also going to be building a deck for her," he said.

Tired, angry and so fed up with her children, Teresa said, have fun with your aunt and dad." As she hung up the phone all happiness and joy washed out of her body. It was as if she had melted into the floor she was standing on. She had nothing left to give.

She felt the bitter sting of betrayal and disappointment. Was this payback for her walking away from her mother? "God, are you trying to teach me a lesson!" she screamed as tears poured from her eyes.

"I protected them from my unstable mother," she whispered to her dog as she petted him. "I wanted to give them a better life than I had, and this is how they treat me?"

It had been many years since her heart had felt this much pain. She was devastated and the pressure cracks in her brick wall were beginning to show.

One summer day, Teresa and Don were out buying some flowers from their favourite garden centre.

"Oh, your son was just up here yesterday buying plants," the owner told her.

"Really," Teresa replied. She now had proof that her second son was avoiding her.

"Yes, he was buying some herbs from me," her friend told her.

Teresa had reached the boiling point with her sons. Her anger woke up inside her like a grizzly bear.

She went home and pulled the phone off the cradle to call her son. There was no answer. Not thinking clearly, Teresa left him a heated message.

"I heard you were in town buying plants. Funny how you always say it's too far to visit me, but when you are in town, you still don't stop in. I would be happy with a five-minute visit to see you and say hi!" she yelled into his answering machine.

She knew the last few years of anger and stress where flying out of her but she was unable to control herself.

"My boys only use me when it's convenient for them," she ranted at her poor husband. "Don't they understand how much I love them?"

She loved them, taught them, protected them, helped and comforted them at the expense of her own health, only to now be slapped in the face with the realization, "They were just using me." They were using her just like their father had done. "They learned well," she said into her hands as her grief consumed her.

Over the next few weeks, Teresa sank into depression: She sank deep and felt like a drowning animal. There was no joy in her life. Nothing she could cling to for hope. Just the black hole of misery as her walled crumbled around and in on her. She welcomed the abyss.

Another Try at Life

"Until we have met the monsters in ourselves, we keep trying to slay them in the outer world. And we find that we cannot. For all darkness in the world stems from darkness in the heart. And it is there that we must do our work."

Marianna Williamson

Angry at the world and tired of life, Teresa remembered the whispered words of her angel, **"You're not finished here yet."** She clung to these words knowing she had been saved for a reason. "I have to try again," she thought. "But how?"

After having a coaching session from a gifted Tony Robbins coach, Teresa decided she would try life as an entrepreneur.

Armed with a very small budget, she attempted and tried a home business but soon learned the economy would not support it. Thinking that entrepreneurship wasn't for her she worked a minor contract position doing some admin work from home. Most of the time work was accomplished virtually.

At times she would go into their location. It was good to connect with people again. As the contract came to an end, Teresa frantically searched for another position. She searched day and night. Few would take a chance on her and she received the standard, "you are over-qualified for this position." She applied for jobs she could perform in her sleep. "I just wanted to do some part time work to help with the bills and get out of the house," she said to a friend. But no one would give her a chance.

Until one day she was interviewed by a church looking for a receptionist. Teresa accepted the job. She was thrilled. Three days per week were now filled with her contribution to the world. Her confidence was returning. The other two days she decided to devote to her health.

Six weeks into the job, Teresa received a call from a recruiter. She was invited to interview for a job in Brantford. "It is an accounting clerk job," she was told. "There is huge potential here," they said. "This company is big in Europe and have just opened a Canadian facility. Even though she disliked accounting she went for it. "It's full time," she told Don. "I have to help you. I have to help myself!" she told him. Teresa's determination had returned. Within hours of the interview she was offered the job. She signed the contract and two weeks later she began her new career. She was hopeful for her future.

"Finally I can lift some of the financial burden off Don's shoulders," she said to her friend.

As it turned out, she was expected to not only do the finances, but also manage the office, play hostess to all guests, and all of the admin work. The company was growing and she worked ten hours a day applying pressure to herself to perform at her highest level.

Teresa created a Human Resources Department and worked hand in hand with the employees, the plant manager and appropriate agencies to provide a quality workforce.

What she was not able to tolerate was the owner's wife. Each time they flew in, the frivolous demands on Teresa began. "Order our lunch; make and serve fresh coffee; where is the chocolate; clean the kitchen," these were orders barked out by this woman.

Still having her own job to do, Teresa found the other demands ridiculous. "I'm not their babysitter," she told her coworker. "I'm being used, and this is not how we treat people here in Canada."

The stress and pressure was mounting. Repeatedly she turned down trips to Europe to train at the home office. "I will not go and be at their mercy," she told Don.

Each day she became more exhausted. As they now worked in the same city, Don drove to work, while Teresa slept in the car. She slept on the way home. Every evening after dinner she would fall asleep while quilting. "Hun, go to bed, please," Don would say. "You fell asleep with your hand up in the air sewing."

The pressures at work continued with changes and visitors from Europe. She now had to learn a massive computer program to do the accounting, still use the old program for payroll, meet with agencies who supplied temporary labourers and benefit packages.

With her energy now depleted and unable to think clearly, Teresa went to see her family doctor.

Teresa was sick and she knew it.

"Your blood pressure is high," he told her. "That's a first!" Then he looked her straight in the eyes and said, "When are you going to stop doing this to yourself? That job isn't worth it."

"I know," she replied. "But I have to help Don." Their savings wasn't going to last forever! Beaten down, Teresa broke into tears.

When she returned to work, her friend and co-worker from Europe asked, "Are you alright? Did everything go alright for you?"

Over the last few months they had worked closely together and had become fast friends. He confided in her and she listened. The man missed his family and wanted to go back to his own life, but no one dared speak up to the owners.

They sat in his office and talked over a cup of coffee like they had done many times before.

He seemed to show genuine concern for her. Teresa understood the pain in this man's heart. She tried her best to support and comfort her friend, but every day here was another day away from his wife and children. "If they don't let me go home to see my family, I'm going to quit!" he said to Teresa one afternoon.

To help break up his loneliness, Teresa and Don invited him to their home for dinner. They had a nice visit and learned about his homeland. "When you come over, we will show you around," he promised them. "It's a beautiful country."

"Thank you," the both replied.

Then the owner's wife hired a friend of hers to 'work' in the company. Everyone knew the real reason she was there. She was hired to spy on the employees and report back. That was the final straw! After voicing her concerns to her friend, Teresa felt a bit better. He understood and agreed. "That is how the wife operates," he said. "There is nothing we can do about it. No one tells them anything. If we don't follow her rules, we would lose our jobs."

"Well that's wrong!" Teresa replied. "We don't operate like that here. They want to be a Canadian company and I was hired to help them follow the rules, but spying on your employees, taking detailed notes and reporting back to the head office is wrong!"

After another trip to her doctor, Teresa had a "melt down." Something inside her exploded. Her body shook as tears of anger and disappointment erupted. **"I can't take it anymore,"** she said to Don through her tears. She cried for hours. It was a breakdown. Don held her and did his best to console her.

"It's ok baby," he said. "Let it out."

"But I have to keep working," she said in between painful sobs. "I can't let you down. I feel like a failure."

"Not if this is what it's going to do to you," he replied, "You are not letting me down!"

The next day Teresa wrote her letter of resignation.

Very early Monday morning, she laid a personal letter to her friend on his desk with the building keys and her company cell phone. "He'll understand," she thought. She truly believed this, especially after everything he had said to her, and how they had supported each other.

Once back home after cleaning out her office, Teresa emailed her resignation letter to the owner of the company in Europe.

"I've made the right decision," she said to Don. "I feel free."

"Yes, you have," he replied as he squeezed her hand.

Now she waited for the fallout. She waited for some comment from the owner and her friend, who had returned home two days after Teresa quit. No one contacted her. Two weeks later she emailed her friend; but she received no reply.

Another friend from Europe did contact her. She and Teresa had bonded and developed a lifelong friendship. When Teresa questioned her girlfriend she was told, "he doesn't like what you did. He doesn't understand."

"What?" Teresa asked astonished. "He felt the same way!"

Her other friend from work explained that he could not believe what Teresa had done. "He's angry that you left him to deal with the fallout."

"I am truly sorry he feels that way," Teresa replied. "I defended him and everyone there, to the best of my ability."

"Maybe in time he will talk to you," her friend said. "Don't worry."

"Thank you for being honest with me," Teresa said.

Saddened by the loss of people she believed were friends, and admitting to herself that she was unable to work outside of the home for someone else, Teresa had the long task of rebuilding herself yet again. "I have to recover my health first," she told her girlfriend. "I have nothing left to give anyone."

What she didn't expect was a visit from a very old acquaintance. Depression had moved back in and became part of her life. She locked herself away from the world.

"All people do is stab you in the back, or heart," she said to her little dog. Closing her eyes in prayer, she asked, "How do I fix this?"

An Opportunity for Business

"When you know better... You do better."
Maya Angelou

Now at 54 years old, Teresa tried again to rebuild. "I'm tired of being knocked down," she said to Don. "I can't take this anymore!"

They agreed she should take a few months off to regroup and get control of her blood pressure. All her life her blood pressure had been low; dangerously low at times. Seeing the surprise in her doctor's eyes, she knew a change was in order.

Steadily she regained her health and her strength.

One afternoon in April a friend stopped by for a visit.

"Have you ever considered becoming a Virtual Assistant?" the woman asked.

"I've never heard of that before," Teresa replied. The conversation continued as the woman discussed her business ideas.

"This would give you the freedom to work from home and do the work of your choosing," her friend said.

Teresa thought this was an interesting idea. She was tired of working for people who undervalued her and her talents.

Looking into the field of a Virtual Assistant, Teresa soon discovered she could recover her former business name and work for herself.

Excited with the prospect of a new business venture, Teresa decided the timing was right.

"I can work from home, take the time necessary to look after myself when I need to," she told Don that evening.

Two weeks earlier, Teresa had received the results of a CT scan on her spine. Because she had fallen down the steps several times, from the loss of balance from the accident, her spine suffered ten more herniated discs. She knew of two from her heavy farm work and injury as a child but this news overwhelmed her, although it provided her with answers for her severe back pain. The news painted a bleak picture for her future. On top of herniated discs, she has arthritis and scoliosis.

"I'm truly not up for a fight," she told her doctor. "But what choice do I have? The alternative is giving in, and I refuse to do that!"

Knowing she had to take control of her life, Teresa felt the virtual work was a great choice.

It began with some general administration work and then quickly branched into coordinating an internet radio program highlighting women and their many accomplishments. Soon other clients were asking for her help. "This is great," she said to Don. "I love what I'm doing and I am connecting with magnificent people."

Emerging from her black hole of depression, Teresa began to envision a bright and positive future.

She rejoined a business women's networking group and made great friends and contacts.

One afternoon while discussing the struggles of their early lives, her friend connected Teresa with a woman who practices N.L.P. work and uses Hypnotherapy to assist her clients in overcoming their shattered pasts. Trusting her friend and hoping that finally she could overcome the horrors of her past, Teresa made the call.

That single call turned her life around. Her journey into healing began.

After several months of sessions, Teresa found she was a new person. "Finally I'm going to put my past where it belongs...in the past," she told her husband. "I'm going to take back my power and take proper ownership of my life."

Her therapist listened, helped and made suggestions, all the while telling Teresa to be kind to herself and to learn to love herself. "I'm not sure I can do that," Teresa told her. "I don't know how."

The two women worked together towards Teresa's healing. She respected and trusted her therapist. Learning how to care and protect herself, Teresa began to grow. Sometimes the work was extremely difficult and caused some backwards steps, but she remained steadfast in her faith and her therapist. Little by little they peeled away the painful memories of her past traumas that **were** Teresa's life. As she acknowledged each memory she placed it where it belonged...in the past. Leaving each session, she felt more empowered and in control of her destiny. "That's something I've never felt before," she told a trusted friend one day.

As time passed, more life situations happened. Now both her sons had turned away from her. One because of anger and the other because she didn't live up to his expectations. "I won't fall into the trap of forcing them to be a part of my life," she told Don. Through intense discussions, she finally understood that her sons had grown up watching their father disrespect and belittle her. Even though she protected and defended them, and loved them both beyond belief, she knew in her heart she couldn't fix this. "I can't do it alone," she thought. "They have to want to be a part of a relationship."

Facing a life without her children hurt her deeply. Teresa desperately wanted to see her little granddaughter, but that meant stepping back into the unhealthy territory with her son. "I want to spend time with her and love her, but I will not put myself in his space," she told Don. "It's unhealthy for me. The boys need to face their own truth before I will step in as their mother again."

The bold steps she was taking empowered her daily. She was no longer willing to be victimized by her past and the secrets and lies of centuries past. Teresa felt brave and resilient.

As part of her new attack on life, she starting taking courses and setting goals. "I'm going to write this book," she said to Don. "This is my healing and one of my life goals. "By exposing the century long secrets and lies, I am going to reveal the truth. I must protect future generations and others who have lost their power," she declared emphatically.

Day by day, her courage grew. It was a transformation that her husband and friends watched with joy and anticipation.

"It's **My** time to step into a bright new future!"

Rainbows and a Bright Future

"All the adversity I've had in my life, all my troubles and obstacles, have strengthened me...You may not realize it when it happens, but a kick in the teeth may be the best thing in the world for you."

Walt Disney

"You are not finished here," **"You are not finished here**.*"* What is the answer?

So many times throughout my life I heard those words. I heard them when I was in my deepest despair with serious thoughts of committing suicide. These words were also spoken to me during high points in my life. I now believed there definitely was a plan for me. God and my Guardian Angel had protected me all my life. I was beginning to awaken to my purpose.

"I'm need to help people!" I told my husband. "I've always helped those in need."

"I think so too," he said. "You have a gift with people."

"I just need to figure out how," I replied.

"I'm not sure I have enough confidence in myself yet. I've silenced the demons of my past and can now bring forth the brilliant light that is love and faith. In time I know I **will** learn to use these gifts."

"You can do this, Teresa," Don said to her. "Your gifts and passion for helping people are genuine and from the heart."

Looking up at my husband with love and admiration, I saw the belief in his eyes.

"At times I still struggle when those hideous demons rise up causing self-doubt. Sometimes, I still look in the mirror her hear the humiliating names my sister called me, but I refuse to let the past define me!" I replied.

"You will be great," he told her affectionately. "You will! I have every faith in you!"

"I trust you," she told him. "You are the only person on this earth I trust completely."

When I was doing the inner child work with my therapist, I created a safe place for my, "little me." My fascination for old castles, secret gardens and mythical animals filled my heart. The safe place I created was a beautiful walled garden surrounding a massive castle. Inside the walls were beautiful birds that sang to their hearts content filling the air with beautiful music. Gorgeous flowers that consumed the surrounding air with their heady perfume, and many types of animals wandered the grounds, drinking from the crystal clear stream and fountains. My favourite of the animals was a beautiful, majestic unicorn.

As the unicorn walked around the garden surveying its kingdom it sniffed flowers, did some play-jousting with deer and ceremoniously held court. After a great deal of encouragement, my 'little self' emerged from behind the secret garden gate. Slowly and cautiously I approached the unicorn offering my hand up for approval. The unicorn recognized me and bowed. "Thank you," I said with happiness and complete love. "You are safe with me, as I know I am with you."

Since experiencing that vision, I have developed a true fondness for unicorns. To me they represent a beautiful mythical creature that is eternal. ***"They aren't finished here either,"*** I thought as joy spread in my heart.

Every once in a while, Don surprises me with little gifts of stuffed unicorns. They are treasured little beings that stand guard in my office. As I approach my new life and goals, these colourful little beings are constant reminders that possibilities and magic must be part of my life. Some may think it silly to treasure stuffed animals at my age; but to me they represent the healing gift I gave my little self. The little girl who was abused and psychologically beaten down at such a young age can finally heal and put her past away. With the aid of the unicorn, I was able to nurture the young girl, giving her security, love and compassion. She flourished under my care and grew into the woman I am today.

As my confidence and possibilities grew, so to did my personal empowerment. I poured myself into courses on Courage and Daring offered by Brené Brown. Working through her courses forced me to face the personal demons of my past head on, examine them and file them in their proper place. One of my favourite quotes from Brené Brown's Courage Works courses is, "There is no greater threat to the critics and cynics and fearmongers than those of us who are willing to fall because we have learned how to rise."

"Those demons may still be a small part of me, but **they no longer own me!**" I told a friend one day during lunch.

Looking deep inside myself, I found my true courage and determination. "I have to tell the story," I said to my husband. "If I can help one person in this world who is struggling, then my life's mission is complete." This was my purpose and that is what I intend to do.

I continued to write the story, with determination and passion.

"Writing about the horrors of my past gave me a new found freedom I never thought possible. "It has been a tremendous healing experience," I told my husband. "Those past traumas no longer affect me or control me. I've taken their power away and silenced them forever."

With my courage in place, I began taking the necessary steps toward living a brave life; a bold life.

Armed with a new outlook on life, I participated in courses designed to teach you to live to your highest energy; I have received my level 1 Reiki training; I practice meditation daily and have started on a path where I take care of 'me.' I am a student of humanity and my goal is to change lives.

I religiously follow motivational leaders and power-changers like BrenéBrown and Anthony Robbins, to name a few. Their inspirational quotes speak to my heart.

I really resonated with this quote: *"Power was given to you at the moment you were born. Its source is unlimited. When you seize it, you'll have everything you need to create a life filled with more passion, excitement, confidence, and joy than you've ever dreamed. Isn't it time to unleash the power within you?" - Anthony Robbins*

My soul is moved by this quote.

Through a friend and great coach in his own right, I connected with an authorship coach. Adam Mortimer, author of The Secrets of As a Man Thinketh, has helped me beyond measure. I've seen my value and true gift as a writer and so much more.

Working with my coach is an experience I will never forget.

"I'm an author," I told Don one day with actual belief in my own words. "I am achieving one of my lifelong goals. What an amazing feeling it is."

Coaching is exactly what I needed to motivate me to complete this book. My life is turning around and for the first time, **I am** in charge!

Positive changes are beginning to happen in my life. I was granted a scholarship to the Aspiring High Potential Leaders Program by the Co-founder of the Acacia Institute, Anne Miner, a woman whom I admire and respect. She is not only a brilliant businesswoman and a published author, but a friend and mentor.

As I move forward, my successes are growing daily. Since taking my power back and bursting forth from the 'old' life, I have been a guest on four internet radio programs and one local cable television show. On my new life path, I am freely exposing the truth of how living with Chronic Pain affects every aspect of my life. It no longer owns me even though I battle with it daily. No longer will I hide the fact that I hurt, but at the same time, the pain will not define me. I believe the opportunities to share my journey are gifts and I am forever grateful even though some of the experiences I have had throughout my life were extremely painful and very unwanted.

While brainstorming for a client one day, I heard the voice of my former physiotherapist, Gloria. Her voice echoed in my mind saying, "You need to help educate people about Chronic Pain and Brain Injury. Others need to know it doesn't have to control their lives: Inspire them." The care and tough love I received from Gloria during my rehabilitation process, has been playing a constant loop in my mind for almost ten years since the car accident. I wanted to help; to make a difference for others; but my fear and limiting beliefs and lack of energy kept me a prisoner of my own self-doubt.

Allowing myself to remain a prisoner of my own self-doubt was no longer an option. I focused on my goals. My courage and strength returned tenfold. I learned about the practice of self-compassion and developed self-respect for the first time in my life.

"I'm taking control of my own destiny," I told my coach. "Yes, you are, and I am so proud of you," he replied.

Through self-empowerment and a strong will I am growing and changing my destiny.

Recently I created **F.I.T.S.** (***Friends in Trauma Support***). **F.I.T.S.** is a social media page where people can go to discuss their trauma or painful experiences and receive compassion, support and understanding in a safe judgment-free environment. This group is very important to me. I often imagine the "what ifs," of what my life would have been like if I had been given love, understanding, support, compassion and help when I was a little girl. I think of the benefits and understanding the support of my family would have given me during the recovery from my accident. They will never know what their lack of understanding and compassion has cost me.

F.I.T.S. is also a place to discuss relevant topics; a place to educate the public, treatment providers and trauma survivors.

It is **NOT**, "all in my head," as I had been told many times over the years. These traumas are real and we can no longer ignore them! I will no longer remain silent.

That is one step of my life plan. My desire to help others to not feel abandoned and alone has taken flight.

"I'm so excited," I told Don. "I'm actually making my childhood dreams come true. I am going to learn from all the abuses I have experienced and use that knowledge and compassion to mentor others."

"I'm so proud of you hun," he said as he smiled at me. I saw truth in his blue eyes. He has gone through every step of this journey with me. I appreciate his support and belief in me. He watches as my unicorns grow wings and morph into beautiful beings.

While chatting with my coach, Adam Mortimer, Director of Achieve Today, during an Authorship session one day, I expressed my strong desire to help others.

"How long have you felt this strongly?" he asked.

"All my life, but over the last several months the feeling has gone from want to strong desire," I told him.

"We have a coaching certification program at Achieve Today. I would love to recommend you for the program," Adam said to me.

"Really!" I said. I was shocked and thrilled all at the same time. "Are you serious?," I asked again.

"Yes," he replied. "I have felt your gifts of intuition and compassion over the phone. I really want you to be part of the program. Let's make it happen," Adam said.

Excited and thrilled beyond belief that my goals and dreams could be realized, I called Don to share the news. I told him of the opportunity Adam presented to me.

"I'm very afraid of spending that amount of money," I told him. "Can we afford for me to do this?" I asked.

"Teresa, we can't afford for you **NOT** to do this," *he replied.* "You have a gift and you need to share it."

Never having such a strong conviction of "the right thing," before, I agreed to take the leap of faith and join the Achieve Today Personal Development and Executive Level Coaching Certification Program.

"Everything is falling into place for me. I can't believe this is all happening! My life has been supercharged with possibilities."

If my coach Adam believes in me this much, then I need to continue to dig deep and believe in me!

"I signed up to begin my training for my new career. This is my next step into helping myself and my first major step into helping others," I told a friend.

Life is good, life is great! I felt the energy of positivity for the first time. It is a true permanent feeling now. No one will ever take my personal power away again.

Now I have written several articles and I still write some poetry. My crowning glory is this, my first book, *A Century of Secrets*. This is the beginning of my life's dreams.

My book has healed my soul and freed the soul of my grandmother. She was a woman who faced insurmountable horrors in her life and still had a huge capacity for love. Her courage and strength has been passed down to me, as I will pass it on to future generations. Writing has gifted me with the ability to pour out the pain that has been locked away deep inside my soul for a lifetime.

Through this book, *A Century of Secrets*, my goal has always been to empower my readers. Believe in yourself and have faith. Do not let your past define you. Deep inside your heart, you have the gift of strength, of courage and beauty. Find it and take control of your power. With faith, determination and love the possibilities are endless! **I am living proof that a brilliant future is possible!** For the first time in my life I am excited for my future. I have put the fear and pain aside and, "*I love it!*" Believing in unicorns, and the pot of gold at the end of each rainbow has shown me how to begin to enjoy life.

All of this, I discovered was just the tip of the iceberg. As I complete this book, my coaching certification course, from Achieve Today, is nearing its completion as well. My coaching company Sterling Silver Coaching has been created and launched. It is my mission to help other women recover their power and strength, find their purpose in life and to learn that they are Enough!

After recently receiving my certificate from the Acacia Institute, and thinking I would have spare time on my hands, fate has a way of presenting gifts when you least expect them. I have been awarded another scholarship for coaching, this time from The Community of Women for Change. Also, joining forces with my husband, I have launched Encouraging YOU Radio; an internet radio station where together with our hosts, 'We Are Motivating the World Through Conversation.'

As 2017 approached, it was suggested that I develop a theme for the year. This was an easy decision for me. I claim 2017 as, 'My Year of Fulfillment.' Since deciding on this theme, my year has exploded. I have been asked to be a contributing author for three compilation books, two of my articles have been picked up by other publications and I have launched my own internet radio show called, 'Powering Through Life.' This part was easy. It wasn't until just prior to New Year's Eve 2016, that another loss would rock my world. We sent our faithful and loving Pekingese, Bruno to pet-heaven. His passing has caused me major grief and loneliness, but it has also given me the gift of showing me how to grieve. I have a lifetime of grief I had never faced or felt; always being forced to bottle it tightly away inside, for if I showed tears, I was weak or made fun of. When Bruno left us, I truly believed his purpose of seeing me through the difficulties of the accident and life traumas since we first brought him home was over. I suddenly learned his mission was not complete. His death has given me the courage and ability to face the grief I feel from his loss, and to face this with compassion for myself. I now know it's alright to grieve: to feel it, experience it, and show it. Bruno's mission is not complete. He has taken his place as my fur-angel, beside my papa, my grandmother and my ever-present guardian angel. I am protected and I know my future is bright and waiting for me.

A Century of Secrets is a multi-generational story of how one family's struggle with abuse, personal identity and deep-seated family secrets has caused suicide, alcoholism and lasting family scars.

This book is one woman's journey to uncover the lies, overcome adversity and finally set her soul free.

This book has bared the soul of one woman's history and shown how she has powered through to her future. She has broken through the lies and multi-generational secrets. "They no longer own her."

"She is NOT finished here yet."

God Bless!

About the Author

Teresa Syms

Entrepreneur, Author, Aspiring Leader
and Personal Development
and Executive Coach.

Teresa over the years has become a master as a Life Change Catalyst. Every so often when tragedy or life altering situations happen, she manages to reinvent herself, stonger, more determined and full of compassion.

Teresa's entrepreneurial heart started a long journey from Human Resources, Accounting, Hairdressing and being a mother and a caregiver.

Given the chance to rethink her life several years after a near-death motor vehicle accident, Teresa focused on working from home. She entered the virtual world and excelled at Coordinating two Internet Radio Shows through her company Syms Solutions.

Soon she discovered the need for a good internet Radio Station. Teresa partnered with her husband, Don, and **Encouraging You Radio** was born. Together, their mission is, **Motivating the World Through Conversation**.

Teresa's has had two main missions throughout her life. One has been to write a book, which she has done. *A Century of Secrets*, takes you four generations into the core of family life; shows you it is possible to survive brutality from those we call family, and rise above where we come from. Her other main mission is to help guide those who have survived trauma, lost their personal power, or those looking for personal growth. Her company, Sterling Silver Coaching, was launched in the fall of 2016. "Life transformational... Sterling Silver Coaching can help you transform yours."

In January 2017, Teresa began hosting her own show on **Encouraging You Radio**. Weekly, Teresa and her guests will explore how other people found ways of "**Powering Through Life.**"

Teresa's education was in Business, Majoring in Human Resources with extra emphasis on Employment and Labour Law. Recently she completed a certificate program from the Acacia Institute, as a High Potential Aspiring Leader. Always one to be learning, Teresa completed an Authorship course, instructed by Joe Vitali and Adam Mortimer, as well as her Personal Development and Executive Coaching Certification through Achieve Today and Adam Mortimer.

This book would not be possible without the true love and support of her husband, Don, who has always been a source of love, trust and inspiration; her 'Editor in Chief,' Bruno the ever faithful Pekingese. Bruno was always ready to assume his role as my 'editor' while he sat in front of my monitor as I wrote. Bruno's life hung in the balance while writing the end of the book. There are no words to describe the happiness, inspiration and pure love you have given me for the last ten years.

Don and Bruno, you both are my motivation and my rocks. Your gifts to me have been many and I will be forever grateful.

To connect with Teresa, visit **TeresaSyms.com**

Made in the USA
Columbia, SC
22 August 2C